The New Cold War, China, and the Caribbean

Scott B. MacDonald

The New Cold War, China, and the Caribbean

Economic Statecraft, China and Strategic
Realignments

Scott B. MacDonald
White Plains, NY, USA

ISBN 978-3-031-06148-6   ISBN 978-3-031-06149-3   (eBook)
https://doi.org/10.1007/978-3-031-06149-3

This Palgrave Macmillan imprint is published by the registered company Springer Nature
Switzerland AG
The registered company address is: Gewerbestrasse 11, 6330 Cham, Switzerland

This book is dedicated to my wife and partner of many years, M.M. Kateri Scott-MacDonald and to the memory of my mother, Anita B. MacDonald. They are two women that most influenced my life and hopefully made me a better person.

PREFACE

My first venture into the Caribbean came when I was young, traveling with my parents to St. Croix, in the U.S. Virgin Islands in the late 1960s. I do not remember much about the visit except that the islanders stored rainwater, that it was really hot during the day, and I got to see the ruins of an old sugar mill, part of which was under considerable tropical vegetation. I also got one of the worst sunburns of my life in St. Croix, a memory made stronger by the fact that I still have the freckles on my shoulders from that encounter with the Caribbean sun. As I grew older and read more what really fascinated me about St. Croix and the region was that its history was made up of numerous battles for control between the Spanish, Dutch, English, and French. As a sugar island, St. Croix found its place in the sun, for a brief time its elite becoming one of the wealthiest in the region. The tragedy of that was that the wealth generated by King Sugar came from a brutal system of African enslavement, which still has profound legacies in the Caribbean.

My introduction to St. Croix left me hungry to know more about the region and people south of the United States that functioned as a critical crossroads of empires. Indeed, the Caribbean's role as a strategic crossroads remains. In the first part of the twenty-first century, the region witnessed a return to great power competition not seen since the end of the Cold War. Indeed, it is the interplay between the Caribbean and external actors, namely the United States and China and, to a lesser extent, Russia, that drove the writing of this book and its focus on the "new Cold War" and how it is playing out in the region. The Sino-American rivalry in the Caribbean must be observed as part of a much broader competition between two powers with very different ideas of what the world system should look like. This becomes all the more important to understand considering that the Caribbean is undergoing substantial change: the region faces climate change, the need to digitalize economies, diversify from a top-heavy dependence on tourism in many countries, and confront new risks carried by transnational diseases (such as Covid-19 in 2020–2022). Where applicable, those issues will be put into the context of the new Cold War, which appears to be in its early stages. The main focus remains on the geopolitical landscape that is being created, seen through the lenses of the major actors, i.e. the United States, China, and the Caribbean and, to a lesser extent, Russia, Europe, Canada, and Iran. Although there remains an ongoing denial of a new Cold war trajectory, the train of events over the past several years points in that direction. One need only look at the coziness of Presidents Vladimir Putin and Xi Jinping sitting together at the Beijing 2022 Winter Olympics, which come to a backdrop of record trade between the two countries in 2021, Chinese support for Russia over halting further NATO expansion in Europe, and their mutual support for corrupt, authoritarian regimes in Cuba, Nicaragua, and Venezuela. The two leaders represent a world that is radically different from the West. Russia's decision to invade Ukraine in February 2022, followed by a tough response by the United States, the North Atlantic Treaty Organization and European Union with economic sanctions and the supplying of large amounts of weapons to the government in Kyiv has served to reinforce the idea of a new Cold War.

And the Caribbean once again finds itself brought back to one of its more traditional roles in global geopolitics, a crossroads of empires. Indeed, the last several years have observed the Caribbean's place on the map change from being a relative, (yet nice-to-visit) economic backwater into a zone of great power rivalry that increasingly feels like the old Cold War. However, we are no longer in 1989, the year the Berlin Wall fell; we are in the tumultuous 2020s, which have already been marked by the chaotic U.S. retreat from Afghanistan, political upheaval and repression in Cuba, a diplomatic flip of Nicaragua from Taiwan to China, a Russian attempt to destroy the Ukrainian state and force a return to Cold War spheres of influence in Eastern Europe, and a Russian-led military intervention in Kazakhstan (in January 2022). For the Caribbean, Russia's musing over upping its military assets in Cuba, Nicaragua, and

Venezuela and China's tacit support reflect that times are changing. Thus far, economic statecraft dominates the nature of the rivalry and has been a cornerstone of Chinese policy. Yet China's drive to be a major power in a region that the United States' considers as its strategic backyard and Washington's willingness to contain that rise, has set the stage for a longer duel that increasingly involves the Caribbean. This is not to argue that the Caribbean lacks its own international relations dynamic, but that years of more intense geo-economic and geopolitical competition are heading in its direction like dark clouds on the horizon. It is difficult to discern whether those dark clouds are going to disperse or bring a new storm. We hope for the former. Caribbean policymakers and their counterparts in North America and Europe should take heed of the words of U.S. statesman Benjamin Franklin, "By failing to prepare you are preparing to fail."

White Plains, USA   Scott B. MacDonald

Acknowledgments

The research for this book was conducted in the Caribbean, the United States, and Europe. Sadly travel was hindered by the Covid-19 pandemic, which precluded any travel to Asia. I was forced to become adept in the use of Zoom. The research was helped considerably by a grant from the Smith Richardson Foundation (SRF), which was most gracious in extending the completion date. Special thanks go to SRF's Christopher Griffin who had faith that I would complete the project. Appreciation is extended to Global Americans, first under the guidance of Christopher Sabatini (who moved to London's Chatham House) and then under Guy Mentel. Global Americans was willing to give me a place to hang my hat as a Global Americans Research Fellow. The Center for Strategic & International Studies in Washington, DC, where I was a Senior Associate (non-resident), was also important in helping provide access to experts in a number of different areas, including China and Taiwan, and international energy politics. I would be remiss not to mention Terry Smith and Pam Smith, who provided an important and flexible platform from which to work, Smith's Gradings & Research. My sometimes spirited discussions with Terry Smith were most useful in deeper thinking on some key issues.

Many others were helpful, providing constructive criticism in helping me gain a better understanding of the changes occurring in the Caribbean. Among those who gave their time to help make this a better book through either sharing their viewpoints, formal interviews, or reading through various parts of the manuscript were founding members of the Caribbean Policy Consortium, of which I was fortunate to be a founding member. This illustrious group includes Dr. Georges Fauriol (formerly of the National Endowment for Democracy and the Center for Strategic & International Studies); Dr. Tony Bryan (a senior fellow at the Institute of International Relations at the University of the West Indies, St. Augustine, Trinidad and Tobago and well-known energy consultant); Dr. Ivelaw Griffith (former Vice-Chancellor of the University of Guyana and an expert on Caribbean security, drugs and crime); Dr. David Lewis (Vice President of Washington, DC-based Manchester Trade and former Assistant Secretary of State of Puerto Rico, and Deputy Executive Director of Caribbean/Latin American Action); and Bruce Zagaris (partner at Berliner, Corcoran & Rowe LLP and internationally renowned expert on white-collar criminal defense, corporate social responsibility, and international tax law as well as editor-in-chief of the International Enforcement Law Reporter). Bruce, Georges, and Ivelaw get special appreciation as they were good sports in suffering through various chapters (sometimes more than once), offering helpful criticisms and encouragement to finish the book.

Thanks also go to former Barbados' Ambassadors Peter Laurie and Michael King, who were generous with their time when I visited them in their country. Ambassador Laurie was very helpful in providing feedback on various chapters. Also in Barbados, appreciation is extended to Dr. DeLisle Worrell, the former Governor of the Central Bank of Barbados, for his insightful comments and a delightful lunch at Champers Restaurant. Appreciation is also extended to former Ambassador Crispin Gregoire of Dominica. Others who provided insights and were generous with their time include the following: Mavrick Boejoekoe in Suriname; Rasheed Griffith, a non-resident senior fellow with the Asia & Latin America Program at the Inter-American Dialogue (in Panama); Dr. Rosemarijn Hoefte, Director at the Royal Netherlands Institute of Southeast Asian and the Caribbean Studies (Netherlands); Frans-Paul van der Putten, Coordinator at the China Centre, the Clingendael Institute, The Hague, The Netherlands; Tycho de Feijter, also of the Clingendael Institute; U.S. Ambassador Philip Hughes (to Barbados and the Eastern Caribbean); Robert Looney, Distinguished Professor in the National Security Affairs Department, Naval Postgraduate School, Monterey, California; Margaret McCuaig-Johnston, Senior Fellow, Institute for Science, Society and Policy, University of Ottawa and Canada China Forum Advisory Board; Professor Andrew Novo at the National Defense University in Washington, DC; Mitchell A. Orenstein, Professor of Russian and East European Studies at the University of Pennsylvania; Professor of Political Science and International Relations and International Relations Chair Zhiqun Zhu, at Bucknell University; Maximilian Hess, Central Asia Fellow in the Eurasia Program at the Foreign Policy Research Institute and Head of Political Risk at Hawthorn Advisers (London); Jean-Marc F. Blanchard, Founding Executive Director Mr. and Mrs. S.H. Wong Center for the Study of Multinational Corporations and General Editor, Routledge Series on the Political Economy of Asia; and Professor Jared Ward, Associate Lecturer and Historian at the University of Akron. Dr. Christopher Sands, Director of the Wilson Center's Canada Institute, was helpful in pointing the way on who to talk Caribbean issues in Canada. Government officials from the United States and Taiwan were also helpful and generous with their time.

No set of acknowledgments would be complete without expressing my gratitude to my wife Kateri Scott-MacDonald, who was often my first-time reader. Her incisive (yet sometimes ego-popping) editing skills were a huge help. Despite her bout with cancer, her support was a tremendous help, especially at times when my own health faltered. Thanks go to my daughter, Estelle, who has been a huge help in making our lives better and my son Alistair who has often forced me to think about the world through different perceptual lenses. I would also like to extend my appreciation to "Orange Joe" (also known as JoJo and Mr. Jinx), the family cat, who often kept me company in the wee hours.

All the comments and criticisms were seriously weighed, appreciated, and applied in one way or another. While many hands helped stir the creative broth, the ultimate product is the responsibility of the author.

CONTENTS

LIST OF TABLES

CHAPTER 1

Introduction

This chapter explores the slide of the Caribbean into a new Cold War in the Caribbean. The primary argument is that the Caribbean's geopolitics have shifted from a period of relative great power disinterest in the aftermath of the Cold War to a gradual movement into a new Cold War in which a global rivalry between the United States and China is acted out regionally. The result of this is a gradual polarization of countries in the Caribbean as they are increasingly pressured to choose between Washington and Beijing. The chapter also discusses the debate on the idea of a new Cold War, the importance of economic statecraft, and sharp power as well as providing an outline of the following chapters.

There is a new Cold War in the Caribbean—or something that increasingly resembles such a strategic realignment. It pits the world's two leading powers, the United States and China, against each other. The mode of competition is generally dominated by economic statecraft, the use of economic tools in the form of loans, foreign assistance, technical help, corporate expertise, and the wiring of regional telecommunications systems. Propaganda, misinformation, and disinformation, the combination of which is sometimes referred to as "sharp power" also play a role. To be certain, many policymakers and academics do not see a new Cold War, but a more traditional great power rivalry. No matter how one wishes to define it, many in the Caribbean regard China as a potential alternative to the United States, which has long dominated the region

S. B. MacDonald, *The New Cold War, China, and the Caribbean*,
https://doi.org/10.1007/978-3-031-06149-3_1

economically, politically, and militarily. Indeed, some Caribbean policy-makers are talking of a Caribbean "pivot to Asia," a reference to the attempted U.S. strategic pivot to Asia under the Obama administration. How far down the road to a new Cold War we have traveled can be debated, but the United States and China are locked in competition for power and influence globally and in the region. Equally important, there is a connection between what is happening in the Caribbean and in other parts of the world where U.S. and Chinese influence collide (MacDonald 2019a, b).

China's economic statecraft has been a powerful instrument in gaining new friends. As noted in a report by the Caribbean Investigative Journalism Network in 2019: "A hotel. A highway. A port. The prime minister's house. For Caribbean countries, one of the most visible, expansive, and expensive forms of Beijing's engagement with the region is its financing of large-scale infrastructure projects" (Bridglal et al. 2019). This has included Chinese investment in Antigua and Barbuda, the Bahamas, Jamaica, Trinidad and Tobago, and Guyana. Indeed, in 2018 the attractiveness of Chinese development aid was a key factor to entice the Dominican Republic to drop its relationship with Taiwan, considered by China as a breakaway province. Beijing had used similar tactics in Central America with Panama, El Salvador and Nicaragua to have them drop Taiwan in favor of Beijing, in 2017, 2019, and 2021, respectively.

China has been willing to extend cheap loans and make available other investments throughout the region. According to the American Enterprise Institute's China Global Investment Tracker, Chinese investment in and contracts with Jamaica from 2005 to 2019 stood at $2.68 billion; at $1.7 billion for Trinidad and Tobago; $1.85 billion for Guyana; and $800 million for Cuba. And the Caribbean does need financing for infrastructure. In 2014, the Caribbean Development Bank estimated that the region needs around $30 billion to upgrade infrastructure over the next decade (Caribbean Development Bank 2014). Many of those needs are still there. Considering the reduction in development assistance from many Western sources (including the United States) and the brutal economic impact of the 2020–2022 Covid-19 pandemic, Caribbean infrastructure spending could be tight in the years ahead.

For their part, Caribbean countries have been quick to acknowledge the role that China can play in their economies. In 2018 Trinidad and Tobago became the first country in the Caribbean to officially sign on to China's Belt and Road Initiative (BRI), a massive development program to convert the Eurasian landmass into an economic trade zone linking China to Europe and extending trade links outwards into Africa and the Americas. Trinidad and Tobago was followed by others, including Antigua and Barbuda, Barbados, Guyana, Jamaica, and Suriname. Both Trinidad and Tobago and Jamaica have tapped loans from the China Development Bank and the China Export–Import Bank, while one of Suriname's major creditors is also China.

China is aggressively pumping out its worldview of itself as a constructive leader of a multilateral world, compared to the United States that is falling apart under the weight of its domestic problems and is led by old political leaders (much like the Soviet Union was in its late stages). The narrative is simple—the United States is in decline; China is on the rise and everyone wants to be on the side of the winner. One of China's more urbane mouthpieces, Eric Xun Li (a Shanghai venture capitalist and trustee of Fudan University's China Institute) provides an example of the Chinese narrative in an editorial in The Washington Post in 2018: "I dare say Xi has done more for China in five years than Bill Clinton, George Bush and Barack Obama combined did for the United States in 25 years. On the watches of those three American leaders, with slow and incompetent reforms and major catastrophes such as the Iraq War and the financial crisis, the U.S. managed to squander what was arguably the greatest advantage any nation ever had in history at the end of the Cold War and is now mired in dysfunction and losing its leadership position in the world" (Li 2018). Generally speaking, China's more substantial profile has not radically changed the political behavior of most Caribbean countries. But China has established a larger presence in the region, which gives it greater leverage in global affairs.

While China may not be looking for a new Cold War, its actions in the Caribbean and elsewhere in the world are perceived in the United States as setting the stage for such a development. Indeed, China's increased role in Caribbean affairs has become a concern for the United States. This has much to do with a change of perceptions about China: the country was initially seen as on a path of more market-oriented development that would eventually make it more like the United States and the West politically, that is, democratic. The development of what Handel Jones called "Chinamerica," an uneasy partnership between the two countries based on strong and deepening economic interdependence, was looked upon as a future path for the global system (Jones 2010). This, however, was not to be.

While tensions rose between the United States and China during the Obama administration, the Trump administration took on China in a more frontal way, using tariffs and other measures to decouple economically. In the Caribbean, now perceived as an important geostrategic region by Washington, the United States took to warning local governments about China, re-invoking the Monroe Doctrine (of keeping external forces out of the Western Hemisphere) and adopting a tough policy against countries which it sees as proxies of China and Russia, which include Cuba, Venezuela, Iran, and Nicaragua. Although the Trump administration is gone, the Biden presidency is facing the probability that China is an ongoing challenge to the United States in the Caribbean. Indeed, at the Summit of the Americans, held in June 2022 in Los Angeles, President Biden and other U.S. officials articulated their concern over increasing Chinese influence and the need to strengthen Washington's democratic partners in the region.

China has not shrunk away from the threat of a new Cold War with the United States. In the Caribbean, it gives overt support to Cuba and Venezuela (in the face of U.S. hostility to those regimes), put pressure on Guyana in 2021 to prevent Taiwan from opening a trade mission, and continued to push its telecom equipment on regional markets. China's providing of medical equipment during the Covid-19 pandemic was meant to demonstrate the Asian country's partnership with countries in the region (despite the virus originating in China, that some of the equipment failed to work and its vaccines were less effective than their Western and Russian rivals). At the same time, China has a tougher, some would argue more aggressive, stance, which it has yet to fully reveal in the Caribbean. That tougher side has been called "wolf warrior" diplomacy (named after a movie in which tough-guy Chinese Special Forces deal with bad guy U.S. mercenaries). This tone of Chinese foreign policy was probably best caught by China's ambassador to Sweden, who stated: "We treat our friends with fine wine, but for our enemies we have shotguns" (The Economist 2020). Another more diplomatic version of China's tougher stance was articulated by China's foreign minister Wang Yi during an interview with CNN in 2020: "We never pick a fight or bully others. But we have principles and guts. We will push back against any deliberate insult, resolutely defend our national honor and dignity, and we will refute all groundless slanders with facts" (Westcott and Jiang 2020).

Purpose of the Book

It is the purpose of this book to examine the slide into a new Cold War in the Caribbean. The primary argument is that the Caribbean's geopolitics have shifted from a period of relative great power disinterest in the aftermath of the Cold War to a gradual movement into a new Cold War in which a global rivalry between the United States and China is acted out regionally. The result of this is a gradual polarization of countries in the Caribbean as they are increasingly pressured to choose between Washington and Beijing. It can be argued that the U.S. focus on the Caribbean in the late 1990s through the early twenty-first century faded, leaving the region open to a China ready and eager to do business. Beijing's growing influence in the Caribbean, as well as the hardening of overall U.S.–China relations, eventually led to a more muscular hardening of U.S. policy during the Trump administration, at first based on the suggestion of military might and then an effort at more coherent economic statecraft to counter China. Key to the perspective of this book is that the global political economy is seen through the lens of competition between countries, which can veer into outright rivalry and at times conflict. As the realist political scientist John J. Mearsheimer observed:

> The sad fact is that international politics has always been a ruthless and dangerous business, and it is likely to remain that way. Although the intensity of their competition waxes and wanes, great powers fear each other and always compete with each other for power. The overriding goal of each state is to maximize its share of world power, which means gaining power at the expense of other states. But great powers do not merely strive to be strongest of all the great powers, although that is a welcome outcome. Their ultimate aim is to be the hegemon—that is, the only great power in the system. (Mearsheimer 2014)

At the core of this story is China's rise, its push to regain its stature as the center of the global system, and its related penetration of the Caribbean. The United States is also a key part of this story: under the Trump administration, there was a process of redefining Washington's approach to the rest of the world as constructed around the mantra of "America First," de-globalization and pulling back from the longstanding multilateral system that brought stability and prosperity during much of the postwar era. A more active U.S. approach toward the Caribbean was enacted, initially with a narrower Cold War-like objective of containing

Chinese as well as Russian and Iranian influence. Another part of the U.S. approach was to strike at Beijing's and Moscow's regional allies, Cuba, Venezuela, and Nicaragua. The Biden administration inherited a challenging geopolitical landscape in the Caribbean as well as a politically polarized society and struggling economy at home. Thus far the rivalry between China and the United States has been played out through economic statecraft, but the Trump years focused some of this rivalry on the Maduro regime in Venezuela and the Castroite state in Cuba, with an echo of the proxy wars in the Cold War fought between the United States and the Soviet Union in Africa, the Middle East, Latin America, and the Caribbean. The Biden administration has its work cut out for it in this regard, even with a preference for multilateralism.

Another important dimension of the book's narrative is the role played by Caribbean countries in the increasing polarization between China and the United States. Although small players on the greater international stage, Caribbean countries are key actors in the new Cold War drama in their region. In policy debates over Venezuela, Cuba and China, Caribbean countries have struggled to find a united front. This reflects the inability to establish more robust regional institutions able to provide consensus on policy vis-à-vis external forces on a number of issues (Lewis 2020). It also highlights the vulnerabilities that face small countries when dealing with larger countries. Considering the scope of challenges facing the Caribbean, ranging from a critical reassessment of globalization, climate change, and transnational disease (brought home with a vengeance by the 2020–2022 Covid-19 pandemic), the new Cold War only reinforces the need to find a more unified front.

The role of the Caribbean in the new Cold War is similar to other regions which are caught in the struggle for influence between the United States and China and Russia. In this, the Caribbean is not unique. The Cold War-like flavor of this was caught by Mitchell A. Orenstein, professor of Russian and East European Studies at the University of Pennsylvania, who observed Eastern Europe in 2019: "With the stakes raised, Russia and the West are entering a dangerous time in their relations. They are engaged in a pitched battle to determine the political future of Europe. Either the West's vision of a rule-bound, liberal order or Russia's vision of a great-power Europe dominated by authoritarian rulers will prevail. Nowhere is this conflict felt more than in the lands in between Russia and the EU, which sit literally on a knife's edge balanced between two competing geopolitical zones" (Orenstein 2019: 79). Whereas Orenstein is discussing Belarus, Moldova, Georgia, and Ukraine, this book's focus is on Dominica, Grenada, Guyana, Jamaica, and the Dominican Republic.

It should be added that geography still plays a role as do domestic politics. The United States cannot "leave" the Caribbean, considering that it marks much of its southern border. Furthermore, domestic U.S. politics now has sizable immigrant communities from the region that tend to show up at the voting booth, as reflected by the 2020 presidential election. This also means that the U.S. tolerance of foreign powers seeking to gain influence and control over such strategic locations as the Panama Canal or the Bahamas port facilities is low. For a Biden administration all of this has to be carefully weighed as it crafts the next stage of U.S.–Caribbean relations and it is to be balanced with the rivalry with China on a grander, global scale. For the purposes of this book, Panama and Venezuela are given a quasi-Caribbean status, meaning that while they are very much part of Latin America, they still play an important role in shaping Caribbean affairs, much more so than Colombia and Mexico, both of which also have Caribbean coastlines.

OPERATIONALIZING TERMS

Before advancing further it is important to define our terms. The Caribbean is the region that encompasses the Greater and Lesser Antilles, the Dutch islands of Aruba, Bonaire, and Curacao (just north of Venezuela), Belize in the Central American mainland (as it is a former British colony, English-speaking, and a member of the Caribbean Community or CARICOM), and the three Guianas on the northeastern shoulder of South America. Although Guyana, Suriname, and French Guiana share borders with Brazil and Venezuela and look out into the Atlantic, their respective cultures are more Caribbean and they have participated in regional Caribbean institutions. In the broader sense, Venezuela and Panama are included as part of the thematic definition as discussed above.

New Cold War?

Another key term is the new Cold War. There is a debate about whether there is a new Cold War or not. Although the United States and

China may not be entirely there yet, Henry Kissinger, speaking in late 2019, probably got it right in arguing that the two countries are now in the "foothills of a Cold War" (Brown 2019). The question is: do China and the United States move from the foothills to the mountains of a full-fledged Cold War? The potential for such a development is likely to increase through the next decade. The Russo-Ukrainian War has certainly done much to reinforce the idea of a new Cold War, especially as it has made a starker contrast between authoritarian and democratic governments and pushed along the de-globalization of trade and investment.

For the purposes of this book, the new Cold War refers to a geopolitical and economic rivalry between a set of Western liberal democratic and market-oriented countries and their competitors who represent an alternative set of guiding political principles which embrace authoritarian or autocratic regimes and usually favor a larger state role in the economy (which can generally be described as capitalist in the broad sense but are driven more by close relationships between major state and private sector representatives). The rivalry between these two sets of countries is global in nature and runs the risk over the long term of shifting from a Cold War-like situation to a hot one (i.e. military conflict). Potential flashpoints include the South China Sea, Taiwan Strait, Syria, and Venezuela. That stated, the main protagonists at this stage are the United States and China, but there is a process of pulling other countries into competing camps. This was reflected by the June 2021 G7 and NATO meetings, which issued wide-ranging warnings to China on disinformation, military cooperation with Russia, and rapid expansion of its nuclear weapons arsenal (Peel and Warrell 2021). Indeed, the NATO communiqué warned that the above constituted "systemic challenges" to the "rules-based international order." For its part, China criticized the G7 countries for "sinister intentions" and "artificially creating confrontation and friction" (Peel and Warrell 2021).

To be certain, the new Cold War is not an exact repeat of the last Cold War. Rather we subscribe to a view often attributed to Mark Twain, "History doesn't repeat itself but it often rhymes." This is a new Cold War of sorts, complete with two large competitors, with strongly different ideological views (at least in terms of political systems), but each seeking to dominate the economic system, not to replace it. The rivalry is taking place planet-wide as well as in cyberspace and outer space. Propaganda and fake news are playing their part in forming opinions and seeking to sway targeted audiences. The new Cold War has reverberations in global supply chains, transnational pandemics, and technology. And it is likely to intensify.

A system of competing alliance systems has not yet been fully created, but there is room for strategic realignments as the United States, under both the Trump and the Biden administrations, has sought to better coordinate policies against China with a number of European and Asian countries. One result of this has been the creation of the Quad, a loose military-political alliance between the United States, Australia, India, and Japan. Another key element of coalition-building is "Five Eyes," an intelligence alliance consisting of Australia, Canada, New Zealand, the United Kingdom, and the United States. Yet another example is the G7 launch of B3W (Build Back Better World) Partnership, which places an emphasis on Western help for infrastructure projects in key developing countries. In 2022, NATO received a substantial revival due to the Russo-Ukrainian War, including the potential expansion to Include Finland and Sweden. The pressure is also on the Caribbean to pick a side, though it may be more politely framed by the Biden administration.

For its part, China has formed an increasingly closer working relationship with Russia, which has become engaged in the Caribbean and elsewhere. Indeed, the Russian relationship was officially moved closer during the 2022 Beijing Winter Olympics when presidents Xi and Putin declared a "new era" in the global system, which challenges the United States as a world power, NATO as a cornerstone of international security, and liberal democracy as a model for the world (Wright 2022). The Russo-Ukrainian war has strained relations with Russia, but China still maintains a high level of trade and is carefully monitoring the situation. Relations between China, Russia, and Iran have also moved closer. China also has "friends" in the Caribbean, Cuba, Venezuela, and Nicaragua. Moreover, there has been a gradual effort to expand beyond its traditional spheres of influence, establishing its first military base in Djibouti in 2017 and there was discussion in 2021 of another base in Equatorial Guinea, which would bring Chinese naval power into the Atlantic. Both the African countries have received considerable attention from Chinese banks and building companies, helped in the construction of a major port to function as a deeps-sea port facility (Tanchum 2021). In 2022, China also turned its attention to the South Pacific countries, offering many of the same incentives (both through public and private companies) as well as looking to port development. Chinese companies have sought to entice some Caribbean countries with the same idea.

To this broad definition of the New Cold War should be added that China's quest for world domination is very different from that of the Soviet Union during the Cold War. There is no question that President Xi Jinping wants to make China great again or the leading global hegemon. This policy stance fits into a certain historical and civilizational approach. In this China's role in the world was caught by Michael Schuman, author of *Superpower Interrupted: The Chinese History of the World*, in which he asserted: "…China wants what it always had. China was a superpower for almost all of its history, and it wants to be a superpower again…In their view, the Chinese have a right to be a premier power in the world, and they want to return to their proper position at the apex of the global order (Schuman 2020: 4; Lawler 2019). This fits the traditional view that China has had of itself as the center of the world, the Middle Kingdom.

China's view of the Middle Kingdom has not left it. This was well noted by Martin Jacques' *When China Rules the World: the End of the Western World and the Birth of a New Global Order*: "Until its engagement with Europe in the nineteenth century, China saw itself in terms quite different from those of a nation-state. China believed that it was the center of the world, the Middle Kingdom, the 'land under Heaven' (*tianxia*), on an entirely different plane from other kingdoms and countries, not even requiring a name. It was the chosen land not by virtue of God, as in the case of Israel or the United States, but by the sheer brilliance of its civilization" (Jacques 2009: 240–241). In this system, the world rotated around China, with its influence reaching out first to those states that were civilized (having found their way through Chinese enlightenment) to the semi-civilized and finally to the barbarians. What is significant here is that this is not a world order of nation-states, but one based on a combination of conquest, assimilation and leading by superiority of civilization, which led in a sense to its "civilizing mission." Thus, China's mission is more one of hegemony and dominance, an ability to control the world around it, than outright conquest or the overthrow of world capitalism (though that could be modified to a more Sinocentric form).

The nuances of the new Cold War are important to understand; this author fully admits the term has differences from Soviet-American competition. China's leaders want to return to the pre-Trump world, which means establishing dominance over key elements of the future global economy and society such as 5G and internet governance, crushing support for liberal democratic norms at home (including Hong Kong) and undermining them overseas. It also wants to break up the U.S. alliance system and bring international forums under its dominance to help maintain a pro-China narrative and crush any critical voices (Doshi 2021). As *Axios* reporter Bethany Allen-Ebrahimian observes, "When Chinese government officials criticize what they explicitly call a 'Cold War mentality' in the U.S., they aren't calling for an end of ideological competition or great power rivalry, but rather to stop U.S. attempts to stymie Beijing's plans" (Allen-Ebrahimian 2020). In this, China is not necessarily exporting its development model overseas, but encouraging countries in the developing economies to adopt its governance practices in order to make them better client states (Rolland 2021). Government, party and military officials as well as state-run media foster influence and favorable elite and public opinion in a wide range of countries. Democratic government is seen as a major challenge to China's ability to reach this objective. At home, it would mean the end of the Chinese Communist Party's monopoly on power.

Two other points are worth mentioning. First, China's views about reclaiming its role at the helm of world order have been conditioned by a deep sense of grievance toward the West, which humbled it during the imperialist era (including the defeats in the Opium Wars, the sack of the Summer Palace in 1860 in Beijing, and the creation of treaty ports). The second point is that in securing control over Eurasia via the Belt and Road Initiative (BRI), Beijing also needs the resources and markets offered by Africa and the Western Hemisphere, including the Caribbean. In this, an aggressive approach in the U.S. backyard serves to keep its main rival off-balance, especially as such actions can be paired with ever closer relations with Russia to reinforce Beijing's and Moscow's revisionist ambitions in their respective spheres of influence.

The idea of a new Cold War is not limited to China hawks in the Democratic and Republican parties in the United States, but also has a following in China, especially in the Chinese Communist Party and with some of the leading intellectuals. While China's leadership is hardly monolithic in its worldview, the new Cold War idea appears to have taken root. One Washington, D.C.-based U.S. China specialist who declined to be identified noted of the Chinese Communist Party: "Perhaps they never gave up the idea of global revolution, but have taken a long view. The old Cold War has blurred into the new Cold War."

There is an echo of this in the views of Yao Yang, dean of the National School of Development at Peking University and a leading voice on U.S.–China relations, in an April 2020 interview in the Beijing Cultural Review: "To a certain degree we already find ourselves in the situation of a new Cold War. There are two basic reasons for this. The first is the need for Western politicians to play the blame game about the origins of the pandemic. The next thing is that now Westerners want to make this into a 'systems' question, saying that the reason that China could carry out such drastic control measures is because China is not a democratic society, and this is where the power and capacity to do this came from" (Ferguson 2020).

The Chinese line is that the United States, in seeking to contain China's rising power, has started a new Cold War. This struggle will end the same way as the last, with the United States being the aging superpower (led by old leaders and not able to keep up in terms of technology) and China will assume the role of the United States. As Eric Li, a trustee of the China Institute at Shanghai's Fudan University, forecast, "By contrast, China today is the opposite of what the USSR was decades ago. It is practical, ascendant and globally connected" (Rachman 2020).

One other element of the Chinese view of a new Cold War is that it will be a purely technological competition, without proxy wars and nuclear brinksmanship. According to Yan Xuetong, Dean of the Institute of International Studies Tsinghua University, the parameters of such a struggle will keep the United States–China competition more like a cold war than the run-up to the two world wars. Considering the Chinese government's active assistance of its domestic technology sector (such as with Huawei and ZTE) and U.S. counter-measures to balance out Chinese state aid against concerns over the ability of those companies to eavesdrop on other countries' governments and companies, there is more than a faint echo of a new Cold War.

There Will Be No Cold War?

There is a counter-argument to the idea of a new Cold War; the global system is now in the grips of great power competition. The idea of a new Cold War is wrong. Accordingly, the two rivals generally acknowledge the broader rules of the game and wish to preserve the main characteristics of the global system, trade, investment, and a degree of political stability.

To put it mildly, a real new Cold War threatens massive wealth generation between the two countries. The interdependence that was created between the world's two largest economies is expected to be maintained. This is a major contrast to the old Cold War, which as Thomas J. Christensen, Professor of International and Public Affairs and Director of China and the World Program at Columbia University, observed, "…was marked by a full-spectrum effort that went beyond the military realm. U.S. containment policy was designed to limit economic contact with those countries and cripple their economies at home while frustrating their diplomacy abroad" (Christensen 2021). It is not clear where cyber-attacks on U.S. private sector and government institutes would fit in his assessment.

Another point in the argument against the idea of a new Cold War is that China has played a key role in the development of the global economy since the late 1990s and the first two decades of the twenty-first century. China has not advocated, as the Soviet Union did in the old Cold War, overturning and replacing the world capitalist system. In many ways, China has sought to be a responsible stakeholder on the international stage as reflected by the critical role it played in 2008 by implementing a massive stimulus package to its economy. That effort buffered the downside of the Great Recession as the strong appetite for natural resources helped re-stimulate growth in many floundering economies.

One last point is that the complexity and interdependent nature of the global economic system do not easily render a detachment of countries into two sharply defined economic and military blocs. In this there will be no equivalent to NATO and the Warsaw Pact. Reinforcing this is a view that China has no allies, let alone a bloc of client states to lead (Mearsheimer 2014b). At the same time, the U.S.–European relationship, especially between Berlin and Washington, is fading as national interests increasingly diverge.

The points listed above seek to discredit the new Cold War idea. As Christensen noted, "So although China's rise carries real challenges for the United States, its allies and its partners, the threat should not be misunderstood. The voices calling for a cold war containment strategy toward China misunderstand the nature of the China challenge and therefore prescribe responses that will only weaken the United States" (Christensen 2021). According to him the main threat from China is the potential for the Asian country to stumble economically at home, which would have global consequences (including in the Caribbean).

Christensen is not the only one viewing the rivalry between the United States and China as overblown. Carol Wise, Professor of International Relations at the University of Southern California and author of *Dragonomics (2020)*, dismisses the Chinese strategic challenge to U.S. interests in the Western Hemisphere. As she noted:

> From the standpoint of the Western Hemisphere, I dispute hawkish, so-called realist interpretations of China's rise in Latin America as a security threat or affront to US hegemony. Realists fret that China's rapid economic catch-up with the US and its aggressive military buildup could destabilize the world order. It is true that China could wreak havoc on the international system but perhaps for reasons that have more to do with some of the inherent weaknesses in the Chinese economy. (Wise 2020)

Despite the strong resistance to the idea of a new Cold War, among those who believe that the international system is already in a new Cold War or heading in that direction are energy expert Daniel Yergin, Chile's former ambassador to China Jorge Heine, economic historian Niall Ferguson, and geopolitical thinker Robert Kaplan (most recently named to the Robert Strausz-Hupé Chair in Geopolitics at the Foreign Policy Research Institute in Philadelphia).

The so-called misunderstood nature of the new Cold War school notwithstanding, it does appear to be a factor that some in Latin America are considering. As former Chilean diplomats Carlos Fortín, Jorge Heine, and Carlos Ominami observed: "We are at the dawn of a Second Cold War, this time between the United States and the People's Republic of China. In this new version, the year 2020 is the equivalent of 1950" (Fortín et al. 2020). Each of those individuals has a deep understanding of China and global politics and economics. From a non-U.S. view, the three Chileans see a new Cold War in motion. The questions that lingers is that for those who do not see a new Cold War, what exact conditions would determine such an outcome? Although the argument is likely to continue over whether or not there is a new Cold War, what is evident is that U.S.–China competition over the Caribbean is set to continue in the years ahead. Both sides of the argument have merits, leading to our assessment that the global system is heading toward a new Cold War, but still has room to avoid such a development.

Economic Statecraft

A third key term used throughout the text is economic statecraft (Baldwin 1985; Blanchard and Ripsman 2008; Blanchard 2018). This is broadly defined as one country's ability to use economic means to influence other countries into doing what it wants them to do. Stated in another way, this falls under the realm of political economy, providing a perceptual lens through which to observe how economic forces influence state policies, including national security goals. In China's case, cheap loans, less stringent lending guidelines, infrastructure development, trade agreements, and other means of assistance boost the Asian country's soft power by demonstrating it to be an economic and political leader and benefactor (Blanchard and Lu 2012). This has had a particular resonance in much of the Caribbean, which have found access to capital from the United States and other Western countries challenging. In return for Chinese largesse, a number of Caribbean countries have opted to provide support for China in international forums, especially when it has come to Taiwan, Hong Kong, and criticism of China's human rights record.

Economic statecraft is not all about providing economic goodies to needy countries. There is another, the negative side of economic statecraft. If a country receiving Chinese assistance takes a stance regarded as contrary to Chinese national interests, there can be punitive actions. In 2021 Guyana ran afoul of China when it moved to allow Taiwan to open a trade office. To be fair, the United States and European countries have also used tough economic statecraft, including economic sanctions, targeting of certain individuals and their offshore financial holdings, tariffs, and non-tariff trade barriers. Examples of this include the United States' longstanding economic sanctions regime against Cuba and the effort against the Maduro regime in Venezuela, while the European Union has been active in the same fashion vis-à-vis Russia after that country's invasion and annexation of Crimea from Ukraine and against Belarus in 2020 over fraudulent elections.

China and the United States engage in economic statecraft. Russia is less inclined to do so considering its smaller economic capacity compared to the United States and China. While a number of studies have captured the Asian country's economic statecraft in action in Africa and Latin America, the focus has been more limited in terms of Chinese and, for that matter, Russian, economic statecraft in the Caribbean. In this context, the works of Richard Bernal, Jorge Heine, Margaret Myers, and Robert Ellis are noteworthy (Bernal 2014; Heine and Anson 2014; Myers and Wise 2017; and Ellis 2018). Each of them emphasizes the rise of China in the Americas, with Bernal more narrowly focused on the Caribbean. Central to each of these studies is the emphasis placed on economic statecraft in achieving Beijing's goals as opposed to military means. China has thus far indicated that it has little inclination to precipitate a military conflict over the Caribbean with the United States; the South China Sea or Taiwan could be an altogether different matter. However, Beijing can tie down U.S. resources by garnering greater influence in the Caribbean, especially considering that Washington's role as a dependable ally is seen throughout much of the region as more questionable due to the Trump years. Indeed, Trump's period in office cast uncertainty over what had been seen as a relatively constant partner, making the work of the following administrations more challenging.

The Caribbean is also at a time when economic statecraft is being carefully weighed with military action, which extends to the Venezuelan crisis and that country's threats vis-à-vis its neighbor, Guyana. This is something Caribbean leaders have to consider. The question arises: when do soft power options end and hard power options begin? Political scientist Joseph Nye, Jr. addresses this issue in his *The Future of Power* (2011) when discussing what is more effective, the workings of the market or the use of military force: "Both sides have a point…whether one or another type of resource produces power in the sense of desired behavior depends upon the context. A carrot is more effective than a stick if you wish to lead a mule to water, but a gun may be more useful if your aim is to deprive an opponent of his mule" (Nye 2011).

For the Caribbean, the new Cold War potentially represents a lot of carrots. Most Caribbean countries have significant needs in terms of critical infrastructure, such as roads, ports, and dependable electrical power generation and distribution. They need to broaden their economic base beyond tourism, a tough challenge and near impossible in some cases. Financing has always been a challenge. One of the key developments in the new Cold War is that China's penetration into the Caribbean has gone hand in hand with its willingness to construct everything from presidential offices and sports stadiums to hospitals and airport upgrades. Access to cheap loans with no political (human rights) requirements or often with no environmental preconditions has only eased China's penetration into the region. As Jochen Bittner, a political editor for the German weekly newspaper *Die Zeit*, noted, "Unlike the West, China doesn't let human rights and the rule of law get in the way of investments" (Bittner 2018). This has relevance for the Caribbean, especially when contrasted with U.S. administrations' unwillingness to match Chinese aid money.

Sharp Power

Another term used in the upcoming chapters is sharp power, which broadly incorporates misinformation, disinformation, and propaganda, all of which could fit under the flag of fake news. One definition of this is provided by a Global Americans study (2021), which focused on Chinese, Russian, Cuban, and Venezuelan activities in Argentina, Chile, Colombia, Mexico, and Peru. Accordingly, sharp power is "a new phenomenon that is often used by non-democratic regimes seeking to attract, distract, and manipulate audiences in democratic countries through their communications outlets, cultural centers, and global learning institutes. Sharp power effectively creates a positive image of the regime via targeted messaging at the international level and influence exertion at the national level" (Global Americans 2021). To this could be added the following from Christopher Walker at the *Journal of Democracy*: "This approach takes advantage of the asymmetry between free and unfree systems, allowing authoritarian regimes both to limit free expression and to distort political environments in democracies while simultaneously shielding their own domestic public spaces from democratic appeals coming from abroad" (Walker 2018).

In the 2021 Global Americans study, it was found that Chinese and Russian sharp power were active in Latin America, especially during the height of the Covid-19 pandemic. Chinese and Russian actors were active in promoting the effectiveness of their countries' vaccines vis-à-vis those from the United States and Europe. At the same time, Russian actors (usually connected to an official media outlet) were active in seeking to augment tensions as during social disturbances in Colombia (2021) and Chile in 2019–2021. Although a deep study like that conducted by Global Americans (with four major Latin American research organizations) has not been done in the Caribbean, it is probable that Chinese sharp power was active in demonstrating the superiority of Beijing's approach to Covid and development in general over that of the United States and the West.

Geography Still Matters

Although this point should not be over-emphasized, geography does play a role in U.S. considerations vis-à-vis the Caribbean. Despite inconsistency in policy focus, the United States does care about the Caribbean. Part of the problem is that the North American perceptual lens of the Caribbean often paints it as a place where people go to party or conduct offshore finance. That stated, the Caribbean Sea occupies considerable strategic space. Retired U.S. Admiral James Stavridis notes: "The Caribbean is a big sea – if you include the Gulf of Mexico, which we will do for our purposes, it surpasses the Mediterranean as the world's largest body of water that is not categorized as an ocean (after the Pacific, Atlantic, and Arctic oceans in that order). It is roughly 1.6 million square miles, about half the size of the continental United States" (Stravidis 2018).

The Caribbean's significance is even greater when considering that it sits due south of the continental United States and is a major transit point for U.S., European, Asian, and Latin American trade. A number of ports in the Caribbean are among the largest and busiest in handling global trade, including Kingston, Jamaica, San Juan, Puerto Rico, Caucedo, the Dominican Republic, and Freeport, the Bahamas. Geographical proximity has also contributed to longstanding cultural links to North America due to migration from the islands to the mainland.

The Caribbean also remains a key area for U.S. investment, especially in travel and leisure, and is also a market for agricultural exports. Because of this, when change ripples through the Caribbean other countries, in particular the United States, pay attention. They have to. Geography still matters. China's stepped-up role in the region is therefore worth noting.

The new Cold War geopolitical environment will probably intensify into the foreseeable future and it is likely to see shifting alliances among the major and regional powers as well as hitting a number of tipping points. At the same time, the Caribbean faces major economic challenges; it will have to contend with the slow-motion train wreck of Venezuela and its refugees (over 6 million in 2022); deal with an economically struggling Cuba; and is vulnerable to powerful transnational criminal organizations and cybercrime. The 2020–2021 coronavirus pandemic has added one more problem to be resolved. Many countries in the region still suffer from low vaccination levels, partially due to the slowness of gaining access to vaccines. All of these have an international component, especially if both the United States and China continue down the road to more Cold War-like policies.

Outline of the Book

The book is broken into 10 chapters including an introduction and conclusion. The second chapter focuses on how China became a significant force in the Caribbean, discussing the Asian country's economic transformation and containing a brief account of the forces driving Chinese companies and banks out into the larger world as well as strategic considerations. It is important to add that while Chinese companies often serve as an extension of Chinese government influence, they are mainly driven by the need to make profits and management must balance business and political considerations. Failure to consider the political considerations can leave management teams at the mercy of measures taken by the Chinese Communist Party.

Chapter 3 "China, Venezuela, and Cuba: The New Cold War" discusses two of the states where China has become the most engaged (for different reasons). Venezuela has emerged as a pivot in U.S.–Caribbean relations as well, especially as Washington imposed economic sanctions on the Maduro regime. China is also a supporter of Cuba's creaky Marxist experiment. There is another twist in this; Cuba is one of the major supporters of the Maduro regime, which puts it on the same side as China (and for that matter Russia and Iran). At the same time, China reluctantly helps prop up the Castrorite regime in Havana. In many ways, the nexus of China–Venezuela–Cuba is where the idea of a new Cold War is the most intense. Chinese and Russian sharp power are their most powerful in these two countries, especially as the Maduro and Castroite regimes are also active in misinformation, disinformation, and propaganda at home and in the neighborhood (as in Colombia) (Global Americans 2021).

Chapter 4 "China and the English-Speaking Caribbean and Suriname" discusses the Asian power's penetration into this part of the region based mainly on economic statecraft. Chinese banks and companies have played and continue to play an important role in this. Although the Caribbean lacks the size and scope of Argentina, Brazil, and Peru, it possesses oil, natural gas, uranium, gold, and timber as well as geo-economically important sea lanes starting on the Pacific side of Panama and ending in the Atlantic. In China's push into the region, it has played its economic statecraft well and is generally perceived as a good partner (in some countries more so than others). Suriname is also brought into this chapter, considering that the Chinese role in that country's economy expanded considerably through the 2010–2021 period, with the Asian country emerging as one of its largest creditors and home to a growing population of Chinese settlers.

Chapter 5 covers how Caribbean countries are responding to the New Cold War. Some are in denial that such a struggle is occurring; some believe that it exists but is manageable; and others are concerned, especially about China's rising influence and uncertainty over long-term U.S. policy in the region. While Chapter 4 discussed specific Caribbean–Chinese interaction, this chapter focuses more on how people in the Caribbean perceive China's role in their home countries. As Jamaica's former ambassador to the United States, Richard L. Bernal, noted, "Whether or not China replaces the U.S. as the dominant superpower, it will still be a major and increasingly influential superpower. By now it should be pellucid to even the most Sinophobic person in the Caribbean that the region can benefit from a strong relationship with China if the relationship is handled properly" (Bernal 2014).

Chapter 6 analyzes the themes of China's embrace of the Caribbean through its competition for diplomatic supremacy with Taiwan. The role of Panama, the Dominican Republic, and Haiti will be discussed in the context of the new Cold War through the China–Taiwan prism. Taiwan has a role to play in the region, especially as it is also a relatively small island state forced to deal with larger, more powerful neighbors. It is also an important U.S. ally. Panama has been added in this chapter; though it is not a Caribbean country per se, if Beijing has any long-term geostrategic ideas for the Caribbean, Panama has to be part of them. It is an important transit point and geopolitically it would be an important piece of real estate in case of a war, if for nothing else but to deny the use of its canal to the United States.

From chapters two through five the key narratives will touch upon how China's BRI and other contacts are related to the Caribbean. China has sought to portray itself as a generous international force, but it is also fiercely nationalistic and willing to use pressure when it does not get its way. This generally has not been seen in the Caribbean, but considering the Chinese track record in Asia, Africa, and Europe, the harder-nosed side of Beijing's behavior is something that could eventually be revealed, especially if a Caribbean country fails to follow Beijing's dictates on core policy objectives and votes in international bodies.

Chapter 7 covers Russia and Iran's engagement with the Caribbean. Although Russia's foreign policy has been oriented to restoring Moscow's influence in Eastern Europe and the Middle East, it has a longstanding relationship with Cuba and, like China, regards the United States as a strategic rival. To be certain, Russia's engagement in the Caribbean is more limited than that of China and is more narrowly focused in terms of the sectors it is involved in with its Caribbean counterparts, such as energy. It has also been willing to send military equipment and advisors to Venezuela and Nicaragua. The Caribbean serves another purpose; the United States has become engaged in Russia's "front yard," i.e. the Baltics and Ukraine, hence Russian involvement in the Caribbean has its usefulness. Russia's war in Ukraine against Ukraine saw Russia reaching, out to Cuba, Nicaragua, and Venezuela prior to the outbreak of fighting. They have not moved from their strong support of Russia.

As for Iran, the focus on the Caribbean has largely been on deepening relations with Venezuela, especially during the Maduro years. Both nations have been hit by U.S. economic sanctions, leaving them to look for greater trade between them. Iran has sent tankers to Venezuela as well as supplied military equipment for the South American country's navy. Iran has also sought to engage Guyana with an eye to that country's supply of uranium. As with Russia, Iran's role in the Caribbean is one of asymmetry. Since the 1979 Islamic Revolution which brought the Islamic Republic into being, the United States and Iran have been locked in a tense relationship, occasionally coming to blows. At the same time, Iran has been happy to pursue its own national interest by engaging in its own Cold War with U.S. ally Saudi Arabia in the Middle East. Backing distant Venezuela places some of the battle between Tehran and Washington in the latter's own backyard. It also creates a policy area where Tehran, Beijing, and Russia generally share objectives.

Chapter 8 "Europe and Canada: Caribbean Relations and the New Cold War" covers two things. Europe's and Canada's changing perceptions of a new Cold War and the role played by these countries in the Caribbean. Three European countries still have holdings in the region (France, the Netherlands, and the UK), while Spain maintains relations in the Spanish-speaking Caribbean, including Cuba. Germany is very reluctant to be engaged in a new Cold War, especially against China, considering its economic links. This raises questions over long-term European policies vis-à-vis the Caribbean as well as how much coordination can be expected between Berlin and Washington, and quite possibility between Berlin and Madrid, The Hague, Paris, and London.

Canada has longstanding relations with the English-speaking Caribbean, sharing a colonial history and trade relations. It has also seen its relationship with China become tenser over human rights in Hong Kong, the activities of Chinese companies in Canada, and trade issues (such as canola and other agricultural goods). As tensions have risen between China and the United States, they have also brought many of the same concerns to Canada. The Caribbean retains some importance to Canada.

Chapter 9 "U.S. Policy in a Choppy Caribbean Sea" covers the shift of U.S. policy from a low-level sense of urgency about the Caribbean to one shaped by growing geopolitical concerns as China's profile in the Caribbean (and elsewhere) rose. The policy is focused heavily on China's role in Venezuela and Cuba as well as in the English-speaking Caribbean, particularly in Jamaica, Trinidad and Tobago, Guyana, and Suriname. The Biden administration has signaled a return to a more multilateral approach, but the challenge posed by China remains. Moreover, U.S.–China relations do not appear ready for a reset. While the Biden administration is seeking to back away from new Cold War terminology, the trajectory in relations seems to be still on the same course toward a more bipolar world. This presents major challenges to U.S. policymakers, covering everything from assistance with infrastructure development to vaccine diplomacy (Griffith 2021).

Chapter 10 looks at the three different scenarios for the mix of the Caribbean, China, and the United States as well as U.S. policy options. During the Trump years, the Monroe Doctrine was re-invoked as well as the articulation of a preference for regime change in Cuba, Nicaragua, and Venezuela. The Biden administration signaled a different approach, returning to more traditional, multilateral strategy (though much of the administration's regional policy lacked any long-term vision). The United States needs to give more serious thought to the benefits of economic statecraft, especially if it wants to compete with China and Russia. While the threat of force is one option for foreign policy outcomes, there is also something to be said for soft power options, something that is expected to have a greater role in the Biden administration (which has been slow in formulating a coherent and meaningful Caribbean policy). This is more urgent in the face of the coronavirus pandemic in 2020–2022 and its devastating impact on Caribbean economies.

Any new policy initiatives for the Caribbean must go beyond the U.S. government's *Caribbean 2020: A Multi-Year Strategy to Increase the Security, Prosperity, and Well-Being of the People of the United States and the Caribbean*, a nice-sounding document, but with little real substance beyond existing programs (U.S. Department of State 2019). The 2020s are set to be a challenging decade. The United States faces rebuilding its own economy in the aftermath of the coronavirus pandemic, which means that on the foreign policy front it will have to make tough decisions about which areas are priorities and which areas are not. That does not mean a full-scale pullback from the post-World War II international relations construct, but a fine-tuning and more precise focus on great power rivalry. It also means increased attention given to helping meet regional needs for such agenda items as infrastructure and climate change assistance as well as helping to counter Chinese and Russian sharp power. In this, the Caribbean remains an important crossroads of geopolitical competition and could play a more significant economic role as the United States continues to decouple from China and bring its supply chain either back to home or in the neighborhood through nearshoring. And the Caribbean has its own needs in dealing with climate change, how to retrain young people from becoming a part of a brain drain to the north, and broadening economic activity from a heavy dependence on tourism to a broader-based approach reflected by blue economies.

A new Cold War or great power competition is something that can derail global economic growth and raises the prospects of war. Although both the United States and China want to dominate the commanding heights of the global economic and political order, it is questionable that either country wants to risk outright warfare, which would be highly destructive for everyone. For the Caribbean, the return to a sharper-edged great power rivalry is not good news if the main protagonists allow nationalist jingoism to override prudent policy options. In this regard, there is an onus on Caribbean states to make clear to Beijing and Washington that they have little wish to be caught in a "with us or against us" world. This is going to be a tough challenge in the years ahead.

It was Barbados-born novelist, essayist, and poet George Lamming who stated, "The architecture of our future is not only unfinished; the scaffolding has hardly gone up." Although this was said a number of decades ago, Lamming's words still have resonance in the third decade of the twenty-first century for the Caribbean—and the United States. The world faces considerable uncertainty in the decades ahead. The advent of a new Cold War-like situation as well as major changes facing the Caribbean in the wake of the Covid-19 pandemic all call for a new architecture to guide local leaders and the United States and China. Failure to find the right architecture could open the door to upheaval; moving beyond the scaffolding stage could open a brighter future for the Caribbean, where its role as a crossroads brings it to a better state of development.

REFERENCES

Alden, Chris. 2007. *China in Africa* Zed Books.
American Enterprise Institute, China Global Tracker. https://www.aei.org/china-global-investment-tracker/ (Accessed on June 22, 2021a).
American Enterprise Institute, *China Global Tracker*. https://www.aei.org/china-global-investment-tracker/ (Accessed on June 22, 2021b)
Baldwin, David A. 1985. *Economic Statecraft*. Princeton: Princeton University Press.
Bernal, Richard. 2014. *Dragon in the Caribbean: China's Global Re-Positioning: Challenges and Opportunities for the Caribbean*. Ian Randle Publishers.
Bittner, Jochen. 2018. Who Will Win the New Great Game?, *The New York Times*. April 27: A27.
Bittner, Jochen. 2020. America and Europe Are Split on China. They Must Come Together. *The New York Times*, July 1. https://www.nytimes.com/2020/07/01/opinion/europe-china-united-states.html.
Blanchard, Jean-Marc F. and Fujia Lu. 2021. Thinking Hard About Soft Power: A Review and Critique of the Literature on China and Soft Power. *Asian Perspective* 36(4): 565–589.
Blanchard, Jean-Marc and Norrin M. Ripsman. 2008. A Political Theory of Economic Statecraft. *Foreign Policy Analysis* 4(4) (October): 371–398.
Blanchard, Jean-Marc. 2018. *China's Maritime Silk Road Initiative and South Asia: A Political Economic Analysis of its Purposes*. Perils and Promise: Palgrave Macmillan.
Brautigram, Deborah. 2011. *The Dragon's Gift: The Real Story of China in Africa*. Oxford University Press.
Bridglal, Carla, Ivan Cairo, Steffon Campbell, Alix Lewis and Neil Marks. 2019. China's Opaque Caribbean Trail: Dreams, Deals and Debt, *Caribbean Investigative Journalism Network*, December 5. https://www.cijn.org/chinas-opaque-caribbean-trail-dreams-deals-and-debt/.

Brown, Andrew. 2019. Foothills of a Cold War, *Bloomberg*, November 19. https://www.bloomberg.com/news/newsletters/2019-11-21/-foothills-of-a-cold-war.

Caribbean Development Bank. 2014. USD30 Billion Needed to Modernize Caribbean Infrastructure over Next Decade. Caribbean Development Bank. June 20. https://www.caribank.org/newsroom/news-and-events/usd30-billion-needed-modernise-caribbean-infrastructure-over-next-decade.

Chaitram, Samantha S.S. 2020. *American Foreign Policy in the English-Speaking Caribbean: From the Eighteenth to the Twenty-first Century*. Palgrave Macmillan.

Christensen, Thomas J. 2021. There Will Not be a New Cold War, *Foreign Affairs*, (March 24) https://www.foreignaffairs.com/articles/united-states/2021-03-24/there-will-not-be-new-cold-war.

Doshi, Rush. 2021. *The Long Game: China's Grand Strategy to Displace American Order*. Oxford University Press.

Evan Ellis. 2009. *China in Latin America: The Whats and Wherefores*. Lynne Reiner.

Evan Ellis. November 2018. *The Future of Latin America and the Caribbean in the Context of the Rise of China*. Center for Strategic & International Studies.

Ferguson, Niall. 2020. America and China Are Entering the Dark Forest. *Bloomberg Opinion*. July 5. https://www.bloomberg.com/opinion/articles/2020-07-05/is-the-u-s-in-a-new-cold-war-china-has-already-declared-it?sref=8VBJk9tz.

Fortín, Carlos, Jorge Heine and Carlos Ominami. 2020. Latin America Between a Rock and a hard Place: A Second Cold War and the Active Non-Alignment Option. *Global Policy*. October 2. https://www.globalpolicyjournal.com/blog/02/10/2020/latin-america-between-rock-and-hard-place-second-cold-war-and-active-non-alignment.

French, Howard W. 2014. *China's Second Continent: How a Million Migrants Are Building a New Empire in Africa*. Knopf.

Gallagher, Kevin. 2016. *The China Triangle: Latin America's China Boom and the Fate of the Washington Consensus*. Oxford University Press.

Global Americans. 2021. Measuring the Impact of Misinformation, Disinformation, and Propaganda in Latin America, Executive Summary. *Global Americans*. https://theglobalamericans.org/wp-content/uploads/2021/10/2021.10.28-Global-Americans-Disinformation-Report_Executive-Summary.pdf.

Griffith, Ivelaw. 2021. Vaccination and Vaccine Diplomacy in the Caribbean. Forthcoming Global Americans.

Heine, Jorge and Cynthia Anson. 2014. *Reaching across the Pacific: Latin America and Asia in the New Century*. The Wilson Center.

Hoss, Ryan. 2021. *Stronger: Adopting America's China Strategy in an Age of Competitive Interdependence*. Yale University Press.

Jacques, Martin. 2009. *When China Rules the World: The End of the Western World and the Birth of a New Global Order*. The Penguin Press.

Jones, Handel. 2010. *Chinamerica: The Uneasy Partnership that Will Change the World*. McGraw-Hill Education.

Kaplan, Robert D. 2019. A New Cold War Has Begun. *Foreign Policy*. January 7. https://foreignpolicy.com/2019/01/07/a-new-cold-war-has-begun/.

Kaplan, Robert D. 2012. *The Revenge of Geography: What the Map Tells Us about the Coming Conflicts and the Battle Against Fate*. Random House.

Lawler, Dave. 2019. China's Blueprint for Global Dominance. *Axios*, April 8. https://www.axios.com/china-plan-global-superpower-xi-jinping-5954481e-02c8-4e19-a50c-cd2a90e4894f.html.

Lewis, Patsy. 2020. The Challenging Path to Caribbean Integration. *Current History*, February: 54–59.

Li, Eric Xun. 2018. Opinion: Why Xi's Lifting of Term Limits is a Good Thing. *The Washington Post*. April 2. https://www.washingtonpost.com/news/the worldpost/wp/2018/04/02/xi-term-limits/.

MacDonald, Scott B. 2019a. Sino-Caribbean Relations in a Changing Caribbean Geopolitical Sea. *Journal of Chinese Political Science*. December 24(4): 665–684.

MacDonald, Scott B. 2019b. The Return of the Cold War in the Caribbean. Center for Strategic & International Studies. May 8. https://www.csis.org/analysis/return-cold-war-caribbean.

Maingot, Anthony P. and Wilfedo Lozano. 2004. *The United States and the Caribbean: Transforming Hegemony and Sovereignty*. Routledge.

Myers, Margaret, and Carol Wise. 2017. *The Political Economy of China-Latin American Relations in the New Millennium*. Routledge.

Mearsheimer, John J. 2014a. *The Tragedy of Great Power Politics*. W.W. Norton & Company.

Mearsheimer, John J. 2014b. Can China Rise Peacefully? *National Interest*. October 25. https://nationalinterest.org/commentary/can-china-rise-peacefully-10204.

Nathan, Andrew J. 2021. Book Review of Rush Doshi, Stronger: Adapting America's China Strategy in an Age of Competitive Interdependence. *Foreign Affairs (September/October)*: 258–259.

Nye, Joseph S. Nye, Jr. 2011. *The Future of Power*. Public Access.

Orenstein, Mitchell A. 2019. *The Lands in Between: Russia v. the West and the New Politics of Hybrid War*. Oxford University Press.

Peel, Michael and Helen Warrell. 2021. NATO Leaders to Issue Tough Warning to China in Sign of Rising Security Fears. *Financial Times*, June 14. https://www.ft.com/content/f454033a-9975-4efd-92eb-9cf63306af7f.

Rachman, Gideon. 2020. A New Cold War: Trump, Xi, and the Escalating US-China Confrontation. *Financial Times*. (October 5).

Rolland, Nadege. 2021. A New Great Game? Situating Africa in China's Strategic Thinking. National Bureau of Asian Research (Washington, D.C.). June 8. https://www.nbr.org/publication/a-new-great-game-situating-africa-in-chinas-strategic-thinking/.

Schuman, Michael. 2020. *Superpower Interrupted: The Chinese History of the World*. Public Affairs.

Stallings, Barbara. 2020. *Dependency in the Twenty-First Century?: The Political Economy of China-Latin America Relations*. Cambridge University Press.

Stavridis, James. 2018. *Sea Power: The History and Geopolitics of the World's Oceans*. Penguin Books.

Sun, Irene Yuan. 2017. *The Next Factory of the World: How Chinese Investment is Reshaping Africa*. Harvard Business Review Press.

Tanchum, Michael. 2021. China's New Military Base in Africa: What It Means for Europe and America. December 14. https://ecfr.eu/article/chinas-new-military-base-in-africa-what-it-means-for-europe-and-america/.

The Economist. 2020. How Sweden Copes with Chinese Bullying. *The Economist*, February 20, 2020. https://www.economist.com/europe/2020/02/20/how-sweden-copes-with-chinese-bullying.

United States Department of State. (2019). U.S. Strategy for Engagement in the Caribbean. Bureau of Western Hemisphere Affairs.

Walker, Christopher, Shanthi Kalathil and Jessica Ludwig. 2020. The Cutting Edge of Sharp Power. *Journal of Democracy*. (January)

Walker, Christopher. July 2018. What is 'Sharp Power'. *Journal of Democracy*.

Westcott, Ben and Steven Jiang. 2020. China Is Embracing a New Brand of Foreign Policy. Here's What Wolf Warrior Diplomacy Means. *CNN.com*, May 29. https://www.cnn.com/2020/05/28/asia/china-wolf-warrior-diplomacy-intl-hnk/index.html.

Wise, Carol. 2020. *Dragonomics: How Latin America is Maximizing (or Missing Out On) China's International Development Strategy*. Yale University Press.

Wright, Robin. 2022. Russia and China Unveil a Pact against America and the West. *The New Yorker*. February 7. https://www.newyorker.com/news/daily-comment/russia-and-china-unveil-a-pact-against-america-and-the-west.

Wright, Thomas. 2020. The Folly of Retrenchment: Why America Can't Withdraw From the World. *Foreign Affairs* (March–April).

Yergin, Daniel. (2020). *The New Map: Energy, Climate, and the Clash of Nations*. Penguin Press.

CHAPTER 2

China's Caribbean Adventure

It is the purpose of this chapter to focus on the forces that brought China to the Caribbean, its strategic goals, and how these have changed over time. It is worth understanding how China came to be such an important and powerful actor in global affairs and how an earlier entry into other parts of the developing world, including Latin America, helped open the door to the Caribbean. The dominant narrative of China in international affairs has been of its economic transformation, embrace of globalization, and finding new markets, critical to its continued economic advancement. China's use of economic statecraft has been effective in carving out a place on the Caribbean geopolitical map, helping its secure natural resources and markets in sync with its international development strategy, while advancing political goals of offering China's model of development (authoritarian-capitalism) as an alternative to Western liberal democracy and to reducing Taiwan's diplomatic representation. Also to be discussed is the role of Confucius Institutes in supporting economic statecraft.

China's role in the Caribbean came on the back of its economic transformation and "Go Global" strategy that eventually brought Chinese banks and companies to the region. China's economic statecraft has generally cast the Asian country as a good partner, a trajectory that worked well through the first decade and half of the twenty-first century. However, in view of a more assertive stance taken by Beijing in global affairs in the late 2010s and early 2020s, Caribbean regional leaders are increasingly aware that going against Chinese wishes may place them to

© The Author(s), under exclusive license to Springer Nature Switzerland AG 2022
S. B. MacDonald, *The New Cold War, China, and the Caribbean*, https://doi.org/10.1007/978-3-031-06149-3_2

a less friendly policy track. Thus far, the economic imperative dominates China's considerations in the Caribbean, especially the region's strategic materials and vital commodities.

CHINA'S ECONOMIC LANDSCAPE CHANGES

China's rise to power and its eventual entry into the Caribbean is very closely linked to the country's economic transformation in the late twentieth century. By any benchmark that change was exceptional in its size and scope, especially considering the low point from which the transformation commenced. According to the World Bank, "Since initiating market reforms in 1978, China has shifted from a centrally-planned to a market-based economy and has experienced rapid economic and social development. GDP growth has averaged nearly 10 percent a year – the fastest sustained expansion by a major economy in history – and has lifted more than 800 million people out of poverty."[1]

How did China achieve this? The early years of China's Communist Revolution were marked by the consolidation of power for the Communist government, during which there was often an emphasis on ideological purity over economic needs. This played out in such policy disasters as the Great Leap Forward and the Backyard Furnace Campaign and was bolstered by such inspirational slogans as "Better Red than Expert." Among the outcomes of this were a massive famine (1959–1961) and considerable socioeconomic dislocation. While Mao Zedong is regarded as the revolution's "Great Helmsman," his long years in power (he died in 1976) left the Chinese economy inward-looking, disorganized, and dominated by large state-owned industrial companies. Many Chinese were poor and living in rural areas. China moved in a radically different direction under the guidance of the pragmatically inclined Deng Xiaoping who became the country's paramount leader from 1978 to 1992.

Deng's reform program came to a country that was exhausted by the political ructions of the Red Guard Movement and Cultural Revolution during the 1960s and early 1970s and yearned for social stability and economic growth. The opening of relations with the United States in 1972 helped remove a major international obstacle to China rejoining the global economy. Under Deng foreign investment was welcome through a system of special economic zones in selected coastal provinces; a gradual introduction of market forces into the economy by permitting state-owned enterprises to sell their surplus on the market; and opening a space to small-scale private entrepreneurs (Economy and Levi 2014: 20). Other reforms opened up the agricultural sector, giving farmers greater freedom to plant crops and sell produce.

Deng's reforms also looked to exports as a means of powering economic expansion. This was a path already used by other Asian countries, including Japan in the 1950s and 1960s, which was then followed by Hong Kong, Singapore, the Republic of Korea (also known as South Korea), and Taiwan in the 1970s. Through the subsequent decades, East Asian and Southeast Asian countries opted to pursue export-oriented economic strategies. Initially, much of this was linked to Japanese and U.S. companies, looking for cheaper labor costs. China had several decades to watch other countries experiment and fine-tune their export strategies. China coupled this export approach with a foreign policy guided by Deng's view of "Hide your strength, bide your time." In terms of foreign policy, it translated into an economics-driven approach to the world and building Chinese power over time. The exception to this was that matters on China's borders still required a strong hand as exemplified by China's bloody intervention against Vietnam in 1979, which followed Vietnam's earlier invasion of Beijing's ally Cambodia.

With an eye to the Caribbean (and other natural resource-endowed countries) China's restructuring into an industrial giant resulted in a voracious appetite for natural resources. By 1990 China became a major importer of raw materials, ranging from copper and iron ore to coal. By 1993 China started to import oil, which helped push Chinese companies into Asia, Latin America, and the Middle East.

Hand-in-hand with China's emergence as a natural resource-hungry industrial economy was the need for the Chinese corporate sector to develop sales outlets outside of its home market. This came from the problem of overcapacity of Chinese goods (the Chinese market only had so many consumers) and the need to generate employment. An important component of this was the government's "Go Global" policy launched in 1999, which saw globalization as a means to project China's influence and power beyond its borders. While Deng Xiaoping was a primary force in getting this policy off the ground, his efforts were followed by his successor President Jiang Zemin (1993–2003) and helped by Zhu Rongji, who served as First Vice Premier and then Premier from 1998 to 2003. Hu Jintao, who followed Jiang as president (2002–2013), maintained the policy, which proved highly successful in creating a cadre of

Chinese multinational corporations. Xi Jinping followed Hu in office in 2013 and headed the country as it went into the 2020s.

China's going global strategy received a major step forward with its membership in the World Trade Organization (WTO) in 2001. Membership in that international organization gave Chinese trade a major boost as foreign consumers were able to buy Chinese goods at lower prices. This also meant that U.S., European and Japanese companies set up plants and production centers in China that could export goods that paid low international duties and undercut labor costs in their own countries. Although U.S. and European workers were squeezed on the job front and saw their wages fall (which was to become a major political issue in the 2010s), their consumer counterparts benefited from cheaper prices.

There was another important aspect of China gaining WTO membership; it brought the Asian country into a rules-based organization, which expected transparency and disclosure. WTO membership stated clear rules for greater transparency and disclosure. However, China did not fully embrace the spirit of the agreement. China's trade regime was filled with rhetoric about free trade, which barely disguised the reality of managed trade in a dense web of deals and bargains among national interests and social policies (Gelber: 402). In 2011 Chris Smith, Congressman from New Jersey, noted at a U.S. Congressional Hearing: "So how is China doing by WTO standards? Awful. China has agreed to abide by the WTO principles on non-discrimination and transparency, however, U.S. exporters face many barriers when trying to sell products to China, starting with customs delays and other problems at the border. Those problems extend into China's markets. Companies in the large and growing state-owned sector operate under a set of policies that favor Chinese producers. Also, it is extremely difficult for our companies to access government procurement" (U.S. Government 2011). Much the same could be said about China and its adherence to WTO standards in 2020. Indeed, China's economic model is akin to mercantilism, which in its most stark form seeks to maximize exports and minimize imports, helped along by an activist government. In this, China was highly successful in boosting exports as well as attracting foreign investment that was channeled into increasing productivity.

One of the important results of China's economic success was that it regained international stature, something very important to a country with a deep sense of historical grievance. The upward trajectory of China's growing power was evident as the size of its economy progressively surpassed Italy, the United Kingdom, France, and Germany. One of the most noteworthy benchmarks came in 2010 when China passed Japan to become the world's second largest economy, the end of a 42-year position for the Asia Pacific island country.

China's greater economic weight was also underscored by two other developments in 2013, the establishment of the Asian Infrastructure Investment Bank (AIIB) and the launching of the Bridge and Road Initiative (BRI). The AIIB was created to provide loans for Asian infrastructure development projects without having to go through more stringent investment guidelines including human rights and environmental considerations demanded by the Western-dominated European Bank for Reconstruction and Development (EBRD), Asian Development Bank (where Japan plays a major role), and World Bank. The AIIB's mission was also to complement the BRI.

The BRI's size and scope are, to put it mildly, ambitious. As a type of massive regional development program, it is meant to deliver a degree of shock and awe. As political scientist Zhiqun Zhu observed: "First unveiled by Xi Jinping in 2013, the BRI has become one of the largest infrastructure and investment mega-projects in human history, covering over 70 countries, equivalent to 65 percent of the world's population and 40 percent of the global GDP as of 2018. The BRI consists of the land-based Silk Road Economic Belt and the ocean-going twenty-first century Maritime Silk Road and aims to enhance connectivity and cooperation among countries" (Zhu 2019: 5; Blanchard 2018; Hillman 2020). The sweep of business to be done includes hydropower, pipeline, port, power plant, railway, and road projects in the landmass stretching from China to Europe. To back this the BRI is designed to invest between $500 billion and $1 trillion in long-term financing across more than 60 Asian, European, and African countries (Organization for Economic Cooperation and Development 2018).

The BRI also reflected China's wish to dominate Eurasia, much like attempts by a number of earlier Chinese dynasties. While this is not a territorial grab, it is an effort to recreate a China-centric world order that existed before the arrival of the West. As historian Michael Schuman notes of President Xi, the force behind the BRI: "Xi has embraced this rejuvenated, expansive vision of China's position within all under Heaven. The Chinese emperor never accepted other peoples as equals and Xi sees no good reason to start to do so today. His favored diplomatic program – called the Belt and Road Initiative – is designed to re-create the

China-centric trade links of the overland Silk Road and the old maritime routes once sailed by the mariner Zheng He by building ports, roads, roads, and other infrastructure across the Eurasian landmass and beyond" (Schuman 2020: 314). And those maritime routes include the Caribbean, a key crossroads.

Important to China's expanded outreach to the world beyond Eurasia is the development of a global network of shipping lanes and ports, either through Chinese-owned companies like Cosco (China Ocean Shipping Company) and Orient Overseas Container Line (OOCL) and their Hong Kong counterparts, such as Hutchison. Chinese-run ports extend from the mainland through the Strait of Malacca to Hambantota, Sri Lanka; Gwadar, Pakistan; and on to Piraeus, Greece. Chinese companies are also active in the management of ports on both sides of the Panama Canal. Chinese shipping has emerged as a global heavyweight. By 2015, close to two-thirds of the world's top 50 container ports had some degree of Chinese investment, up from one-fifth in 2010 (Kynge et al. 2017). Since 2015 the amount has grown.

China's push into waters beyond its coastline is backed by the creation of military bases in the South China Sea, the creation of what is probably the largest maritime law enforcement fleet, one of the world's largest seafaring fishing fleets (estimated at over 200,000 ships) and a rapidly expanding navy, complete with aircraft carriers and nuclear submarines. All of the above is reinforced by the establishment of an overseas military base with port facilities in Djibouti in the Horn of Africa.

Although China claims that its development of ports is strictly for commercial purposes, there is the possibility of their conversion to military use, something that has left other countries nervous (Agarwal 2020; Singh 2022, 2020). Considering China's willingness to provoke a military confrontation with India along their lengthy mountainous border, its clampdown on Hong Kong's freedoms, and bellicose threats to Taiwan, the ability to convert commercial ports into military bases has gained considerable attention from other countries. While China is seeking to be the dominant economic and ultimately political force in Eurasia it has come to regard control of sea lanes as important as well. Although China's blue water navy lacks the scope of its U.S. counterpart, it is increasingly competitive in Asian-Pacific waters and is a major factor in the Indian Ocean.

Still Authoritarian After All These Years

While China's economic restructuring was highly successful, it maintained an authoritarian political personality. In the West, it was expected that as China played a larger role in the international economic system and benefited from the economic freedoms linked to market economics, it would also move in the direction of becoming a more open and democratic society. The Chinese authorities were willing to extend a certain degree of economic freedom to their citizens; that largesse did not extend to political freedoms. In a sense, the Communist Party's bargain with its population was that it would bring them economic prosperity (which it generally delivered), but politics were best left to the Party. No other institutions or groups were to be allowed to challenge Communist Party dominance, including groups like Falun Gong or big business. An important strand of thinking in the Communist Party was that too much political freedom could be manipulated by external forces, which could lead to chaos, a central theme in China's dynastic history.

If there were any doubts about the Communist Party's commitment to remaining in control one had only to look to the outcome of the pro-democracy Tiananmen Square protests in 1989, which were brutally crushed by the Communist Party. The Party's resolve not to relinquish political power was, no doubt, further strengthened by the demise of its sister party in the Soviet Union in 1991–1992 as well as the end of Eastern Europe's Communist states during the same period. Since then, the Communist Party has worked hard to enhance its means of control over the population, making use of artificial intelligence, facial recognition, and other surveillance techniques. This was evident in the 2020–2022 clampdown on Hong Kong's freedoms.

There is another dimension to Chinese authoritarianism and that is the creation of a middle class that identifies with the Communist Party system. Unlike the famous thesis of American political sociologist, Barrington Moore, "no bourgeoisie, no democracy," China's middle class has demonstrated a close identification with and institutional ties to the state, which has helped maintain the state's legitimacy through considerable economic changes. It has been argued that the lack of support for democracy among middle-class Chinese is rooted in the ability of the Communist Party to address this social group's economic well-being as well as its concerns over political instability (Chen 2013: 20; Pei 2006; Li 2010). This is important in terms of foreign policy; as China faces the world the government and the Communist Party are seen as legitimate in the eyes of the majority of its people, a situation secured by an activist state keeping the rest of the world's bad influences (such as Western ideas of liberal government) out.

The Communist Party has worked hard to control the flow of information into China, including via the internet. Under Xi this has gone hand in hand with the creation of a new history of the country. In the new official version of "A Brief History of the Communist Party" many of the mistakes and purges conducted under Mao are played down. Mao is restored as the wise and benevolent great helmsman of the revolution, which serves as an acknowledgment that strong, autocratic leaders are a good thing (and certainly fit in Chinese political history and culture). This is, of course, a nod to President Xi who done much to recentralize power at the top of the country's power pyramid through a new cult of personality.

President Xi has also done much to reinvigorate the Communist Party, which had become highly corrupt in the early 2000s, was increasingly seen as out of touch with the citizenry, and was losing legitimacy. Since coming to power in 2013, President Xi has launched anti-corruption campaigns, reduced official misconduct, and created a cadre system that motivates local officials to pursue "green" economic development in their cities and expand social welfare programs (Nathan 2021). To a degree, President Xi has sought to make the Party more accountable to the average citizen. This has included giving officials the right to lock away entrepreneurs and other citizens whom they perceive to have gained too much wealth or influence independent of the party. Considering China's income disparity, the fall of the rich and powerful has a certain attraction. Along these lines, a number of companies and their top management teams have been humbled by the government.

In 2020 and 2021 the authorities focused their efforts on going after the country's high-flying tech companies by complicating stock offerings outside of the country, while putting the "Bridle on the horse" of big name business leaders. One of the most obvious of these was Jack Ma, the founder of Alibaba (China's largest tech company) and Ant Group (the largest fintech company in the world) (Calhoun 2021). Well known inside and outside of China and generally liked, it is likely that his profile was too big for President Xi and the Communist Party. The government moved to cancel an initial public offering in the United States for The Ant Group (which was set to be a massive capital raising), dissembled his companies, leveled a "record" fine of $2.8 billion against Alibaba, and launched other penalties on his other companies.

Beyond reducing other potential sources of power and cleaning up the Communist Party, President Xi also pushed to further reduce poverty in the country, give the appearance of greater social equity, and rein in the power of big business. Ideologically supported by his political thought, in particular, the "China Dream," President Xi brought the Communist Party in line and through that institution the rest of the country. Although China's political system is hardly monolithic, President Xi towers over any potential usurpers and expects to be around into the next decade having changed the constitution to allow more terms in office. As American political scientist Andrew Nathan astutely noted in 2021: "Xi is presented in voluminous propaganda as the all-knowing, benevolent, serenely smiling sage who guides China unerringly toward inevitable greatness" (Nathan 2021). This is the China that since 2013 has faced outwards to the rest of the world, economically successful, nationalistically proud, and ruled by a new emperor and his court, President Xi and the Communist party. Consequently, Beijing can point to political stability at home and socioeconomic improvements over several decades to demonstrate the superiority of the Chinese development model.

China's International Development Strategy

As China emerged in the early twenty-first century, the message from Beijing was that it was showing up around the world to conduct business not revolution. China's approach has been referred to by political scientist Carol Wise as its "international development strategy," broadly defined as a comingling of commercial and strategic interests, which is geared to acquire those agricultural, energy, and minerals commodities that are in short supply in China (Wise 2020). Evan Ellis helps flesh out this strategy: "…the Chinese state is pursuing a principally economically-oriented strategy which, at its core, seeks to capture value added and orchestrate global flows of wealth primarily beneficial to itself. It leads and supports these efforts through employing State Owned Enterprises as the principal repository of value and capability, using the Chinese state's ability to coordinate deals across sectors, regulation of the Chinese market, and through the contributions of the Chinese intelligence services" (Ellis 2022).

Three results came out of China's growing role in other developing countries, sometimes referred to as the South. First, China's need for commodities created a commodities boom that lasted from the early 2000s to roughly 2013–2014. Second, Chinese demand resulted in a significant spurt in economic growth throughout the developing world. Third, China's growing economic role hit different countries in different ways. While Chinese investment and trade were well managed by some countries, others found themselves on the path to indebtedness to China.

China's economic surge provided both positive and negative reviews. On the negative side, debt-trap diplomacy is seen by some analysts as China intentionally ensnaring recipient countries with loans that they cannot repay. It is argued that this increases Chinese influence. When the borrowers default, China seizes strategic assets. The case that has drawn the most attention has been Sri Lanka's Hambantota Port. The story goes as follows: the ambitious and corrupt Sri Lankan prime minister proposed the construction of a new port in his district despite questions over its viability; the project eventually became a white elephant contributing to the South Asian country's buildup of debt to unsustainable levels; and when Sri Lanka defaulted, China reached an agreement with its debtor for a Chinese state-owned enterprise to assume the management of the port.[2] Indeed, the port was leased to China for $1.1 billion, which was used to repay debts owed to other creditors.

While Hambantota is seemingly devoid of any overarching plot, China has made clear its intentions to play a dominant role in the Indian Ocean. Control over a port in Sri Lanka, next door to its primary strategic rival, India, is a major shadow cast over regional geopolitics. If anything, China proved to be pragmatic and opportunistic. In the case of a major conflict between China and India, having access to the port could be important if for nothing more than monitoring Indian Navy movements. China's alleged debt-trap diplomacy has also been brought up concerning other countries.

In Asia, Laos and Pakistan come to mind as debt-trap countries; both nations have racked up considerable debt with China being the major creditor with loans earmarked for infrastructure. In the former, the $20 billion economy has close to $13 billion in foreign debt, of which close to half ($5.9 billion in 2020) was owed to China. As the *Nikkei Asia's* Marwaan Macan-Markar observed: "China's rise as the country's leading lender has been fueled by billions of dollars to finance a building spree of megaprojects, spanning large hydropower dams and economic zones to a flagship high-speed railway" (Macan-Markar 2021). As for Pakistan, its external debt rose from $44.35 billion in June 2013 to

$90.12 billion by April 2021, with $24.7 billion owed to China (Younos 2021). Much of the debt in Pakistan went to bail out an ailing power sector causing perennial electricity shortages; it now produces a surplus of energy, which the country can ill-afford. The situation in Pakistan has been further complicated by terrorist attacks on Chinese officials (with some deaths), corruption, and the inability of some Pakistani companies to make repayments.

China also plays a major role in Africa, where its total loans to the region from 2000 to 2018 have been estimated at $148 billion, making it a leading bilateral lender in 32 countries and the top lender to the continent as a whole (Chaudhury 2021). The main drivers for investment have been mining, energy, and infrastructure development. Africa is a key source for such strategic natural resources as oil, copper and cobalt. While China has done much to advance infrastructure development in a number of countries, its role in local economies has become a political issue with the criticism echoing earlier claims about European and American companies being exploiters. Indeed, African criticism has centered on many things that have also been heard in the Caribbean, a disregard for local environmental standards, the purposeful isolation of Chinese workers and managers from the indigenous population, and corruption (Dok and Thayer 2019).

While China has explained its international development strategy in win–win terms, it has often come off less like South-South solidarity and more like old imperialist North–South economic exploitation. Indeed on the Latin American side there has been concern that their economies are undergoing reprimarization. According to Brown University's Barbara Stallings, this is a process "where the region sells petroleum, metals, and soy to China in return for industrial goods" (Stallings 2020: 2). China's answer is that the benefits of economic growth resulting from its investment depend on how other countries manage the process. At the same time, China has not been shy in pushing its own foreign policy agenda, sometimes including issues distinctly political in nature, especially when they concern Hong Kong, Taiwan, the South China Sea, and criticism of its authoritarian political system, including the repression of ethnic Uighurs. It also demonstrated a thin skin to any international criticism of its role as the starting point for the Covid-19 pandemic.

Chinese efforts to regain popularity by sending medical equipment and personnel to both developing and advanced economies failed to turn around an increase in negative sentiment vis-à-vis China. In October

2020, a Pew Research survey of a number of advanced economy countries gave China its highest negative evaluations since 2002, with 81% of Australians having an unfavorable view; 86% of Japanese; 85% of Swedes; and 73% of Americans. The same survey of 14 countries found that 61% say China has done a bad job in dealing with the Covid-19 outbreak and 78% had little or no confidence in President Xi to do the right thing regarding world affairs (Silver et al. 2020). That said, China's reputation in Africa initially took a battering, but Beijing's strategic vaccine distribution and PPE donations rebuilt goodwill in a number of cases, especially as Europe and the United States were slow to respond to African needs.

China and Latin America

China and Latin America have a long historical relationship, dating back to the 1570s when Sino-Latin American trade crossed the Pacific involving the Spanish Empire on one side and the Qing dynasty on the other. As Chinese academic Jiang Shixue observed: "China exported silk, porcelain, and cotton yarn to Mexico and Peru in exchange for silver coins and other items."[3] Beyond that and some migration of Chinese workers to the Caribbean (more on that later) and parts of Latin America, relations remained largely unimportant for lengthy periods. As Chinese companies globalized in the late twentieth century, however, Latin America loomed large, having many key natural resources that China wanted.

Trade between Latin America and China exploded from $17 billion in 2000 to $306 billion in 2018 (Shixue 2008: 27). During this period China became the top trading partner of Brazil, Chile, Peru, and Uruguay and was significant in Colombia and Venezuela. At the same time, foreign direct investment (FDI) by China in Latin America and the Caribbean started at modest levels; in 2004 it was barely noticeable, by 2012 China's FDI flows attained a high of $87.8 billion (Chen and Pérez Ludera 2014). This placed China among the world's three largest outward investors for the first time. But there was more to come in the period between 2012 and 2015, which was probably the peak of Chinese bank lending.

Much of Chinese lending and investment was focused on acquiring firms or assets in mining and agro-industry, power generation, utilities (electricity), gas and water utilities, and other infrastructure (Sullivan and Lum 2019; Wise 2020). According to China's Global Energy Finance database at Boston University, China committed $58.4 billion to Latin America and the Caribbean's energy sector between 2000 and 2019

(Boston University Global Development Policy Center). This surge in Chinese capital flows was reflected by a substantial increase in Latin America's mineral exports to China, which increased from 19% of total exports in 2006 to 45% in 2016. As for metal exports, those increased from six percent of total exports in 2006 to 20% in 2015 (Vasquez et al. 2018).

Chinese construction and infrastructure companies found work in upgrading harbors, roads, airports, and power utilities. Ports were seen as particularly important to China. According to strategic intelligence company Pointe Bello's Gabriel Alvarado, "A good place to look are ports, which are key trade nodes that, if they are deep enough, could host naval vessels. Chinese state-owned enterprises (SOEs) have been involved in building, renovating, and operating ports in Latin America. These include Margarita Island Port on the Atlantic side of the Panama Canal, TCP Port of Paranaguá – Brazil's second largest port – the Posorja Deep-water Port in Ecuador, and the Santiago de Cuba Port" (Alvarado 2019). The latest port development venture, launched in 2019, is the construction of a megaport in Chancay, Peru. The $3 billion project has been undertaken by Cosco and seeks to redraw trade flows on South America's Pacific coast and reduce reliance on the Panama Canal. Chancay will be Latin America's megaport and plans to be a key hub for the movement of goods between South America, Oceania, and Asia.

Chinese foreign direct investment in Latin America tapered in 2019 and 2020, though it has been difficult to fully ascertain the amount considering the use of third country-registered entities (such as those operating out of Luxembourg, Hong Kong or Cayman Islands). Rounding out the picture, Chinese banks (mainly the large state-owned institutions such as the China Development Bank and China Export–Import Bank) became the largest lenders to Latin America, with accumulated loans having topped $140 billion in the 2005–2018 period. Although Chinese loans extended to Latin America appeared to have peaked in 2015 (when the full impact of the end of the commodity boom was confirmed by ongoing depressed prices) and no loans were made in 2020 (due to Covid-19 and a focus on pandemic project management), the development banks remain important creditors for a number of countries.

China's entry into Latin America was a major contributor to the region's economic expansion. Indeed, China's active entry into Latin America was referred to as the "China boom." While demand from the United States, Europe, and Japan remained important in pushing commodity prices up, it was China that pushed demand to new levels. Chinese mining companies, driven by the need for copper and coal, showed up in Chile, Peru, and Colombia, while other companies found Brazil open to business in iron ore and soybeans. Argentina also had soybeans to sell as well as wheat and beef. Oil and natural gas drove Chinese expansion into Venezuela and Peru.

For many Latin American countries, the surge in Chinese business was generally attractive. China's massive demand for natural resources was important to elevate economic growth rates, help government finances and increase national wealth. Moreover, China did not put up many of the restrictions on lending to which the West and Japan were prone (which was to have its own set of problems as will be reflected in upcoming chapters). Another factor that helped matters was that China's entry into Latin America came at a time when regional debt levels (with the exceptions of Argentina and Venezuela) were more manageable than they had been in the troubled 1980s and 1990s.

Complementing the economic side of relationships, China actively courted Latin American governments and their citizens. This included regional summits, one-on-one visits of Latin American leaders, and an upswing in cultural diplomacy including student exchanges and the spread of Confucius Institutes. China also pursued and obtained the position of a permanent observer at the Organization of American States (OAS) in 2004. The OAS is based in Washington, DC, was founded in 1948, and has served (to varying degrees) to enhance solidarity and cooperation among its member states within the Western Hemisphere. During the Cold War, the United States sought to use the organization as an instrument against the spread of Communism. At the end of the Cold War, the OAS mission changed to function more as a force for electoral monitoring. For China, OAS membership was intended to be a positive signal that Beijing was interested in the region's development.

As with the entry of any new economic power into a region, there were downside risks. As Latin America opened up to a flood of Chinese manufactured and consumer goods, many local companies found it increasingly difficult to compete. If it caused some displacement of less efficient local companies, Chinese goodwill infrastructure projects and soft loans papered over some of the discomforts. At the same time, trade balances in a number of countries fell sharply in favor of China. Additionally, many Chinese companies did little in terms of meeting environmental rules and regulations; oftentimes Chinese companies brought Chinese workers, which did little to help the local employment picture and was resented. Chinese companies also gained a reputation for sacrificing social progress and environmental safety for economic advancement and were willing to pay local government officials to look the other way.

Latin America and China also shared the experience of having been at the receiving end of Western imperialism, which helped bring the relationship closer. This was reinforced in the aftermath of the 2008–2009 global financial crisis. That crisis hit the advanced economies hard, making the financing of infrastructure projects by U.S. and European capital in short supply. At the same time China, with over $1 trillion in reserve assets in 2007, was willing to spend money. As will be observed in the Caribbean, China's economic statecraft, backed by a large pocketbook, made the visitors from Beijing welcome partners in regional economic development. China also became a member of the Inter-American Development Bank in 2009, contributing $350 million to various programs (Inter-American Development Bank 2009).

Despite China's declarations of having no ideological interest it was inevitable that as Beijing's involvement in the region deepened, ideological elements crept into the web of relations woven throughout the Americas. One of the important developments on the ideological front was the rise of the so-called "Pink Tide" in Latin America. This included the election of Hugo Chávez in Venezuela (1999), Luiz Inácio Lula da Silva in Brazil (inaugurated in 2003), and Evo Morales in Bolivia (inaugurated 2006); leaders identified in Beijing as leftist fellow travelers. While business was to remain business, it was easier to deal with governments that shared similar ideological mindsets and worldviews.

China's reach into Latin America also included the signing of Free Trade Agreements (FTAs) with a handful of countries. The China–Peru FTA, which went into effect in 2010, was the first comprehensive FTA China signed with a Latin American country. It was to follow through with Costa Rica, Mexico, and Chile and opened up talks with Panama in 2017 (as of 2022 the two countries had yet to reach an agreement).

On another trade front, China emerged as a competitive arms seller to Latin America. According to the Arms Transfers Database maintained by the Stockholm International Peace Research Institute, China's arms sales from 2009 to 2019 accounted for almost five percent of total arms exports to the region. Although this put it behind the United States and Russia, it was a significant advancement, especially important to countries like Venezuela, Ecuador, and Bolivia.

China's growing presence in Latin America eventually stirred up concern in the United States. China's response has been to argue that its presence in the region is not driven by ideological factors nor has it sought to disadvantage third parties engaged in Latin America, like the United States and Europe. Loss of market share, however, often belied these comments. Most U.S., European and Japanese companies operating in Latin America saw the Chinese for what they were, another rough and tumble economic rival. Others, like U.S. economist Barbara Stallings, saw the Chinese as putting Latin America backwards into the ranks of being primary commodity exporters as opposed to manufacturers and service providers (Stallings, 2020).

U.S.–Latin American relations through the 2010s became increasingly focused on China's rising presence in the region. The basic message from the United States, as conveyed by President Trump's first Secretary of State Rex Tillerson and his successor Mike Pompeo, was that China was a corrosive agent for Latin American development, engaged in creating dependency based on cheap loans as part of a well-thought-out debt trap. This left a stark contrast between the United States and China as they are seen in Latin America—U.S. delegations to the region come to lecture on the evils of doing business with China; Chinese delegations come to talk about trade and investment (often with an open checkbook). Moreover, the U.S. message is seen as paternalistic: most Latin Americans believe that they understand what China represents, both positive and negative. The dominant attraction is that Latin America has considerable infrastructure needs that Washington is not going to finance; China will. This goes for green project financing (Yuan and Gallagher 2016). The United States is seeking to rebalance its ability to help finance green infrastructure projects, but lending requirements remain more onerous than those o9ffered by Chinese institutions. The lessons learned in Latin America have an impact on the arrival and penetration of the Chinese in the Caribbean.

CHINA COMES TO THE CARIBBEAN

China's approach to the Caribbean was conducted in much the same fashion as in Latin America, with large corporations, backed by state development banks, seeking out natural resources as well as construction projects. As in Latin America, Caribbean nations had substantial economic needs, including infrastructure that was not likely to be financed any time soon by the West. Caribbean leaders, many of them participating in larger regional forums (that mixed Caribbean and Latin American governments), were increasingly aware that China was stepping up as U.S. interest waned. As Alicia Nicholls, a Barbados-based international trade and development consultant captured how a number of her Caribbean colleagues saw matters: "In the midst of declining US presence in the Caribbean, Beijing has sought to fill the void through mainly bilateral engagement with individual Caribbean governments. China has become an increasingly important source of foreign direct investment, government loans, and development aid and cooperation. A growing number of infrastructure projects throughout the region have been built with Chinese funding and labour" (Nicholls 2018).

For its part, China initially perceived the Caribbean as an outlet for construction and engineering firms, with an eye on infrastructure and tourism. It also was drawn to Guyana, Suriname, and Trinidad and Tobago for oil, natural gas, and other commodities. Equally important in this situation was that whether or not Caribbean countries had economies heavily dependent on tourism or extractive minerals, Chinese corporate engagement and investment were welcome.

One of the earliest Chinese forays into the Caribbean came with the creation and first ministerial meeting of the China–Caribbean Economic & Trade Cooperation Forum, which was held in Jamaica in 2005. China's Vice President Zeng Qinghong attended the opening ceremony. On the Caribbean side were the prime ministers from Jamaica, Antigua and Barbuda, Dominica, and high-ranking officials from Cuba and Suriname. The platform intended to "deepen China-Caribbean friendship and expand their reciprocal cooperation" (Foreign Ministry of the People's Republic of China 2005). It was also a signal that China was beginning to take a serious look at the Caribbean for business prospects.

The 2005 meeting was followed by several more through the years, with the second being held in China in 2007 and a third in Trinidad and Tobago in 2011. The last was important from the standpoint that China made very clear that it regarded the Caribbean as a place where it wanted to play a greater role. At the meeting, China announced that it would take six measures to deepen the relationship: over the next three years it would provide $1 billion in preferential loans through the Caribbean Development Bank; offer capacity-building courses for at least

2500 Caribbean trainees; augment cooperation on environmental issues; enhance cultural and educational exchanges; promote trade and tourism, including Chinese tour groups going to the Caribbean; and increase cooperation on agriculture and fisheries. Together with bilateral cooperation agreements between China and Barbados, Jamaica, the Bahamas, Guyana, Suriname, and Antigua and Barbuda, China was signaling that it intended to establish an enduring relationship with the Caribbean apart from Latin America. The London-based Caribbean Council noted of the 2011 Trinidad meeting: "...what is clear is that China is in the process of establishing a long term relationship that will permeate every aspect of these Caribbean nations that are prepared to engage in dialogue" (Caribbean Council 2012).

It should be added that what China promised at the 2011 Trinidad meeting was a more Caribbean-focused and updated version of China's First White Paper on Latin America and the Caribbean in 2008. Considering the difficult nature of the global economy in 2008, China's commitment to helping Latin America and the Caribbean was well received. The 2008 document also played to the sentiment found among many of the region's foreign policymakers in that it emphasized a multipolar world order, win–win cooperation, and nonintervention in the affairs of other countries.

President Xi returned to the Caribbean in 2013, being the first Chinese president to visit Trinidad and Tobago. He would be followed by other high-ranking Chinese officials in the ensuing years. At the same time, there was a succession of Caribbean leaders traveling to Beijing to meet with President Xi, including those from Antigua and Barbuda, Dominica, Suriname, and Jamaica. Those official visits to China were meant to establish warmer relations between Caribbean countries and China and were to demonstrate that Beijing was open to the region's needs and took its leaders seriously enough to have official state visits with the top leaders.

During the early 2000s and 2010s, Chinese trade focused generally on the Caribbean's larger economies, in particular those with mineral resources and sizeable populations. While the United States remains by far the largest trade partner to the Caribbean, China's role in Caribbean trade has become more significant, with overall trade expanding from $1 billion in 2002 to $8 billion in 2019, with three-fourths of that accounted for by a rise in Chinese exports (Ellis 2020). The trade balance usually runs in favor of China. As the IMF Direction of Trade Statistics shows below, China is not in the top three export destinations for Caribbean goods. Where China factors significantly is on the import side, much of it consumer goods (Table 2.1).

Table 2.1 Direction of trade—selected Caribbean Countries Top 3 trade partners in export and imports (2020)

Country	Top 3 export partners	Top 3 import partners
Bahamas	U.S., Singapore, Panama (**China** was #4)	U.S., Brazil, **China**
Barbados	U.S., Jamaica, Guyana	U.S., Trinidad and Tobago, Netherlands
Cuba	Venezuela, Belgium, Russia	Spain, **China**, Argentina
Dominican Republic	U.S., Switzerland, Haiti	U.S., **China**, and Mexico
Guyana	Uruguay, Canada, Jamaica	Uruguay, Qatar, Tunisia
Jamaica	U.S., Canada, Netherlands	U.S., **China**, Brazil
Suriname	United Arab Emirates, Belgium, U.S	U.S., Trinidad and Tobago, Netherlands
Trinidad and Tobago	U.S., Guyana, Brazil	U.S., **China**, Brazil

Source https://data.imf.org/?sk=9d6028d4-f14a-464c-a2f2-59b2cd424b85&sId=151561 9375491. As accessed on February 6, 2022

Chinese companies that entered the Caribbean in the first two decades of the twenty-first century varied in size and scope of operations. While most companies that gained public attention were state-owned and closely linked to the Chinese state, there were also smaller and medium-sized companies, some of them privately owned, that ventured into the region. Considerable attention is given to Chinese companies for functioning as an extension of Chinese government policy (to which there is a degree of truth), but most company management teams are also guided by the need to select viable projects and ultimately profits; there are business considerations. Moreover, Chinese companies have to compete with other companies for business, which often involves open bidding. That sometimes includes state-owned Chinese companies competing against each other.

One of the most active Chinese companies in the Caribbean is the China Harbour Engineering Company (CHEC), which is a subsidiary of the much larger state-owned conglomerate, China Communications Construction Company. Founded in 1980 and guided by the "go Global" mantra, CHEC has developed a global presence. According to the company, it has more than 70 overseas branch offices or subsidiaries in over 80 countries, with over 10,000 employees undertaking $10 billion

worth of projects. https://www.cccme.cn/shop/cccme12721/introduct
ion.aspx. In the Caribbean, CHEC has become one of the public faces
of China, with a regional headquarters in Kingston, Jamaica and projects
throughout the region including in the Bahamas, Jamaica, and Guyana.
Another well-known Chinese infrastructure/engineering company active
in the Caribbean is the China Civil Engineering Construction Corporation (CCECC), which was spun out of the Ministry of Railways in 1979
and since expanded its operations to over 40 countries, including in the
Caribbean.

As Chinese companies fanned out throughout the Caribbean, talking
with various governments and assessing different projects, Chinese development banks played an important supporting role, offering loans at low
rates. Equally important, Chinese banks do not place the same emphasis
on conditionality that European, Canadian, and U.S. aid agencies and
multilateral lenders, like the World Bank and the Inter-American Bank,
do (as with the case of human rights and environmental concerns). As
an Inter-American Development Bank report noted: "What distinguishes
Chinese loan and grant capital is that it is not accompanied by policy
conditionality as is the case sometimes with the more established international financial institutions such as the International Monetary Fund, the
World Bank, and regional development banks as well as bilateral donor
organizations. China is a pragmatic partner in foreign relations, willing
to engage with a wide spectrum of regimes, irrespective of the quality of
governance, political conditions, financial conditions, or state of development. Most importantly, China is open to accepting repayments in
physical commodities, especially oil, which broadens access to countries
that may be illiquid or have a history of loan defaults and thus have no
access to traditional capital markets" (Wenner and Clarke 2016).

By 2020, China was a major lender and trade partner to many countries
in the Caribbean. Looking back to 2000, China was not an active lender
in the Caribbean. That changed radically by 2020 as demonstrated by the
following table. For a country like Suriname, it is estimated that after the
Inter-American Development Bank, China is the second largest lender to
the country, holding close to 20.0% of total debt (Munevar, European
Network on Debt and Development: 2021, 16). Although loan size is
smaller than Venezuela's debt, Caribbean countries are well-represented
in the top ranks of borrowers from China in Latin America and the
Caribbean (Table 2.2).

Table 2.2 China–Latin American and Caribbean Loans 2020

Country	No. of loans	Amount
1. Venezuela	17	$62.2 billion
2. Brazil	12	$29.7 billion
3. Ecuador	15	$18.4 billion
4. Argentina	12	$17.1 billion
5. Bolivia	10	$3.4 billion
6. Jamaica	**11**	**$2.1 billion**
7. Mexico	1	$1.0 billion
8. Dominican Republic	**1**	**$600 million**
9. Suriname	**4**	**$580 million**
10. Costa Rica	1	**$395 million**
11. Trinidad and Tobago	**2**	**$374 million**
12. Cuba	**3**	**$240 million**
13. Guyana	**3**	**$240 million**
14. Barbados	**1**	**$170 million**
15. Antigua and Barbuda	**2**	**$128 million**

Bold marks Caribbean countries as opposed to Latin American countrues
Source The Dialogue. https://www.thedialogue.org/map_list/. Accessed on February 6, 2022

Although it is difficult to pin down fully accurate numbers, China has emerged as the second in the world with the most capital invested beyond its borders. According to the American Enterprise Institute's (AEI) China Global Investment Tracker, the total value of China's overseas investment and construction combined since 2005 to 2021 exceeds $2 trillion, despite slowing through the Covid-19 pandemic. The AEI places Chinese investments in the 2005–2021 period at $1.67 billion in Guyana; $1.178 billion in Trinidad and Tobago; and $1.17 billion in Jamaica. These numbers differ from the table above, which is more defined by loans. Whatever the exact amount of Chinese capital flowing into the English-speaking Caribbean, Suriname, Cuba, and the Dominican Republic, it is having a significant impact.

Another line of Chinese policy was to deepen its role in the Caribbean by joining the Barbados-based Caribbean Development Bank as a non-borrowing member with 5.58 percent of that body's total shares. The contrast to China's rival in the Caribbean was clear; the United States is not a member. Canada, Germany, Italy, and United Kingdom are also non-regional members.

China's awareness of the importance of the Caribbean Development Bank was furthered by the development of a closer working relationship between the Export–Import Bank of China and the Caribbean institution. The good partner tone of Chinese policy was evident in the comments of Yu Wen, Deputy General Manager, Corporate Business Development, Export–Import Bank of China, in 2017 when her bank signed a memorandum of understanding with its Caribbean counterpart in 2017: "CDB and EXIM Bank, we share the same target, to improve the economic development of Caribbean countries. I am quite sure that by signing this MOU we will expand this kind of cooperation and achieve the given result, the economic cooperation between China and Caribbean agencies" (Caribbean Development Bank 2017) China's move to join the Caribbean Development Bank was an astute move. Although there was little action on this front going forward, for a small amount of capital, China reinforced its image as a good partner to the region, especially as the matter quickly dropped out of public perception.

China's economic statecraft is not limited to trade and lending. It has other important components, one of which deserves further examination, Confucius Institutes.

THE ROLE OF CONFUCIUS INSTITUTES

Confucius Institutes (CIs) were created in 2004 by China's Ministry of Education with the mission to advance the Chinese "voice" in the world, through language training, instruction of Chinese history and other aspects of Chinese civilization, and to develop ties with local communities. As of 2021, there were 548 CIs around the world, most located at universities and in major cities. In the marketing of Chinese culture to the world, China is hardly alone in the use of soft power as the United States and France have long engaged in the same process, fulfilling what the French have in the past called their "mission to civilize." While CIs' general functions are readily acceptable as what countries often do to provide their own narrative of their development, China's cultural centers have assumed a more "sinister" role to some in that they are controlled by the Chinese government and Communist Party and, as such, are seen as propaganda machines and active in stifling any scholarship in other countries which is deemed to be detrimental to Chinese interests. In the

United States, detractors have warned that CIs are used as "a platform for China's intelligence collection and political agenda" (Paterson 2018).

In the Caribbean, CIs are generally seen in a positive light and are located in capital cities and at national universities. CIs opened their doors in Jamaica in 2009, Trinidad and Tobago and the Bahamas in 2013, Barbados in 2015, Suriname in 2017, Antigua and Barbuda in 2018, and the Dominican Republic in 2019.

While there should be concern about CIs functioning as propaganda machines and possibly espionage, what is often missed is their role in advancing Chinese economic statecraft. According to Jennifer Hubbert, Associate Professor of Anthropology and Asian Studies at Lewis & Clark College: CIs "are the most extensive and most future-oriented" components of China's "massive international soft power campaign" and they have "the greatest long-term potential impact" (Hubbert 2019: 10). The key point of Hubbert's analysis is that the CIs work to counter the Western narrative that colors China's rise as a threat to the global community by revealing its "true nature" to the world, something that can be accomplished by sharing its culture, philosophies, and language with the global community. While this sounds very much like what the United States and a number of European countries do with their cultural outreaches, the economic statecraft part quietly slips into the CIs function in a number of ways. Many CIs in the Caribbean and Latin America offer job fairs, and instruction in Business Mandarin and provide forums to discuss new business projects in the region being advanced by Chinese companies. They also work with local universities, business leaders, and governments to hold conferences or symposiums that promote trade and investment. Where this crosses over from cultural to political lines is that such activities seek to create long-term support for the advancement of Chinese business and political objectives. As Jake Gilstrap observed in a research paper for the U.S. National Defense University: "...it is my analysis that China seeks to create a generation of future political and business leaders that will support its ascent and serve as diplomatic allies in the international order. By increasing Mandarin language abilities and cultural influence in Latin America, China hopes to establish long lasting ties that will lead to individuals in the region wanting what China wants, becoming valuable allies" (Gilstrap 2021: 21).

It can be argued that China has already accomplished some of this through the diplomatic shuffles of Panama, El Salvador, and the Dominican Republic from Taiwan to China. It has also helped build up a positive image of China throughout the English-speaking Caribbean. The activity of CIs should also be seen as operating in tandem with the offering of scholarships for local students to study in China. Scholarships have included airfare to and from China, free accommodation, free tuition, a yearly living stipend, and offer instruction in International Business, Public Policy, Educational Management, Tourism and Hotel Management, Environmental Engineering, Project Management, Social Work, Fishery Science, International Communications and Theoretical Economics. Although CIs and educational offerings are not the same as building roads, harbors, and cricket stadiums, they do provide a long-term soft power instrument in the increasingly new Cold War environment in the Caribbean.

CHANGING STRATEGIC CONSIDERATIONS

In the early twenty-first century the global geopolitical landscape for China changed radically. Although the old Cold War ended, China had a new rival, the United States. During the 2000s the Bush and Obama administrations maintained some degree of faith in the necessity of the multilateral institutions that had emerged from the Second World War. These institutions as well as alliances were seen as systems to avoid the mistakes that led to World War II: the gutting of international mechanisms, like the League of Nations, led to more head-to-head confrontations pushed along by more narrow nationalistic goals. Although the postwar system struggled in the aftermath of the Cold War, it provided a format for global discourse. Under pressure from Russia (which rejected the post-Cold War status quo in recent years) and China (which embraced multilateralism while seeking to gain hegemony), the Trump administration made a move away from the old system and its alliances. China looked upon the Trump administration's effort to ditch the post-World War II multilateral system as an opportunity to take the lead as the defender of a multilateral world order, but with Beijing in the driver's seat, not Washington (which appeared tired and bent on isolation).

China's efforts are not solely related to intensifying economic and political cooperation, but also follow a strategic goal of developing its own sphere of influence in Latin America and the Caribbean and reducing Taiwan's diplomatic footprint. This helps elevate its hard and soft power to a more systemic level. As political scientist Lei Yu noted in an article in *International Affairs*, "With access to Latin American markets, resources and investment destinations, China may sustain its economic and social progress that bases its cherished dream of restoring its past glory of *fuqiang* (wealth and power) and rise as a global power capable of reshaping the current world system" (Yu 2015). The Caribbean fits as part of this strategic consideration; by playing an active role in the region China gains more soft power in and leverage over its economic partners, which helps it rise in the global power hierarchy.

The trade war unleashed by the Trump administration against China in 2018 came as a surprise. Much of Chinese thinking was that with Trump being a businessman he would be easier to deal with, and willing to strike deals. When the United States began to raise tariffs on Chinese goods, Beijing initially found itself caught off guard; while most Chinese policymakers expected this would happen, they had not expected it so soon. This was a major change in strategic alignments as the trade war nudged the two countries closer to a new Cold War. It also added pressure on other countries to pick a side, something that most governments in the Americas, Europe, and Asia dreaded considering how it would complicate trade and investment relations.

The trade war remains a factor in the shift from the Trump to Biden administrations. This has led China to understand that relations with the United States are going to remain tense for the foreseeable future, which has led China to make shifts in policy goals. While the international development strategy remains very much in place, there are three other key planks in Chinese policymaking. Ryan Hass, a Senior Fellow at the Center for East Asia Policy Studies at the Brookings Institute, suggests the following: "Chinese officials recognize that they will need to overcome obstacles in their country's pursuit of its national goals. To do so, China appears to be pursuing a three-pronged medium-term strategy: maintaining a non-hostile external environment in order to focus on domestic priorities; reducing dependence on America while increasing the rest of the world's dependence on China; and expanding the reach of Chinese influence overseas" (Hass 2021). The Russo-Ukrainian War has complicated this, but not derailed these goals. However, the brutal nature of Western sanctions has given Beijing a degree of apprehension, considering China's desire to lead the global order. That stated, China continues to press ahead in the Caribbean, Latin America, Africa and Asia with trade and investment programs.

China has clearly made its presence felt in the Caribbean, with waves rippling to Washington. Yet for all of the Asian giant's harnessing of economic power and political influence, it is not a monolithic actor. President Xi has amassed the most political power since Mao, but he still has to work with other groups inside the Communist Party, the military and business. President Xi has to balance more nationalistic factions within his base with those who are more globalist in orientation. Chinese nationalism is a core element of the Xi regime, but there are different levels of patriotism and how they interface in policy matters. Backed by the second largest economy in the world and military power that has considerably grown in sophistication and deadliness since the late 1970s, President Xi, with aircraft carriers and space weapons at his disposal, has clearly buried Deng's "Hide your strength, bide your time." Instead China new maxim appears to be "Show your strength, this is your time." In the Caribbean, thousands of miles away from the opaque politics of the Communist Party, China matters. And China will continue to shape a narrative that stresses partnership and win–win development, even if that is not always the case. Indeed, China's story in the Caribbean must be carefully scrutinized to discern between facts and what is misinformation, disinformation, and propaganda.

CONCLUSION

This chapter outlined in broad brushstrokes how Chines banks, companies, and government arrived in the Caribbean. It has covered the transformation of China from a closed and struggling economy into a global economic power as well as its move from being a minor business partner to Latin America and then the Caribbean to becoming a major economic and geopolitical force in their regions. Unlike the Soviet Union which vowed to overturn the capitalist order, China is a major stakeholder in that global system, has its own ideological biases as to the order of things, and increasingly is pushing its own agenda. That includes clawing out a political and economic space in the U.S. strategic backyard. It is also advancing its international development strategy of finding and securing critical natural resources to help fuel the country's future economic expansion and conversion from an export-driven to domestic demand-driven economy in which green technologies are significant. Beijing's message to the Caribbean is that China's rise is not a threat, but an opportunity to gain wealth and prosperity, just like the Communist Party has delivered at home. Despite the win–win message from Beijing, Chinese largesse in the Caribbean as elsewhere in the developing world does not come without strings. Just as Chinese companies are driven by their need for profits, President Xi and the Communist Party have geopolitical goals which include the Caribbean and could put governments there at odds with their larger neighbor to the north, a reality governments in the region are increasingly going have to consider as they navigate the decades ahead.

NOTE

1. World Bank, "China At-a-Glance", https://www.worldbank.org/en/country/china/testpagecheck (Assessed December 19, 2021).

REFERENCES

Agarwal, Rupal. 2020. China's Expansion in the Indian Ocean: A Big Worry for India. *The Diplomatist*. July 23.

Blanchard, Jean-Marc F., ed. 2018. *China's Maritime Silk Road Initiative and South Asia: A Political Economic Analysis of Its Purposes*. Perils and Promise: Palgrave Macmillan.

Boston University Global Policy Center, China's Global Energy Finance. https://www.bu.edu/cgef/#/all/Country.

Calhoun, George. 2021. The Sad End of Jack Ma Inc. *Forbes*, June 7. https://www.forbes.com/sites/georgecalhoun/2021/06/07/the-sad-end-of-jack-ma-inc/ (Accessed on July 21, 2021).

Caribbean Council. 2012. Background Paper for the Advisory Committee of the Caribbean Council. *The Caribbean Council* (London), November 12, 2012. https://www.caribbean-council.org/wp-content/uploads/2014/02/China-and-the-Caribbean-Advisory-Committee-Background-article.pdf.

Caribbean Development Bank. 2017. CDB Signs MOU with Export-Import Bank of China. *News and Events Caribbean Development Bank*, July 13: https://www.caribank.org/newsroom/news-and-events/cdb-signs-mou-export-import-bank-china.

Chaudhury, Dipanjan Roy. 2021. Africa's Rising Debt: Chinese Loans to Continent Exceeds $140 Billion. *The Economic Times (India)*. September 23. https://economictimes.indiatimes.com/news/international/world-news/africas-rising-debt-chinese-loans-to-continent-exceeds-140-billion/articleshow/86444602.cms.

Chen, Jie. 2013. *A Middle Class without Democracy: Economic Growth and the Prospects for Democratization in China*. Oxford University Press.

Chen, Taotao and Miguel Pérez Ludena, 2014. *Chinese Foreign Direct Investment in Latin America and the Caribbean*. United Nations Publication: 5. https://repositorio.cepal.org/bitstream/handle/11362/35908/1/S2014011_en.pdf (Accessed May 11, 2020).

Dok, Akol Nypk Akol and Bradley A. Thayer, 2019. Why China is Taking Over Africa's Resources One Country at a Time. *National Interest*, July 3.

Economy, Elizabeth C., and Michael Levi. 2014. *By All Means Necessary: How China's Resource Quest Is Changing the World*. Oxford University Press.

Ellis, Evan. 2020. China's Advance in the Caribbean. Woodrow Wilson China and U.S. in Latin America Program. https://www.wilsoncenter.org/publication/chinas-advance-caribbean.

Ellis, Evan. 2022. Panama: The New Battlefield Between the US and China? *Dialogo-Americas*. March 25

Foreign Ministry of the People's Republic of China. 2005. "Zeng Qinghong Attends 'China-Caribbean Economic & Trade Cooperation Forum' and Delivers Speech". February 3. https://www.fmprc.gov.cn/ce/ceee/eng/dtxw/t184238.htm.

Gabriel Alvarado, 2019. Beijing Seeks to Rapidly Solidify Its Position in Latin America Amidst Spat with Washington. *Global Americans*, February 11. https://theglobalamericans.org/2019/02/beijing-seeks-to-rapidly-solidify-its-position-in-latin-america-amidst-spat-with-washington/.

Gilstrap, Jake. 2021. *Chinese Confucius Institutes in Latin America: Tools of Soft Power*. William J. Perry Center for Hemispheric Defense Studies, October.

Hass, Ryan. 2021. How China Is Responding to Escalating Strategic Competition with the US. China Leadership Monitor, Brookings Institute, March 1, 2021. https://www.brookings.edu/articles/how-china-is-responding-to-escalating-strategic-competition-with-the-us/ (Accessed July 19, 2021).

Hillman, Jonathan E. 2020. *The Emperor's New Road: China and the Project of the Century* Yale University Press.

Hubbert, Jennifer. 2019. *China in the World: An Anthropology of Confucius Institutes, Soft Power, and Globalization*. University of Hawaii Press.

Inter-American Development Bank. 2009. China Joins IDB in Ceremony at Bank Headquarters. Inter-American Development Bank, News Releases, January 12. https://www.iadb.org/en/news/china-joins-idb-ceremony-bank-headquarters

Kynge, James, Chris Campbell, Amy Kazmin and Farhan Bokhari, 2017. How China Rules the Waves. *Financial Times*, January. https://ig.ft.com/sites/china-ports/.

Li, Cheng, ed. *China's Emerging Middle Class: Beyond Economic Transformation* Brookings Institution Press.

Macan-Markar, Marwaan. 2021. Laos Shifts to China Equity from Loans as Party Congress Starts. Nikkei Asia, January 12. https://asia.nikkei.com/Economy/Laos-shifts-to-China-equity-from-loans-as-party-congress-starts.
Munevar, Daniel. 2021. European Network on Debt and Development. 2021. Dam Debt: Understanding the Dynamics of Suriname's Debt Crisis. January. https://d3n8a8pro7vhmx.cloudfront.net/eurodad/pages/1997/att achments/original/1611155073/suriname-dam-debt-final.pdf?1611155073.
Nathan, Andrew. 2021. An Anxious 100th Birthday for China's Communist Party. The Wall Street Journal, June 26–27: C2.
Nicholls, Alicia. 2018. US-China Trade Tensions: What May These Mean for the Caribbean?. Caribbean Trade Law and Development. February 9. https://caribbeantradelaw.com/2018/09/23/us-china-trade-tensions-what-may-these-mean-for-the-caribbean/.
Organization for Economic Cooperation and Development. 2018. China's Belt and Road Initiative in the Global Trade. Investment and Finance Landscape (Paris: Organization for Economic Cooperation and Development. https://www.oecd.org/finance/Chinas-Belt-and-Road-Initiative-in-the-global-trade-investment-and-finance-landscape.pdf.
Paterson, Rachelle. 2018. China's Rebranding its Confucius Institutes. Real Clear Education. July 22. https://www.realcleareducation.com/articles/2020/07/22/china_is_rebranding_its_confucius_institutes_110445.html.
Pei, Minxin. 2006. China's Trapped Transition: The Limits of Developmental Autocracy Cambridge University Press.
Schuman, Michael. 2020. Superpower Interrupted: The Chinese History of the World. Public Affairs.
Shixue, Jiang. 2008. The Chinese Foreign Policy Perspective. Riordan Roett and Guadalupe Paz, editors, China's Expansion into the Western Hemisphere: Implications for Latin America and the United States. Brookings Institution.
Silver, Laura, Kat Devlin and Christine Huang. 2020. Unfavorable Views of China Reach Historic Highs in Many Countries. Pew Research Center, October 6. https://www.pewresearch.org/global/2020/10/06/unf avorable-views-of-china-reach-historic-highs-in-many-countries/.
Singh, Abhijit. 2020. India Has a Bigger Worry Than LAC. China Now Expanding Footprint in the Indian Ocean. The Print, June 12.
Singh, Antara Ghosal. 2022. China's Evolving Strategic Discourse on India from Dokham to Galwan and Beyond. Stimson Policy Center, May 4. https://www.stimson.org/2022/chinas-evolving-strategic-discourse-on-india/.
Stallings, Barbara. 2020. Dependency in the Twenty-First Century: The Political Economy of China-Latin American Relations Cambridge University Press.
Sullivan, Mark and Thomas Lum. 2019. China's Engagement with Latin America and the Caribbean, Congressional Research Service, April 11. https://fas.org/sgp/crs/row/IF10982.pdf.

U.S. Government. 2011. Ten Years in the WTO: Has China Kept Its Promises?, Hearing before the Congressional-Executive Commission on China One Hundred Twelfth Congress, December 13. Opening statement of Hon. Chris Smith, a U.S. Representative from New Jersey; Chairman, Congressional-Executive Committee on China. https://www.govinfo.gov/content/pkg/CHRG-112hhrg74026/html/CHRG-112hhrg74026.htm.

Vasquez, Patricia I. with David Humphreys and Ana Elizabeth Bastida, 2018. China's Engagement in the Mineral Sector in Latin America: Lessons Learned and Opportunities for International Cooperation, European Policy Brief, Strategic Dialogue on Sustainable Raw Materials for Europe (STRADE), November. http://stradeproject.eu/fileadmin/user_upload/pdf/STRADE_China_engagement_LATAM.pdf.

Wenner, Mark D. and Dillon Clarke, 2016. *Chinese Rise in the Caribbean: What Does It Mean for Caribbean Stakeholders?* Inter-American Development Bank. https://publications.iadb.org/publications/english/document/Chinese-Rise-in-the-Caribbean-What-Does-It-Mean-for-Caribbean-Stakeholders.pdf.

Wise, Carol. 2020. *Dragonomics: How Latin America Is Maximizing (or Missing Out on) China's International Development Strategy.* Yale University Press.

Younus, Uzair. 2021. Pakistan's Growing Problem with Its China Economic Corridor. United States Institute of Peace, May 26. https://www.usip.org/publications/2021/05/pakistans-growing-problem-its-china-economic-corridor.

Yu, Lei. 2015. "China's Strategic Partnership with Latin America: a Fulcrum in China's Rise", *International Affairs*, Vol. 91, Issue 5, September: 1047–1068.

Yuan, Fei and Kevin P. Gallagher. 2016. Repositioning Chinese Development Finance in Latin America: Opportunities for Green Finance. Boston University Global Economic Governance Initiative, GEGI Policy Brief. August. https://www.bu.edu/pardeeschool/files/2016/05/ChineseDevelopmentBankingLAC.pdf.

Zhu, Zhiqun. 2019. *A Critical Decade: China's Foreign Policy (2008–2018).* World Scientific.

CHAPTER 3

China, Venezuela, and Cuba: The New Cold War?

The Caribbean's slide into the new Cold War is observable in a number of countries, but in the cases of Cuba and Venezuela, the authoritarian kinship between like-minded states is most evident. It is in the dynamics of how Cuba and Venezuela interact with China that the lines of polarization are most evident in the region. At the same time that Cuba and Venezuela share a high degree of political affinity with China, the gross mismanagement of their economies has also been problematic for Beijing. Moreover, Beijing has demonstrated a willingness to be more invested in Venezuela's fortunes than those of Cuba as the former has one of the world's most significant reserves of oil, still important in a global energy scene that remains in transition. China's willingness to support both governments has also set it up in an adversarial position vis-à-vis the United States, which maintains economic sanctions against the Cuban and Venezuelan regimes.

Cuba and Venezuela are the odd ones in the Caribbean. The two countries have dictatorial governments, dysfunctional economies, and share a strong dislike of the United States, which has sanctions against both countries. Cuba and Venezuela share another factor—in the early twenty-first century China has become a major economic and diplomatic prop for their governments, providing support for them in international forums and being a major trade partner and source of investment. In Venezuela's case, China is helped by Russia and Iran, two other authoritarian regimes each with their own motivations for being engaged with the South American country. Their role in the new Cold war will be taken

© The Author(s), under exclusive license to Springer Nature Switzerland AG 2022
S. B. MacDonald, *The New Cold War, China, and the Caribbean*, https://doi.org/10.1007/978-3-031-06149-3_3

up in Chapter 7. Despite the perception among the Caribbean's largely democratic governments that China is a well-intentioned partner, it is in Cuba and Venezuela where Beijing most starkly demonstrates its support for leftwing authoritarian governments that have little regard for their citizens.

China is attracted to Venezuela for its oil (as part of its international development strategy) and Cuba for its strategic location close to the United States. Both countries have joined the BRI and proudly host Confucius Institutes, indicating their engagement in the budding Chinese world order. However, these are not easy relationships. In a sense, China is locked into its relationships with Caracas and Havana; playing a role in both countries makes geopolitical sense, and backing down under U.S. pressure to abandon them would be a loss of face that Beijing is no longer willing to accommodate. At the same time, China has considerable reluctance to liberally bankroll bad economic managers as found in Cuba and Venezuela. The lending extended to the latter has been a scarcely disguised headache for Chinese policymakers. Complicating the picture further, China has to contend with considerable political uncertainty regarding the future of both regimes. Cuba's and Venezuela's governments preside over restless populations, have badly eroded their legitimacy in the eyes of their citizens, and rely on military/police coercion to remain in power. And China supports these unpopular regimes, something that no doubt would come into consideration if these governments were replaced by more open, democratic societies.

Putting Venezuela into Context

Although Venezuela is not usually considered to be "Caribbean" in the same sense as the Bahamas or Suriname, Caribbean waters lap its coastal areas and it plays an important role in regional affairs. In many regards, it is difficult to separate Venezuelan history from that of the Caribbean, considering that the country's founder, Simón Bolívar, spent time in exile in Jamaica and Haiti. The latter country also helped Bolívar with ships, men, and weapons. In more modern times, Venezuela has loomed large—Cuba sought in the 1960s to topple its democratic government; it was a place of exile for Leslie Manigat in 1979 (who briefly became president of Haiti); and has been a major supplier of oil (both during the democratic and Chávez-Maduro periods) to Caribbean countries, and, most recently, it has provided a massive stream of refugees (over

6 million) into neighboring countries. Venezuela will continue to play a role in Caribbean affairs, a situation reinforced by overlapping national interests and geographical location. At the same time, Venezuela is the country in Latin America and the Caribbean that has attracted the most Chinese investment. Venezuela alone accounted for 45 percent of total Chinese development bank lending to Latin America and the Caribbean since 2005, though since 2017 China has considerably reduced the credit stream (Myers and Ray 2021).

Formal relations between China and Venezuela commenced in 1974, when Caracas recognized the People's Republic of China, dropping the Republic of China (Taiwan). Over the next several decades, Chinese–Venezuelan relations were largely uneventful and not of any great consequence to either country. Trade existed between the two countries, but China's key energy needs were met through either domestic oil production or coal as well as imports from Indonesia and the Middle East. Moreover, throughout the Cold War Venezuela was considered a U.S. ally, which precluded the development of much closer ties.

Hugo Chávez's arrival was a major catalyst for Chinese–Venezuelan relations. To understand the full implications of his rise to power and how this was to play out in the triangle of Venezuela, China, and the United States, it is useful to understand the pre-Chávez era. Venezuela was a petro-state, an economy largely based on the production and export of oil. As a founding member of the Organization of Petroleum Exporting Countries (OPEC), Venezuela maintained close relations with most major oil companies, including those from the United States. The Unites States' role was important as much of Venezuela's heavy crude was shipped north where it was refined. At the same time, the United States was a major source of food imports and other North American companies were well represented throughout the Latin American country's economy.

The sustainability of U.S.–Venezuelan relations as well as the country's politics became increasingly fragile in the late 1980s and early 1990s when oil prices were low and the country ran into problems repaying its debt. Another layer of problems came from massive corruption in the Venezuelan economy and considerable social inequality, paving the way for someone like Chávez, who could channel popular anger and frustration with the country's elites (Naím 1993: 139; Gallegos 2016: 57–78). The late democratic period was marked by considerable turmoil, mirrored by two coup attempts (one led by Chávez) in 1992 and the impeachment of President Carlos Andrés Pérez in 1993 for embezzlement of government funds. Two interim presidents lasted until elections, leaving the old republic's last act in the hands of Christian Democrat Rafael Caldera, who was unable to come to grips with Venezuela's problems. Things were soon to change and radically.

In 1998, Chávez won the presidency with 56 percent of the vote, indicating that the country wanted a change from the traditional parties. They were to get their wish. Through the first decade of the twenty-first century, Chávez took Venezuela down a socialist-populist rabbit hole, admonishing the wealthy, nationalizing businesses (both local and foreign), and upping social spending. He took on the power of the country's state-owned oil company, PDVSA, broke its powerful unions, and put in ideological loyalists and cronies to run it (driving out many experienced managers and workers in the process). Narrowly surviving a coup attempt in 2002, Chávez increasingly shut down freedom of the press, packed the judicial system with loyalists, harassed opposition figures, and put the United States on notice that he considered it a foe. Chávez won re-election in 2001 and 2007 and served until his death of cancer in 2013. While he was intensely disliked by Venezuela's wealthy and much of its middle class, Chávez was popular with much of the lower classes, something bolstered by his strong charisma and generous state handouts.

Chávez's time in office coincided with an extended run of high oil prices (from 2004 to 2014). He used oil-fueled financial largesse to augment social spending, disregard more conventional economic advisers, and outspend any political rivals in the country's elections. He also benefited from a badly divided opposition and a relative disinterest by the United States in becoming involved in Venezuelan politics, especially when other foreign policy challenges were more pressing. Despite Chávez's ongoing rhetoric, Venezuela remained a major oil exporter to the United States and large U.S. energy companies continued to be in the country. It appeared that as long as the oil business between the two countries remained largely intact, the mutual interests trumped geopolitical differences. This dynamic was to change as China increasingly became a factor in Venezuela's economic landscape.

Chávez's was the major force behind better relations with China. The addition of a new economic partner gave the Venezuelan leader an opportunity to reduce his country's dependence on the United States. At the same time, China, which had earlier shifted from having demand met from domestic oil production, needed to secure new sources to maintain its industrialization process. Venezuela also represented an opportunity to reduce the political risk that was often evident in the Middle East. Chinese and Venezuelan national interests converged. In 2000, Chávez visited China, meeting with President Jiang Zemin and announcing that Mao Zedong had been an influence on his thinking. In 2001, Zemin went to Venezuela, meeting with Chávez and setting the tone of closer ties. This was reflected in the creation of the China–Venezuela High-Level Commission, which helped lower barriers, allowing Chinese energy companies easier entry and expanded opportunities for trade and investment. This was a significant move as it provided China with a beachhead in the country's economy. The companies benefiting from this opening included some of China's largest state-owned energy enterprises, China National Petroleum Corporation (CNPC), China National Offshore Oil Corp., and China Petroleum & Chemical Corporation (Sinopec). Oil exports to China rose from less than 90,000 barrels per day in 2005 to more than 320,000 in 2014 (Kaplan and Penfold 2021).

Equally important to Beijing's engagement in Venezuela was the massive extension of credit by China's development banks for various projects. Access to Chinese credit was important as it helped finance Chávez's post-2006 re-election round of nationalizations and expropriations in the non-oil sectors, which extended to mining, electricity, financial, telecommunications, agriculture, and industrial sectors. This continued over the next several years, helping to facilitate Chávez's "Socialism of the 21st Century" campaign. As Stephen Kaplan and Michael Penfold observed: "By 2013, China had provided the Venezuelan government with more than $30 billion in oil-backed loans, which enabled sectoral investments on state priorities beyond the most economically important oil and mining industries, including infrastructure, construction, agriculture, telecommunications, housing and forestry" (Kaplan and Penfold; Liu and Wang 2012). This was to leave the Venezuelan state with a growing inventory of economic enterprises spread across the economy, including cattle ranches, large housing projects and cellphone assembly, which in many cases were headed by Chávista loyalists with little or no business or management experience (Gallegos 2016).

While China's loans helped Chávez's takeover of the economy, Beijing sympathized with Caracas' foreign policy, which was centered around the creation of an anti-U.S. bloc of like-minded socialist and social democratic countries in the Western Hemisphere. This was accomplished with the formation of the Bolivarian Alliance for the Peoples of Our America

(Alanza Bolivariana para los Pueblos de Nuestra América or ALBA) and Petrocaribe. ALBA was created by Venezuela and Cuba in 2004 and came to include Antigua and Barbuda, Bolivia, Dominica, Grenada, Ecuador, Nicaragua, St. Kitts-Nevis, St. Vincent and the Grenadines, and Suriname. Chávez used ALBA to offer his ideological regional allies subsidized fuel and financing for infrastructure projects. Much of this was done in an opaque fashion, which is believed to have later helped ALBA be used to assist Venezuelan evasion of U.S. sanctions and engage the Maduro regime in a wide range of criminal enterprises (Farah and Yates 2019).

Petrocaribe was established in 2005 with the objective of helping the energy-challenged Caribbean and Central American countries through concessionary pricing for Venezuelan oil. The member states were able to access 25-year loans with interest rates of between 1 and 2 percent from Petrocaribe whenever world oil prices exceeded $50 a barrel. For many energy-dependent countries, this provided an important cushion as international oil prices rose from a low of $18.41 in May 1998, peaking at close to $160 a barrel in May 2008 and trading at over $100 a barrel until prices collapsed in 2014 (Macrotrends 2021).

The Caribbean representation in Petrocaribe was extensive, including Antigua and Barbuda, the Bahamas, Belize, Cuba, Dominica, the Dominican Republic, Jamaica, St. Lucia, and Suriname, with Haiti and Nicaragua joining later. While the concessionary financing helped deal with the surge in oil prices, it also raised the debt levels of a number of countries. Like ALBA, Petrocaribe was known for its opaque finances and eventually became a source of scandal, in particular in Haiti where $2 billion of oil funds went missing and contributed to that country's destabilization of the country in 2020–2022.

The combination of ALBA and Petrocaribe extended Venezuela's influence into the Caribbean, where Caracas was seen as a counterpoint to U.S. power up until 2014–2015. In exchange for Venezuela's helping hand, goodwill was earned from recipient countries, which was tapped when votes came up at such forums as the OAS. Petrocaribe members voted together to support the Maduro government in April 2014 at the OAS, when an effort was made to discuss the country's political crises stemming from accusations of cheating in the 2013 elections that gave Maduro a narrow victory (Trinkunas 2014).

The Chávez government developed a close working relationship with Cuba, also a Chinese friend. Following the failed 2002 coup in Venezuela in 2002, Chávez deepened his relations with Cuba. Fidel Castro provided advice as well as security personnel to keep control over the Venezuelan military (of which Chávez was suspicious after the attempted coup). Cuban doctors and other medical staff showed up in Venezuela, as part of an exchange for cheap Venezuelan oil, which Cuba could refine and then sell on international markets for badly needed foreign exchange. Cuba's shambolic communist economic experiment was saved by Venezuelan oil, at least for another decade.

THE BEST OF TIMES AND THE WORST OF TIMES

Chinese–Venezuelan relations deepened during Hu Jintao's presidency (2002–2012). It was during this period that China became Venezuela's major foreign banker, eventually leading to an estimated $63 billion in debt for the Latin American country. The bulk of that lending came during the Hu years, which thus far have proved to be the high point in the Beijing–Caracas relationship. It was in those heady days in the late 2000s that China displaced the United States as the Latin American country's primary economic partner.

While the energy sector dominated China's attention, other Chinese businesses became involved in power plants, transmission lines, and railways. Huawei won contracts to support and build telecommunications networks in Venezuela. And support for a massive new iron project in the state of Bolívar in the southern part of the country was established in 2009 under a contract in which the China Development Bank provided a $1 billion credit line to the Venezuelan Economic and Social Development Bank or BANDES. At the end of 2012, China and Venezuela had reached the apex of their relationship. The Chinese were comfortable with Chávez and Venezuela regarded China as a friend, international ally, and source of funding for development projects. Oil prices were high; China had a friend in power, and a precious commodity was secured. What could go wrong?

China badly miscalculated Venezuela's political risk. The Chinese approach to lending is that Western creditors place too much emphasis on the macroeconomic and institutional environment. The former would encompass such items as economic growth, inflation, fiscal performance, debt management, and trade. The latter fits into the broader rubric of governance issues, like transparency and disclosure in government finances, corruption, the rule of law, and coherent and relatively consistent government policies. To Chinese creditors, the Western approach is overly political and impinges on the sovereignty of borrowing countries. This approach also allowed Chinese companies to conduct business in countries where Western lenders and companies often opted not to tread, like Venezuela and Cuba.

China's approach to lending is based more on commercial considerations that seek to promote long-term opportunities by linking their investments to guaranteed contracts for its state-owned firms, content requirements to stimulate Chinese machinery exports, or the use of labor or commodity guarantees (Penfold and Kaplan). In their excellent study on Chinese lending to Venezuela, Penfold and Kaplan quote from the *Chinese Academy of Social Sciences'* (CASS) *Journal of Latin American Studies,* the Chinese government's think tank's regional studies publication: "The primary reason that the World Bank and other development financial institutions overlook Venezuela and other such countries is that they are so-called high-risk nations. This type of judgment is based upon a political perspective and not an economic perspective. In reality, Venezuela is South America's largest oil exporter and maintains a relatively strong ability to repay debt" (Kaplan and Penfold 2021). The upside to China's international development strategy was that it was able to secure a very large source of oil and potentially other resources. The downside was that the era of high oil prices came to an end in 2014, revealing Venezuela's economy as a chaotic mess, a problem compounded by Chávez's death and his replacement by Maduro, a former bus driver and union organizer, who had little experience in economic management and proved to be inflexible, slow in making important decisions, and doctrinaire in policy matters.

When the Venezuelan economy slid into negative territory in 2014 there was no easy way of turning the situation around. The costs of a too-heavy dependence on oil exports and poor economic management came home. Part of the latter was evident at PDVSA, which was starved for funds needed for maintenance, exploration, and qualified personnel. According to BP, oil production in thousands of barrels per day fell from 3038 in 2009 to 2692 in 2014 to 918 in 2019 (BP 2020). Venezuela would endure almost a decade of economic contraction, hitting the bottom in 2019, when real GDP fell by 35 percent. This meant that Venezuela became increasingly constrained in its ability to repay Chinese loans, even those backed by oil. U.S. sanctions, which commenced in 2014 under the Obama administration and gained considerable momentum under the Trump administration, only added further misery to the sinking of the Venezuelan economy. The mutual interests that had bound U.S.–Venezuelan relations largely dissolved, due to China's rising importance as a customer and the shale revolution in the United States, which reduced that country's dependence on imported energy.

As the Venezuelan economy sank, some of the problems in the relationship became evident. One of the more well-known corporate disasters came with Chávez's plans to diversify the economy, which led to a deal in 2009 between the state-run mining company CVG Ferrominera Orinoco, part of a larger state-own conglomerate, Corporación Venezolana de Guayana (CVG), which would deliver 42.96 million tons of iron ore to the Chinese steel company Wuhan Iron and Steel Corporation (Wisco) (Segovia 2021). This transaction was to last for eight years. A $1 billion line of credit from the Chinese Development Bank to BANDES was to help facilitate the project's development and iron ore exports. The line of credit would be repaid by Venezuela with the proceeds from the sale of the iron ore.

The project's problems were numerous. The shipment's targets were too high for the Venezuelan mining group to meet on time; the Venezuelan port where Wisco's ships were to pick up the ore did not have the capacity needed; and there was considerable corruption (including extortion, money laundering, and criminal association) on the part of Ferrominera's top management in 2013. Moreover, international iron ore prices increased, but the Venezuelans were stuck at a negotiated lower price, which benefited the Chinese. The iron ore project ultimately became an embarrassment to both sides, with some commentators regarding it as part of a Chinese debt trap. As one observer noted: "China had paid just $1 billion dollars for securing 42.95 million tonnes of iron ore, whose cost according to markets rates in 2009 was close to $4 billion. Not only were the Venezuelans short-changed by the Chinese, but the seemingly overwhelming requirements of the deal had a deteriorating effect on the company's capacity" (OpIndia 2021).

The dysfunctional nature of the Maduro regime rippled into other parts of the relationship. Although Venezuela looked upon China as a critical financial lifeline, the Chinese did not feel the same way. Indeed, delays in Venezuelan payments eventually provoked a legal response from China. In 2017 in a court in Houston, a U.S. subsidiary of Sinopec sued PDSVA for $23.7 million-plus punitive damages over a May 2012 contract to supply steel rebar for $43.5 million, half of which the Chinese company claimed was unpaid (Kassaai 2017). As part of a larger deal in which Sinopec agreed in September 2013 to invest $14 billion in a Venezuelan oil field, the suit was a small change. However, it signaled that for the Chinese business is business, a view that trumped socialist solidarity. According to Sinopec's complaint, PDVSA was using "an undercapitalized shell with the sole purpose of preventing Sinopec from having a remedy" and that the Venezuelan company's conduct "constituted intentional misrepresentations, deceit, and concealment of material facts," involving "willful deception" and a coordinated conspiracy among several units of PDVSA (Wheatley 2017). This can hardly be construed as friendly words between two allies.

China's increasing wariness was evident in other ways. While President Hu had been happy to let Chinese credit flow into Venezuela, his successor President Xi was warier. The policy framework adopted by Beijing from 2014 forward was shaped by a refusal to offer any new major loan-for-oil deals; Chinese attention was given more to recovering something from their previous bilateral loans. China also advanced with caution when the opposition-held National Assembly let it be known that it would consider any new loans from major international banks (like Goldman Sachs and JP Morgan Chase), multilateral development banks, and Chinese creditors as illegal. To stress the point to China, the National Assembly sent a letter directly to the Chinese embassy in Caracas.

Greatly complicating the picture was the increasingly tangled political mire. Although dying of cancer Chávez won the 2012 elections, which were seen by some as fraudulent. In 2013, when Chávez died and was replaced by Maduro new elections were held. Maduro narrowly won the contest, but there was considerable fraud. China remained supportive of Maduro, despite growing political volatility (China.org.cn. 2014). The situation became even more problematic with the 2015 congressional elections which were won decisively by an opposition coalition. The National Assembly, previously held by Maduro's party, was converted into an anti-regime body. Various efforts were taken to dilute the National Assembly's authority. In 2019, the National Assembly declared one of its own, Juan Guaidó, as interim president, which launched the country into an extended period of political upheaval, brought about new rounds of economic sanctions, and internationally challenged Maduro's position as the legitimate head of state. Riots and demonstrations, border tensions with Colombia and Brazil, and crackdowns functioned to make the country's already dire economic situation even worse.

While China continued to publicly support the Maduro regime, it also sought to hedge its bets with the Venezuelan opposition, with Chinese officials meeting the opposition candidate Henrique Capriles. Chinese officials also let it be known that opposition leaders were welcome to visit Beijing. In 2019, China was willing to have some low-level contacts with the National Assembly interim president Guiadó. With a sizable, though reduced, exposure in Venezuela China followed a relatively pragmatic path based on national interests just in case Maduro was toppled.

THE TIES THAT BIND

China did not abandon the Maduro regime. Through a combination of financial sleight-of-hand, diplomatic activity, maintenance of trade, weapons sales, and helping Venezuela introduce digital control over its telecommunications system, China has worked to keep a highly unpopular regime in power. Certainly, the size of what Venezuela owes China is a consideration (probably somewhere around $20 billion as of 2020), but there is a long-term game at play (Hernández 2020). China's international development strategy still places an emphasis on energy, even if it is from fossil fuels. And there remains the allure of having an ally in the Americas which is strongly anti-United States. This was reflected by President Xi's July 2014 visit to Caracas, in which he clearly indicated that relations between the two countries remained strong (China.org.cn. 2014). This was important as the visit came after Chávez had died and Maduro had claimed victory in an election that many believed was stolen. Equally important was that while Chinese credit available to Venezuela was reduced, China kept a lifeline open. As Kaplan and Penfield observed: "Shortly after his visit [Xi], the China Export–Import Bank and China Development Bank replenished tranches A and B respectively (totaling $9 billion) of the China-Venezuela Joint Fund (FCCV). This financing was vital to helping Venezuela cover its financing shortfalls and avoid a balance-of-payments crisis. From 2014 to 2015, Chinese funds provided nearly one-third of Venezuela's total financing needs, often directly padding its international reserves" (Kaplan and Penfold 2021). China also provided a two-year repayment moratorium on state-to-state debt.

Anyone looking for China's commitment to keeping a thuggish and corrupt regime afloat has to look no further than the strategic lending. China also released some bank lines in 2016, though the credit spigot was turned off in 2017 and subsequent years. Part of the reason for China not extending more loans was probably related to the growing role of Russia during this period, another external player willing to prop up an anti-U.S. dictatorship. In subsequent years, China's and Russia's roles would also be helped by technical assistance from Iran to breathe life back into Venezuela's oil industry (which will be covered in a following chapter).

Lacking Chávez's charisma, Maduro was increasingly forced to rule through police and military repression (helped by Cuban security forces and armed supporters of the regime). China no doubt hoped for the situation to stabilize. But that was not to be: Venezuela's political and economic situation deteriorated further. From 2016 through 2021 Venezuela underwent hyperinflation (with inflation moving from 62.2 percent in 2014 to over 66,000 percent in 2018 before heading down to 6500 percent in 2020); a massive contraction in economic life almost to barter levels; and high unemployment (around 54.4 percent in 2020) (International Monetary Fund 2020). As crime skyrocketed, many Venezuelans opted to leave, contributing to an exodus of over 6 million people. Venezuela's humanitarian crisis, its spillover into neighboring countries, including Colombia (which created tensions along the border), Ecuador, Peru, Brazil, and Trinidad and Tobago), the widespread public hatred of the regime, and the massive corruption conducted by members of the Maduro government (including drug trafficking and illegal gold smuggling), helped mobilize international support for a transition. U.S., Canadian, and a number of European government imposed economic sanctions on Venezuela and along with most Latin American countries backed Guaidó. In this context, China remained supportive of the Maduro regime as a diplomatic backer at the United Nations, a provider of technical advice, and a supplier of weapons.

Some of the weapons used by the Maduro regime against its own people came from China, which was a major seller of military equipment to the South American country. The Stockholm International Peace Research Institute has estimated that between 2011 and 2015 Venezuela purchased $373 million of Chinese weaponry (Nixon 2016; Tian and da Silva 2019). Many of these purchases were made when oil prices were high and Venezuela had money. The sales included trainer aircraft, light tanks, and infantry fighting vehicles. A major order for $500 million was placed in 2011, marking China's largest arms sale to the region.

Chinese assistance in keeping the Maduro regime afloat is its export of digital authoritarian infrastructure, and information technology used for surveillance. The Venezuelan government contracted ZTE to build a national ID card, payment system, and "fatherland database" to track individual transactions alongside personal information such as birthdays and social media accounts (Polyakova and Meserole 2019). The "Carnet de la Patria" (developed by ZTE) was introduced in 2016. While the card is supposed to be voluntary, possession of the card is necessary to access a wide range of goods and services, ranging from doctor's appointments to government pensions (Moreno 2021). Considering the authoritarian nature of the Venezuelan government, ZTE's activities have left opposition groups deeply concerned about the implementation of what could be a version of China's "social credit system," which is broadly defined as a national surveillance system that is capable of aggregating bank data, hospital records, real-world movements, online activity, and other records into a single "trustworthiness" score (Berwick 2018; Horsley 2018).

China's support for the Maduro regime has also been manifest in international diplomacy, where China, often working in tandem with Russia, has blocked Western attempts at the United Nations to condemn Caracas. Moreover, China has been consistent in urging the United States to lift sanctions on Venezuela. As articulated by Ministry of Foreign Affairs spokesperson Hua Chunying in 2020: "China has always believed that the sovereign equality of nations and non-interference in other countries' internal affairs are some of the most significant principles of the UN Charter...We firmly oppose unilateral sanctions and other means to coerce the Venezuelan people to change their path of development" (Xinhua 2020).

What keeps the Chinese–Venezuelan relationship intact? China could have walked away from Venezuela once oil prices imploded and the regime struggled. Instead, China stayed the course, albeit with considerably more caution. All the same, while Venezuela was watching 20 percent of its population leave, China was happy to open a Confucius Institute in Caracas in 2016 and Venezuela officially joined the BRI in 2018. While China is not deeply enamored with Maduro and probably would not be sad to see him replaced by someone more competent, Beijing has sunk considerable capital into Venezuela, the South American country remains a major oil producer, and, if the situation can be turned around, China can wait it out (Rendon 2020). China's commitment to the Maduro regime has provided it another advantage—the use of Venezuela as a base from which to further penetrate the region and carry out disinformation activities. In a study conducted by Caracas-based Medianálisis, China was pegged as an active social media user (as well as using other means of communication) to spread inaccurate information about all Western vaccines during the Covid-19 pandemic and influence public opinion in favor of its own vaccine (Global Americans 2021: 272–284).

China's support for Venezuela has undergone considerable transformation through the 1999–2022 period. The halcyon days paralleled the Chávez period (1999–2013) when oil prices were high. Chinese national interest was well-served by being allied to one of the world's major oil producers and holder of the world's largest reserves. In this respect, China's international development strategy was working. Economic statecraft was a helpful tool in cementing the bonds between the two countries, a situation that was helped along by the two have a similar worldview partially shaped by an adversarial view vis-à-vis the United States. The dynamic changed in the Maduro era (2013–2021), a time marked by economic implosion, political and social unrest, and a massive refugee flow out of Venezuela. Relations have not been helped by the Maduro regime's constant requests for greater Chinese support.

China's economic statecraft was shown its limitations during the Madura era. Yes, China gained considerable influence in Venezuela, but its advice was often not heard and actions had to be taken to protect the loans sunk into the country. Moreover, China's influence was diluted by a more active role played by Russia as the crisis surrounding the Maduro regime's legitimacy deepened with U.S. and European sanctions. China's stepping back also gave space for other countries to step in, including Iran, Turkey, and India (which became a major buyer of Venezuelan crude). Iran, like Russia, has a strong anti-U.S. bias, while Turkey's President Erdogan found a new arena for him to demonstrate his country's playing the role of world power. The involvement in Venezuela by the other countries was a positive development for China as it took some of the pressure off Beijing.

China's support for the Maduro regime has consequences for international politics in the Caribbean, global energy markets, and U.S.–Chinese relations. Considering that Venezuela's political situation became a murky mess, China's heavy engagement with one of the world's largest oil producers continues to be important. Even what limited support China wishes to provide will continue to prop up a regime that has plunged into criminal enterprises, some of which have rippled into the Caribbean. Considering that Russia's ability to maintain a significant role in Venezuela has been crimped by the massive use of its resources in Ukraine, China emerges as even more important for Caracas. Moreover, as long the Maduro regime remains in power, the flow of refugees is not likely to stop (though it has slowed with the Covid-19 pandemic), maintaining pressure on Colombia, Ecuador, Peru, Trinidad and Tobago, and other Caribbean islands.

The other issue that sits on the table is once political change or political stability comes to Venezuela, what happens in terms of the country's reconstruction? While debt obligations form a major block to new lending from international capital markets, what will China's role be as the country's major creditor? Linking all of these challenges together is how does the new Cold War-like environment factor into where Venezuela heads in the rest of the 2020s? For China, Venezuela is likely to be a long-term investment. Despite the country's economic disaster and the massive refugee outflow, there are advantages to be gained in maintaining an outpost in Caracas. In late 2021 it was reported that China National Petroleum Corp. (CNPC) had sent engineers and commercial staff to Venezuela to help in the maintenance work at an oil-blending facility it operates with PDVSA (Zerpa 2021). Almost all of CNPC's production is earmarked to be exported to China and will be used to repay PDVSA debt to Beijing.

The ongoing tensions between China and the United States are not likely to diminish, which means that wherever Venezuela heads, it will remain an arena for competition between Beijing and Washington. Moreover, even if there is a government change in Caracas, both Venezuela and China as well as the United States will have to deal with the fundamental issue that the Asian country remains the South American country's largest creditor. The new Cold War issue remains on the table in this corner of the Caribbean.

CHINA, CUBA, AND THE NEW COLD WAR

In 2019, long-time Cuba watcher and professor of Political Science at American University William LeoGrande observed: "Cuba faces a much tougher international environment today than it did just a few years ago. Relations with Latin America have cooled as relations with Washington have regressed to a level of animosity reminiscent of the Cold War. In response, Havana is looking to old ideological comrades in Moscow and Beijing to compensate for the deterioration of ties in its own backyard" (LeoGrande 2019). Indeed, Cuba has faced considerable change, especially in U.S. policy from the Obama to Trump administrations, which gave Cuban–Chinese relations a push to develop a closer relationship. China is an important component in keeping the Communist government afloat in Cuba, though this role is not as deep as in Venezuela and shows little prospect of developing a military dimension any time soon. (Such a development could be left to the Russians.) That said, it is to China's advantage to have an ally in the Caribbean like Cuba.

Cuba's relationship with China began in the eighteenth century when it was still part of a Spanish Empire that spanned the globe, including the Caribbean, Europe, and the Philippines. Cuba's economy at the time was heavily geared to plantation agriculture, which was reflected by the need for a sizable labor force especially in the sugar industry. Cuba stopped participating in the slave trade in 1867 and the institution of enslavement was abolished in 1886. As the supply of slave labor became problematic there was a brief experimentation with Chinese workers. Between 1847 and 1874 it is estimated that some 125,000 Chinese laborers entered Cuba. Such was the inflow of Chinese to Cuba that the Qing dynasty government eventually established a consulate in Havana. When Cuba gained independence Qing China was quick to grant diplomatic recognition.

China's engagement with Cuba through most of the first five decades of the twentieth century was minimal. That was to change with two revolutions thousands of miles apart. The first revolution resulted in the founding of the People's Republic of China in 1949. The newly established PRC's role in the world soon expanded as when it sent forces into the Korean War in 1950 to fight the United Nations and the U.S. forces as well as the promotion of revolutionary groups in Africa and Asia. As an ally of the Soviet Union, Beijing clearly placed itself in the anti-U.S. camp in the Cold War, a situation furthered by Washington's support for Taiwan which effectively thwarted China's bid to take the last Nationalist bastion.

The second revolution took place in Cuba in 1959, which brought into existence a government that was as equally committed to revolution as was China's. Castro's Cuba was willing to export revolution to other countries and was soon profoundly hostile to the United States. Cuba's need for an economic backer, however, guaranteed that the Castro regime ultimately sided with the Soviet Union in its dispute with China, which became increasingly bitter during the 1960s. Considering the massive amount of economic assistance Moscow provided during the 1970s and 1980s as well as preferential trade agreements with the Soviet Union and other Eastern European countries, China remained at arms length through much of this period. The situation changed, however, when the Soviet Union collapsed in the early 1990s. Cuba underwent a substantial economic downturn, referred to as the Special Period (*Periodo Especial*) (Gott 2004: 273–298; Chomsky et al. 2019; Sweig 2016; Domínguez et al. 2017; Morgenstern et al. 2018). Cuba's problem was straightforward; the Castro regime long refused to make painful, market-oriented economic reforms, much of its economy was dysfunctional, the sugar industry was limping along and there was a heavy dependence on the Soviet Union for financial aid, oil, and preferential trade. The combination of the Soviet collapse, an inability to make any major structural reforms, and the longstanding U.S. economic embargo (started in the early 1960s) left Cuba in dire straits. Cuba suffered from fuel shortages, food rationing, and a forced turn to tourism to earn foreign exchange badly needed to pay for food imports. However, it was not until Chávez's arrival in Venezuela in 1999 that Cuba's fortunes improved. Venezuela, flush with money from the surge in oil prices, quickly assumed much the same role as the Soviet Union in supplying Havana with cheap oil, part of which was sold on international markets.

The Havana–Caracas axis was cemented by a close personal bond between Chávez and Fidel Castro, with the former calling the aging Cuban *líder máximo* (maximum leader) his mentor and referring to Cuba as "a revolutionary democracy." That relationship became even closer after the failed 2002 coup attempt that almost succeeded in knocking Chávez from power. The Venezuelan leader turned to Cuba to help his security apparatus, allowing the Caribbean country's G2 (Cuban intelligence) to help secure his position (Naím 2021). The Cuban–Venezuelan relationship quickly developed into a symbiotic one, with Venezuelan oil bolstering the Cuban economy and, in turn, the Cubans providing help in controlling Chavez's personal security and sending its medical corps to Venezuela for payment in hard currency (from which the Cuban state took its cut).

Although Venezuela rose to become Cuba's major trade partner in the 2000s and into the early 2010s, China's role in both economies expanded. By 2011 Cuba had emerged as China's major trading partner in the Caribbean, and China was Cuba's second largest trading partner after Venezuela. China overtook Venezuela as Cuba's major trade partner in 2016, due to the implosion of the South American country's economy. Although China would not remain in the number one trading position through the end of the decade and into the next, it remained a significant source of imports for the island, especially in the area of manufactured goods (much of the consumer goods such as automobiles and home appliances) and food. The trade balance ran starkly in China's direction.

But the sale of Chinese goods to Cuba depended on Cubans having enough money to buy consumer goods. When Cuba's economy was hurt by new economic sanctions imposed by the Trump administration and then Covid-19 in 2020 and 2021, this became more challenging. Between an economy already struggling from government mismanagement and the collapse of tourism, most Cubans were struggling just to find food. As one observer noted in 2021: "Today Cubans have to hustle to survive; many work two jobs. A recent currency change means cash is scarce and many everyday goods are unaffordable" (Holmes 2021).

Chinese investment was also hurt by Cuba's economic downturn. The Asian country's businesses had penetrated much of the island economy, including telecommunications, mining, and energy. Huawei in 2015 became the major seller of smartphones, while most buses used in Cuba were Chinese. However, as the Cuban economy stagnated and contracted in the late 2010s, trade between China and Cuba shrank. According to data from the Chinese Customs Office, Cuba's imports from the Asian country continued their five-year descent in 2020, hitting a low of $483 million compared to $791 million in 2019 (Frank 2021). Cuba's exports to China also fell. Overall trade slipped below a billion dollars, the lowest in more than a decade.

DEFINING CHINA'S ROLE IN CUBA

China's role in Cuba is that of hegemonic power, playing a geopolitical game vis-à-vis its main rival, the United States. While China does not appear to want to be a sugar daddy for the Cuban government in the form of its becoming a "client state," it enjoys having considerable influence in the Caribbean country. This is not to argue that Beijing tells Havana what to do, but it "suggests" a course of action by using economic levers. While the Cuban Communist Party benefits from having the support of Communist China, it does not always follow such advice.

China's role in Cuba has also been to enhance its partner's intelligence/security network (vis-à-vis the Cuban people), sell Chinese goods to Cuban consumers, and explore and exploit anything that could be used in the green energy revolution. On the security front, China has provided the same help it did to Venezuela—the ability of the regime to control what the Cuban people have access to, just like their Chinese counterparts. The equipment used to keep socialist Cuban free of democratic pollution is thought to be made by Huawei, and is part of what a U.S. 2020 Senate Relations Committee report called an extension of China's policy of digital authoritarianism (Moreno 2021). Cuba also provides an excellent outpost from which to eavesdrop on U.S. communications.

China has not been willing to provide the same largesse as the Soviets or Venezuelans, but enough to try to keep Cuba from undergoing the same implosion as occurred in Venezuela. One estimate of China's official development assistance to Cuba from 2000 to 2014 is $6.3 billion, which would make it the leading recipient in Latin America and the Caribbean (Koleski and Blivas 2018). Moreover, China has been willing to write off more than $6 billion in debt owed by Cuba, a substantial policy move on Beijing's part (Rapoza 2019). China does not want to be caught in the same situation as it was in Venezuela, overextending loans to a poorly-managed economy. The challenge is to balance keeping the creaky Cuban regime afloat while not ending up with a large debt exposure.

Beyond the economic parts of the Chinese–Cuban relationship, China's leadership has made repeated visits to the Caribbean island, starting with President Jiang Zemin in 1993, continuing with President Xi first in 2011 as vice president and then again as President in 2014, and then Premier Li Keqiang in 2016. For their part, the Cubans have also traveled to China, with Raúl Castro doing so in 2008 and his successor President Miguel Díaz-Canel in 2018. Through these visits, China and Cuba have sought to maintain their relationship using a personal touch. They have also provided a venue to bring Cuba into the BRI and maintain economic relations with China.

It is in China's interest to see a successful Cuba under the Cuban Communist Party. Thus far China is playing a role similar to the Soviet Union during the Cold War, with the important distinction being that the Asian country's involvement is largely economic (albeit limited) rather than military. That, however, does not change the fact that the most important item Cuba offers China is its strategic location and how that fits into Beijing's larger world view of a new Cold War. In looking at a map of the Caribbean, Cuba is located between two critical sea lane choke-points; between Cuba and the Yucatan Peninsula and between Cuba and Florida. As the United States holds bases throughout the Pacific and the

Indian Ocean as well as having a relationship with Taiwan, China having bases in Cuba does not necessarily mean they have to be used for offensive military action, rather they suggest a threat of such a development. The threat would not impact the West or East Coast, but the Gulf Coast ports, of which the most significant are New Orleans and Houston (Friedman 2021). Cuba with Chinese air and naval forces could also project a threat to shipping heading back and forth to the Panama Canal.

Two areas where Cuba offers potential value to China are biotechnology and is in the mining of chromium. The two countries have established a working relationship in biotechnology, which encompasses a strategy to establish production facilities in Cuba for jointly researched products. Cuba has a sizable medical establishment and wants to attract Chinese pharmaceutical companies to the island. The Covid-19 pandemic helped bring Cuban and Chinese medical researchers closer together and could set the stage for badly needed foreign investment in the island.

Chromium is a steely-gray, lustrous, and brittle transition metal. It is usually used in steel production as an anti-corrosive element. It is also seen as a metal that will be useful in the transition to a global green economy. While South Africa, Turkey, and Kazakhstan dominate global production, China is the world's largest consumer. China has been seeking to diversify its chromium sources, which is reflected in its investment in mining the ore in Cuba in the early 2020s. Considering the problematic nature of so many parts of the Cuban economy, chromium mining holds out some hope for the struggling island. Prospects for the development of this sector should not be overstated, but it does hold out a possible area of mutual benefit. Cuba also has supplies of nickel and zinc which are also seen as important for the transition to a green economy (Marsh 2017).

Cuba benefits from China's expertise in controlling its population. In 2021 when widespread riots broke out in the Caribbean country, the communist regime was able to shut off the internet and telephone services, which effectively disrupted the protesters' connection to the outside world (Lazarus and Ellis 2021). China's involvement in this was reflected in that, the major technology provider for Etecsa (Empresa de Telecommunicaciones de Cuba), the island's only internet access company, is Chinese. The companies providing the technology are Huawei, TP-Linbk and ZTE. As Lazarus and Ellis observed: "China's role in helping the regime cut off communications during the protests has exposed one of the many ways Beijing helps keep the Cuban communist regime afloat" (Lazarus and Ellis 2021). At the same time, China's involvement in upgrading Cuba's telecommunications system could also be a means to deepen Chinese intelligence gathering and broadcasting misinformation and disinformation throughout the Caribbean and Latin America.

China and Cuba already have a degree of military cooperation. As one report by the U.S.–China Economic Security Review Commission observed in 2018: "Militarily, China maintains a strong relationship with Cuba that is characterized by frequent senior-level meetings and technical assistance provided by China's military to Cuba's military. Between 2003 and 2016, Chinese and Cuban military officials met 33 times. China has helped Cuba upgrade its air defense system, purchase more sophisticated communications equipment, maintain its Soviet-era aircraft, and upgrade some of its MIG-21 fighter/interceptor aircraft. In addition, China reportedly has a physical presence at multiple Soviet-era intelligence facilities at Lourdes, Bejucal, and Santiago de Cuba to collect signals intelligence" (Koleski and Blivas 2018: 24).

While China appears to have increased its support for Cuba since 2017 in the face of Venezuela's acute economic and political troubles and the Trump's administration's tougher stance on the Caribbean country, China's help has been calculated. But keeping the Cuban Communist Party afloat is not an easy task. Since Fidel Castro stepped down in 2006, the country has seen considerable change. That includes the tenure of his brother Raúl at the country's helm, an opening of relations with the U.S., President Obama's 2016 visit to the island, Fidel's death in December of that year, Raúl's handing of the presidency to Díaz-Canel, a renewed chill in the relationship with Washington from 2017 through the end of the Trump administration, and significant questions as to the next step in relations with the United States when the Biden administration entered office in 2021.

Cuba's litany of problems bears a strong relationship with external vulnerabilities, including the decline of oil prices in 2014, Venezuela's economic implosion, hurricanes (most notably in 2017), U.S. economic sanctions, and the Covid-19 pandemic, which badly hurt tourism and overall economic life. Cuba's economy contracted by 11 percent in 2020 and barely expanded in 2021. In 2021 demonstrations boiled over in many of the island's major cities due to the severity of the economic situation. Although the Cuban government blamed the United States, the upheaval that rocked the island was sparked by civil disobedience from the

San Isidro Movement, a group of artists and journalists that demanded an end to the dictatorship.

Although progress has been made in developing biotechnology and medical services (a major earner of foreign exchange), much of the Cuban economy is struggling. It is dominated by large state-owned companies. Cuba's largest company is Grupo de Administracíon Empresarial S.A. or GAESA, a holding company owned by the armed forces. It controls or has stakes in more than 50 companies spanning hotel chains, shipping, car dealerships and real estate. How can a private sector compete with this massive conglomerate which has political clout in economic decision-making?

Among the major problems facing Cuba are a technologically obsolete manufacturing base, a near-terminal sugar industry (China remains a buyer of Cuban sugar), a struggling agricultural sector and dependence on food imports (some of which comes from the United States), a generally flat to negative economic growth trajectory through much of the 2010s and into the 2020s and an aging population with a similar demographic profile as Italy and Japan (not a good thing). While these factors are daunting, they are symptoms of a deeper problem, the inability of the Cuban Communist Party to make the necessary reforms and adhere to them to revitalize the economy. This is not for lack of trying. Cuba's special period in the 1990s saw a loosening of government controls over certain activities, largely because without external assistance the state's approach had failed miserably and extreme measures were required to spark any activity.

The periodic reform efforts to introduce market incentives into the economy have usually been successful, at least until the government decides to intervene. The Caribbean island's entrepreneurs have demonstrated a strong ability to respond to any openings, setting up a large segment of small and medium-sized businesses where allowed, which has usually been in tourism (small hotels, restaurants, and food suppliers) and agriculture. While there has been a grudging willingness to allow a private sector, the Cuban Communist Party has looked upon anything that smacks of market economics as odious. This has meant that efforts to streamline state-owned enterprises have had mixed success, distribution chains are transfixed by red tape, and through the end of the first two decades of the twenty-first century, the entire system struggled to get any goods to consumers, including basic staples.

The challenge ahead is that the island's ruling establishment—a combination of the Communist Party, managers of the state-owned enterprises, bureaucrats, military elite, and the revolutionary families—finds major changes threatening. The nature of the threat is twofold. First, if the Cuban people are given too much freedom in the economic sphere, they may wish for the same in the political sphere, something that cannot be tolerated in a Leninist state. Second, if a Cuban private sector is allowed to grow, it could threaten the economic status quo and state-run enterprises could find competition in their areas of commerce. The bottom line in all of this is that the accumulation of economic power could see the leverage of that power in the political realm. While the state can control the inflow of foreign competition by forcing joint ventures and other ways of limiting competition, it has little interest in fostering the means of its own demise by local private sector agents. At the same time, members of the Cuban leadership are painfully aware that their economic experiment is a house of cards, which is reflected by low levels of economic activity, slowness of foreign investment (also hurt by U.S. sanctions and other measures), and young Cubans postponing having families as they wait for better economic conditions (which is resulting in a population decline in absolute numbers and a growing aging population). The island-wide demonstrations and riots that shook Cuba in 2021 reflected the strong social malaise of the country and eroded the nature of the regime in the eyes of its population.

Cuba's inability to make lasting and significant economic reforms is a point of irritation for the Chinese. China and, for that matter, Vietnam, both have maintained their Communist parties in power and successfully introduced well-controlled market incentives into their respective economies. In both cases, the standard of living has improved, national economies have grown, and the ruling elite's legitimacy has been reinforced. If the deal between the Chinese Communist Party and the Chinese people over economic freedom and political control and stability has worked in the Asian country, why can't it work in Cuba? (Pérez-López and Xiao 2018: 85–116; MacDonald 2018). Both sides have been frustrated by the inability of certain projects, once launched with considerable excitement, to materialize. The two more prominent of these were the failure of a proposed $500 million Chinese investment in the Caribbean island's nickel mining sector and a $6.6 billion project to modernize the Cienfuegos oil refinery (with a letter of intent signed in 2010).

Yet there are advantages to being a friend to Cuba. This was proven in 2020, when China faced criticism for its passage of a National Security Law for Hong Kong. When Hong Kong was returned to China in 1997 by the United Kingdom, it was agreed that the city-state would maintain certain political freedoms inherited from the British as well as its legal system. Indeed, the "one country, two systems" framework that China agreed to uphold was meant to provide a way for the people in the Special Administrative Region to become integrated with China. It was also intended to maintain a system that had allowed Hong Kong to become one of the world's major financial hubs, business centers and transit points for foreign companies wishing to conduct business on the mainland and Chinese firms looking to do business with the larger world.

China's clampdown on Hong Kong brought considerable international condemnation, mainly from the United States, Canada, Europe, and a handful of other countries. At the United Nations 44th Human Rights Council meetings in July 2020, the issue of China's new repressive law for Hong Kong came up in an assembly divided into two blocs. A bloc of 27 governments critical of the new security law, which criminalizes political dissent, was led by the United Kingdom and included Australia, a number of European countries, Belize, Canada, and Palau.

China did not wish to be embarrassed by any United Nations censure and mobilized some 53 countries to vote for its position. On behalf of those countries, Cuba welcomed the adoption of China's new National Security law and fended away any risk of censure. The Cuban representative stated, "In any country, the legislative power on national security issues rests with the State, which in essence is not a human rights issue and therefore not subject to discussion at the Human Rights Council" (The Nation 2020).

Cuba also made certain to reaffirm that Hong Kong is an inseparable part of China, and Hong Kong's affairs are China's internal affairs and that this should allow no interference from the outside. The Cuban position also closely echoed China's stance that external forces (i.e. the United States, United Kingdom, and Europe) should stop using Hong Kong to meddle in China's domestic affairs. Venezuela also voted in China's favor.

Despite Cuba's economic shortcomings, China remains invested in the Caribbean country. In 2022 a new economic cooperation agreement was signed between the two countries, which seeks to promote BRI construction on the island as well as financial integration between the two countries, which might include the use of China's digital current and an alternative international payments system from SWIFT which is run by the West. China has not made the same commitment to Cuba that the island's other patrons did, but is a critical partner. China contributes on the economic side which helps keep the Cuban establishment afloat, hopefully to the period when they finally make China-like changes to reinvigorate the country's economic energy and tap its people's innovative creativity. This was readily reflected in prompt Chinese declarations of support for the communist regime in July 2021, following the island-wide anti-regime riots, blaming the U.S. embargo for the shortages of medicine and energy in Cuba, and calling for an immediate end by Washington of its economic embargo (Xinhua 2020). The narrative expressed by the Chinese government echoed its Cuban counterpart; the riots were not because of decades of bad economic management on the part of the regime, but because of U.S. actions. In the meantime, China's main benefit is the geopolitical backing of one of the world's most dogged anti-U.S. regimes.

China's position in Cuba has also gained over Russia's. The Russo-Ukraine War has greatly complicated Russia's ability to project its power to the Caribbean. On the one hand, Russian resources are tied up in Eastern Europe; on the other hand, Russia will be more hard-pressed to give Cuba what it wants in terms of financial assistance. Short of the United States removing some of the sanctions (which is a possibility), Cuba's best chances are China as a strategic partner and the hope for a long-term spike in oil prices that could allow Venezuela to once again boost the Cuban economy.

CONCLUSION

China has established two important beachheads in the Caribbean, Cuba, and Venezuela. Both countries are clearly part of an anti-U.S. alignment around the world that includes China, Russia, Iran, North Korea, Syria, and Hezbollah. China's economic investment has been strategically guided, helping to bolster two of the most non-democratic regimes in the Americas. However, the benefits must be observed through the prism of the long-term goals of China's position in the international system. In this, the failure of U.S. policy to enact regime change in either state over the past ten years can be seen as a Chinese victory. China has maintained friendly regimes in the backyard of its major global rival, something to balance U.S. power and influence in East Asia and Southeast Asia. Moreover, a deeper relationship with Cuba could expand China's ability to listen in on U.S. communications as well as to better monitor the rest of the Caribbean or to disseminate anti-U.S. propaganda. From Cuban and Venezuelan perspectives, the view is likely that they feel that China could do more to help them economically, but there is a certain comfort in knowing that in international forums they have an ally that is the world's second largest economy and has one of the most rapidly expanding militaries. For China, Cuba and Venezuela will continue to represent a careful balancing act between possible involvement in a major crisis with the United States over the two countries and not becoming the economic sugar daddy for the two regimes.

References

Berwick, Angus. 2018. How ZTE Helps Venezuela Create China-Style Social Control. *Reuters*, November 14. https://www.reuters.com/article/us-ven ezuela-zte-specialreport/special-report-how-zte-helps-venezuela-create-china-style-social-control-idUSKCN1NJ1TT.

BP. 2020. *Statistical Review of World Energy 2020*. https://www.bp.com/con tent/dam/bp/business-sites/en/global/corporate/pdfs/energy-economics/statistical-review/bp-stats-review-2020-full-report.pdf.

China.org.cn. 2014. China, Venezuela Lift Ties to Comprehensive Strategic Part-nership. *China.org.cn* (originally from Xinhua), July 21. http://www.china.org.cn/china/2014-07/21/content_33009951.htm.

Chomsky, Aviva, Barry Carr, Alfredo Prieto, and Pamela Maria Smorkaloff, eds. 2019. *The Cuba Reader: History, Culture, Politics*. Durham: Duke University Press.

Domínguez, Jorge I., Omar Everleny Pérez Villanueva, and Loreana G. Barberia (eds.). 2017. *The Cuban Economy in a New Era: An Agenda for Change Toward Durable Development*. Harvard University David Rockefeller Center for Latin American Studies.

Farah, Douglas, and Caitlyn Yates. 2019. Maduro's Last Stand: Venezuela's Survival Through the Bolivarian Joint Criminal Enterprise, IBI Consul-tants, May 2019. https://www.ibiconsultants.net/_pdf/maduros-last-stand-final-publication-version.pdf.

Frank, Marc. 2021. Cuba's Imports from China Slump 40% in 2020, Extending Long Decline. *Reuters*, February 5. https://www.reuters.com/article/cuba-china-trade/cubas-imports-from-china-slump-40-in-2020-extending-long-dec line-idUSL1N2K919P.

Friedman, George. 2021. China's Search for a Negotiated Settlement. *Geopolit-ical Futures*, July 6. https://geopoliticalfutures.com/chinas-search-for-a-neg otiated-settlement/.

Gallegos, Raúl. 2016. *Crude Nation: How Oil Riches Ruined Venezuela*. Sterling: Potomac Books.

Global Americans. 2021. Medición del Impacto de la Información Falsa, la Dsinformación y la Propaganda en América Latina. https://theglobalameric ans.org/wp-content/uploads/2021/11/2021.11.03-Global-Americans_Rep orte-Desinformacion.pdf.

Gott, Richard. 2004. *Cuba: A New History*. New Haven: Yale University Press.

Hernández, Alicia. 2020. China Remains Quiet and Pragmatic on Venezuela Crisis. *Diálogo Chino*, January 20. https://dialogochino.net/en/trade-invest ment/32971-china-remains-quiet-and-pragmatic-on-venezuela-crisis/.

Holmes, Catesby. 2021. Cuba Protests: 4 Essential Reads on Dissent in the Post-Castro Era. *The Conversation*, July 13. https://theconversation.com/cuba-protests-4-essential-reads-on-dissent-in-the-post-castro-era-164456.

Horsley, Jaime. 2018. China's Orwellian Social Score Card Isn't Real. *Foreign Policy*, November 20. https://foreignpolicy.com/2018/11/16/chinas-orwell ian-social-credit-score-isnt-real/.

International Monetary Fund. 2020. *World Economic Outlook October 2020: A Long and Difficult Ascent*. International Monetary Fund. https://www.imf. org/en/Publications/WEO/Issues/2020/09/30/world-economic-outlook-october-2020.

Kaplan, Stephen, and Michael Penfold. 2021. China–Venezuela Economic Relations: Hedging Venezuelan Bets with Chinese Characteristics. In Cynthia J. Arson, *Venezuela's Authoritarian Allies: The Ties That Bind?*, 76. Washington: Woodrow Wilson International Center for Scholars. https://www. wilsoncenter.org/sites/default/files/media/uploads/documents/Venezuela% E2%80%99s%20Authoritarian%20Allies_The%20Ties%20That%20Bind_June% 202021_0.pdf.

Kassaai, Lucia. 2017. Venezuela–China Relationship Sours as Sinopec Sues PDVSA. *Bloomberg*, December 7. https://www.bloombergquint.com/china/ venezuela-china-relationship-sours-as-sinopec-sues-pdvsa.

Koleski, Katherine, and Alec Blivas. 2018. China's Engagement with Latin America and the Caribbean—U.S.–China Economic and Security Review Commission Staff Research Report, October 17. https://www.uscc.gov/ sites/default/files/Research/China's%20Engagement%20with%20Latin%20A merica%20and%20the%20Caribbean_.pdf.

Lazarus, Leland, and Evan Ellis. 2021. How China Helps the Cuban Regime Stay Afloat and Shut Down Protests. *The Diplomat*, August 3. https://thediplomat.com/2021/08/how-china-helps-the-cuban-regime-stay-afloat-and-shut-down-protests/.

LeoGrande, William. 2019. Cuba Must Contend with a New Cold War in the Western Hemisphere. *World Politics Review*, January 24. https://www.wor ldpoliticsreview.com/articles/27270/cuba-must-contend-with-a-new-cold-war-in-the-western-hemisphere.

Liu, Ming, and Fajun Wang. 2012. Zhongguo Zai Ladingmeizhou de Daikuan [China's Loans in Latin America]. *Lading Meizhou Yanjiu* [Journal of Latin American Studies] 34 (4, August): 14–19. https://www.wilsoncenter.org/sites/default/files/media/uploads/documents/Venezuela%E2%80%99s%20Authoritarian%20Allies_The%20Ties%20That%20Bind_June%202021_0.pdf.

MacDonald, Scott B. 2018. Why Cuba Isn't Getting Much from Russia or China, November 27. https://nationalinterest.org/feature/why-cuba-isnt-getting-much-russia-or-china-37282.

Macrotrends. 2021. Crude Oil Prices—70 Year Chart. https://www.macrotrends.net/1369/crude-oil-price-history-chart.

Marsh, Sarah. 2017. Cuba Seeks to Revive Mining Sector with New Lead and Zinc Mine. *Reuters*, July 22. https://www.reuters.com/article/us-cuba-mining/cuba-seeks-to-revive-mining-sector-with-new-lead-and-zinc-mine-idUSKBN1A70K3.

Moreno, Jaime. 2021. China Seen Backing 'Digital Authoritarianism' in Latin America. *Voice of America*, January 4. https://www.voanews.com/a/china-seen-backing-digital-authoritarianism-in-latin-america-/6398072.html.

Morgenstern, Scott, Jorge Perez-Lopez, and Jerome Branche (eds.). 2018. *Paths for Cuba: Reforming Communism in Comparative Perspective*. University of Pittsburgh Press.

Myers, Margaret, and Rebecca Ray. 2021. Shifting Gears: Chinese Finance in LAC, 2020. *The Dialogue and The BU Global Development Policy Center*, February. https://www.thedialogue.org/analysis/shifting-gears-chinese-finance-in-lac-2020/.

Naím, Moisés. 1993. *Paper Tiger & Minotaurs: The Politics of Venezuela's Economic Reforms*. Carnegie Endowment.

Naím, Moisés. 2021. Venezuela's Fatal Embrace of Cuba. *The Wall Street Journal*, December 11–12.

Nixon, Allan. 2016. China's Growing Arms Sales to Latin America. *The Diplomat*, August 14. https://thediplomat.com/2016/08/chinas-growing-arms-sales-to-latin-america/.

OpIndia. 2021. Chinese Debt Crisis: After Sri Lanka, Venezuela the Next Target of China's Debt-Trap Diplomacy? *OpIndia*, February 16. https://www.opindia.com/2021/02/sri-lanka-venezuela-the-next-target-of-chinas-debt-trap-diplomacy/.

Pérez-López, Jorge, and Yu Xiao. 2018. Foreign Investment and Economic Growth in Cuba: Lessons from Cuba. In *Paths: Reforming Communism in Comparative Perspective*, ed. Scott Morgenstern, Jorge Pérez-López, and Jerome Branche, 85–116. University of Pittsburgh Press.

Polyakova, Alina, and Chris Meserole. 2019. *Exporting Digital Authoritarianism: The Russian and Chinese Models*. Brookings Institute.

Rapoza, Kenneth. 2019. China Has Forgiven Nearly $10 Billion in Debt, Cuba Accounts for Over Half. *Forbes*, May 29. https://www.forbes.com/sites/ken rapoza/2019/05/29/china-has-forgiven-nearly-10-billion-in-debt-cuba-acc ounts-for-over-half/?sh=71f03158615b. Accessed 15 July 2021.

Rendon, Moises. 2020. The Fabulous Five: How Foreign Actor Prop up the Maduro Rehime in Venezuela. *Center for Strategic and International Studies*, October 19.

Segovia, María Antonieta. 2021. A Dream Deal with China That Ended in Nightmarish Debt for Venezuela. *Diálogo China*, February. https://dia logochino.net/en/trade-investment/40016-a-dream-deal-with-china-that-ended-in-nightmarish-debt-for-venezuela/.

Sweig, Julia E. 2016. *Cuba: What Everyone Needs to Know*. Oxford University Press.

Tian, Nan, and Diego Lopes da Silva. 2019. The Crucial Role of the Military in the Venezuelan Crisis, April 2. https://www.sipri.org/commentary/topical-backgrounder/2019/crucial-role-military-venezuelan-crisis.

The Nation (Pakistan). 2020. Cuba, 52 Countries Voice Support for China's National Security Law in Hong Kong. *The Nation* (Pakistan), July 1. https://nation.com.pk/01-Jul-2020/cuba-52-countries-voice-support-for-china-s-national-security-law-in-hong-kong.

Trinkunas, Harold. 2014. Assessing the Risks Associated with the Possible End of Petrocaribe Oil Subsidies. Paper delivered at the LACC/ARC/U.S. Southern Command Policy Roundtable Series, June 16. Miami, Florida. Latin American and Caribbean Center, Florida International University. https://lacc.fiu.edu/research/publications/security-roundtable-trinkunas-final-paper.pdf.

Wheatley, Jonathan. 2017. Lawsuit Shows China Losing Patience with Venezuela. *Financial Times*, December 6. https://www.ft.com/content/d627460a-da8e-11e7-a039-c64b1c09b482.

Xinhua. 2020. China Urges U.S. to Lift Sanctions on Chinese Enterprises. *Xinhuanet*, December 1. http://www.xinhuanet.com/english/2020-12/01/c_139556222.htm.

Zerpa, Fabiola. 2021. China's Top Oil Producer Prepares to Revive Venezuela Operations. *Bloomberg*, September 1. https://www.bloomberg.com/news/articles/2021-09-01/china-s-top-oil-producer-prepares-to-revive-venezuela-operations?sref=8VBJk9tz.

CHAPTER 4

China and the English-Speaking Caribbean and Suriname

The following chapter focuses on China's engagement with the English-speaking Caribbean and Suriname. Although each Caribbean country merits attention, the limits of space have narrowed the focus to the following English-speaking countries—the Bahamas, Trinidad and Tobago, Guyana, and Jamaica. They were selected based on their relative size of the economy, type of economy, and population size as well as their varied experiences with China. In each case, the experience with China was generally positive, but there were and remain certain tensions. Equally important, geopolitical considerations, driven by each country's national interests, are examined. Caribbean leaders have demonstrated their willingness to engage China, to benefit from its partnership, while seeking to balance the concerns of their largest trade and foreign direct investment partner, the United States. As demonstrated, this has not always been an easy process.

Driving through the University of the West Indies Campus at Cave Hill, Barbados, one comes across the Confucius Institute. It is discreetly nestled off the main road, a tasteful and distinctly Chinese-looking building, with its red and green colors blending with the rest of the campus. Through the Confucius Institute, young Barbadians are gaining insights into Chinese culture and language. Although Confucius Institutes have become controversial in Australia, Canada, Japan, Sweden, and the United States due to concerns over improper influence in teaching

S. B. MacDonald, *The New Cold War, China, and the Caribbean*, https://doi.org/10.1007/978-3-031-06149-3_4

and research, industrial and military espionage, their role in Barbados is perceived as generally positive (Myre 2019; Myklebust 2020; Power 2021).

The spread of Confucius Institutes in the Caribbean is part of China's push to cultivate new friends and potential allies. The English-speaking Caribbean, a group of countries that emerged from the British colonial empire, and Suriname, which gained its independence from the Netherlands in 1975, are part of the slow-motion shift into a new Cold War. Unlike Cuba and Venezuela, the English-speaking Caribbean countries and Suriname have regular and often hotly contested elections, peaceful transfers of power, and articulate and often critical media. Human rights, rule of law, and good governance matter. In some respects, this presents an interesting contrast between a handful of the world's smallest and democratically oriented states with one of the world's largest countries which is run by an authoritarian government that brooks no internal dissent and increasingly seeks to punish those governments that challenge its national interests.

It is the purpose of this chapter to examine the implications of China's higher profile in the economic and political development in the English-speaking Caribbean and Suriname. China's involvement with the region is largely economic, driven by its international development strategy, which showcases trade and investment. At the same time, China is quietly pushing its own objectives, including its struggle with Taiwan, gaining diplomatic support in international forums, and long-term geo-economic logistical support for trade and potentially military ventures. We have opted to narrow our examination of China's interaction to a handful of countries: the Bahamas, Guyana, Jamaica, Suriname, and Trinidad and Tobago. These are some of the larger economies in the region and have experienced a high degree of Chinese engagement. Chinese involvement in some of the other smaller Caribbean states will be treated in later chapters. Although Chinese involvement in the Caribbean is perceived through a different perceptual lens by the United States, most Commonwealth Caribbean countries have approached their relationship with the Asian power "with their eyes wide open" according to one former Caribbean diplomat. While Caribbean officialdom may sometimes give an impression that they are not worried about rising Chinese power in their region, they are closely watching the state of play, with one eye on Beijing and the other on Washington. China is also actively surveying the Caribbean, especially as the region slowly moves into a post-Covid-19 pandemic period filled with substantial economic challenges and opportunities as well as ongoing political friction between Beijing and Washington.

Better in the Bahamas?

Since the Bahamas recognized the People's Republic in 1997, China has become an important factor in the Caribbean country's economic development. Located in the northernmost part of the Greater Antilles and east of Florida, the Bahamas has a population of over 300,000 people, with one of the region's highest per capita incomes as well as a functioning democracy. Tourism is the dominant sector of the economy, accounting for 75–80 percent of GDP on an annual basis. The main tourist markets are American and Canadian, but there are also a significant number of Europeans. During the twentieth century, the Caribbean country also became one of the world's most significant offshore financial centers, offering a combination of political stability, no taxes paid by Bahamian citizens and resident aliens, and a ready cornucopia of financial services.

The Bahamas was an early test for the Chinese in the English-speaking Caribbean and was focused on two areas—port/infrastructure and tourism. In the late 1990s Chinese companies, many of them of Hong Kong origin but well-connected to the Chinese state, became active in the Caribbean. The most important of these was Hutchison Whampoa, through its subsidiary Hutchison Port Holdings Limited (incorporated in the British Virgin Islands). The company has a long track record in running container ports around the world, including container ports at either end of the Panama Canal. Considering the Bahamas' strategic location and the importance of trade between China and the United States, the Caribbean country's deep-water Freeport container facilities were a major point of interest. According to the company, "Freeport is the closest offshore port to the east coast of the United States, at the cross-roads of routes between Europe and the Americas and through the Panama Canal" (Ruddy and Archer 2000).

With the geo-economic importance of Freeport in mind, in 1995 Hutchison entered into a 50–50 partnership with the Grand Bahama Development Company, a privately owned Bahamian company, to develop and expand the then small Freeport facility that was catering to cruise ships. Also part of the deal, the Hong Kong firm bought a 50 percent share in the airport as well as three hotels and land on what is known as the "Lucayan Strip."

Hutchison moved quickly to dredge and expand the port, with the objective of making it capable of handling the largest container ships in the world. By 2000, the Freeport Container Port occupied 88 acres of the 530-square mile Grand Bahama Island, offering 3400 feet of berthing, seven large Post Panamex cranes, and other up-to-date facilities, making it one of the most modern and efficient container ports in the world (Collins 2001).

Hutchison's involvement in the Bahamas was not without controversy. In the United States, the extension of Hutchison Whampoa to Freeport was a concern that it could potentially be used to put some of its American competitors out of business; that it ultimately gave China a potential base in the Caribbean (65 miles northeast of Miami); and that the large investment in the port ($2.6 billion) was payment for the Bahamas dropping its recognition of U.S. ally Taiwan and recognizing the People's Republic in 1997. The Chinese connection was manifest in the form of Hong Kong's reversion to the control of the People's Republic in 1997 and that Hutchison's chairman, Li Ka-Shing, had close relations with senior leaders of the Chinese government and the Communist Party. Ultimately the United States did not make a major issue of the port. The dominant thinking about China in the Clinton administration was that Beijing was a concern, but not a major geostrategic risk. Weighing heavily on the discussion was that the development of the port in the Bahamas, a longtime U.S. ally, was beneficial for the development of trade, the main driver in China–U.S. relations.

While Hutchison has managed the port facility for many years with few problems with the Bahamians, the tourist sector was more of a challenge[1] (Smith 2017). The hotels that were part of the initial deal with Hutchison ran at a loss and in 2016 the company opted to sell them, beginning a lengthy process of finding a buyer.

---

[1] Hutchison Whampoa eventually moved to sell the three hotels that it initially purchased. In 2016 the company began a search to sell Lighthouse Pointe, the Grand Lucayan Beach and Golf Resort and Memories Grand Bahama and Casino Resort. The Hong Kong company was selling the hotels as part of a plan to streamline its investments in Grand Bahama. While the port venture worked for the company, the hotels ran at losses. The hotels were part of negotiations between Canada's Wynn Group and Hutchison, but not all of the properties are part of an eventual package yet to be hammered out.

While the Lucayan properties were a sore point, their significance was dwarfed by the construction of Baha Mar, which opened its doors for business in 2017. The resort has become a showpiece for Bahamian tourism as it boasts three major hotels, a Grand Hyatt, SLS Baha Mar, and the Rosewood. It also has a Tournament Players Club golf course designed by Jack Nicklaus and a 100,000 square-foot casino. Yet for all the grandeur, Baha Mar's creation was a long and painful saga.

The initial idea for Baha Mar was announced in 2005, but took until 2010 for a Swiss-born Bahamian investor (Sarkis Izmirlian) and the government (then headed by Prime Minister Perry Christie) to team up to help revitalize the core development for Baha Mar and Cable Beach, a highly popular beachfront destination on New Providence Island. What drove the idea from the Bahamian side was the need to remain competitive in global tourism. In this, the Bahamian government was willing to help get the Baha Mar project launched. The problem was that such an undertaking was costly. Moreover, relations between Prime Minister Christie and Izmirlian deteriorated. Making matters worse, the Great Recession (2008) hit and Baha Mar was at risk of sinking. At this point, the Bahamian government turned to the Export–Import Bank of China and China State Construction and Engineering Corporation. The former was to provide a $2.54 billion loan, while the latter contributed $150 million for the project.

At the time of the initial Chinese involvement, Izmirlian stated, "It became quickly apparent during the selection process that one organization stood out above all the others, China State Construction and Engineering Corporation. This is because they saw Baha Mar for what it is: a unique world-class resort that they could build, and in the process, showcase to the world China State's ability to deliver an intricately designed, and complex, resort metropolis on a somewhat remote island in the Caribbean" (Simon 2015).

Although the project would be completed and parts of it opened in 2017, the process became acrimonious, including a brief bankruptcy, opening delays, lawsuits, and tensions between the Chinese and Bahamian governments. In the process, Izmirlian was ousted from the project and replaced by Hong Kong-based Chow Tai Fook Enterprises, a family-owned conglomerate with close ties to Beijing.[2] While this was China's largest overseas commercial real-estate project up to that date, many Bahamians resented the roughly 4000 Chinese workers brought into their island country during the project.

At the opening of the resort, Prime Minister Christie indicated that relations between his government and China had been "tumultuous" and that there had been "endless and tedious negotiations" (King 2017). However, the Bahamian leader also stated, "Baha Mar's opening is not a mirage. It is not some ostentatious effort of misrepresentations. It is real, and it is the most significant economic event ever to occur in a single phase in the Bahamas and in the Caribbean region."

Baha Mar was a mixed result for the Chinese experience in the Caribbean. On the positive side, it demonstrated that Chinese companies could build a major tourist complex in the region and play an important role in the local economy. This certainly helped to market Chinese construction companies in the rest of the tourist-oriented Caribbean. Importantly, Baha Mar was finished. At the same time, there was considerable criticism, which could not be overlooked, especially as the Chinese would often repeat the same pattern in other countries (Cohen 2016). One critical voice was that of Carey Leonard, an associate with the law firm Callenders & Co., in Freeport, Grand Bahama, who stated, "With investors, other than the Chinese, the Bahamas has been able to rely on their moral sense of doing the right thing. It is clear that the Chinese have no moral sense at all. They don't care who gets hurt as long as they can screw every last penny out of anyone they come in contact with, be they the very Bahamians who have allowed them into their country" (Leonard 2017).

Despite criticism of Chinese companies and Baha Mar, China's involvement in the Bahamas hardly ended. Beginning in 2009 the Bahamas was again on the radar screen for China, with then-Vice Premier Hui Liangyu

---

[2] The Chow Tai Fook business empire is expansive and has been around for a considerable period of time. The various companies that fall under the family banner include jewelry, property development, hotel, department stores, transportation, energy, telecommunications, port and casinos. Some of the businesses are privately held, but others are traded on international stock exchanges and have been incorporated in the British Virgin Islands and the Cayman Islands.

visiting the Caribbean country that year and signing a number of agreements. Among the projects that spilled out of the closer relationship were a $30 million grant to construct the Thomas A. Robinson National Stadium, loans to build a four-lane highway from the Sir Lyden Pindling Airport to Nassau's city center, and loans for further port construction. Moreover, Huawei upgraded the Bahamas' digital infrastructure, linking the island's grid to 4G service and the surrounding region. Considering the geopolitical sensitivity that was to later surround Huawei, its ability to gain a foothold in the Bahamian telecommunications system has become a sensitive issue with the United States.

Although Chinese investment has continued in the Bahamas beyond the Baha Mar experience, the seeming lack of interest from the United States has helped Beijing maintain influence. At the reception celebrating the 2018 Chinese Spring Festival, the Chinese ambassador to the Bahamas felt comfortable enough to state, "The economic and trade cooperation have flourished. The Baha Mar Resort has achieved its completion and opening last year, which will create more than 5,000 jobs and bring new vigor and vitality into the Bahamian economy" (People's Republic of China 2018). That may be true, but both sides have become more cautious in dealing with each other.

China's involvement in the Bahamas eventually spilled over into the country's politics. In the run-up to the 2017 elections, China was an issue. K. P. Turnquest, an opposition leader, worried about the government's giving away of Bahamian sovereignty because of its laser beam focus on China, questioning the long-term prospects for the economy were being sacrificed in favor of its preelection campaign "given that it was seemingly pinning all of its hopes on Chinese-related investment to drive an economic revival" (Hartnell 2015; Cohen 2016). In the election campaign of Hubert Minnis (for the opposition Free National Movement or FNM), part of the platform was to hold Chinese companies more accountable. At that point China's massive involvement in Baha Mar and the British Colonial Hotel had become the subject of national discourse, while many Bahamians felt that the Chinese were taking over the national economy, illegal Chinese immigrants were moving in and putting small enterprises out of business, and that Bahamans were at risk of no longer being masters in their own house. Minnis and the FNM won by a landslide, taking 57 percent of the vote and capturing 35 of 39 seats.

Although the Bahamas remained cautious of China, Nassau found Beijing a persistent suitor compared to the United States. Indeed, the

United States has lacked an ambassador to the Bahamas since 2011 due to domestic American politics that prevented the passage of a candidate through the Senate. The seeming lack of interest from Washington has left a bad taste. Other issues complicated relations: the Trump administration's views on climate change (the Bahamas has suffered major damage in 2019 from Hurricane Dorian), his comments on "shit-hole countries" (which were taken to be racist in nature), and the overall U.S. shift from multilateralism to America First. Even with the change in the United States to the Biden administration, tensions remained over the United States' support for the Organization for Economic Cooperation and Development (OECD) effort to impose a global taxation system, which calls for a global minimum corporate income tax with a minimum tax rate of 15 percent. As the *Nassau Guardian's* Paige McCartney noted: "The changes would impact the vibrant but dwindling financial services sector, which has shrunk year over year for the past five years" (McCartney 2021). Furthermore, the slow U.S. response to Bahamian requests for help during the Covid-19 pandemic did not play well in Nassau, especially considering the brutal impact the medical crisis had on the country's tourist-based economy.

The state of play between a United States seemingly not caring about them and a China that is ready to provide more (and gain more influence) has left Bahamians cautious in steering their way between the two larger countries. Prime Minister Minnis was one of the handfuls of Caribbean leaders invited to meet with President Trump at Mar-a-Lago in Florida in early 2019. When asked about China and the United States, the Bahamian leader stated, "The issue with China came up during one of the earlier meetings. I pointed out very clearly that China and the Bahamas are allies and we have a good working relationship, and that will not change" (Eyewitness News [The Bahamas] 2019).

Despite the penetration of Chinese money and influence into the Bahamas, the economic reality is that the island state is strongly linked to the United States. The Caribbean country relies heavily on imports from the United States to meet food and fuel needs for local and tourist consumption, which is reflected in that over 80 percent of the country's international trade is with the United States, which is also home to most of its tourists. At the same time, the U.S. private sector remains a major presence in the Bahamas. In 2018 Royal Caribbean International invested $200 million in renovating its properties on CocoCay, an island that it leases; Walt Disney Company purchased a large part of Eleuthera Island from another U.S. company and planned to spend between $250 and $400 million to construct a port for its cruise ships and other facilities; and Margaritaville Enterprises announced plans to construct a new luxury hotel complex in Nassau (ECLAC 2019: 67).

The Bahamas' role in the new Cold War does not pivot on ideology. China is not about to colonize the island country, but it is eroding the U.S. position. Much of diplomacy is about showing up—the United States has not had an ambassador for over 10 years. As Patrick Griffin, who was an assistant to President Clinton and a professor at American University noted in 2021, "A positive first move would be to send an ambassador who wants to work with the Bahamian government as they rebuild from the dual tragedies of the hurricane and pandemic" (Griffin 2021).

Chinese companies may have emerged over the last two decades as rivals, but the playing field is still dominated by the United States. The challenge ahead for the Bahamas is how to recover from the Covid-19 pandemic, revive its tourist sector and weigh its needs with an eye to what the U.S. and China are willing to offer in terms of economic assistance and investment. For China, the Bahamas can be regarded as a success story; the Chinese are perceived as a partner (though carefully watched) and have given them access to one of the world's best ports just off the coast of the United States, its main rival in global geopolitics.

TRINIDAD AND TOBAGO—REALPOLITIK AND MUTUAL INTERESTS

Trinidad and Tobago was the first Caribbean country to sign up for the BRI in 2018, while there has been a steady train of high-ranking officials of both countries paying their mutual respects, and China is an active investor in the dual-island Caribbean country. And during the Covid-19 pandemic, China donated a large number of its Sinopharm vaccines to Trinidad and Tobago, while being highly critical in the Chinese media of U.S. efforts, which were initially comparatively meager (*Global Times* 2021).

For Trinidad and Tobago, China is considered an important strategic partner, a means of diversifying its customer base for its exports (led by LNG), and an important source of economic assistance that does not demand the same levels of conditionality as do Western lenders. Equally important, elements of Trinidadian foreign policy have dovetailed with

China's; Port of Spain has made it clear that it does not want to be involved in interfering in the affairs of other countries, in particular, both countries officially do not favor a forced regime change of Venezuela's Maduro regime, though for very different reasons. The growing closeness between the two countries was evident in 2018 when Trinidad and Tobago became the first Caribbean BRI country.

The main drivers for the development of Chinese–Trinidadian relations are economic, largely rooted in China's need for oil and LNG (as well as the need to diversify its sources of these commodities). China's engagement in Trinidad and Tobago began during the 2000s, but rapidly gained momentum in the 2010s. Although Trinidad is not of the same size and scope as other major LNG exporters, such as Qatar, Australia, the U.S., and Russia, it is in the top 10 group of countries, ahead of larger countries, such as Algeria and Indonesia. While the United States was a longtime the major buyer of Trinidadian LNG (up to 80 percent in 2000), it declined over the next couple of decades as Canadian natural gas imports to the United States were facilitated by pipelines, U.S. fracking diminished the need for a high level of imports, and Latin American and Chinese demand increased for Trinidadian LNG. U.S. natural gas imports began to decline in 2007. According to the U.S. Energy Information Administration, in 2019 about 2 percent of total U.S. natural gas imports came as LNG, 89 percent of which were from Trinidad (U.S. Energy Information Administration 2021). Chinese interest in Trinidadian LNG came at a good time.

The size and scope of China's involvement in Trinidad and Tobago was quickly evident as the Asian country became a major buyer of the Caribbean country's LNG as well as the undertaking of major infrastructure projects. These included a $500 million drydock at La Brea (with China Harbor Engineering Company), a $102 million industrial park in La Brea, a renovation of Piarco International Airport, construction of a new airport on Tobago (China Railway Construction) the Couva Children's Hospital and Medical Multi-Training Center, the rebuilding of a wing of Port of Spain's general hospital, and work being done on the Curepe Highway Interchange (a China Railway Joint Venture). Moreover, it was announced in February 2021 that the National Gas Company of Trinidad and Tobago (NGC) signed an Engineering, Procurement, and Commissioning contract for gas infrastructure for Evolving TecKnologies and Enterprise Development Company's Phoenix Park Industrial Estate (which covers 145-acres) (*Daily Express* 2021).

Trinidad's embrace of China as an alternative economic pole to the United States was something that both of the country's major political parties embraced. The Caribbean country was governed by the People's National Movement (PNM) under Prime Minister Patrick Manning (2001–2010), and followed by the United National Congress (UNC) under Prime Minister Kamla Persad-Bissessar from 2010 to 2015. The PNM then returned under Keith Rowley in 2015 and won re-election in 2020.

Although Manning adopted a warmer approach to China, it was the UNC government that hosted President Xi's visit in 2013. Prime Minister Persad-Bissessar made an official visit to China in 2014, during which she officially opened her country's embassy in China. It was also during her administration that Trinidad and Tobago bought a Chinese-made military patrol ship. Chinese investment in Trinidad and Tobago also increased during her period in office, with one of the more notable transactions being the 2011 purchase by the China Investment Corporation (the PRC sovereign wealth fund) of Atlantic LNG. Indeed, during Persad-Bissessar's 2014 Beijing trip energy was a top issue as Trinidad needed to make up lost exports to the United States and international prices had plunged. The Rowley administration followed the general policy outline of engaging China, which has been reflected by larger infrastructure projects (Government of Trinidad and Tobago 2019).

China has also managed to gain a strong position in Trinidad and Tobago's telecommunications market. Huawei as well as its rival ZTE have established a strong position in local markets. Indeed, one estimate put Huawei's investment in the twin-island state from 2015 to 2019 at $40 million, much of it going to make it an information and communications technology hub (ICT) for the Eastern Caribbean (*Stabroek News* 2019). Huawei performs infrastructure work for Telecommunications Services of Trinidad and Tobago (TSTT), in which the Trinidad and Tobago government is the majority (51 percent) partner. The Chinese company has also teamed up with TSTT to introduce a fixed-wireless 5G solution in the Caribbean country. Moreover, it has been successful in selling its smartphones and other telecommunications devices in the local market. In terms of security concerns, the dependence on Huawei provides China potential access to a wide sweep of information flowing out of Trinidad and Tobago. As one U.S. security analyst observed: "Thus, in terms of both phones and the lines that carry their data, virtually all sensitive, proprietary and personal data transmitted by Trinidad and Tobago government personnel, local and foreign businessmen, and others in the country, passes through Huawei hardware at some point in its journey" (Ellis 2019).

The China–Trinidad relationship has had its share of tensions. Some proposed projects have fallen through, there has been grousing over Chinese workers being used over local workers, and concerns have been raised about moving too close to the Asian country over the United States. Although the perception of China is positive, the Asian country has demonstrated that it can be driven by its own national interests which are tied to economics. The debt issue does rise as a point of concern. According to the IMF, public sector debt to GDP has risen from 37.8 percent in 2016 to over 87 percent in 2021, largely driven by a series of large budget deficits and a steep Covid-19 pandemic-induced economic contraction of 7.4 percent in 2020 and around 1.0 percent in 2021 (IMF 2021). Although this is hardly a blinking red light, it has to be seen in the context of weak growth over the past decade which has forced the government to run a series of large fiscal deficits. Reflecting the erosion in the country's creditworthiness, Trinidad and Tobago's sovereign credit ratings have fallen (hitting non-investment grade with Moody's in May 2020), making international capital markets more costly and difficult to tap.

Considering the erosion of Trinidad's credit position, Chinese loans, with low interest rates and fewer conditions, have maintained their appeal. There is a risk that Trinidad and Tobago's economic recovery from the pandemic takes longer than hoped and problems emerge for debt repayments, though this risk appears to be declining due to higher natural gas prices related to the Russo-Ukrainian War. Although the idea of China's debt-trap diplomacy often is derided as U.S. propaganda, the question must be asked, if Trinidad and Tobago ends up in a dire situation (like a balance of payments crisis) and is unable to repay debt, what will China ask for?

The other dimension of the complex nature of the China–Trinidad relationship is Venezuela and how that impacts the Caribbean country's relations with the United States, still its major trade partner and a key source of foreign direct investment. The Rowley administration remained committed to maintaining positive relations with China and Venezuela. With the latter it shares a maritime border, has taken in an estimated 24,000 Venezuelan refugees fleeing their homeland's economic chaos, and there are potential deals to be made on joint exploitation of offshore areas. Consequently, through the lens of the U.S.–Venezuelan tensions as well as Washington's new cold war with China, Trinidad and Tobago has put itself in the middle. This fell into place over Prime Minister Rowley's disagreement with the OAS backing Guaidó over Maduro; his willingness to engage with the Maduro regime; the Trump administration's designating Trinidad as a Tier 2 country in the U.S. 2019 Trafficking in Persons Report; Secretary of State Mike Pompeo's January 2020 hosting a meeting in Jamaica for other Caribbean heads of state (and seemingly not inviting Trinidad and Tobago, Barbados, and other English-speaking Caribbean countries for their unwillingness to join in the hostility to Venezuela); the criticism of the U.S. embassy over Trinidad's continued support of the Maduro regime (during the Trump administration); and a very negative U.S. reaction to the May 2020 visit of Venezuela's Vice President Delcy Rodríguez to Trinidad, which was complicated by an April 2020 fuel shipment from Trinidad and Tobago's Paria Fuel Trading Company to Aruba, which was then sent to Venezuela.

The Rodríguez visit resulted in the U.S. Ambassador Joseph Mondello criticizing the Rowley government for allowing Rodríguez into the country, a development made worse in U.S. eyes by her also being the head of the Bolivarian Intelligence Service (which reports into the Office of the Vice President). This, in turn, caused Prime Minister Rowley to state in parliament, "I take umbrage. I take umbrage at the United States ambassador making a public statement criticizing the actions of the government of Trinidad and Tobago. As far as taking instructions from the US embassy on Marli Street, leave the People's National Movement (PNM) out of that" (OilNow 2019). This set up concerns about possible U.S. economic sanctions and allowed the Leader of the Opposition Kamla Persad-Bissessar (of the UNC) to take a shot at the Rowley government, "…Rowley even got into a very public row with the US Ambassador to Trinidad and Tobago, Joseph Mondello, when he said Rowley's continued recognition of Maduro's regime was 'deeply concerning.' Now, the alleged illegitimate actions of the Rowley regime is their ongoing, questionable, and dangerous support of Maduro which could cause the US to impose costly and detrimental sanctions for Trinidad and Tobago" (Persad-Bissessar 2020).

Persad-Bissessar was also aware that new elections loomed and it was worth painting the Rowley government as putting the country at risk of a major meltdown of relations with the United States. It further injected uncertainty into Trinidad's politics at a time when the economy was in poor shape and criminal violence against the country's police force had risen to high levels. Nonetheless, Rowley and the PNM went on to win the August 2020 elections (by a narrow margin).

Trinidad and Tobago has emerged as a China-friendly voice in the Caribbean. Although other countries, like Antigua and Barbuda and Dominica, have also emerged as partners with the Asian country, Trinidad and Tobago offers more in terms of its natural resources and geostrategic location as a regional hub. While this should not be overstated, Port of Spain has been a facilitator in advancing China's engagement in Caribbean affairs, especially as it is one of Caricom's largest economies. This has also been a benefit to the Caribbean country—thus far. Chinese–Trinidadian relations have yet to undergo a major test, but if the Caribbean country has major economic problems that impair its ability to repay the Asian one, that crossroads could come.

GUYANA

Long isolated and economically marginal, massive discoveries of offshore oil have placed Guyana on the geopolitical map. Indeed, Guyana is highly attractive to China, which is already buying its oil. Guyana also has other important natural resources, including gold, bauxite, and uranium. Considering the rollercoaster ride Chinese companies, banks and government officials have experienced in neighboring Venezuela, Guyana has much to offer. The Caribbean country's politics are relatively stable, it has huge reserves of oil, and its national infrastructure is in bad need of an upgrade, something which Chinese construction and engineering companies have considerable experience. In turn, China has much that Guyana needs, including funding for infrastructure development, a legacy of involvement in the country dating back to its independence, and a market for what Guyana is going to be exporting in large quantities, oil. While the United States has been active in supporting Guyana through a challenging period of oil discovery, China is not a marginal player.

Guyana is a former British colony that gained independence in 1966, has a population of 737,718 people, and shares borders with Venezuela, Brazil, and Suriname. Beyond oil, bauxite, timber, and oil, the country is also a producer of sugar, rum, and rice. However, the country's economic development has long been problematic, due to past periods of economic mismanagement and a lack of sustained investment. Additionally, the Guyanese economy's heavy dependence on commodities has left it vulnerable to fluctuations in international prices.

The country's political life also has a mixed record as it has been marked by sometimes sharp divisions between the two major ethnic groups, the Afro-Guyanese and Indo-Guyanese, who today make up a little over 29 percent and roughly 40 percent, respectively. Other groups in Guyanese society include "mixed" at around 20 percent, Amerindians at 10.5 percent, and others (Chinese and Europeans). The two largest groups tend to support different political parties, the Progressive People's Party/Civic (PPP/C) for the Indo-Guyanese and the People's National Congress-Reform (PNC-R) for the Afro-Guyanese. Although efforts have been made to form non-ethnically based parties, the ethnic divide has persisted in the country's elections, often with a winner-take-all sentiment.

Guyana was the first in the English-speaking Caribbean to recognize the People's Republic in 1972. At the time it was led by Forbes Burnham, who ran Guyana with a mix of autocracy, ethnic politics (seen as favoring Afro-Guyanese), and quasi-socialist-populist ideology. He was a firm believer in autarky and banned a wide range of imports to the country, including rice and flour as well as nationalizing much of the economy. His efforts did much to kill the country's private sector, drive away foreign investment and park the economy in a developmental cul-de-sac. In terms of international alignments, Guyana was seen as a friend of Cuba but tolerated by the United States. By the time of his death in 1985 Guyana was one of the poorest countries in the Western Hemisphere.

Fortunately for Guyana, two important developments occurred over the next two decades. First, Burnham's autocratic political system gave way to a more competitive pluralistic political system. This did not happen overnight, but progressed through the 1990s and into the first decades of the twenty-first century. Cheddi Jagan, who had early on been ousted by a British coup in 1953 (supported by the Americans), returned and later became the country's first Indo-Guyanese president (1992–1997). Despite pressures from sometimes rancorous divisions between its Indo-Guyanese and Afro-Guyanese communities and corruption, the political system did not revert back to autocracy.

The second development was that after a lengthy period of struggling economically, in 2015 Guyana struck it big with a major offshore oil find. ExxonMobil, a U.S. oil multinational, had persistently searched for offshore oil in what is known as the Guiana Shield. With this discovery, the geopolitical landscape for Guyana changed radically. The country of fewer than one million people and long a geopolitical backwater of South America and the Caribbean, was now on the international oil map, with possible reserves to rival those of Venezuela. The oil discovery was important from another angle in that it suddenly opened up Guyana to badly needed capital. Prior to that Guyana had struggled on the debt management front, with payments falling into arrears. Although Guyana was able to restructure and reduce its debt burden (helped hugely in 2007 when the Inter-American Development Bank canceled nearly $470 million in debt), the country remained cut off from international capital markets—at least until the oil discovery.

Considering Guyana's economic history and relative isolation for many decades, earlier Chinese overtures to provide assistance were well-received. During the earlier period, these included a $32 million loan in 2004 to revive a sugar refinery and a $12 million grant to build the Arthur Chung Conference Center, expansion at the Cheddi Jagan International Airport, construction of a four-lane highway on the East Coast of Demerara, numerous scholarships and training programs and services provided by Chinese medical brigades. Chinese companies also invested in bauxite and timber, though with mixed results. Chinese FDI rose from $5.6 million in 2005 to $183.7 million in 2010, climbing above $200 million in 2013 and beyond (Bernal 2016: 99; Guyana Chronicle 2017). Guyana officially joined the BRI in 2018.

Like the Bahamas and Trinidad and Tobago, Guyana has provided a market for Huawei. In 2017 China and Guyana signed a $37.6 million agreement geared toward boosting Guyana's broadband capabilities covering several sectors and there has been discussion of moving the Caribbean country in the direction of 5G operations. This raised the issue of Guyanese national security, which was reflected in an opinion piece by the *Stabroek News*: "What should be of greater interest to the government here and particularly its Ministry of Public Telecommunications is the growing international concern about whether Huawei is at the beck and call of the Chinese government and can be made to do its bidding against the interests of its clients like Guyana and particularly in security sensitive areas like fifth generation telecommunications" (*Stabroek News* 2018).

Not every Chinese venture in Guyana has worked. One point of irritation has been the slow progress with the expansion project at Cheddi

Jagan International Airport, work on which was expected to be completed by December 31, 2021. Started in 2013, the project has already gone beyond its initial planned $150 million in spending, of which $138 million was financed by the China Exim Bank and the rest from Guyanese taxpayers. The project, managed by China Harbor Engineering Corp., is expected to be completed at some point in 2022. Of this situation, one Guyanese newspaper noted in December 2021: "As the country awaits the completion of the project, which falls way below expectations, taxpayers are still obligated to repay a loan of US$138M to China, which forms part of the contract sum" (*Kaieteur News* 2021).

Another Chinese disappointment has been with Bai Shan Lin Forest Developers. For over a decade in Guyana, the company has struggled. Although given access to 680,000 hectares of timber reserves in exchange for hiring local workers and the construction of a wood processing facility, the company's experience was largely negative (*Kaieteur News* [A and B] 2018a, b; Ward 2020) Indeed, the wood processing facility was never built, a failed housing venture left local banks with bad debt, and in 2017 its forest concessions were taken away. In early 2018 it was charged with illegal logging. Moreover, Bai Shan Lin racked up debt it could not repay. Even support from the Chinese Development Bank could not save the company.

Chinese–Guyanese relations have generally been smooth, but there has been a degree of tension regarding the practices of Chinese companies, the lack of hiring of Guyanese, overstaffing with Chinese workers, and the activities of what is perceived as a big country that sometimes seeks to impose its will on a smaller one. In 2017, the Guyanese Revenue Authority conducted a probe into an alleged racket in which the Chinese Embassy was accused of importing containers of goods for its nationals who operate businesses in the country[3] (*Kaieteur News* 2017). The Chinese embassy strongly denied any such racket, but local merchants

---

[3] "Major Chinese Project Stalled," *Kaieteur News*, November 12, 2017. https://www.kaieteurnewsonline.com/2017/11/12/major-chinese-project-stalled/. The article noted: "Earlier this year, the Guyana Revenue Authority (GRA) started a probe into an alleged racket in which the Chinese Embassy was accused of importing containers of goods for its nationals who are operating businesses here. The Chinese Ambassador vehemently denied the allegation. GRA late last year stumbled on what seemed like an abnormally large number of containers brought in by the Chinese Embassy. GRA reported that the Chinese Embassy brought in more containers than all the other embassies combined. Investigators initially believed that maybe there was a mistake with the number of containers.

were adamant that the containers (as diplomatic mail) passed through Guyanese customs duty free and were hurting their business. Taken together with a mall being constructed and financed by Chinese businessmen in Georgetown, the capital, there is sentiment in some quarters that this was all part of a bid to take over Guyana's commercial activity to the benefit of the Chinese.

Most Chinese companies in Guyana have operated with fewer issues. Indeed, Chinese companies are actively bidding on Guyanese infrastructure development projects and Chinese financial support exists for the country. At the same time, China is willing to play a larger role in Guyana and could find lucrative business opportunities in the infrastructure upgrade surrounding the development of the energy sector. However, the economic landscape is complicated by a number of factors: China is a major backer of Venezuela, which still claims a large part of Guyana. The United States has been more proactive in backing Guyana (no doubt because of oil and the activities of large U.S. corporations); and Guyana's political elite (despite its internal differences) has recognized that things have changed—their country now has something the larger powers want.

China has also demonstrated that the good partnership approach has limits, which became evident in two ways, the 2020 elections and the Taiwan office incident in 2021. In both cases, the Guyanese got a view of the more hard realpolitik that China plays. The March 2020 elections were largely a battle between the incumbent PNC-R government, headed by President David Granger, and the PPP/C opposition, led by Irfaan Ali. The country found itself in a political crisis in December 2018, when the government lost its one-seat majority in parliament and failed to survive a vote of no confidence. The Granger government then challenged the validity of that vote and sent the matter to the country's courts. The matter dragged on through 2019 and 2020 until it was agreed that elections would be held in March of the latter year. The elections took place

However, further checks confirmed that the embassy allegedly used its diplomatic channels to pass the containers through the wharves. Under the diplomatic arrangements, shipments and packages for embassies are not too closely scrutinized. Local businesses have been complaining of being unable to compete in terms of prices against the Chinese especially, no matter how they tried to bring down costs or purchasing directly from the manufacturers."

but were quickly said to be fraudulent in favor of the government. President Granger sought to swear himself in but was stopped by the High Court. Granger was eventually forced to back down and the PPP/C was declared the winner. Throughout this process, considerable external pressure was brought to bear on the Granger government by the Caribbean Court of Justice, the United States, Canada, and the United Kingdom. Indeed, the United States and the European Union made it clear that reinstatement of a Granger government would probably result in sanctions against individuals who stood to gain from the Granger government staying in power. China's response was that it did not intervene in other country's affairs, indicating to some that they would have been quite happy to honor the results of a fraudulent vote.

The second development came with a diplomatic incident in which a large power clearly put a smaller country in its place, complete with a scolding. In February 2021 it became news that Guyana had granted Taiwan the right to establish a trade office in Georgetown. This was perceived in Beijing for what it was in reality; the opening of an informal embassy. This was thought by some to be a push by the United States to help Taiwan claw back diplomatic recognition after its losses of El Salvador, Panama, and the Dominican Republic. Nonetheless, China was not pleased. China's Foreign Ministry spokesman Wang Wenbin promptly indicated Beijing's official displeasure: "We hope the relevant party will abide by the one-China principle, refrain from any form of official exchanges and establishment of official institutions with Taiwan, take concrete actions to correct the error and eliminate the negative effects" (Reuters Staff 2021). Guyana quickly capitulated: "The government has not established any diplomatic ties or relations with Taiwan and as a result of the miscommunication of the agreement signed, this agreement has since been terminated."

Why did Guyana capitulate? The simple answer is that China is an important source of infrastructure finance, a buyer of Guyanese oil, and further trade could be generated. In 2020 according to the IMF Direction of Trade Statistics, China bought only $119 million of Guyanese goods (which made it the 8th largest export partner); Guyana imported $213 million of Chinese goods (which made it the 4th largest source of imports), leaving the relationship clearly in the Asian country's favor (IMF 2022). Guyana hopes to gain further traction on its oil exports to China. Taiwan, a smaller country and ultimately with less to offer, was not worth torpedoing Guyana's relations with China. However, the veiled threat of Chinese action sent a clear message, don't mess with China over core foreign policy issues or there will be consequences. For an example of what China could do Guyana has only to look to Australia. Australia's exports are being held up outside Chinese ports or being stopped because of health considerations due to Canberra's insistence in 2020 that China be investigated for being the point of origin of the Covid-19 pandemic. In 2021, Lithuania's exports suffered the same treatment after the Baltic country is permitting Taiwan to open a business office in its capital.

For all of China's use of leverage on a smaller country, it still has to contend with the United States, which has a strong presence in Guyana. Although CNOOC has part of the same offshore bloc, it is ExxonMobil and Hess that control most of the offshore assets. Moreover, other U.S. oil companies are playing an active role in exploration and production as well as in logistics. The U.S. government has also stepped up its support for Guyana in the face of territorial claims on two-thirds of its territory, including conducting joint maneuvers with the Guyanese military. China has not been active in backing Guyana in dealing with Venezuela.

Although Chinese policy in Guyana underwent a tough patch, Beijing's willingness to remain in the diplomatic mix in what is rapidly emerging as a southern Caribbean energy arc (ranging from Trinidad and Tobago through the Guianas and possibly to the oil refineries in Aruba and Curacao) is likely to keep Chinese companies and banks involved. This was evident in late 2021 when the Guyanese government announced that it is contracting with China Railway Group to construct and fund a reboot of the Amaila Falls hydroelectric project, which was shelved in 2015. Moreover, Chinese companies are in the process of a number of other projects, including a $256 million contract to build a bridge over the Demerara River connecting Guyana and Suriname, a $200 million overhaul to a road link between Annandale to Mahaica and upgrades to segments of roads in Georgetown (Ellis 2021).

The PPP/C government of President Mohamed Irfaan Ali came to power in August 2020, a time marked by a global depression induced by a pandemic and a new Cold War-like international political landscape. The complicating factor for the Guyanese is that both countries are important actors in its economy. Guyana is now on the oil map and must make decisions as to how to navigate difficult new Cold War-like waters. While U.S.-Chinese friction is likely to continue around the world, it appears in Guyana that there is a loose accommodation between the two powers, something that is obviously preferred by the Guyanese government. For

China, Guyana is important due to its oil; although the PRC is committed to going green Beijing clearly recognizes that there will be many years before alternative energy can meet demand. While China may not have a large role in oil exploration and production, it can be an active buyer of oil as well as play a large role in the development of Guyanese infrastructure. The worst case for China would be if Venezuela, its authoritarian friend, opts to invade Guyana, which no doubt would put Beijing in a difficult position, especially if the weapons used in such a venture were Chinese supplied. For Guyana, it is important to get its balancing act between China and the United States right. Indeed the stakes are high as for the first time in many decades the country has a real chance to make some real, long-term gains in its economic development and standard of living.

JAMAICA

Jamaica is one of the larger islands in the Caribbean, blessed with a range of natural resources, and an inventive people and, since independence in 1962, has been governed by elected governments. For all of the country's achievements, it has also faced considerable challenges that have left a mixed track record in terms of its economic development, which is important to understand with an eye to China's engagement on the island. Probably one of the best summaries of the Jamaican experience was penned by Harvard University's Orlando Patterson, himself a Jamaican: "There are few places on earth more confounding than Jamaica. A little island barely the size of Connecticut, it has a larger global profile than countries hundreds of times its size; at times celebrated for the spectacular performances of its stars and the worldwide impact of its cultural creations, it is often condemned for the depravity of its gangsters and racketeers and the failures of its economy" (Patterson 2019).

Jamaica's developmental experience has long been conditioned by its dependence on commodity exports (bauxite, coffee, sugar, and rum) and tourism, challenged public finances, and heavy debt burden. Consecutive governments through the 1980s and into the first decade of the twenty-first century had to contend with austerity, structural reforms, and working with the International Monetary Fund. The country's debt history did not help it as a place to either lend money or invest. A major bank crisis in the mid-1990s and the failure of several large state-owned enterprises helped push Jamaica into a debt spiral, a situation that was compounded by the global financial crisis in 2008–2009. By March 2009, public sector debt had climbed to 124 percent of GDP and interest costs commanded a little over half of the tax revenues. Although the country had turned to the IMF in 2010 for help, the government was unable to maintain the required fiscal constraint; the deal floundered and Jamaica's debt continued to rise, reaching 147 percent of GDP by 2013.

Jamaica had gained the distinction of becoming one of the largest debtors in not only the Americas but in the world. As the country's finance minister Nigel Clarke stated in early 2019, "Another IMF agreement was brokered. However, there was deep skepticism of Jamaica's commitment to the programme goals, so other international partners would provide only limited financing. Jamaica was virtually on its own" (Clarke 2019). Clarke's assessment of the situation was reflected in foreign investment in Jamaica. FDI inflows into Jamaica cooled in the aftermath of the Great Recession, with a total of $228 million in 2010 and an even lower $218 million the following year (ECLAC 2021: 24).

As China ramped up its international development strategy, Jamaica gained attention. Through the first decade of the twenty-first century, Chinese FDI was largely negligible, but from 2008 on it gradually crept upwards hitting $2.16 million that year, $3.37 million in 2010, before taking a sharp move upwards the following year to $39.1 million and heading toward the $100 million mark in subsequent years (Bernal 2016: 93). For a Jamaica struggling with limited access to international capital markets and a mixed track record with multilateral lending agencies, Chinese investment was decidedly welcome.

Chinese investment in Jamaica was largely directed to infrastructure. Indeed, Chinese companies and banks became active in a number of projects ranging from transportation to other large infrastructure ventures, such as the $730 million North–South Highway connecting Kingston to Ocho Rios; the upgrade of an industrial park; and plans were announced for a children's hospital, two infant schools; and the new headquarters for Jamaica's Foreign Affairs Ministry in Kingston. Chinese efforts also went into port upgrades and management, while programs were created for young Jamaicans to travel to the Asian country, learn Chinese and develop an understanding of one of the world's great powers.

Chinese investment was also critical in reviving the island's bauxite industry. In 2017, the Alpart alumina refinery was sold for $299 million to the Chinese state-owned enterprise, Jiuquan Iron and Steel Company (JISCO). The selling company Russia's, UC Rusal, which had suspended

Alpart's operations between 2009 and 2015 due to the collapse in global aluminum prices. We will hear more of Rusal later.

One of the key developments in the Jiuquan purchase was the insistence by the Jamaican government that local people be hired. The initial work of modifying and upgrading the alumina plant to reduce costs and enhance production, however, fell to 200 Chinese technicians. Once that part of the work was accomplished, the next step was to hire Jamaicans and get the refinery back to work full time. Despite good intentions, the refinery purchase did not go according to plan. Residents around the JISCO alumina refinery have complained that the Chinese-owned company has caused environmental damage (in particular with dust pollution) and they demanded the company's relocation. Indeed, in 2019 Jamaica's regulatory agency issued 16 enforcement orders against the Chinese company for non-compliance with environmental regulations. As the Chinese government has clamped down on pollution in China, many of the more heavy-polluting companies, such as those in the aluminum smelting and refining, have opted to export those businesses to other parts of the world where environmental enforcement was not as stringent (Minto 2019). It is probable that Jinquan also found the Jamaican business environment more challenging than initially expected, especially in dealing with the local community.

China experienced other setbacks in Jamaica. Jamaicans have mobilized to halt infrastructure projects sponsored by Chinese lending, and in one case, the Jamaican government opted not to proceed with what would have been a massive container port around Goat Island after environmental groups opposed the project. Local architects also pushed back over talks on the construction of a new parliamentary building by a Chinese company. To fend off public concern over the new building, the Jamaican government opened an international competition to bid on the project: eligible teams had to be led by a Jamaican citizen, residing locally or abroad, who was also a registered and licensed Jamaican architect.

The fine line China walks in Jamaica was reflected by Prime Minister Holness' November 2019 visit to Beijing, which was an important milestone for Chinese–Jamaican relations and indirectly for the U.S.–Jamaican relations. It was the Jamaican leader's first official trip to the Asian country and the first time the Caribbean island participated in the China International Import Expo (CIIE). During the visit, the Jamaica leader met with China's President Xi and Premier Li Keqiang to sign a cooperation plan to jointly promote the BRI, "setting a precedent in the political relations between China and Caribbean countries in the new era," as China's ambassador to Jamaica, Tian Qi, stated (Qi 2019).

Prime Minister Holness' trip to China clearly signaled a "new era" in bilateral relations, made even more evident by the prompt U.S. response to the trip. Speaking to the local newspaper, *The Gleaner*, U.S. Ambassador to Jamaica Donald Tapia questioned the basis on which China has—through direct investment and loans—injected an estimated $2 billion into Jamaica over the past decade, most of which went to infrastructure projects or industries critical to the island's economy. The U.S. ambassador noted China's particular interest in minerals and ports. Ambassador Tapia also shared his concern over China's behavior when countries fail to keep up with their payments, with China usually controlling the narrative on their behalf: "I could tell you horror stories of countries where [China] has taken over ports because those countries could not pay for their investment. China usually has a great propaganda story as to why it has happened."

The U.S. Ambassador's displeasure over Holness' trip to China did not go over well in Jamaica. An editorial from *The Gleaner* noted: "Mr. Tapia should be given a message about where Jamaica's foreign policy is formulated, which oughn't be Foggy Bottom." The editorial also suggested that under the current world order, where new centers of power—such as China—are rising as a result of global realignments, small countries like Jamaica are increasingly interested in "maintaining a viable system of multilateral partnerships" (The Gleaner 2019).

Ambassador Tapia's warnings were perceived as rude or at least over the top by many Jamaicans. At the same time, Jamaicans shared some of his sentiments toward Chinese loans. As one comment on *The Gleaner's* editorial states: "We need to be wary of the kinds of agreements and contracts we enter into with the Chinese. There are countries which are now realizing that the rose that they saw in China is nothing but thorn bush." Moreover, Jamaicans have some concerns over China's involvement in their affairs. Jamaicans have mobilized to halt infrastructure projects sponsored by Chinese lending, and, in one case, the Jamaican government opted not to proceed with a container port around Goat Island after environmental groups opposed the project (MacDonald 2019). Moreover, Prime Minister Holness, in the aftermath of the China trip, indicated that there would be a halt on China's loans for the time being.

In December 2019, following the aftermath of the uproar over Ambassador Tapia's comments, the U.S. government announced the launch of its "América Crece" Initiative (Growth in the Americas), described as being "an innovative approach to support economic growth by catalyzing private sector investment in energy and infrastructure projects across Latin America and the Caribbean, including telecommunications, ports, roads, and airports." Jamaica figured prominently at the launch, joining the U.S. Caribbean Energy Security Initiative, a loan guarantee program that will help to mobilize $25 million in private finance for energy projects in the region in cooperation with the National Commercial Bank of Jamaica, under the umbrella of the Growth in the Americas project. No doubt Prime Minister Holness' trip helped drive the mention of Jamaica during the meetings.

The development of closer China–Jamaica relations and the U.S. reaction underscore the shifting tides in international relations to what increasingly looks like a new Cold War in the Caribbean. The sharpness of the debate over this situation is most likely to intensify the importance of China's economic largesse in Caribbean countries, like Jamaica. While *América Crece* and the subsequent B3W (Build Back Better World) launched by the Biden administration were positive-sounding steps, the former never fully materialized and ended when the Trump administration ended. The latter remains a question mark in terms of implementation and timing. Moreover, both programs fall short of the large-scale aid China has so far pumped into the region and appears willing to continue. If Washington wants to be taken more seriously, it needs a bigger checkbook and less lecturing on accepting Chinese help.

Although concerns were raised about the wave of Chinese investment in Jamaica, Prime Minister Andrew Holness was clear that what is being offered will benefit Jamaicans over the long term. He noted that Jamaicans cannot escape certain realities, one of which is that China is probably the world's largest provider of foreign direct investment across the globe and it would be foolhardy to ignore them. As he stated, "We are claiming independence, but we can only claim and hold that independence when we are economically independent" (Serju 2017). He also noted that it was not just his government that decided to develop a "strategic relationship and partnership with the Government of China," but previous administrations as well.

There is another factor in Jamaica's willingness to assert itself with the United States; the turnaround in the economy. By the late 2010s, years of structural reforms have given hope of sustained future economic expansion. In 2019, when Jamaica ended a $1.66 billion Stand-By Arrangement with the IMF, it was noted by that body that the Caribbean country's unemployment rate was down (to around 7.8 percent, an all-time low); foreign exchange reserves were up to comfortable levels; and the current account and fiscal deficits were subdued (IMF 2019). As a reflection of growing confidence in Jamaica FDI rose from a low of $218 million in 2011 to over $500 million a year from 2013 through 2019, when it was $665 million (ECLAC 2021: 24). Although a large amount of the FDI was from the United States, Canada, and Europe, China played a significant role, especially in the financing of key infrastructure projects.

Jamaica's experience with China has been similar to those of the Bahamas, Guyana, and Trinidad and Tobago; there have been positive developments in terms of upgrading infrastructure, a cheaper flow of consumer goods, and attention from a rising hegemonic power. At the same time, there have been downside factors, which range from irritation over Chinese staffing at the expense of local labor to disregard for environmental considerations, not to mention commentary over the opaque nature of Chinese finances and a willingness to use bribery. From the Chinese perspective, Jamaica provides a market for its construction and engineering companies, a strategic location from which to conduct regional business and a chance to erode U.S. regional hegemony. Although Jamaica has generally been pro-U.S. in its foreign policy, it has at times held itself apart from Washington's direction and stressed its Caribbean identity through organizations such as CARICOM and the Caribbean Development Bank. Considering the above, there is an incentive to partner with China which is ready and able to invest in Jamaica's infrastructure. At the same time, China is not pushing a military alliance, but a relationship based on economic utility in a region that feels its importance to the local hegemon slipping away. The caveat to this is that if globalization continues to be pushed back as major economies decouple, such as Russia with the West, and to some extent China and the West, Jamaica could benefit from a rise in regionalization, spearheaded by nearshoring, the reorganization of U.S. business supply chains to "friendly" jurisdictions.

Suriname

Suriname's experience with China is not radically different from those of the Bahamas, Jamaica, Guyana, and Trinidad and Tobago. For China though, Suriname represented a different challenge as the Dutch-speaking country was marked by a higher degree of political instability from its independence in 1975–2022. Chinese companies and banks have found an economic landscape complicated by coups, civil war and the ups and downs of electoral politics (which have been on a relatively steady path since the 1990s). Suriname's attraction derives from its considerable wealth in natural resources and periodic diplomatic support for China's foreign policy goals. At the same time, competition for influence in Suriname has become more contested, due to the discovery of large amounts of commercially viable oil in 2019 and 2020 (Maliksetian 2020). Moreover, the May 2020 elections saw the exit of President Desi Bouterse from the political stage, which removed a longtime dominant political figure and friend of China from the presidential palace.

In a 2014 paper, Professor Betty Secdoc-Dahlberg advanced the view that China's role in Suriname up to that point had undergone three different stages. These were 1976–1985, when the Netherlands was the preponderant external power based on its aid program, a "Golden Handshake" given at independence which placed the new country in a relatively strong financial position (Secdoc-Dahlberg 1990: 27). This period encompassed Suriname's independence, a brief period of democratic rule, the 1980 military coup that brought Desi Bouterse to power, the December 1982 murders of opposition members, and the subsequent suspension of the Dutch aid package. During this period China's role was negligible.

The second period lasted from 1986 to 2000, which was marked by a declining Dutch role, caused by bad relations with the military regime and human rights violations. To garner support and develop new friends the Bouterse-dominated leftist governments in Suriname turned to the Soviet Union, Cuba, Libya, Grenada, and Iran. During this period China's role expanded, with its companies establishing some of the first commercial projects. While Chinese and banks began to interact with Suriname, a new wave of Chinese immigrants, called the "Xin Yimin" arrived in substantial numbers, starting local businesses.

We have expanded Secdoc-Dahlberg's third period, 2010 to 2014 to 2020. During this time, the Netherlands' role in Suriname was eclipsed and China emerged as the strongest external actor in the Caribbean country. As Secdoc-Dahlberg noted: "This period is characterized by investments and commercial (mainly forestry) projects, involvement in gold exploration as well as continuation of soft loans, donations, and influx of (though reduced number compared with the early 1990s) of Xin Yimin, Chinese migrants" (Secdoc-Dalhberg 2014). It can be argued that China's importance to Suriname was helped considerably by Bouterse's election in 2010 and his re-election in 2015. Although the country remained "democratic," Bouterse's strong political personality dominated the political scene as well as serving as a corrupting influence. Bouterse maintained strong links to the Maduro regime in Venezuela, which is likely to have helped finance his 2015 re-election bid as well as allowing the Caribbean country to be used for the illicit traffic of gold to Turkey and the United Arab Emirates (Farah 2020: 9).

Through the 2010–2020 period China loomed large in Suriname's development. Although the Inter-American Development Bank played an important role in providing finance for development programs (providing $325 million in the 2016–2020 period alone), China was active in supplying financing for a number of infrastructure projects throughout this entire period—or at least announcing projects (Inter-American Development Bank 2021). China Harbour signed a memorandum of understanding with the Suriname government in 2010 for a road and railroad from Paramaribo to Brazil; a deep sea harbor; a sea dam from Albina to Nickerie; and a highway to Zanderij. (Most of these are not completed.) In 2012, plans were advanced to modernize the Martin Luther King Highway with the Chinese road builder Dalian (which would be helped by a loan from a state-owned Chinese bank). In 2018 it was announced that China Harbour Engineering Corporation was involved in discussions to upgrade Suriname's major international airport. Suriname has long wanted to upgrade Johan Adolf Pengel International Airport (JAP), which has been in need of new terminals, a parallel taxiway for aircraft, and a new fire station (to meet international standards). To finance the overhaul, Suriname approached China for a $205 million loan in 2018, but the process was slowed by the Caribbean country's debt restrictions on borrowings. A measure to approve the new borrowing was put forth to Suriname's parliament in 2019, but it remains in limbo especially in light of the change of government, the country's weakened financial position and the negative impact on the economy from the Covid-19 pandemic.

In 2019 Presidents Xi and Bouterse announced the China–Suriname strategic cooperation partnership, bringing Suriname into the BRI. On the diplomatic front, Suriname was one of the 53 countries to support China's National Security Law for Hong Kong. Ironically, Bouterse was on an official visit to China in November 2019 when the courts in his country passed a guilty verdict for his involvement in the December 1982 murders. Despite the embarrassment, he returned to Suriname with a promise of $300 million in loans for 14 projects, on top of roughly $500 million of existing debt. Indeed, China emerged during this period as Suriname's leading sovereign creditor, holding around $1 billion of the country's total debt of $2.4 billion in 2019.

The size and scope of Chinese involvement in Suriname over the past ten years has been impressive. As *The Guardian's* Nicolas Bourcier observed in 2015:

> In less than 10 years the Chinese have set up hundreds of companies, shops, casinos and restaurants in this small South American state, which reaches deep into the Amazon jungle. They have widened and asphalted roads, and built social housing. A television channel, with staff of about 20, now broadcasts in Mandarin Chinese on Surinamese networks. In 2011 the Southern Commercial Bank opened in Paramaribo. A group of Chinese businessmen has just bought out another one, the Fina Bank. Chinese nationals are now estimated to control around 90% of the country's supermarkets, small grocery stores and food shops. (Bourcier 2015)

Chinese companies, from both the local Chinese–Surinamese community and China, became active in the timber sector. Considering the heavy demand for lumber in China to meet the demands of a growing middle class, Chinese companies took advantage of Suriname's vast woodland resources (over 80 percent of the country is covered by forests). Although this helped generate exports for Suriname, there were problems in terms of poor forestry policy on the part of the Caribbean country and Chinese companies having a preference for Chinese workers.

While Chinese investment in Suriname has generally been welcome, it has not come without tensions. There has been a degree of resentment over the rise of Chinese business in the country and its displacement of other Surinamese ethnic groups. This includes the immigration policies that have raised the number of Chinese in the country and made them a more influential group in the local political and business landscape

(Secdoc-Dahlberg 2014: 10). Indeed, the growing Chinese population as well as investment has raised a degree of alarm from some quarters. As one reporter stated: "The number of Chinese in Suriname is increasing rapidly. They own an increasing percentage of Suriname's soil and economy, with support from China. However, China has much bigger plans for Suriname. If it continues like this, China will take over Suriname and we can better call it SuChiname" (Tobacco 2020). The same reporter adds: "The large group of 'new Chinese' who recently moved to Suriname is different. These Chinese are closed, do not integrate, do not speak the language and Surinamese entrepreneurs compete with cheap products from China." Surinamese concerns about China also extend to political influence. As one Surinamer noted in 2018: "China is Suriname's main lender and this increases Beijing's influence in Paramaribo, especially if the loans cannot be repaid. China will not be adverse to influencing the elections in Suriname if it suits her (non-interference in internal affairs is just a slogan" (Balraadjsing 2018).

Despite the misgivings from some quarters of the Surinamese public, Bouterse was a good client for China. Considering his criminal background and violations of human rights, he was relatively odious to Western governments and not a major recipient of foreign aid. Indeed it can be argued that Bourtese's track record made him easier for China to deal with; a former dictator in the 1980s who had waged war on the Maroon segment of the population, Bouterse also had earned an international criminal record. After his involvement in the murders of 15 men in December 1982, he is thought to have directed the Moiwana massacre by the National Army in 1986 of the Maroons, and in 1999 he was sentenced in absentia in the Netherlands to 11 years' imprisonment after being convicted of cocaine trafficking. His role as an international drug dealer with connections to a major drug trafficker in Guyana was tagged in Wikileaks (2006). He is also suspected of having been part of Maduro's international sanctions-busting, helping facilitate the flow of cocaine and gold through Suriname to Europe and the Middle East. Rounding out the picture, Bouterse's son, Dino, who was made head of the Suriname Anti-Terrorist Unit, was arrested in Panama by the U.S. DEA in 2013 for drug smuggling and trying to assist Hezbollah to establish a base in Suriname for $2 million.

Bouterse's two terms in office were marked by a high level of corruption, which included several banks involved in money laundering. Even the central bank was not exempt. In early 2020 it became evident that all was not right with government finances when $100 million went missing from the country's central bank. What generated political heat was that the government had forced the banks to deposit the foreign exchange of private citizens held in their vaults to the safekeeping of the central bank. In the ensuing scandal, the head of the central bank was fired, arrested and eventually would go on trial, while the government's finance minister was implicated. At the same time, the Bouterse government sought to cover its tracks by attempting to slow investigations into the matter. What was probably most galling to many Surinamers were the comments of Vice President Ashwin Adhin, who told the country that some of the money was used by the state to procure basic goods including "onions and potatoes" in addition to meeting monthly foreign debt repayments (Caribbean Life 2020).

In May 2020 Suriname went to the polls and elected a new government. Taking Secdoc-Dalhberg's breakdown of China–Suriname relations one step further, the elections of May 2020 have ushered in a new period in which the strong position of China is being contested by the United States, driven by its sense of a new Cold War and the need to attend to what is likely to be a new petro-power during the 2020s. The Dutch role is also likely to regain lost ground. President Santokhi visited the Netherlands in 2021, where he addressed the Dutch parliament which "is a rarely awarded diplomatic honor in the Netherlands and marks the restoration of good ties with Suriname" (NL Times 2021). Indeed, it can be argued that China's strong role in Suriname was already under considerable pressure prior to the 2020 elections. While U.S.-Suriname relations were cordial, the U.S. role in the Caribbean country was growing. This included support for student scholarships to U.S. universities and programs, governance training seminars, and other forms of outreach. Moreover, the United States, the Dutch, and other European countries were strong supporters of the Suriname court's decision on Bouterse's involvement in the December 1982 murders. The increasing engagement of U.S. and other Western oil companies in the country added an economic interest, especially considering that what was discovered offshore could be in the same volume range as in Guyana. The last factor was that the Trump administration saw China's role in Suriname through the perceptual lens of a new Cold War. This was reflected by Washington's strong support for the results of the 2020 vote to be recognized by the outgoing Bouterse government, which dragged the process out.

In the aftermath of the election, the United States was quick to signal support for the new government of President Chandrikapersad "Chan" Santokhi. The new leader was left with the unenviable task of stabilizing the country's finances, dealing with a default on debt payments, and revitalizing the economy in the middle of the Covid-19 pandemic (Boejoekoe 2021; MacDonald 2020). At the same time, U.S.–Chinese rivalry remained very much part of the foreign policy scene. This was evident during the visit of Mike Pompeo in September 2020 to Paramaribo. The visit, which included a meeting with President Santokhi, was noteworthy as it was the first time a U.S. Secretary of State set foot in Suriname and for the war of words it set in motion with China. While in Suriname, Pompeo asserted that the United States is "eager to be a partner" with Suriname. Moreover, he took a critical shot at China's involvement in Suriname (and for that matter the rest of the Caribbean and Latin America): "No state-owned operation can beat the quality of the products and services of American companies. We've watched the Chinese Communist Party invest in countries, and it all seems great at the front end and then it all comes falling down when the political costs connected to that become clear" (Al Jazeera 2020).

The Chinese embassy in Paramaribo (as well as its counterpart in Georgetown) quickly responded to the U.S. Secretary of State's comments. As China's local representative stated: "We advise Mr. Pompeo to respect facts and truth, abandon arrogance and prejudice, stop smearing and spreading rumors about China" (Youkee 2020). China was not pleased that Pompeo had also worked on making Suriname part of the Trump administration's new infrastructure development plan, the Growth in the Americas Initiative (This will be more thoroughly discussed in Chapter 9).

For China Suriname, no doubt represents a challenge. On the plus side when Suriname was dominated by Bouterse the Caribbean country represented a gain by China. It was a relatively straightforward deal; Bouterse had an autocratic personality, was friends with Cuba and Venezuela, and was willing to align his country with Beijing in global forums. He was also comfortable with allowing Chinese migration. Moreover, Suriname possessed commodities near and dear to China's economic needs. The downside risk for Beijing was that Suriname remained a democracy, retained segments of the political spectrum and society that still adhered to the rule of law, and the United States and the Netherlands still retained a degree of influence, which increased with the 2020 elections. That said, Suriname can hardly disengage from China. Nor has it. The Chinese narrative of being a good partner was reflected in a number of inter-government communications between the two states since the 2020 elections, such as the phone conversation between Chinese Foreign Minister Wang Yi and his Surinamese counterpart, Albert Ramdin in May 2021, the 45th anniversary of the diplomatic ties between the two countries. Wang expressed that China was ready to strengthen cooperation with Suriname to fight the Covid-19 pandemic and that the two countries should strengthen unity and cooperation in international affairs as well as safeguard multilateralism and the common interests of developing countries (Xinhua 2021a, b). For his part, Ramdin responded with what has become a well-used script by Caribbean countries by acknowledging China's achievements in economic and social development and emphasizing that the one-China principle will never be shaken as the cornerstone of Suriname-China relations. Suriname can hardly be regarded as a Chinese satellite, but Beijing retains influence, especially as long as the Caribbean country's debt crisis continues, the oil industry has yet to take off and uncertainty remains over the post-Covid-19 pandemic economic recovery.

CONCLUSION

China's engagement with the English-speaking Caribbean and Suriname has been consistent, partnership-oriented, and backed by financial largesse. For China, there has been a significant transformation in the geopolitical and economic landscape surrounding their engagement in the Caribbean. When the Chinese first arrived in the Caribbean they were new business partners, taking advantage of receding U.S. and European interests. Two decades into the twenty-first century they are now part of the geopolitical and economic landscape. China may not be fully dominant, but it has gained a voice in regional affairs, which is gradually becoming more assertive. With the exception of Guyana, the harder side of Chinese policy, the Wolf Warrior face, has not been used. That, however, does not mean that China will sit back when there are items on its diplomatic agenda that call for votes from its Caribbean partners. For Beijing the easy part of entering the Caribbean is over; now it has to live up to the image of being a good partner, something that may become more difficult

122   S. B. MACDONALD

in the post-Covid-19 pandemic period when the costs of economic revitalization and debt management become more challenging. Moreover, China is also likely to face greater competition for hearts and minds in the Caribbean as the United States and other Western countries refocus on the region increasingly through the lens of a new Cold War, something which has become more intensified with the Russo-Ukrainian War and the Biden administration's strong stance on offering U.S. support to defend Taiwan.

References

Al Jazeera. 2020. Pompeo Asks Suriname, Guyana to Favor US Business Over China, September 18. https://www.aljazeera.com/economy/2020/9/18/pompeo-asks-suriname-guyana-to-favour-us-business-over-china.
Balraadjsing, D. 2018. SuCHINAme. *Dagblad Suriname*, November 12. https://www.dbsuriname.com/2018/11/12/suchiname/.
Bernal, Richard. 2016. *Dragon in the Caribbean: China's Global Re-Dimensioning—Challenges and Opportunities for the Caribbean*. Kingston, Jamaica: Ian Randle Publishers.
Boejoekoe, Mavrick. 2021. Suriname, Post-Election Policies and Challenges for the New Government. *Global Americans*, February 2. https://theglobalamericans.org/2021/02/suriname-post-election-policies-and-challenges-for-the-new-government/.
Bourcier, Nicholas. 2015. China Finds an Eager South American Stablemate in Suriname. *The Guardian*, June 23. https://www.theguardian.com/world/2015/jun/23/suriname-china-business-influence.
Clarke, Nigel. 2019. Lessons from Jamaica for Small Countries with Big Debts. *Financial Times*, February 19. https://www.ft.com/content/04870fa8-2e12-11e9-80d2-7b637a9e1ba1.
Cohen, Muhammad. 2016. How China Rescued—Then Ruined—The Caribbean's Largest Resort Project. *Forbes*, December 14. https://www.forbes.com/sites/muhammadcohen/2016/12/14/how-china-rescued-then-ruined-the-caribbeans-largest-resort-project/#24baab553edb.
Collins, John. 2001. China's Whampoa Lts. Opens Port in Bahamas. *The Washington Times*, November 20. http://www.latinamericanstudies.org/caribbean/whampoa.htm.
Daily Express. 2021. NGC Signs Phoenix Park Deal with Chinese Firm. *Daily Express* (Trinidad and Tobago), February 23. https://trinidadexpress.com/business/local/ngc-signs-phoenix-park-deal-with-chinese-firm/article_c4447b64-7636-11eb-95a8-67e33e2d7298.html.

Economic Commission for Latin America and the Caribbean (ECLAC). 2019. *Foreign Direct Investment: Latin America and the Caribbean 2019*. https://repositorio.cepal.org/bitstream/handle/11362/44698/10/S1900447_en.pdf.

Economic Commission for Latin America and the Caribbean (ECLAC). 2021. *Foreign Direct Investment in Latin America and the Caribbean, 2021*, 24. https://repositorio.cepal.org/bitstream/handle/11362/47148/S2100318_en.pdf?sequence=4&isAllowed=y.

Ellis, Evan. 2019. China's Engagement with Trinidad and Tobago. *Global Americans*, March 26. https://theglobalamericans.org/2019/03/chinas-engagement-with-trinidad-and-tobago/.

Ellis, Evan. 2021. Chinese Engagement in Guyana: An Update. *Global Americans*, November 30. https://theglobalamericans.org/2021/11/china-guyana-update/.

Eyewitness News (The Bahamas). 2019. PM: Zero Pressure from U.S. to Alter China/Bahamas Relations. *Eyewitness News*, March 25. https://ewnews.com/pm-zero-pressure-from-u-s-to-alter-china-bahamas-relations.

Farah, Douglas. 2020. *The Maduro Regime's Illicit Activities: A Threat to Democracy and Security in Latin America*. Atlantic Council. https://www.atlanticcouncil.org/wp-content/uploads/2020/08/The-Maduro-Regime-Illicit-Activities-A-Threat-to-Democracy-in-Venezuela-and-Security-in-Latin-America-Final.pdf.

Government of Trinidad and Tobago. 2019. T&T and China Strengthen Cooperation. Government of the Republic of Trinidad and Tobago News got.tt, April. http://www.news.gov.tt/content/tt-and-china-strengthen-cooperation#.XzmHTehKjcs.

Griffin, Patrick. 2021. U.S. Must Do Better to Engage Bahamas. *Miami Herald*, January 7. https://www.miamiherald.com/opinion/op-ed/article248351090.html.

Guyana Chronicle. 2017. PM: Guyana Open to Chinese Investments. *Guyana Chronicle* (Georgetown), September 23. http://guyanachronicle.com/2017/09/23/pm-guyana-open-chinese-investments.

Inter-American Development Bank. 2021. Overview Suriname (Website). https://www.iadb.org/en/countries/suriname/overview.

International Monetary Fund. 2021. Direction of Trade Statistics (DOTS). International Monetary Fund. https://data.imf.org/?sk=9d6028d4-f14a-464c-a2f2-59b2cd424b85.

International Monetary Fund. 2022. Direction of Trade Statistics. https://data.imf.org/?sk=9D6028D4-F14A-464C-A2F2-59B2CD424B85&sId=1515619375491.

IMF. 2019. Jamaica: ON the Path to Higher Economic growth. *IMF*, November 7. https://www.imf.org/en/News/Articles/2019/11/07/NA110719-Jamaica-On-the-Path-to-Higher-Economic-Growth.

Kaieteur News (A). 2017. Major Chinese Project Stalled. *Kaieteur News*, November 12. https://www.kaieteurnewsonline.com/2017/11/12/major-chinese-project-stalled/.

Kaieteur News (A). 2018a. Chinese Bank Cannot Save BaiShanLin—Concessions Will Be Reallocated—GFC. *Kaieteur News*, February 21. https://www.kaieteurnewsonline.com/2018/02/21/chinese-bank-cannot-save-baishanlin-concessions-will-be-reallocated-gfc/.

Kaieteur News (B). 2018b. BaiShanLin Busted for Illegal Logging in Berbice River. *Kaieteur News*, February 18. https://www.kaieteurnewsonline.com/2018/02/18/baishanlin-busted-for-illegal-logging-in-berbice-river/.

Kaieteur News. 2021. Ten Years On...CJIA Expansion Project Still Milking Treasury. *Kaieteur News*, December 6. https://www.kaieteurnewsonline.com/2021/12/06/ten-years-on-cjia-expansion-project-still-milking-treasury/.

King, Danny. 2017. After Two Turbulent Years, Baha Mar Looks to Fulfill Potential. *Travel Weekly*, April 21. http://www.travelweekly.com/Travel-News/Hotel-News/After-two-turbulent-years-Baha-Mar-looks-to-fulfill-potential.

Leonard, Carey. 2017. Lost Opportunity: A Case of What Could Have Been. *Tribune 242*, May 2. http://www.tribune242.com/news/2017/may/01/lost-opportunity-case-what-could-have-been/.

MacDonald, Scott B. 2019. The Shifting Tides in Caribbean International Relations: Jamaica, China and the United States. *Global Americans*, December 19. https://theglobalamericans.org/2019/12/the-shifting-tides-in-caribbean-international-relations-jamaica-china-and-the-united-states/.

MacDonald, Scott B. 2020. Suriname's Changing of the Guard? *Global Americans*, June 17. https://theglobalamericans.org/2020/06/surinames-changing-of-the-guard/.

Maliksetian, Vanand. 2020. The Battle for Suriname's Oil Is About to Begin. *Oil Price.com*, January 13. https://oilprice.com/Energy/Energy-General/The-Battle-For-Surinames-Oil-Is-About-To-Begin.html.

McCartney, Paige. 2021. Bethel: Bahamas Won't Move on Global Corporate Tax Before Rest of the World. *The Nassau Guardian*, July 15. https://thenassauguardian.com/bethel-bahamas-wont-move-on-global-corporate-tax-before-rest-of-the-world/.

Minto, Jevon. 2019. Jamaica Issues Enforcement Orders Against Chinese Mining Giant. *Dialogo Chino*, April 19. https://dialogochino.net/en/extractive-industries/26051-jamaica-issues-enforcement-orders-against-chinese-mining-giant/.

Myklebust. 2020. Sweden—Confucius Institutions Close as China Relations Deteriorate. *University World News*, May 16. https://www.universityworld news.com/post.php?story=20200513092025679.

Myre, Greg. 2019. As Scrutiny of China Grows, Some U.S. Schools Drop a Language Program. *NPR*, July 17. https://www.npr.org/2019/07/17/741 239298/as-scrutiny-of-china-grows-some-u-s-schools-drop-a-language-pro gram.

Hartnell, Neil. 2015. Economic Sovereignty Fear Over PM's 'laser beamed' Focus on China. *The Tribune*, January 16.

NL Times. 2021. Surinamese President to Address Dutch Parliament. *NL Times*, August 3. https://nltimes.nl/2021/08/03/surinamese-president-add ress-dutch-parliament.

OilNow. 2019. US Ambassador Frowns on TT's Support for Maduro: Rowley Lashes Back. *OilNow*, January 26. https://oilnow.gy/featured/us-ambass ador-frowns-on-tts-support-for-maduro-rowley-lashes-back/.

Patterson, Orlando. 2019. *The confounding island: Jamaica and the postcolonial predicament*. Cambridge, MA: The Belknap Press of Harvard University Press.

People's Republic of China, Ministry of Foreign Affairs. Remarks by H.E. Huang Qinguo at the Reception Celebrating 2018 Chinese Spring Festival, February 2. Embassy of the People's Republic of China in the Commonwealth of the Bahamas. http://bs.china-embassy.org/eng/dszl/dsjh/t1533402.htm.

Persad-Bissessar, Kamla. 2020. Trinidad and Tobago Faces US Sanctions. *Caribbean News Global*, May 2. https://www.caribbeannewsglobal.com/tri nidad-and-tobago-faces-us-sanctions/.

Power, John. 2021. Confucius Institutes at Australian Universities Could Be the Next Casualty of Strained Beijing-Canberra Ties. *South China Morning Post*, May 28. https://www.scmp.com/week-asia/politics/article/3135021/ confucius-institutes-australian-universities-could-be-next.

Qi, Tian. 2019. Jointly Advance High-Quality Belt and Road Cooperation…A New Chapter of China-Jamaica Friendship. *Jamaica Gleaner*, November 13. https://jamaica-gleaner.com/article/commentary/20191113/tian-qi-joi ntly-advance-high-quality-belt-and-road-cooperation-new.

Reuters Staff. 2021. Guyana Nixes Taiwan Office After Beijing Criticizes 'Mistake'. *Reuters*, February 3. https://www.reuters.com/article/us-taiwan-guyana/guyana-nixes-taiwan-office-after-beijing-criticizes-mistake-idUSKB N2A404T.

Ruddy, Christopher, and Stephan Archer. 2000. Chinese Company Completes World's Largest Port in Bahamas. *Sightings*, January 20. http://www.rense. com/politics6/chinabahamas_p.htm.

Secdoc-Dahlberg, Betty. 1990. *The Dutch Caribbean: Prospects for Democracy*. Gordon and Breach.

Secdoc-Dahlberg, Betty. 2014. Chinafication of the Global South? The Case of Suriname. Working Paper, International Studies Association, p. 10. Buenos Aires, July 2014. http://web.isanet.org/Web/Conferences/FLACSO-ISA%20BuenosAires%202014/Archive/f17baf3c-1c51-4427-bf3b-a377e14ce4a2.pdf.

Serju, Christopher. 2017. Chinese Good for Jamaica—Holness. *The Gleaner*, August 11. http://jamaica-gleaner.com/article/news/20170811/chinese-good-jamaica-holness.

Simon. 2015. The Baha Mar Saga: The Major Players. *Bahama Pundit*, July 15. http://www.bahamapundit.com/2015/07/the-baha-mar-saga-the-major-players-.html.

Smith, Xian. 2017. Attorney: Govt Must 'Put Its Foot Down' with Hutchison Whampoa in GB. Company Hired by Hutchison Whampoa to Oversee Sale of Its Freeport Resorts. *The Nassau Guardian*, June 28. http://nassauguardian.cyberitas.com/bahamas-business/40-bahamas-business/74352-attorney-govt-must-put-its-foot-down-with-hutchison-whampoa-in-gb.

Stabroek News. 2018. Guyana and Huawei. *Stabroek News*, December 17. https://www.stabroeknews.com/2018/12/17/opinion/editorial/guyana-and-huawei/.

Stabroek News. 2019. Huawei Looking to Boost Trinidad & Tobago's ICT. *Stabroek News*, August 21. https://www.stabroeknews.com/2019/08/21/news/regional/trinidad/huawei-looking-to-boost-trinidad-tobagos-ict/.

The Gleaner. 2019. Editorial: Call in Donald Tapia. *The Gleaner*, November 13. https://jamaica-gleaner.com/article/commentary/20191113/editorial-call-donald-tapia.

Tobacco, Annechien. 2020. SuChiname. *Geografie.nl*, April 8. https://geografie.nl/artikel/suchiname.

U.S. Energy Information Administration. 2021. Natural Gas Explained: Natural Gas Imports and Exports. https://www.eia.gov/energyexplained/natural-gas/imports-and-exports.php.

Ward, Jared. 2020. China and Guyana: A Special Relationship in the Making. *Global Americans*, February 27. https://theglobalamericans.org/2020/02/china-and-guyana-a-special-relationship-years-in-the-making/.

Wilkinson, Bert. 2020. Bank Money Gone. *Caribbean Life*, February 13. https://www.caribbeanlifenews.com/bank-money-gone/.

Xinhua. 2021a. China Ready to Enhance Cooperation with Suriname: Chinese FM. *Xinhaunet*, May 8. http://www.xinhuanet.com/english/2021-05/09/c_139934448.htm.

Xinhua. 2021b. Xi Eyes Closer Partnership with Trinidad and Tobago. *Xinhuanet*, March 17. http://www.xinhuanet.com/english/2021-03/17/c_139815142.htm.

Youkee, Mat. 2020. US Makes Fresh Pitch to Latin America in Bid to Counter China's Influence. *The Guardian*, October 1. https://www.theguardian.com/world/2020/oct/01/us-latin-america-china-beijing.

Yuwei, Hu, and Juecheng Zhao. 2021. US Gift of 80 Vials of Vaccine Mocked in Trinidad and Tobago After Receiving Over 300k Chinese Shots. *Global Times*, June 15. https://www.globaltimes.cn/page/202106/1226145.shtml.

CHAPTER 5

Caribbean States and the New Landscape

This chapter examines the drift into a new Cold War from Caribbean perspectives, ranging from the nature of economic engagement to geopolitical considerations. It is advanced that the idea of a new Cold War is not readily accepted and certainly not wanted in the region. At the same time, as the experiences explored in the following pages demonstrate, policymakers, economists, and businesspeople are keenly aware that China has emerged as a significant actor. In this, the Caribbean message has been one that it has developed a partnership with China with 'its eyes wide open." While China's economic statecraft is a factor in shaping Caribbean sentiment, U.S. policy is another important factor. This was certainly the case with U.S. Covid-19 policy and how it was perceived in the Caribbean. At the same time, China has had its own image problems from a Caribbean perspective.

"We have always been very strong on one-China policy and I think they appreciate what Trinidad and Tobago has done." Prime Minister Kamla Persad-Bissessar of Trinidad and Tobago, 2013 (South China Morning Post 2013).

The decade ahead is likely to be one of the most challenging for the Caribbean due to the confluence of mega-trends that include climate change, the green economic revolution, the potential for new transnational diseases, and major geopolitical challenges from a number of directions. As stated in the previous chapter, what happens elsewhere in

S. B. MacDonald, *The New Cold War, China, and the Caribbean*, https://doi.org/10.1007/978-3-031-06149-3_5

the world, like in the South China Sea or Taiwan Straits, has a geopolitical echo in the Caribbean. The quote above clearly demonstrates that as it was the re-affirmation of Trinidad and Tobago's prime minister of her country's one-China policy during President Xi's 2013 visit.

This chapter examines how the Caribbean perceives the drift toward a new Cold War, with an emphasis on the views of Caribbean policymakers, academics, and business people through their writings and interviews. The view is hardly uniform, but the main threads running through the various commentaries are that a new Cold War is a risk; the region can make its own decisions about how it interfaces with the new global power (China); the United States is less of a factor than prior for a number of reasons; and that the United States does not focus on the Caribbean unless there is a crisis. There is also a sentiment that Caribbean countries do not wish to become overly dependent on China, switching one hegemonic power for another.

THE RETURN OF GEOPOLITICS AND THE CARIBBEAN

Most Caribbean leaders and policymakers are reluctant to embrace the idea of a new Cold War. Sir Ronald Sanders, Antigua and Barbuda's veteran ambassador to the United States and the Organization of American States, sums up the position of many Caribbean countries, "…Latin American and Caribbean countries, concerned about their economies and advancing the social and economic conditions of their people, do not subscribe to a rivalry between China and the U.S. in their region and hemisphere. They would all declare that there is ample room for economic and other forms of mutually beneficial cooperation between China and U.S." (Sanders 2021).

Both the United States and China offer something to the Caribbean, especially if they are at peace and support globalization. However, there is a concern that the era of globalization is over and that a new one marked by the return of geopolitics has begun. The preference is to avoid using the term "new Cold War". However, like it or not, the Caribbean faces a world in the midst of a major realignment and pressure to pick a side is likely to increase. And if the Caribbean does not necessarily seek out more aligned relations with the United States or China, those two countries are likely to take their own headcount as to who they can rely upon as partners and those whose loyalty is questionable. The Caribbean has a voice in this but must do more to coordinate its message to the great powers and make use of its numbers in defining and pursuing a "national" interest (no matter how broadly defined it is). Considering the Caribbean's track record of attempting to speak with one voice on policy matters, this is a daunting challenge even in English-speaking countries.

But the lacuna in the Caribbean–U.S. relations is not entirely because of Caribbean shortcomings. At the same time, there is considerable frustration with the United States; even if the Caribbean spoke with the weight of one voice, it is felt the United States often does not listen, a point made in Richard Bernal's *Corporate versus National Interest in US Trade Policy: Chiquita and Caribbean Bananas*, where it was repeatedly pointed out to the Clinton administration in the 1990s that the end of banana quotas preferential to Caribbean countries (namely Jamaica and the Eastern Caribbean) used by the European Union would be harmful to the region. The Clinton administration was pushed by Chiquita, then the major U.S. multinational banana company, which wanted greater access to European markets. Despite considerable concerns articulated by Caribbean leaders, the Clinton administration forced the issue at the World Trade Organization, which set in motion Europe's dismantling of its banana trade regime. The consequence was a decline in economic activity throughout the Eastern Caribbean, resulting in a challenging decades-long period for much of the region, as the island states underwent economic structural adjustment—causing popular resentment toward the United States to build—and become more susceptible to external forces like drug trafficking. These consequences were written off by U.S. policymakers as "collateral damage," but over the long run they opened the door to increasing Chinese influence in the Caribbean (Bernal 2020).

In discussions with former Caribbean diplomats, regional academics and business people, the following points emerge around the idea of a new Cold War. First, there has been a feeling that the Caribbean's traditional foreign policy partners, namely the United States, Canada, the United Kingdom, and Europe have generally neglected the region since the end of the Cold War with the exception of focusing on transnational crime. The sentiment is that U.S. treatment of the Caribbean went from being a place to vacation to a war zone with international crime lords. An editorial in the *Antigua Observer* stated in October 2018: "We went from being the playground to the hood. Our countries were labeled as drug pushers, money launderers, and all sorts of negativity were attached to anything we attempted to do to help develop our economies" (Antigua Observer 2018). The same editorial continued by saying, "Now, like a jealous lover, the United States seems uneasy with the fact that China has picked up where it has left off."

While Caribbean countries have found the U.S. and, for that matter, European interest in their region "fickle" (according to one regional academic), over the past twenty years China has maintained a strong interest and provided badly needed support. This message came out loud and clear in 2019 when the Prime Minister of Antigua and Barbuda, Gaston Browne, stated at the groundbreaking ceremony for China's new embassy compound, "...the People's Republic of China has shown far more interest [in Antigua and Barbuda], even more than other countries in this hemisphere with superior resources. They have shown greater interest in our development. It stands to reason that we must stand with the People's Republic of China" (Browne 2019). The prime minister further mentioned key areas of mutual interest: the Caribbean debt problem (to be made worse by the Covid-19 pandemic in 2020–2021); climate change; and reform of the UN.

Browne's sentiments are also evident in a response from Sir Ronald Sanders to U.S. Congressional concerns articulated in October 2021 over "the growing influence of the Chinese Communist Party in both Latin America and the Caribbean trade and economic development." As the ambassador responded: "The U.S. Congresspersons have come to this realization years after Caribbean representatives in Washington – me included – have been saying to successive U.S. Government and Congress that the U.S. has been absent as a meaningful contributor to Caribbean development for almost two decades" (Sanders 2021).

Second, there is a feeling in the Caribbean that its political stability and commitment to democratic governance are taken for granted (excepting Cuba and Haiti). The smooth and uneventful running of government amid challenges from climate change, more severe weather, and transnational pandemics is not given much thought—or at least that is how it often appears in the Caribbean to U.S., Canadian and European policymakers. It is easy for people in the Caribbean to point to the fact that President Obama was the last U.S. leader to visit the region, an indicator of the low level of importance Washington attaches to the region. President Trump did visit Puerto Rico in 2017 in the aftermath of Hurricane Maria, but that island is a territory of the United States and the visit was not a high point of his administration.

A third factor is that the United States is still generally seen in a positive light, but many in the Caribbean are sensitive to their northern neighbor's track record of being overly involved in their affairs, sometimes in an unwanted capacity. U.S. reasons for this are many, ranging from security and political/ideological reasons to economic dominance. In realist political circles in the United States, the Caribbean occupies an important strategic geography; in liberal political circles, the largely island states represent a like-minded community in their adherence to democracy (with few exceptions), market-orientation, and preference for multilateralism—even if those countries receive less attention than they feel they deserve as friends, allies, and neighbors.

The post-Cold War period was an unexpected break from the United States acting like a big brother in the region; instead many regarded U.S. policy more along the lines of "benign neglect." However, the Trump years brought an abrupt change, especially Washington's retreat from globalization and multilateralism. This was complicated by a reactivation of U.S. policy in the Caribbean, galvanized by China's larger profile in regional affairs. While the Bush and Obama years passed in a relatively quiet manner, the Trump years were marked by the steady application of pressure and the use of the U.S. Navy to show the flag. This situation was complicated by what was perceived as racism out of the Trump administration as well as concerns over the U.S. leader's autocratic leanings. Indeed, President Trump tended to evoke a strong response from the Caribbean, most of it negative in nature.

As the United States and other traditional partners reduced aid and their banks pulled out of the Caribbean due to de-risking, Chinese economic statecraft was welcome. This comes despite warnings of the Chinese debt trap and a growing awareness that China's national interests can cut across local interests. Moreover, Chinese engagement is not as threatening as it is in parts of Latin America, such as Brazil and Mexico, which have found their local manufacturing sectors under siege by floods of often cheaper-priced imports. This has set off a debate in Latin America about the potential threat from China coming in the form of "reprimarization" of their economies. Reprimarization is broadly defined as a condition under which "…the region sells petroleum, metals, and soy to China in return for industrial goods," which points back to concerns about Latin America becoming dependent on yet another industrial metropole, this time, China (Stallings 2020). In the Caribbean, U.S. warnings have been centered on the issue of having China assume control over the strategically key parts of a national economy—transport infrastructure, telecommunications, and public utilities.

There is some resentment from Caribbean policymakers that see U.S. criticism of taking aid from China as bad judgment. Caribbean policymakers believe that they can make their own decisions as to who they receive aid from. An example of the above came in October 2020 in Antigua and Barbuda, when there was U.S. criticism over Chinese involvement in the two-island country. Antigua and Barbuda is one of the more pro-Chinese nations in the region, has followed Beijing's lead in votes in some international forums, and is home to what has been described as "a sprawling 'Chinese colony' complete with factories, homes and holiday resorts across a pristine marine reserve" (Handy 2019). In 2014 the above-mentioned project was undertaken by Yida Zhang, a Chinese entrepreneur, for whom the project became locally know, and supported by the government of Prime Minister Gaston Browne. The entire project is expected to cost around $2 billion and take 10 years to complete (Joseph 2021).

The Yida project fits into Browne's vision of making his country into an "economic powerhouse" in the Caribbean (Browne 2014) and China has been happy to help: beyond the Yida project, Chinese assistance came in the form of $255 million in plans to rebuild St. John's Port. In 2015 the Antigua Port Authority signed a financing agreement with China Civil Engineering Construction Corporation (CCECC) to dredge the harbor. CCECC also worked on upgrading the airport and was active in the construction of the large new Chinese embassy in 2020.

China was also quick to provide assistance to Antigua and Barbuda in the aftermath of Hurricane Irma in 2017. The growing closeness between the two countries was again evident in 2018 with Antigua becoming the first country in the Eastern Caribbean to join the BRI. As the international environment changed and the United States became more focused on Chinese engagement throughout the region, the mantra from Washington was for Caribbean countries not to accept Chinese gifts. Washington grew even more concerned about the nature of Antiguan-Chinese relations when the twin island-state backed the new Hong Kong national security law in the UN.

Between local environmental criticism over the Yida project and U.S. concerns over Chinese economic statecraft, the Antiguan government in October 2020 responded. Information Minister Melford Nicholas stated:

China remains an important partner to the government and people of Antigua and Barbuda and there is a growing level of paranoia that is being stoked by people who ought to be more responsible and to try to give an impression that the sky is falling. We hosted the World Cup 2007 in the Caribbean of which Antigua was very much a part of the proceedings. That brand new stadium was a gift from the Chinese government and there are a legion of projects that have been granted to us and have been supportive of us from the government and people of China. We want people to be mindful and we can go back as far as the 1950s where the Chinese have played a role in the development of many aspects of the Caribbean. (Caribbean News 2020)

Antiguan national interest has been best served by moving closer to China and letting the relationship with the United States drift. For its part, the United States has maintained a degree of distance, especially in the physical sense as the closest embassy to conduct business between the two countries is in Barbados. In the meantime, China has constructed one of its largest compounds in the Caribbean in Antigua.

China's Economic Statecraft—A Sentiment Shaper

Considering the above sentiments, China's economic statecraft has had a major impact on how the Caribbean perceives China in being a credible economic alternative to the United States and Europe. In *China in the Caribbean's Economic Future*, the former governor of the Central Bank of Barbados and veteran economist DeLisle Worrell argue that China's role has been positive for the Caribbean. While Worrell acknowledges the importance of Chinese foreign direct investment, tourism, and trade, he highlights China's significance as a low-cost producer and a standard-bearer for globalization. As he noted: "The remarkable surge in Chinese economic productivity, especially since the turn of the century, has been of material benefit to every economy in the world trading system, and the Caribbean has shared in those benefits. The most substantial benefit to the Caribbean from the relationship with China has been via the purchase of more affordable products made in China or made with Chinese inputs" (Worrell 2020).

On a more granular basis, Worrell points to China's contribution to key Caribbean needs beyond everyday consumer goods, including products critical for the next wave of global development, involving the transition from fossil fuels to green alternatives. Among the new products are solar photovoltaic panels (PVs) for household use. Through the first two decades of the twenty-first century, the Chinese government put considerable resources (heavy subsidies) into developing PVs, drastically reducing prices (and putting most foreign companies out of business and reducing the scope of potential innovation) (Hart 2020). While U.S., European and Japanese companies have almost entirely folded under Chinese competition, Caribbean households and society generally have benefited. Noting that a solar panel module which carried a price of $3.50 at the turn of the century (U.S. Department of Energy, 2012), and was 23 cents in April 2019, Worrell stresses the following: "At today's prices, middle income households are able to afford home installation, and there has been a significant increase in the use of solar PV in private businesses and residences. Not only has this been of material benefit to the companies and households concerned, it has also made a contribution to energy interdependence and the green economy" (Worrell 2020).

Worrell makes two other points in favor of China:

1. China is a world leader on the cleaning up of the environment as it is a leading user of renewable sources of energy, a leader in establishing eco-friendly high-speed rail systems, and is a leader in electric vehicles. (He does not mention that China is also one of the world's major polluters, being the largest user of coal, the second largest user of oil, and second largest user of natural gas) (BP 2021).

2. China is a firm believer in globalization and a supporter of key multilateral organizations like the World Trade Organization, World Health Organization, the International Monetary Fund, and World Bank. In the Americas, it is also a member of the Caribbean Development Bank (which the United States is not) and the Inter-American Development Bank.

The punchline in Worrell's essay is that while the West moves into isolation, China remains a beacon of globalization. Never mind that one reason for the shift away from globalization in the West is partially due to China's mercantilism; the Chinese government has worked hard to vocalize its support for key elements of a globalized world economy, at a time when the United States veered sharply into protectionism and isolationism under Trump, which continued (at least in trade policy) under the Biden administration.

Worrell urges the Caribbean to undertake a number of strategies, such as the adoption of a regional program for sea and air transportation; for the development of large international ports and airports throughout the region (to break up the dependence on Miami for Caribbean travel); the putting into place of strategies for a switch to renewable sources of energy; and the development of a digital currency to establish a monetary and economic bloc. As he concludes: "...the greatest benefit to the Caribbean comes from the worldwide diffusion of gains from Chinese productivity, gains which are under threat from the surge in Western sentiment against globalization. The stronger and more persistent the anti-globalization tide, the more the benefits of the Chinese connection are attenuated. However, Caribbean strategies for transportation upgrades and investment, renewable energy adoption, use of digital currencies and universal use of the US dollar offer promise of reaping benefits for the Caribbean from the China connection in the medium term, even in the face of Western isolationism" (Worrell 2020).

If one were to extrapolate from Worrell's report, the United States has moved into isolation, while China has emerged as the new champion of globalization. Along these lines, the Chinese model of development is highly successful and it has benefited the rest of the world, the Caribbean included. Although this may be an overstatement, the United States is the spoiler of a global economy influenced increasingly by China that is bringing goodies to Caribbean countries and making a cleaner and more affordable future for countries like Barbados, the Dominican Republic, Jamaica, and Trinidad and Tobago.

Worrell is not alone in the view that China offers significant benefits to the Caribbean. A paper written by University of the West Indies law students through TradeLab law clinics in 2020 was given considerable attention. Titled *A Proposal for a Comprehensive Economic and Trade Agreement between CARICOM and China*, the report sought to carve a position for CARICOM which would create a more level of playing field for both economies. One concern for CARICOM, mentioned early in the report, has been the decrease in the region's trade performance, "...a large part of this decrease is due to CARICOM States' dependence on their long-standing trading relationships with Europe and the United States of America (USA)" (Baksh et al. 2020).

Looking from the Caribbean, the logical solution is to increase trade with China. The report clearly recognizes that the trade relationship between China and CARICOM is lopsided in the direction of the Asian economy, but a trade agreement could address many of the concerns of Caribbean countries. As the report observed: "...it cannot be ignored that development and economic sustainability is only achievable between CARICOM and China provided there is a reformulation of the dynamics of the trade and economic relationship. This can be achieved through a formalized agreement whose provisions would set out the dynamic of the trade and economic relationship, ideally giving CARICOM some advantage since it is outmatched by China's global dominance" (Baksh et al. 2020). These concerns include the build-up of unsustainable levels of debt, the environmental challenges, and the risk of causing a disruption in relations with the United States. Ultimately Baksh, et al. regard China as an opportunity, but with the necessary bells and whistles to make any trade deal more equitable.

For many Caribbean policymakers, China, if managed properly, can help their region find a path to sustainable growth and greater socioeconomic equity. Simply stated, China's importance cannot be ignored. Indeed, as Ambassador Bernal wrote in 2014: "The formulation and execution of the foreign policies of the Caribbean will have to be diversified and re-balanced to accord greater significance to Asia, in particular China and India" (Bernal 2016). China's attractiveness is enhanced by its willingness to pursue Caribbean nations with visits by top leadership as well as providing opportunities for Caribbean leaders to be given official welcomes in Beijing. Equally important, China also sends business and cultural delegations to the Caribbean. Moreover, the Chinese have been persistent with a longer term goal of creating a pro-Chinese cadre of local leaders and opinion-makers through paid for trips and scholarships to China. For many Caribbean government officials, members of the press, and academics this approach is educational and fosters a positive image of China.

TRIGGERS TO THE GEOPOLITICAL DEBATE

Considering that considerable attention has already been paid to China's relationship with the Caribbean through its use of economic statecraft. The region generally has not had any major incidents with the Asian power as have occurred in Africa or Asia. However, three developments are worth examining from a little deeper perspective of the Caribbean actors: the Covid-19 pandemic, the 2020 UN vote on China's national security law for Hong Kong, and China's prompt, intimidating behavior with Guyana over its intention to let Taiwan open a trade office in Georgetown in 2021. While the key threads in Chinese–Caribbean relations are economic, the China relationship raises questions over support for democracy, the importance of good governance, and dealing with social inequalities.

Covid-19 Diplomacy

The 2020–2022 Covid-19 pandemic began in China and spread around the world, eventually bringing the global economy to a halt. In the Caribbean, this was felt through the shutdown of international travel, which hurt economies based on tourism and exports of commodities. The initial reaction to China as a point of origin was negative, but the Chinese government's strong propaganda and misinformation effort helped counter the story of China's culpability. Indeed, the Chinese government has worked through its state-owned media organizations to discredit the story of China as a point of origin, calling it "immoral, irresponsible and reprehensible" (Cao Siqi 2021). At the same time, China embarked upon what is referred to as "vaccine diplomacy," which according to Peter Hotez "refers to almost any aspect of global health diplomacy that relies on the use or delivery of vaccines and encompasses the important work of the GAVI Alliance, as well as elements of the WHO, the Gates Foundation, and other important international organizations" (Hotez 2014).

Considering that the Trump administration made the fateful decision to provide masks and other medical equipment and then vaccines for U.S. citizens first, a number of Caribbean governments opted to use Russian (Sputnik V) and Chinese alternatives (Sinopharm and Sinovac). Cuban vaccines were also available. The perceived insensitivity of the Trump administration was a psychological blow to many Caribbean governments, which had long looked to the United States as a critical backup in times of emergency. While actively seeking to discourage the origin story, China was quick to bring badly-medical equipment to a number of countries, such as the Dominican Republic and Suriname, while the Trump administration effectively shut down the shipment of U.S. medical equipment for a period.

China played its game of Covid-19 vaccine diplomacy well in the Caribbean. Beijing was quick to take command of the messaging and response to negative commentaries, a development no doubt helped by its extensive network of embassies throughout the Eastern Caribbean. The message was that China's superior political and economic system was more geared to respond to the crisis than those of the democratic and chaotic West, a narrative backed by the export of its vaccines around the world. Although not as good as Western versions, Chinese and Russian vaccines stepped into a gap. If there was ever to be a new Cold War geopolitical arena, vaccine diplomacy defined it. Indeed, Ivelaw Griffith noted "...less than six months into the pandemic, Russia gave pandemic aid to 46 countries around the world, including the United States. Within the same time frame, China had offered Latin American and Caribbean countries US$ 1 billion in loans to enable them to battle the pandemic. Moreover, China, and India have been offering bilateral aid to several countries in the region" (Griffith 2021).

Among those opting to use these was the government of Antigua and Barbuda, which accepted Sinopharm vaccines in 2021. China made the vaccines a gift, while Venezuela helped transport them from Beijing to Antigua and Barbuda. In June 2021, 20,000 doses of Sinopharm arrived, which were quickly used. With an eye to the advanced economy countries, the Minister of Health Sir Molwyn Joseph stated: "Holding of vaccines is a crime. Why hold vaccines when generosity and solidarity could make them available to people who badly need them? So, in this context, I want to publicly state my appreciation for two governments who understand the meaning of solidarity." His sentiments were echoed by Prime Minister Browne who added that "during a time of need, they are always there to help" (Knight 2021). His reference was China, not the United States or Europe. Dominica was using Sinopharm since March 2021 and that country's Prime Minister, Roosevelt Skerrit, made certain to publicly praise China as "a reliable and sincere partner" of his country (*St. Kitts and Nevis Observer* 2021).

The appreciation for China's vaccine efforts was evident in the Dominican Republic as well. The first round of Chinese medical assistance came in the form of face masks, personal protective equipment for medical personnel, and 10,000 Covid-19 tests. The second round of Chinese medical help came when the government of President Abinader had difficulty in obtaining 400,000 doses of AstraZeneca in early 2021, providing an opportunity for Sinovac to expedite shipment of its vaccines to the island-republic (Ellis 2021). The Chinese company sold the Dominican government one million doses at the cost of $19 million, while China donated an additional 50,000 doses.

The impact of prompt Chinese vaccine diplomacy was significant. As Evan Ellis observed: "In the eyes of many Dominicans, the symbolism of the Chinese vaccine sale was powerful, given President Abinader's declaration that Chinese companies would not be permitted to operate in certain strategic sectors" (Ellis 2021). The Caribbean perception of China as a good partner was evident in comments between Presidents Abinader and Xi, on their first telephone conversation in June 2021 on the anniversary of the Chinese Communist Party's 100th anniversary, in which the Dominican leader stated: "The medical supplies and vaccines provided by China for the Dominican Republic have played a key role in its fight against the virus, for which the Dominican republic expresses sincere gratitude. The Dominican Republic sticks to the one-China policy, and wishes to expand exchanges and cooperation in fields such as economy and trade with China" (Guzmán 2021 and Ministry of Foreign Affairs of the PRC 2021).

From a Caribbean perspective, despite the fact that China was where the pandemic started, the Asian country was quick to step up and send help. The disappointing development was that the United States was slow in reacting and made a point to serve its population first and freeze out Caribbean requests for assistance. Although the Chinese vaccines were less effective than their Western counterparts, they were available. In a world where a pandemic has disrupted travel and commerce as well as killed thousands, a vaccine in the hand is better than none being promised at some time in the future. U.S. assistance eventually came, but was slow in coming, leaving the moral high ground to China and Russia.

Another dimension of the new Cold War in regard to vaccine diplomacy is related to Cuba. While the Cuban economy has many weak points, its biotechnology sector has been a strong point (including being a focus of cooperation with China). During the pandemic Cuba deployed 56 teams to more than 40 countries, bringing medical personnel and equipment and eventually vaccines to a wide range of other Caribbean countries, including Antigua and Barbuda, Barbados, Belize, Dominica, Grenada, Haiti, Jamaica, St. Kitts-Nevis, St. Vincent and the Grenadines, St. Lucia, Suriname, and Trinidad and Tobago (Griffith 2021). Although the extension of Cuban medical aid (which was often paid for in cash) was appreciated in the region, it became a point of irritation within Cuba once the pandemic went into a bad stage.

International Democracy

The issue of the state of international democracy is one that touches the Caribbean. Most nations in the region have democratic forms of government, broadly defined as the holding of regular elections, the peaceful transfer of power, relative freedom of the press, and some degree of accountability of elected officials to their constituencies. Although there is often quibbling as to the extent of just how democratic each Caribbean country is, most people in the region take some pride in local democracy. Support for democracy becomes a more challenging point of debate when the role of Caribbean democracies is discussed vis-à-vis other countries. This issue came up in CARICOM's policy toward Venezuela at the Organization of American States and at the United Nations.

For much of the Caribbean, national sovereignty has been a sensitive issue. Most Caribbean states have followed foreign policies that underscore a belief in noninterference in a country's internal affairs. There is also a degree of realpolitik in this, Venezuela being a case in point. A number of Caribbean countries, such as Trinidad and Tobago and Suriname, have sought to maintain cordial relations with their larger neighbor. This comes despite steady erosion of democracy in Venezuela, a largely self-induced economic crisis of epic proportions, and the emergence of one of the world's worst refugee crises with over six million Venezuelans fleeing their country. While the idea of noninterference is upheld, there is a degree of realpolitik; it is not in the smaller Caribbean countries' national interest to upend relations with Venezuela. This has left a number of Caribbean countries that closely adhere to this policy at odds with most countries at the Organization of American States, an ongoing point of friction between the region and a number of its larger Latin American neighbors.

Not everyone in the Caribbean agrees with the hands-off approach over Venezuela. Indeed, many Venezuelans find the noninterference argument preached by the many of the English-speaking Caribbean states frustrating. As Moises Naím, a former Venezuelan minister of trade and industry and Distinguished Fellow at the Carnegie Endowment for International Peace in Washington, DC stated: "It is one of the world's great diplomatic clichés that the problems of a country are for that country's citizens alone to solve. For Venezuela, penetrated to the marrow by Cuban communism and propped up by this disparate coalition of autocracies, such ritual exhortations are a cop-out – a call to leave Venezuela to the Cubans" (Naim 2021).

While the drama over Venezuela has made headlines, less visible in all of this has been the drama at the UN. The 44th session of the United Nations Human Rights Council in 2020 brought forward the issue of democracy on the international stage, with Caribbean countries coming down on both sides of the issue. In June 2020, Beijing enacted new legislation without input from the government of Hong Kong or the city's population. The 66 article law seeks to safeguard national security (in this case from democratic protests) and "prevent, suppress, and impose punishment" for acts deemed to be secessionist, subversive, terrorist in nature or for collusion with foreign country or "external elements" (Albert 2020). The main thrust of the new law is to provide Beijing the legal means (as Chinese law is taking over Hong Kong law) to crush democratic protests and more tightly weave the city into mainland control.

The Hong Kong security bill became a target by democratic governments at the UN Human Rights Council in 2020. For China, such a vote could not be lost; such a counter-narrative could not be allowed to gain ascendency in any international forum. China position was defended by Cuba, whose authoritarian government is a clear ally. At the same time, the Chinese government worked hard to corral its friends to vote in favor of the Hong Kong security bill as an internal affair not open to outside sanction. Among the 53 countries voting in favor of the Chinese government position were Antigua and Barbuda, Dominica, and Suriname, putting these parliamentary democracies in the same ranks as authoritarian regimes such as Cuba, Eritrea, Guinea, Iran, Laos, Myanmar, Nicaragua, North Korea, Saudi Arabia, Syria, and Venezuela. Those who condemned the draconian security law included most of Europe, Canada, and the United Kingdom, and, from the Caribbean, Belize.

The Diplomat's Eleanor Albert made the following observation in regard to the Hong Kong security vote at the UN: "While many global governance institutions are conceptualized as a forum for countries to consult on shared or transnational issues, some have opined that the UN system, built on the principle of sovereign equality, has become a site for competing nations of international order and norms. While contestation has been previously been less public and taken place at different levels below the international level, China's rising power and greater involvement in the UN may well have altered the vehicles through which diplomatic differences are aired" (Albert 2020). At the UN, China's rising power has clout and its economic statecraft in countries like Antigua and Barbuda and Dominica paid a solid dividend, despite the dubious company in which it put those two Caribbean states.

The vote over Hong Kong's national security law brought out a debate over China's and the West's values and how the Caribbean responds. For some U.S. and European observers (as well as some of those in Latin America), Caribbean support for China in international forums was appalling, seemingly putting a number of Caribbean countries on the same side as authoritarian regimes busy violating human rights. In this, it appears that part of the Caribbean response is to equalize the behavior of the United States and China, which minimizes or undermines the common Western democratic values which the Caribbean and the United States have, but which China does not. Although this may not be the message meant to be emitted from the Caribbean, it is what often gets communicated to the United States. The response is that Americans are hard-pressed to see why any Caribbean government would find any common values in China's authoritarian and mercantilist system.

At the same time, the calling out of Caribbean democracies by the United States over China's national security law is seen in the region as hypocritical: the North American country has trade and investment relations with many countries, including a number deemed authoritarian, including China and Vietnam. In other cases, as with Saudi Arabia and Egypt, two distinctly non-democratic states, there have long been close working relationships.

The United States also has its defenders in terms of the discussion over international democracy. As one Guyanese voice asserted: "While it's questionable that the United States may have a double standard and should not lecture other nations on democracy and human rights, yet it was the United States, Canada, the UK and the EU that saved democracy when the People's National Congress (PNC), from March to July 2020, violently and brazenly tried to steal the 2020 election. It was also the U.S. government involvement in the restoration of democracy in Guyana in 1992 that was brokered by President Jimmy Carter" (Chickrie 2021). The same person asserted: "Guyana should not become dependent on autocratic nations, like China, India, Russia or Saudi Arabia because these countries will remain silent when democracy and human rights are trampled upon in Guyana and elsewhere." Indeed, China and Russia both had little to say in making certain that a democratic transition occurred in Guyana in 2020.

Taiwan, China, Guyana, and Being Bullied

Caribbean countries have had the room diplomatically to play to their national interests while not disrupting their relationships with either the United States or China. Simply stated, it is in the national interests of various Caribbean countries to take the benefits offered by China and the United States to create a competition between the two great powers from which the smaller states can extract economic goodies. The risk is that if this game is played too hard, either China or the United States could exercise their leverage, in trade, investment, or assistance. As already demonstrated Guyana found itself in an awkward position with opening a Taiwanese trade office in 2021.

For those looking for the risk posed by the growing power of China in the Caribbean, Guyana's slap down clearly indicated that the Asian power has a hard side when its interests are challenged. China can be a bully. In the Caribbean China had long shown its sunny face; with Guyana, it showed its wolf warrior side. China saw its national interests challenged and acted accordingly demonstrating that not all sovereign states are equal. China got its way because it was a much more powerful international actor than Guyana. The United States, which was thought to be possibly behind the effort to give Taiwan a diplomatic victory, did not feel it was worth escalating matters with China over the issue.

Will China resort to more Wolf Warrior antics in the Caribbean? China's stance in the Caribbean as a good partner, a geopolitical construct upheld by economic statecraft, is likely to remain intact through the rest of the decade, but that is contingent on developments elsewhere. Most Caribbean commenters give the impression that as long as China does not impinge too much on their own political domains, they can live with China's more aggressive side, be it pushing maritime claims against Japan, asserting its sovereignty against Vietnam, the Philippines, Malaysia, Indonesia, and Singapore in the South China Sea or further suppression of democratic governance in Hong Kong. One is left wondering how Caribbean states would respond to a Chinese invasion of Taiwan, a functioning democracy.

The Chinese in the Caribbean:
Negative Perceptions

While national security concerns are often mentioned in regard to Chinese businesses and lending, there is another aspect to the role of China in the Caribbean, the role of the local Chinese populations. The largest populations are concentrated in Jamaica, the Dominican Republic, Cuba, French Guiana, Belize, Suriname, Trinidad and Tobago, and Guyana. Hard data on actual numbers is difficult to obtain, but there has been a movement of non-state enterprise-related Chinese finding the Caribbean an agreeable place to settle. The Chinese are now thought to make up a 10th of Suriname's total population, though that number is questionable.

While broad aspects of China's economic statecraft have been appreciated by much of the Caribbean, frictions have emerged where the Chinese have moved into small-scale trading and commerce. Ambassador Bernal notes: "Locals view them an unwelcome competition and indeed, in some circumstances, as unfair competition. In Latin America, 80% of the negative comments about Chinese business relate to unfair, illegal, immoral and abusive practices" (Bernal 2021: 199). To this, Ambassador Bernal adds: "Trade unions and contractors in Barbados, architects in Trinidad and Tobago, and engineers have complained about the employment of Chinese workers on projects being executed by Chinese firms" (Bernal 2021: 199). Other complaints have included the use of official diplomatic mail to bring in goods into Guyana, which were then sold to the locals; that some parts of Caribbean towns have seen their shopping streets converted into "mini-Beijings"; and that the newer Chinese are cliquish and do not seek to integrate and have their own radio stations and schools (Kaieteur News 2017).

Another negative perception of the Chinese in the Caribbean relates to the environment. In this, the Chinese are said to be involved in the hunting of jaguars in Suriname for Chinese medicine, polluting around bauxite operations in Jamaica (which has been a cause of tension with the local population), and conducting illegal timber operations in Suriname (Stabroek News 2020). In the case of Suriname, it has been alleged that Chinese criminal cartels illegally harvest timber, which is moved through a supply chain that includes local customs officials, which by implication have been regarded as corrupted by the Chinese cartels (Holm 2021).

Although this should not be overstated, there is a divide between official perceptions of China and actual Chinese interaction with local populations. Chinese economic statecraft has brought about an official approach to China as a good partner. At the same time, not every person in the Caribbean has a positive view of or experience with the newcomers. The Chinese have their own way of how they want things done, which at times steps on local sensitivities. Indeed, it can be argued that the Chinese have acted as later versions of aggressive North Americans and Europeans. Having China as a power in the Caribbean leaves many in the region requiring patience and pragmatism in dealing with the many issues the new situation represents. The situation also places an onus on Caribbean governments to manage the interchange with the Chinese so that they do not become "bought" by Asian companies and banks and ethnic tensions do not become an issue.

CONCLUSION

In the words of one former ambassador from Barbados, Peter Laurie: "CARICOM countries have an enduring partnership with the United States, based on shared values, etc., but we insist that we too will develop economic relations with whom we like without being accused of betraying our deep and longstanding friendship with the United States. We may be small and insignificant in the wider geopolitical scheme of things, but we will not be bullied." In this context, the Caribbean voice on the new Cold War is summarized in the following points. First and foremost, Caribbean countries want their national sovereignty respected. They do not want to be part of one bloc or another, but are left to deal with both sides as they see fit even if it means siding with the country regarded as more beneficial to the particular country's national interests. That pertains to China as well as the United States and Europe.

The second element of the Caribbean voice is that the region is aware that if China's entry into their affairs is not well managed there are major risks. These include rising and ultimately unsustainable debt levels, the potential loss of economic autonomy, corruption, and environmental damage. China prefers to let countries manage their relationship with their companies and banks, but the local governments need to demonstrate an awareness that loss of control has a considerable downside.

The third element of the Caribbean voice is that globalization has been generally positive for the Caribbean. This is not to say that everything has benefited the region, but that generally being open economies, historically tied to such sectors as tourism and mining, and energy, the now broadening of trade and investment relationships has helped create new partners. It is generally recognized that a new Cold War is bad for business. If the new Cold War follows a similar path to the last, Caribbean countries could find themselves under pressure to align. Not coming down on the Chinese side risks not being able to take advantage of the future bonanza of multitudes of Chinese tourists. Trinidadian, Guyanese, or Jamaican goods could be forced to sit offshore a Chinese port as Beijing opts to play a regulatory card to punish one of those countries for not voting in its favor or challenging it on issues like human rights. The Chinese government has already demonstrated a willingness to use such tools to hurt other countries, something it did to Australia over that country questioning the origins of Covid-19, the role of Chinese propaganda and misinformation inside its borders, and human rights violations. The Caribbean faces some major challenges ahead, one of which is to figure out what the dominant Caribbean voice is going to be vis-à-vis China and the United States. The risk for China is that growing familiarity and hard questions over its global mission could take some of the shine off the good partner sentiment it is earned. As the Caribbean looks to the United States it generally sees a major partner falling short of what it could be doing. Obviously, there are differences in how each Caribbean country looks upon the potential for a new Cold War, but one point of agreement is that no one wants one to emerge.

References

Albert, Eleanor. 2020. Which Countries Support the New Hong Kong National Security Law? *The Diplomat*, July 6. https://thediplomat.com/2020/07/which-countries-support-the-new-hong-kong-national-security-law/.

Antigua Observer, 2018. Editorial: Say It Like It Is. *Antigua Observer*, October 24. https://antiguaobserver.com/editorial-say-it-like-it-is/.

Baksh, Sarah, Mikayla Darbasie, Shannon Potter, and Carissa Rodulfo, 2020. A Proposal for a Comprehensive Economic and Trade Agreement between CARICOM and China, Shridath Ramphal Centre, University of the West Indies and TradeLab, July 1. https://www.tradelab.org/single-post/2020/07/01/a-proposal-for-a-comprehensive-economic-and-trade-agreement-bet ween-caricom-and-china.

Bernal, Richard L. 2016. *Dragon in the Caribbean: China's Global Re-Dimensioning Challenges and Opportunities for the CaribbeanLin Randle Publishers.*

Bernal, Richard. 2020. *Corporate versus National Interest in U.S. Trade Policy: Chiquita and Caribbean Bananas*. New York: Palgrave Macmillan.

Bernal, Richard. 2021. China's Increasing Role in Central America and the Caribbean. In *Handbook of Caribbean Economies*, ed. Robert E. Looney, 193–203. New York: Routledge.

BP. 2021. Statistical Review of World Energy 2021. https://www.bp.com/content/dam/bp/business-sites/en/global/corporate/pdfs/energy-economics/statistical-review/bp-stats-review-2021-full-report.pdf.

Browne, Gaston. 2014. Inaugural Address by the Honorable Gaston Browne, Prime Minister of Antigua and Barbuda, June 18. St. John's, Antigua. http://www.caribbeanelections.com/eDocs/articles/ag/Gaston%20Browne%20Inaugural%20Address%202014.pdf.

Browne, Gaston. 2019. PM Speech at China Embassy Groundbreaking Ceremony, January 19, 2019. https://www.facebook.com/abstvradio/videos/406098033269538/?video_source=permalink.

Chickrie, Ray. 2021. Guyana Should Not Be Dependent on Autocratic Nations. *Caribbean News Global Media*, June 15. https://www.caribbeannewsglobal.com/guyana-should-not-be-dependent-on-autocratic-nations/.

Cao Siqi. 2021. Referring to the Global Times Exclusive, FM Spokesperson Condemns US Coercing China's Neighbors With Vaccines to Join Virus Origins Smear Camapign as 'Immoral, Irresonsible'. Global Times, August 19. https://www.globaltimes.cn/page/202108/1231970.shtml.

Ellis, Evan. 2021. Chinese Engagement in the Dominican Republic: An Update. *Global Americans*, May 7. https://theglobalamericans.org/2021/05/chinese-engagement-in-the-dominican-republic-an-update/.

Griffith, Ivelaw Lloyd. 2021. Caribbean Geopolitics in the Age of COVID-19. Lead Paper Prepared for the FIU LACC-Caribbean Policy Consortium Webinar on Geopolitical Competition and Cooperation in the Caribbean in the Age of COVID-19, May 13. https://lacc.fiu.edu/research/publications/lacc-caribbean-working-paper-series/griffith_health-geopolitics-in-contemporary-caribbean_wps2-2021.pdf.

Guzmán, Sandra. 2021. Detalles de la conversación entre Luis Abinader y el president chino Xi Jinping. *Diario Libre*, June 2. https://www.diariolibre.com/actualidad/politica/detalles-de-la-conversacion-entre-luis-abinader-y-el-presidente-chino-xi-jinping-FH26654771. Accessed 12 Oct 2021.

Handy, Gemma. 2019. Antigua: Sprawling 'Chinese Colony' Plan across Marine Reserve Ignites Opposition. *The Guardian*, June 20. https://www.theguardian.com/world/2019/jun/20/antigua-yida-project-chinese-colony-controversy.

Hart, David M. 2020. The Impact of China's Production Surge on Innovation in the Global Solar Photovoltaics Industry. Information Technology & Innovation Foundation, October 5, 2020. https://itif.org/publications/2020/10/05/impact-chinas-production-surge-innovation-global-solar-photovoltaics.

Holm, Carl. 2021. China's Illegal Timber Business Is Stripping Suriname's Forests. *Asian News International*, May 22: https://www.aninews.in/news/world/others/chinas-illegal-timber-business-is-stripping-surinames-forests20210522154932/. Originally from a story in the German government-owned DW News Agency.

Hotez, Peter. 2014. Vaccine Diplomacy: Historical Perspectives and Future Directions. *PLoS Neglected Tropical Diseases* 8, June. https://go.gale.com/ps/i.do?id=GALE%7CA383176597&sid=googleScholar&v=2.1&it=r&linkaccess=abs&issn=19352727&p=AONE&sw=w&userGroupName=nysl_oweb&isGeoAuthType=true.

Joseph, Kadeem. 2021. Govt Urges Yida to Start Golf Course Project. *Antigua Observer*, March 5. https://antiguaobserver.com/govt-urges-yida-to-start-golf-course-project/.

Kaieteur News. 2017. Chinese Embassy Container Imports Attract GRA's Attention. *Kaieteur News,* February 23, 2017 https://www.kaieteurnewsonline.com/2017/02/23/chinese-embassy-container-imports-attract-gras-attention/.

Knight, Carlena. 2021. Country Receives 20K Does of Chinese Sinopharm Vaccine. *Antigua Observer*, June 30, 2021. https://antiguaobserver.com/country-receives-20k-doses-of-chinese-sinopharm-vaccine/.

Ministry of Foreign Affairs of the People's Republic of China. 2021. Xi Jinping Speaks with Dominican Republic's President Luis Abinader. Ministry of Foreign Affairs of the People's Republic of China, June 3. https://www.fmprc.gov.cn/mfa_eng/zxxx_662805/t1881143.shtml.

Moises Naim. 2021. "Venezuela's Fatal Embrace of Cuba". *The Wall Street Jounral*, December 10. https://www.moisesnaim.com/my-columns/2021/12/10/venezuelas-fatal-embrace-of-cuba.

Sanders, Sir Ronald. 2021. For the Caribbean, Relations with the US and China Is Not One or the Other. *The St. Kitts Observer*, October 15. https://www.thestkittsnevisobserver.com/for-the-caribbean-relations-with-the-us-and-china-is-not-one-or-the-other/.

Sheri-Kae McLeod. 2020. Antigua and Barbuda Defends Relationship with China. *Caribbean National Weekly*, October 5. https://www.caribbeannationalweekly.com/caribbean-breaking-news-featured/antigua-and-barbuda-defends-relationship-with-china/.

South China Morning Post. 2013. Xi Jinping Arrives in Trinidad to Boost Caribbean Trade with China. *South China Morning Post* (Hong Kong), hea5 CARIBBEAN STATES AND THE NEW LANDSCAPE 151

June 13. https://www.scmp.com/news/china/article/1251310/xi-jinping-arrives-trinidad-boost-caribbean-trade-china.

St. Kitts and Nevis Observer. 2021. Dominica Gets China COVID Vaccine Shipment. *St. Kitts & Nevis Observer*, March 5. https://www.thestkittsnevisobserver.com/dominica-gets-china-covid-vaccine-shipment/.

Stabroek News. 2020. Suriname's Jaguar Trade: From Poaching to Paste. *Stabroeak News*, October 5. https://www.stabroeknews.com/2020/10/05/news/guyana/surinames-jaguar-trade-from-poaching-to-paste/.

Stallings, Barbara. 2020. *Dependency in the Twenty-First Century?: The Political Economy of China-Latin American Relations*. Cambridge University Press.

Worrell, DeLisle. 2020. China in the Caribbean's Economic Future. Working Paper, August 2020. Barbados. https://papers.ssrn.com/sol3/papers.cfm?abstract_id=3668058.

CHAPTER 6

The China–Taiwan Duel: Caribbean Echoes

One of the major reasons for China to be active in the Caribbean is to reduce the number of countries that still provide diplomatic recognition to Taiwan. While this falls under the rubric of domestic Chinese politics in Beijing (as Taiwan is a breakaway province), it has become a pressing issue in the slide toward a new Cold War. For Taiwan, the Caribbean, which holds a number of its remaining diplomatic official relations, is a critical geopolitical arena. This easily assumes a new Cold War dimension in that democratic-capitalist Taiwan does not want to be "re-unified" with authoritarian mainland China and is a U.S. ally. It is argued that China's gains in diplomatic recognitions are Taiwan's losses, which in a new Cold War sense, make them U.S. losses. In the China–Taiwan rivalry in the Caribbean, economic statecraft is very much front and center.

"The People's Republic of China is the only legitimate government that represents all of China, and Taiwan is an inalienable part of Chinese territory" (Sevastopulo and Hille 2021). That came from Nicaragua's Foreign Ministry as it announced on December 9, 2021 that it was dropping its diplomatic recognition of Taiwan and replacing it with the PRC. This is a major blow to the island state and a diplomatic victory for Beijing. The change in diplomatic recognition also indicates that China continues to make inroads into the Caribbean and Latin America at the expense of the United States in the new Cold War.

© The Author(s), under exclusive license to Springer Nature Switzerland AG 2022
S. B. MacDonald, *The New Cold War, China, and the Caribbean*,
https://doi.org/10.1007/978-3-031-06149-3_6

Taiwan is now down to 14 countries that recognize it. That could change if Honduras were to flip, which is possibility. The situation becomes even bleaker if any of the remaining Caribbean and Latin American countries can be flipped. Those remaining loyal (thus far) to Taiwan are Honduras and Guatemala in Central America, Paraguay in South America and Belize, Haiti, St. Vincent and the Grenadines and St. Kitts and Nevis in the Caribbean. In this the Caribbean counties constitute the largest bloc of countries that recognize Taiwan, making this a supreme test for the Asian island state to maintain those ties. For the United States, Taiwanese closest ally, further Chinese gains in the Caribbean and Latin America represent the ongoing erosion of its dominant hegemonic position.

It is the purpose of this chapter to examine the role played by Taiwan in the Caribbean through the lenses of the new Cold War-like environment. The stakes are high. Taiwan is a strong U.S. ally, is an important force in the global high-tech supply chain, and a symbol of democratic governance in sharp contrast to its neighbor, China. Taiwan's foreign policy also supports many of the same ideals that drive the United States, including a preference for democratic rule and a robust private sector. In this context, what happens with Taiwan's diplomatic recognition is important to the United States because its gains are shared...as are its losses. Consequently, the Caribbean looms large for Taiwan. Equally important, Panama is key to U.S. security and Taiwan's lost diplomatic recognition has been more than filled by Chinese banks and companies engaged in trade and infrastructure development.

Three major elements are at play for Taiwan as it approaches the Caribbean (1) compared to China, Taiwan has fewer resources to draw upon in foreign assistance, which means that it must pick and choose wisely what projects it agrees to undertake in the region; (2) there is an importance given by the Taiwanese to longstanding personal relationships between its ambassadors and local leadership; and (3) Taiwan benefits from United States in the region as Washington works to halt the shrinkage of the list of countries which represent Taiwan.

There is also an ideological element to Taiwan and the Caribbean. Taiwan offers a democratic-capitalist alternative to China's authoritarian-mercantilist approach. It is also an island, like much of the Caribbean and has struggled to convert what was a relatively poor country into a technological power. This leaves China and Taiwan locked in a battle for hearts and minds (and pocketbooks), both using economic statecraft and soft diplomacy (such as medical training and equipment as occurred during the Covid-19 pandemic as well as educational assistance). An important difference between China and Taiwan, however, is that the former can offer a package of state-owned companies and cheap Chinese labor, backed by large state-owned bank loans, while Taiwan's economy relies on private sector companies, which can gain support from the Taiwan Export–Import Bank, though hardly on the scale or ease as their mainland counterparts. Over time it is increasingly logical from a national interest sense for Caribbean countries and their counterparts in Central America to establish relations with China if no other reason than the deeper menu of economic incentives that can be offered by the world's second largest economy to countries with relatively meager natural resources. This situation puts the Caribbean on one of the key fault lines of the new Cold War.

FROM REPUBLIC OF CHINA TO TAIWAN—A BRIEF LOOK

To understand Taiwan's role in the Caribbean it is important to have an understanding of the Asian island's political and economic development. In the aftermath of China's civil war (1946–1949) prospects for Taiwan were poor. The Kuomintang or KMT (the Nationalists who claimed to represent China) was a defeated force, while the local population resented the addition of a large number of mainlanders. Indeed, in 1947 the island was rocked by a major insurrection by the local Taiwanese against the KMT. Although the rebellion was crushed, it is seen by many as the birth of Taiwan's independence movement, a historical strand that is still at play in relations between Beijing and Taipei and within Taiwanese domestic politics.

Despite its rocky beginning Taiwan was to emerge as one of Asia's "miracle economies." Taiwan's transformation from the last bastion of the KMT to one of Asia's most dynamic economies occurred in part from a unique set of circumstances. Historically Taiwan (also known as Formosa) often had a tenuous relationship with mainland China and its imperial dynasties. Often forced to contend with barbarian invasions from inner Asia's hinterlands, dynastic China generally regarded Taiwan though as peripheral. The island was to change hands a number of times as it was fought over by European powers, Japan, and pirates. It settled back to Chinese rule from 1683 to 1895. Taiwan was then lost to a modernizing and militarily superior Japan in the first Sino-Japanese War (1894–1895).

Taiwan's period as part of the Japanese Empire (1895–1945) was important as it had much to do with forging the island's future as Japan sought to develop the island economically, which meant creating an industrial foundation and badly needed infrastructure as well as providing a relatively lengthy period of political stability. Although Japan was forced out of Taiwan in 1945, it maintained an interest in its former colony's fortunes through foreign direct investment and trade.

Taiwan's relationship with the United States was also critical. Threatened by a militarily more powerful China, flush with victory on the mainland, Taiwan had few friends in 1949. Despite concerns about Chiang Kai-shek, who was seen by many in U.S. policymaking circles as corrupt and a liability, the outbreak of the Korean War (1950–1953) changed circumstances. The subsequent clash of U.S. and Chinese forces on the Korean Peninsula reinforced Washington's perception that Taiwan was useful to contain the spread of Chinese Communism. U.S. policy would therefore be guided by providing diplomatic, economic, and military support to Taiwan. This, of course, was to have long-term consequences for Taiwan and its relationship with the Caribbean. In the early Cold War most Caribbean countries followed the U.S. lead in maintaining their recognition of Taiwan as the Republic of China. The exception to this was Cuba; following its revolution in 1959 the new communist government broke relations with Taiwan and recognized the People's Republic. Indeed, in 1961, Cuban President Osvaldo Dorticós Torrado was the first leader from the Caribbean and Latin America to visit China.

What was important in Taiwan's economic development is that it offered a successful developmental model for smaller island nations. In the 1950–1990 period, Taiwan underwent a far-ranging change that brought it up through the value-added economic chain, based on education, exports, and strategic planning. It was able to attract considerable foreign direct investment and eventually took the economy from heavy industry to high tech. This success on the economic front gave Taiwan the ability to use economic statecraft in maintaining diplomatic ties to much of the world.

Taiwan's politics also underwent a substantial reconfiguration. From 1950 until his death in 1975, Chiang Kai-shek ruled Taiwan as an authoritarian regime. Power was kept in the hands of the KMT, a largely former mainland Chinese group. The KMT government also worked hard to maintain control over local Taiwanese aspirations for independence. At the same time, Taiwan and China had reached a loose arrangement for co-existence. As long as Taiwan maintained its claim to represent China and not seek independence (anathema to Beijing's hardliners), the two states could find some space for trade and commerce. Beijing was also clear that if Taiwan did declare independence it would most likely resort to military means to resolve the island's future status.

Taiwanese politics radically changed during the 1980s and 1990s, with a shift away from authoritarian rule to a more open political system as Taiwanese politics became increasingly competitive and less ideological. The main dividing line has become independence, with the KMT (which remained one of the major political parties) opposed, while a number of other parties, in particular the Democratic Progressive Party (DPP), favoring independence from the mainland, ending all pretense to eventual unification.

As Taiwan faced outwards to the rest of the world, needing markets, foreign investment, and diplomatic recognition, its relationship with the United States underwent considerable changes. The major shock for Taiwan was the strategic shift undertaken by the Nixon administration, which put Washington on track to recognize Beijing and the Communist regime. Although this made sense in the Cold War game that brought China on the side with the United States against the Soviet Union, Washington maintained de facto recognition of Taiwan and supported the island with military equipment. With U.S. diplomatic ties finalized to China in 1979 by President Jimmy Carter, Taiwan found itself in a more complicated and precarious position. Many countries opted to drop Taiwan in favor of China, a situation that deteriorated with the wind down of the Cold War. China's economic takeoff in the 1990s and first decade of the twenty-first century only worsened this situation, especially as Beijing quickly learned the importance of economic statecraft.

A GLOBAL GAME

The diplomatic game played between Beijing and Taipei is global. While Taiwan lost formal diplomatic ties with the Soviet Union and members of its Eastern bloc as well as India, Switzerland, and Pakistan in the 1950s and others followed through the next several decades. In the Caribbean throughout the 1960s, Cuba alone recognized the People's Republic. That changed, however, in the 1970s. Left-leaning governments in Guyana and Jamaica ended recognition of Taiwan in 1972. They were followed by Trinidad and Tobago in 1974, Suriname in 1976, and

Barbados in 1977. In this shift, the Caribbean states were hardly alone in the Americas: Argentina, Mexico, and Venezuela all recognized China during the decade. Despite further defections in the 1980s (Antigua and Barbuda in 1983 and Grenada in 1985), the rest of the Caribbean remained as firm for Taiwan until 1997 when the Bahamas and St. Lucia dropped Taiwan for China.

What changed the tone of China–Taiwan competition over diplomatic recognition was the rise of pro-independence forces in Taiwan. The KMT was willing to improve cross-straits relations as a pragmatic approach to dealing with a larger and more powerful neighbor. In 1992, President Lee Teng-hui's KMT government and China agreed on a "one-China" policy, in which both governments claim sovereignty over mainland China and Taiwan, but critically neither recognizes the other's legitimacy. This allowed a status quo on the diplomatic front as well as helping open up China to badly needed Taiwanese foreign direct investment.

As long as KMT governments were in office the one-China policy was the basis of cross-border relations and Beijing pressed less hard on other countries to drop their recognition of Taiwan. However, a major juncture was reached with the election of Chen Shui-bain as president in 2000. Chen had earlier repudiated the idea of one China, which greatly displeased China. Although Chinese foreign policy at the time was reluctant to appear to be too aggressive in global affairs, the situation was different when it came to Taiwan. The thought of pro-independence leaders in command of the "breakaway" province led to greater pressure from Beijing on isolating Taiwan. During Chen's presidency the numbers shifted drastically, with the loss of eight countries in 2000–2008 period, including Dominica (2004) and Grenada (2005) in the Caribbean and Costa Rica (2007) in Central America.

The China–Taiwan rivalry eventually percolated into local Caribbean politics. In 2004 Dominica Prime Minister Roosevelt Skirrit decided to end relations with Taiwan and embraced China. This action ended 20 years of diplomatic relations between Roseau and Taipei. The main motivation was economic. The island's economy entered a recession in 2000 and between 2001 and 2004 it shrank by 9.0 percent. Although Taiwan had lent Dominica money, the recession was biting deeply into the government's finances. China, sensing an opportunity, was willing to provide Dominica with fresh loans. For the hard-pressed Dominican government the decision was straightforward, especially considering that Taiwan was reluctant to increase its exposure to the struggling Caribbean country.

An unintended consequence of the China–Taiwan rivalry was that when Dominica went to a general election in 2005, the issue of diplomatic recognition emerged as a dividing point between the country's two major political parties, Skirrit's Dominica Labour Party (DLP) and its rival, the United Workers Party (UWP). According to one report, "Taiwanese flags adorned the homes of opposition supporters" (Thorburn 2007). Skirrit and the DLP went on to win the elections and the decision on the new diplomatic relationship with China was upheld. To all appearances the Skirrit government played China and Taiwan off against each other to see which state would provide the better deal for Dominica, lending some credence to pocket book or "yuan" diplomacy.

Chinese pressure on Taiwan on the diplomatic front eased somewhat with the return of the KMT into government under President Ma Ying-jeou. Winning the 2008 election, Ma's win brought back a degree of calm in cross-straits relations. All the same, Chinese influence in the Caribbean, surged during this period (as outlined in Chapter 3). China worked hard to consolidate its presence throughout much of the region. Losses for Taiwan were contained to Africa (Gambia, South Sudan and Sao Tomé and Principe). In the Caribbean, the status quo held.

The dynamic changed again in 2016 when Tsai Ing-wen became President, leading the DPP back into office. Tsai, the island state's first woman chief executive, won with 56.1 percent of the vote, despite warnings from China during the campaign that such a development would be problematic for cross-straits relations. In Tsai's inaugural speech she identified two issues related back to mainland China's interests in Taiwan: she underscored Taiwan's commitment to democracy, calling it a value "deeply ingrained in the Taiwanese people" and the tenuous relationship with Beijing. The new leader noted that both sides "have a responsibility to do their utmost to find mutually acceptable ways to interact…and ensure no provocation and no surprises" (Hunt and Stout 2016).

China's response to Tsai's electoral win was frosty. Beijing's apprehension about Taiwan taking a more independent stance was deepened when President Donald Trump took a call from President Tsai, who congratulated the U.S. leader on his victory in the 2016 election. This was the first direct communication between the leader of the island and a U.S. president or president-elect since relations were officially ended in 1979. A statement from Trump's team stated, "During the conversation they noted the close economic, political, and security ties that exist between Taiwan and the United States. President-Elect Trump also congratulated

President Tsai on becoming president of Taiwan earlier this year" (Phillips et al. 2016).

Although China played down the phone call, it put Beijing on alert that the new U.S. president was likely to take a different approach than previous occupants of the White House. In particular, it raised deep concerns that the Trump administration would abandon the one-China policy and possibly recognize Taiwan as an independent state.

China's apprehension over the incoming Trump administration also took into consideration that one of the incoming U.S. leader's chief advisers was Peter Navarro, a China hawk, who traveled to Taiwan in the first half of 2016 at the invitation of its Ministry of Foreign Affairs. Navarro had earlier written in *Foreign Policy* magazine that President Obama's treatment of Taiwan had been "egregious," adding: "This beacon of democracy in Asia is perhaps the most militarily vulnerable US partner anywhere in the world" (Gray and Navarro 2016). Considering where the Trump administration would head in terms of China policy, launching a tariff war in 2017, and seeking closer ties with Taiwan, the phone call with Taiwan's President Tsai was a signal of bigger changes to come in U.S. China policy, with implications for the Caribbean.

PANAMA, THE NEW COLD WAR, AND THE CARIBBEAN

Panama is a key chokepoint in world trade as its canal provides the passage of ships and cargo from and to the Pacific and Atlantic Basins. The actual canal stretches for 51 miles, cutting across the Isthmus of Panama. On both sides it is surrounded by the Canal Zone, which includes busy economic free trade zones filled with foreign companies drawn by incentives and location. Although not considered a Caribbean country, Panama abuts the Caribbean, it plays a key role in that region's trade, and there is a sizable community of Panamanians who are of Caribbean descent.

U.S.–Panamanian relations have a long history. Although France began work on the canal in 1881, it was the United States that finished it, opening the waterway in 1914. Along the way (in 1901), the United States also helped the Panamanians achieve their independence from Colombia. The United States long controlled the land surrounding the canal, but in 1977 agreed to hand over control to Panama. This was done in 1999, when Panama formally assumed control of one of the world's engineering marvels that split its country in two. Due to its importance, the Panama Canal remains a point of keen interest to the

United States, which militarily intervened in 1989 to oust the dictatorial Manuel Noriega, who was a one-time U.S. intelligence asset and long-time facilitator of the Latin American drug trade. U.S.–Panamanian relations remained generally positive through the subsequent decades.

Like other countries in Latin America and the Caribbean, China's first connection with Panama came through the export of labor, with the first group of Chinese arriving in 1854 to work on the Panama Railroad. Still more Chinese came in the later decades of the nineteenth century to work on the Panama Canal. In 1912 official diplomatic relations were established between China and Panama. Official Chinese–Panamanian diplomatic relations date back to 1912. During the Cold War the Central American country loomed large to Taipei as a regional business and financial hub. At the same time, Chinese immigrants to Panama came from mainland China and have been Cantonese-speakers (though Mandarin and Hakka speakers exist among later immigrants). Numbers vary on the size of the ethnic Chinese community in Panama, but it appears to be in excess of 200,000 out of a total population of 4.2 million. This makes Panama's ethnic Chinese population the largest in Central America and the Caribbean.

China's growing influence in Central America was first noticeable in 2007 when Costa Rica dropped Taiwan in favor of China. Although official diplomatic relations with Taiwan were severed, Costa Rica and the island state continued to trade with each other, something that other countries in the region noted. In Panama trade with China grew, with Beijing establishing a trade office in 1996. Panama reciprocated later in the same year. In 2010 Panama sought to establish diplomatic relations with China. China, however, turned down Panama at that point due to the interest in improving relations with the Taiwanese government of President Ma Ying-jeou.

The catalyst of change for China vis-à-vis Panama was the victory of President Tsai. Her win, followed by a decision not to affirm the 1992 Consensus (on China) and her congratulatory telephone call to the President-elect Trump in December 2016 pushed President Xi's government to renew the push against Taiwanese diplomacy.[1] It was shortly after this sequence of events that China snatched diplomatic recognition

---

[1] The 1992 Consensus on Chain or "one China" is a political term used by the KMT leader, Su Chi, referring to the result of a meeting in 1992 between the semiofficial representatives of the PRC and Republic of China (Taiwan). The key point is that this

from one of Taiwan's longstanding African allies, Sao Tomé and Príncipe. The message was clear; President Xi was implementing a more aggressive policy to isolate Taiwan as a part of a broader plan to pull all things Chinese under Beijing's control. Indeed, President Xi has consistently been a hardliner on reunification, repeatedly asserting: "The historical task of the complete reunification of the motherland must be fulfilled, and will definitely be fulfilled" (BBC 2021; Xinhua 2019).

To the backdrop of deteriorating China–Taiwanese relations Panama loomed large. As the London School of Economics' Alvaro Mendez and Chris Alden observed: "The small state of Panama is a key node in the global trading system that can make an unexpectedly large contribution to China's national security and international influence" (Mendez and Alden 2019). China is the second largest user of the Panama Canal, behind the United States. Much of China's oil is brought through the canal. This is significant in that Latin America and the Caribbean as of 2018 accounted for 13.5 percent of China's total energy needs, 95 percent which came from Colombia, Venezuela, and Brazil as well as Guyana and Trinidad and Tobago (International Trade Centre 2019). Largescale discoveries of oil in offshore fields in Guyana and Suriname are likely to push that up. Additionally, China imports food from Argentina and Brazil, some of which, like oil, travels through the Panama Canal.

And while trade is important for China, the canal has obvious military considerations. In the case of war between the United States and China, the U.S. Navy regards the Panama Canal as critical. If China opted to invade Taiwan and force reunification, it is likely that the United States would respond militarily. In a widely read 2001 article, "How the United States Lost the Naval War of 2015," by Professor James Kraska at the U.S. Naval War College, Beijing uses its commercial control of the ports on either side of the Panama Canal to close off the use to U.S. ships (Kraska 2001). Although this is a fictional account, much of the conjecture in the article is based on real factors. Indeed, John Hemmings (an Adjunct Fellow with the Japan Chair at the Center for Strategic and International Studies) and Janjan Sun (a researcher at the Asia Studies Centre, Henry Jackson Society) pointed out:

meeting provided a context for deeper relations between mainland China and Taiwan, with a view that both states represented China, though they held different interpretations.

Presently, a Chinese company CK Hutchison Holdings (formerly Hutchison Whampoa) does own and operate the two Panamanian ports through its subsidiary Hutchison Ports. In 1996, a U.S. State Department cable alleged that Panama's 1996 auction for the operating rights over the canal had been facilitated by a Chinese state-owned enterprise, the China Resources Enterprise, which gave $400 million to Hutchison Whampoa Limited to clinch the deal. Despite a bid that was fourth, behind a Kawasaki bid, a Bechtel bid and a M.I.T. bid, the Chinese won the deal and now have a twenty-five year lease, with an automatic renewal for another twenty-five years. (Hemmings and Sun 2017)

That was written in 2017; in 2020 China assumed direct control over Hong Kong, which means that the lines of control between Beijing and a Hong Kong conglomerate are more direct. With China now more keenly interested in cutting Taiwan down to size and less concerned about provoking the United States, playing the Panama card advanced national interests, especially considering the strategic value of the canal.

For Panama the incentive for flipping Taiwan was largely economic. Although President Juan Carlos Varela denied his action had nothing to do with economic incentives, it clearly did. The denial of economic motivations was also heard from Zhao Bentang, then Director-General of the Department of Latin American and Caribbean Affairs of the Foreign Ministry, "China and Panama establishing ties is a political decision made by both sides on the basis of political principles and looking at long term benefits. There are no economic or financial strings attached" (Chansoria 2018).

But Panama's economic condition clearly was a factor. The Panamanian economy was struggling. In the post-Great Recession era global trade was only slowly recovering, a situation not helped by rising protectionism. There were also complications related to the running of the canal after a major multi-year overhaul and the country's financial sector was undergoing a crisis related to the Panama Papers. The last were released in 2016, consisting of more than 10 million documents belonging to the Panamanian law firm and corporate service provider Mossack Fonseca. The Panama Papers revealed the names of those who had used Mossack Fonseca to create offshore companies to help them place funds beyond the eyes of local tax authorities. While much of what is done in offshore financial centers is legal, the papers demonstrated that many of the shell corporations (a large number incorporated through the law firm's British

Virgin Island's office) were used for illegal purposes, including fraud, tax evasion, and circumventing international sanctions (Bernstein 2017).

Mossack Fonseca, which had thrived on secrecy, was soon out of business. At the same time, the reputational damage to Panama was severe, especially as the files were collectively named after their country. Offshore company formation in Panama evaporated. Many U.S. banks moved quickly to de-risk from Panamanian correspondent banks (i.e. cutting off their lines of credit). As international banks and other financial actors scrambled for the exits in Panama, the country found itself on blacklists from the European Union, the Organization for Economic Cooperation and Development (OECD), and the Financial Action Task Force.

To keep the Panamanian economy on the growth track and take the canal to the next stage, President Valera embraced a plan to capture greater value-added production by creating large assembly facilities in free trade zones, upgraded port facilities, and new road and rail links into Central America. Also part of the picture was a new cruise terminal at Panama City's Amador Causeway, near the Pacific entrance to the Panama Canal (which was started in 2016 and designed by Cruceros del Pacífico consortium which consists of the Belgian company Jan De Nul and Chinese firm China Harbour Engineering). In all of this the idea of Chinese loans had a tremendous appeal; Taiwan could hardly compete.

Valera's gamble of flipping Taiwan for China despite the risk of incurring U.S. anger was worth the gamble. As one observer noted: The facts and figures state otherwise, however. China and Panama ended up signing 19 deals while upgrading economic and commercial ties. Chinese enterprises "with full governmental support are participating proactively in energy, infrastructure construction, and maritime transport agreements with a special focus on transport infrastructure in Panama" (Chansoria 2018; Ellis 2018). Among the other commitments acquired by Panama from China were a loose agreement for the establishment of a China Development regional headquarters in Panama; a formalization of cooperation between the Banco Nacional de Panamá and Bank of China; and a feasibility study for a passenger and cargo train from the capital to the western port of Chiriquí (Herrera et al. 2020).

China's approach to Panama was well-thought out, clearly stressed the importance of economic statecraft, and excellently executed. Chinese companies, either via Hong Kong, Cayman Islands (offshore registrations), or mainland, had been approaching Panama for a lengthy period of time. This was helped by a sustained penetration of the local Chinese population in Panama by mainland organizations, such as the Confucius Institute and the state-controlled press, such as *China Daily* and *Xinhua* news agency. It has been asserted that *Xinhua* has become a standard go-to source of news for many high levels of Panamanians, all part of providing China with a positive image in the build-up to diplomatic recognition and serving as a platform for Beijing's narrative on the COIVID-19 pandemic. As China moved toward actual signing the diplomatic deal with Panama, the stage had been set vis-à-vis the public. Moreover, China and Panama worked hard to keep any leaks about their talks to reach the United States and Taiwan.

President Varela, who made the decision to move ahead with diplomatic recognition of China, had been one of the key negotiators with that country in Panama's earlier effort to establish relations during the presidency of Ricardo Matinelli (2009–2014). In the game of checkbook diplomacy, China was clearly a favorite for Valera. With the United States seemingly disinterested in the Caribbean and Latin America, Panama pulled the trigger. Five months after Panama's recognition of China, Varela visited China, meeting with President Xi. The two countries signed a multitude of agreements touching upon shipping, tourism, and justice, many of which involved Chinese state banks and state-owned economic enterprises (Blanchard 2017). The way was also clear for Panama to join the growing list of Caribbean and Latin American countries that signed on to the BRI. President Xi returned the favor, visiting Panama in 2018.

While Taiwan was taken by surprise by Panama's move, so was the United States. President Valera had concealed his move to recognize China from the United States until less than an hour before his public announcement of the change. From the U.S. perspective this was another loss of ground in a strategically important region in what was becoming an increasingly visible new Cold War with China. For Taiwan the loss of Panama was a bitter development. However, President Tsai in her official statement went to the heart of the matter, saying "Our refusal to engage in a diplomatic bidding war will not change" (Republic of China 2017).

It is worth noting that Beijing's diplomatic gain did not automatically lead to Panama becoming a Chinese satrapy (despite the worry of some U.S. policymakers). At the same time, the Panamanian government's action had left the country's public taken aback. There was a decided gap between government policy and public sentiment, which soon became evident with the eruption of an intense national debate over allowing China to build an embassy overlooking the Panama Canal.

As a report by three Panamanian academics stated: "This gap, between political and economic opportunism and citizen perceptions illustrates the challenges facing Panamanians seeking to ensure that relations with the PRC are in their interest" (Herrera et al. 2020). Together with intense U.S. pressure, public opinion forced the Chinese to seek another less sensitive location. China's position was also checked by the departure of President Valero and his replacement by the more pro-U.S. Juan Carlos Laurentino Cortizo in 2019. The new administration dismissed a Chinese $4.1 billion proposal for a high-speed train. A major electrical transmission project (which included a Chinese company as one of the last two bidders) was canceled and recast as a public–private partnership. A number of other major infrastructure projects did not fall in China's way. Trade talks stalled. The motivation for Panama was twofold: one, U.S. pressure was intense on containing the spread of Chinese influence in the Panamanian economy and two, the Cortizo government had its own agenda, which was to bargain with China from a stronger position. Despite the seeming halt of further Chinese gains of influence in Panama, there were no indications that the Cortizo government had any intention to restore relations with Taiwan.

THE "LOSS" OF THE DOMINICAN REPUBLIC

The loss of Panama put Taiwan on the defensive in the Caribbean and Central America. China was proving to be hard to resist. The next major target was the Dominican Republic. Long faithful to Taiwan, the Dominican Republic has emerged as one of the Caribbean's stronger economies during the first decades of the twenty-first century, with trade being a key element to success. On April 30, 2018 Beijing scored a major victory in finally winning the Dominican Republic's diplomatic recognition. By pulling Santo Domingo into its orbit, Beijing managed to bring into its diplomatic fold one of the economic success stories in the Caribbean.

As with Panama China's attraction to the Dominican Republic is multiple. Beyond the importance of stripping away one more precious diplomatic relationship from Taiwan, the Dominican Republic has long tapped foreign investment to build up its manufacturing base and competitive tourist industry. Its trading and manufacturing platform has been rendered more competitive by the DR-CAFTA (Dominican Republic-Central America Free Trade Agreement made with the U.S.). China could find such investments worth its while, especially if could induce more of its nationals to travel the distance to the Caribbean (though this was set back by the 2020–2021 Covid-19 pandemic and will have to wait for a post-pandemic era). Additionally, China is interested in the Caribbean country's natural resources, namely aluminum and nickel, while it maintains a sizable trade surplus with the Caribbean country.

Important to both China and the Dominican Republic are the Caribbean's country's interest in developing into a regional logistics hub: Hispaniola marks a boundary between the Greater and Lesser Antilles, being close to Cuba and Puerto Rico and commanding a number of sea lanes that connect the Caribbean and Atlantic. Considering the Dominican Republic's geostrategic location, it has for many years nurtured the development goal of becoming the Caribbean's logistical and business gateway to and from South America. To make this objective a reality various Dominican governments have pumped funds into major infrastructure projects. Los Americas airport was privatized and an air cargo city was added to its operations. Furthermore, new marine ports for cruise ships were constructed and older facilities were upgraded. The Dominican Republic's position as a key regional hub was helped by heavy volume of passenger travel out of Punta Cana airport.

The Dominican-China diplomatic deal was long in coming. As Iván Gatón, an international relations expert at the Autonomous University of Santo Domingo noted, "Since the administration of President Fernandez (2008–2012) contacts had already been made. So let's say that it was something that one way or another was bound to happen" (Castillo 2019). Again, the primary incentive was economic. To achieve the regional transportation hub the Dominicans hoped Chinese loans could be tapped to build a railway between the Dominican Republic and Haiti, dams in the Monsenor Nouel province; the modernization of the Port of Arroyo Barril; new sewage and wastewater systems in several northern provinces; and aqueducts in Cotuí. Considering the above, it was reported that China offered a package worth $3 billion in exchange for the Dominican Republic's diplomatic recognition, with $1.6 billion earmarked for infrastructure development projects.

China's muscling Taiwan out on the Dominican Republic was greeted in Taipei as another case of China's yuan diplomacy, strongly hinting that these "vast financial incentives" were akin to bribery. China's response, taken up in Beijing's mouthpiece publication, *The Global Times*, was to call Taiwan's allegations as a "malicious smear," with no merit (Ding Gong 2018). Considering the high stakes nature of politics between China and Taiwan it is more than likely large sums of cash helped move the deal along.

The Medina administration and elements in the business community also observed the normalization of relations as an opportunity to boost Dominican exports to China. In 2019 trade with China was worth a little over $4 billion, with the trade balance heavily in favor of China. One of the first things that China did was to authorize the importation of Dominican rum; the expectation was that other Dominican products will follow, including mango, avocado, and coffee. Indeed, President Medina noted in November 2018: "It is our interest to increase Dominican exports to the Chinese market, which is also among the largest and most dynamic in the world."

In a different area from the economy China was also supportive of the Dominican Republic's longstanding effort to get a non-permanent seat on the Security Council at the United Nations. The Dominican Republic had made two earlier attempts (in 2002 and 2007), but failed. The Dominicans took their seat for a two-year tenure on January 1, 2019, with Chinese backing (as well as U.S. support).

China's success in the Dominican Republic was another geopolitical victory. It further cut Taiwan down to size and poked its influence further into a region considered by Washington as its backyard. The Dominican Republic's relationship with the United States has been long and in the twenty-first century the northern country is the Caribbean country's largest trade partner (accounting for close to 50 percent of its total exports and imports), the home to most of its tourists and foreign direct investment. In terms of foreign policy the Dominican Republic usually sides with the United States on most issues. Further cementing the relationship, there is a large community of Dominicans, more than two million, who have moved to the United States. President Medina's decision to drop Taiwan quickly caused tension with the Trump administration, especially as this came in the aftermath of Panama's defection. The Dominican action put into play a wide range of concerns within the U.S. government, including the potential of Chinese companies to make greater use of the DR-CAFTA to access the U.S. market. This was linked to concerns that the U.S. position in the Dominican Republic would be weakened by China in everything from losing out on business deals to shifts in Dominican foreign policy to a pro-Beijing stance in key votes in international forums.

As for the Dominican Republic and Taiwan, the Caribbean country had recognized Taipei since 1949, being one of the few countries that maintained ties for several decades after the People's Republic gained U.S. diplomatic recognition. Throughout the twentieth century and into the first two decades of the twenty-first century Taiwan was an active trade partner and provided economic assistance on a regular basis. In contrast, China's foreign direct investment was small, though there was a steady expansion of trade. In addition, China's assistance represented a greater chance for Santo Domingo to realize its dream of becoming a critical Caribbean hub. In the aftermath of the split, Taiwan cut its various aid programs to the Dominican Republic. It did, however, maintain its trading relationship with the Caribbean country.

In the aftermath of the announcement of a new era in relations between China and the Dominican Republic, President Medina became the first ever Dominican chief executive to visit China in November 2018. There he participated in the opening of his country's embassy. Moreover, 18 agreements were signed between China and the Dominican Republic to cooperate in a range of areas from finance to civil aviation. The Dominican Republic and China also signed an Memorandum of Understanding (MOU) for the Caribbean country to join the BRI.

The Dominican Republic's China deal injected hope in Santo Domingo that the island country had taken a major step in diversifying its economic partners and opened the door to new business opportunities. It was also a recognition that China had more to offer them than Taiwan. At the same time, there was probably the calculation that the United States would eventually calm down; after all the United States recognizes Beijing. At the same time, there are concerns about the new relationship. As Philip Hughes, senior director at the White House Writers group and former U.S. ambassador to Barbados and the Eastern Caribbean noted: "Chinese concessional financing will come with strings attached – buy Chinese equipment – and 'gifts' of big, showy projects will come with reminders to be sure that the Dominican Republic votes China's way on international issues, especially now that the Caribbean nation sits on the U.N. Security Council. President Medina's government may find that this regular nudging drives wedges between the Dominican Republic and its traditional friends and largest trading partners, such as the United States, precisely as intended" (Hughes 2019; Myers and Barrios 2019).

Assessing the New Cold War Landscape—China, Taiwan, and the United States

China's diplomatic campaign in the Caribbean and Central America was not over with the Dominican Republic. In August 2018, El Salvador announced that it had severed relations with Taiwan and established ties with China. Following a script used by Panamanian and Dominican leaders before him, El Salvador's president, Salvador Sánchez Céren, proclaimed the "extraordinary opportunities" that came with recognizing China. One such extraordinary opportunity was a special economic zone (SEZ), proposed before a national election and prepared before the break with Taiwan. The SEZ would account for roughly 14 percent of the country and to some analysts was geared to attract Chinese investment, especially considering that the negotiations over the plan had largely been in secret.

El Salvador had earlier asked Taiwan for loans for a major port project that Taiwanese engineers concluded was economically unfeasible. El Salvador had also brought the matter up with China, which apparently was more open to the idea. This left Taiwan's foreign minister Joseph Wu stating: "It is irresponsible to engage in financial aid diplomacy or compete with China in cash" (Horton 2018). The Salvadoran ruling party, however, was voted out of office, leaving the fate of China's status in the hands of the next president, Nayib Bukele, who came into office in June 2019. Although Bukele has been to Taiwan and met with President Tsai before becoming his nation's leader, he maintained the new relationship with the PRC.

In the aftermath of Taiwan's "loss" of the Dominican Republic and El Salvador, the United States began to assume a more active role in supporting its Asian ally in the Caribbean and Central America; efforts were made for better coordination between Washington and Taipei over aid programs vis-à-vis the region (to pool resources and make a more efficient response to China); and a more high-profile Taiwanese effort to woo the Caribbean. The first was done by signaling to Caribbean and Central American countries that they would incur Washington's displeasure by changing sides. Indeed, the White House pulled back its top officials in El Salvador, Panama, and the Dominican Republic for consultations. In direct response to what happened in El Salvador, the White House issued a statement: "The El Salvadoran government's receptiveness to China's apparent interference in the domestic politics of a Western Hemisphere country is of grave concern to the United States, and will result in a re-evaluation of our relationship with El Salvador" (Ching 2018).

In the aftermath of El Salvador's and the Dominican Republic's defections, Haiti loomed large. Considering the choppy nature of regional diplomatic relations, Taiwan granted a $150 million low-interest loan to upgrade Haiti's rural power grids, something that the Caribbean country had long wanted. The issue of enough and regular power dominates any discussion about the country's ability to attract foreign investment in its manufacturing sector as well as make life better for the country's citizens. This loan was granted prior to President Jovenel Moise's visit to Taiwan in May 2018. On the visit the two countries discussed agriculture, energy, infrastructure, and private investments. Although the trip was filled with plenty of photo ops, the Haitians left Taiwan relatively disappointed. Prior to the trip expectations were that Taiwan would put together an aid package of $1–2 billion.

Haiti's needs are considerable; Moise's presidency was under acute pressure to obtain substantial help needed to jump start a struggling economy. Moreover, Haiti is an exceedingly difficult environment to conduct policy, which has resulted in frustration among Taiwanese officials in dealing with Haiti. Part of the problem in Haiti is the country's acute political instability, which made the long-term development of any projects difficult. This was painfully brought home in President Moise's murder in his private residence on the outskirts of Port-au-Prince in July 2021, a development that left the country's political scene in near-chaos. What followed was a combination of gang violence, kidnappings, and political squabbling over who would succeed the dead president. As Caribbean Policy Consortium Fellow Georges Fauriol dismally observed in October 2021: "But what may be most alarming is that the dysfunction that framed Haiti prior to these events, remains unresolved – and arguably is sliding toward complete ungovernability. There is no coherent and sustainable pathway in place to address any of this – whether among Haitian leadership or international actors" (Fauriol 2021).

Despite the long arc of political instability in Haiti, it is still a prize in the China v. Taiwan fight. Part of China's inducements for Haiti was a complete upgrade of Port-au-Prince, the country's down-at-the-heels capital, where according to one journalist, "crumbling infrastructure, terrible gridlock and blackouts are the norm." Two Chinese companies, Southwest Municipal Engineering Design and Research Institute and the Metallurgical Corporation of China, a state-owned construction firm, negotiated with the Mayor of Port-au-Prince over a $4.7 billion plan to reconstruct Haiti's capital city. While the Chinese plan was certainly tempting, the idea that such a plan could be implemented strained credulity, considering the very low levels of development and political instability. Nonetheless, the idea of a massive Chinese aid package caught peoples' attention and left many wondering why Haiti should miss out on the bonanza of Chinese money. As Fritz Jean, an economist who was briefly prime minister of Haiti, noted in 2019: "It's a brave new world out there and mainland China is evolving to be on top of it economically and otherwise. Sooner or later, we will have to concede involuntarily to the new world order, but without the capacity as our neighbors did. And we will receive peanuts." The problem for Haiti is that to be part of that brave new world, it needs to put its house in some type of order. This left the Taiwan-China fight in a suspended state, especially after Moise's assassination as it was difficult to figure out who actually represented Haiti.

Taiwan is aware of the acute pressure it faces in keeping its remaining Caribbean allies, including Haiti. In July 2019 President Tsai made a four-day tour through the Caribbean. Dubbed, the "Journey of Freedom, Democracy, Sustainability," the diplomatic campaign was designed to reassure Taiwan's remaining diplomatic allies that it was still a factor and that they mattered. In this Haiti was again given special attention, with President Tsai meeting with President Moise. Taiwan's assistance to agricultural and energy sectors was praised. Taiwan has already been heavily engaged in helping Haiti try and develop a better working power system, necessary to attract foreign companies for manufacturing as well as making improvements in the daily lives of the Haitian people.

Tsai also visited St. Kitts-Nevis, being the first Taiwanese president to set foot on to the smaller island on Nevis. The trip's next stop was St. Vincent and the Grenadines, where Tsai met with Prime Minister Ralph Gonsalves, the country's longtime leader. She also addressed the Vincentian parliament. Taiwan has had a long and successful relationship with St. Vincent. Through the first two decades of the twenty-first century, Taiwan's banks and Taiwanese companies have helped with the development of the Argyle International Airport and its terminal, the Union Island Airport, the National Library, and a number of other infrastructure projects. Moreover, Taiwan was very active in providing medical training to the island state, which would extend to face masks and other hospital equipment during the 2020 coronavirus pandemic.

President Tsai's final lap of her trip was St. Lucia. She met with government leaders and visited agricultural and infrastructure projects. Taiwan's relationship with St. Lucia has been a little more complicated past than with other Caribbean countries. St. Lucia recognized Taiwan through 1997, but in that year flipped it and went to China. The China–St. Lucian relationship lasted until 2006, when St. Lucia decided to return to its earlier relationship with Taiwan. Taiwan has been active in helping St. Lucia's infrastructure, providing some financial help with the country's $175 million Hewanorra International Airport, $50 million of loans for an island-wide road and infrastructure program, and help for a St. Lucian government-wide wireless network (Zheng 2019).

While Tsai's trip was well-received in the Caribbean, it was questionable as to how much Taiwan could do to rally the region again to its side. In many respects, Taiwan was left playing defense, seeking to hold its diplomatic team together and fending off intense Chinese pressure as with Haiti. China's offers to Haiti were very tempting, especially after seeing the Dominican Republic shifted its relationship for a rumored $3.2 billion in investments and loans (Charles 2018). Ironically Haiti's political instability has reduced the government's ability to make any decision in changing its diplomatic recognition. The other point of concern among the remaining countries is that governments changed in St. Lucia with the 2021 elections, bringing to office the same Labour Party that had earlier broken ties with Taiwan (which was later changed back).

Taiwan clearly benefits by having the U.S. play a greater role in the Caribbean. Although it puts Caribbean countries in the position of having to steer between a China that has thus far been willing to help finance and construct various projects and a United States that is increasingly aggressive in warning Caribbean countries of the negative consequences of dealing with China, Taiwan is likely to find its diplomatic position reinforced. Without U.S. support it faced the prospect of fading as the diplomatic lights on the map of the world go out one by one. At the same time it is worth underscoring that although diplomatic recognition has shrunk to a handful of countries, Taiwan still has important allies, including the United States as well as Japan and Australia. Indeed, as China has ramped up its aggressive behavior against Taiwan in the Asia–Pacific, U.S. support has increased. As Bonnie Glaser, a Taiwan expert at the German Marshall Fund noted: "Taiwan's isolation isn't in the interest of the EU, Japan, Australia and many other countries. So they may take steps to strengthen their ties with Taiwan" (Sevastopulo and Hille 2021).

Although Taiwan's diplomatic situation has deteriorated in the late 2010s and early 2020s, it might benefit from the wolf warrior side of Chinese diplomacy. Generally speaking, China has demonstrated a partnership approach to the Caribbean, provided aid, and helped develop infrastructure. It has also increased its influence as countries have seen their debt with China rise. China has also politely nudged many Caribbean aid recipients to its side of voting in international organizations. While the Chinese reputation is one of advancing win–win policies, it also has a harder side of policy. As discussed in Chapter 4, Guyana flirted with the idea of allowing Taiwan open a trade office, only to be slapped down by China. The message was departures from the Chinese line on a number of issues (like one China) will have a prompt response, followed by consequences. Although Taiwan has not been shy in asserting itself, it could benefit from further manifestations of wolf warrior policies in the region.

Taiwan's Covid-19 Diplomacy

One area where Taiwan has played a strong diplomatic hand has been in its response to the Covid-19 pandemic. It had to considering its rival's active engagement on this front. While China cannot escape the fact that the global pandemic started in Wuhan, it did seek to recoup some lost goodwill by selling medical equipment (some of which has been defective), sending medical personal, and getting doses of its Sinopharm vaccine into the Caribbean. Following the arrival of vaccines in the Dominican Republic, Santo Domingo backtracked on a prior commitment not to include Huawei from its 5G networks. The United States, in contrast, followed a different policy in seeing after its own population first, which meant what supplies that were available went to U.S. citizens first.

Taiwan was effective in dealing with the coronavirus at home. Despite China's efforts to isolate Taiwan (even from the World Health Organization), the island state was active in helping other nations, including those that follow the ones that follow the one China policy. Among the countries receiving Taiwanese medical aid was Haiti. The Taiwanese response to the spread of the pandemic to that Caribbean country prompted sending a first batch of 280,000 masks, seven thermal cameras, and thermometers (Lai 2020). Taiwan also delivered rice to Haiti, helped fund the purchase of new ambulances, helped in medical training, and provided credit for Haiti to purchase medical goods.

Although China had its own medical diplomacy, Taiwan's actions demonstrated that it was still on the global map, especially in the Caribbean. Although the effort was not costly in the great scheme of major infrastructure deals which China usually cuts, Taiwan's medical diplomacy did much to show that the Asian island is still around and can play a constructive role in world affairs. If nothing else, the Chinese-made pandemic gave Taiwan an opportunity to play for hearts and minds in a long and tough diplomatic duel with its larger neighbor.

TAIWAN AND THE CARIBBEAN—A BLEAK 2020S?

There is no hiding it: the December 2021 defection of Nicaragua was a blow to Taiwan as well as the United States. It represented one more cut at U.S. regional hegemony, especially as seen in the light of a new Cold War. It can be argued that the move by the newly re-elected Ortega regime was more leveled against the United States than Taiwan. Relations between the United States and Nicaragua have been strained over the last several years due to the increasingly authoritarian turn of the Ortega regime and its closeness with Russia. A former Marxist guerrilla and president, Ortega and his family have run Nicaragua since he was again elected to office in 2007. In 2021 he was re-elected for a fourth consecutive term along with his wife as the vice president. His victory was regarded as fraudulent, in particular since he had jailed dozens of opposition leaders (including seven potential presidential candidates prior to the vote). The United States was very critical of the vote as was the Organization of American States, the European Union, and United Kingdom. In the aftermath of the vote, Ortega moved quickly to drop Taiwan, embrace China, and pull out of the OAS. Russia, Cuba, and Venezuela expressed their support to Ortega. Chinese vaccine diplomacy was soon activated with 200,000 doses of Chinese-made Sinopharm arriving in the Central American country only days after the diplomatic flip.

The Nicaraguan flip must be seen as mainly about economics, though Nicaragua does provide China another authoritarian friend in the region alongside Cuba and Venezuela. It appears that China offered a package of vaccines, some type of financial assistance, greater trade opportunities, and a potential restart of the Nicaragua Canal (a project led by a Chinese tycoon which would have established a new trans-isthmus canal to challenge the one in Panama) (Everington 2021). Taiwan was aware of the looming shift in relations and it is said that in the run-up to the November 7, 2021 election that President Tsai agreed to provide a new $100 million loan to Nicaragua (Sevastopulo and Hille 2021). The plan hit a snare when Taiwanese banks refused to extend the loan due to such an action being a violation of U.S. sanctions against Nicaragua.

Nicaragua points back to the main question dogging Taiwan's role in the world, its shrinking list of countries that recognize it diplomatically. Because of this the stakes for Taiwan are high in the Caribbean. If no country recognizes Taiwan as an independent sovereign Taiwan, the idea that the island is nothing more than a "breakaway province" becomes more credible. As Chen-shen Yen, an international relations research fellow at Taiwan's National Chengchi University, aptly observed when the Dominican Republic in 2018 shifted its recognition to Beijing, "What will happen if no one recognizes you? Can you still claim to be a sovereign nation?" (Dou 2018).

One line of thinking is bleak. According to Rasheed Griffith, a non-resident Senior Fellow at the Inter-American Dialogue, Taiwan's last remaining allies will swap allegiance to Beijing within the next decade. The reasoning behind this view is largely economic. As Griffith noted: "The opportunity cost of keeping Taiwan as an ally relative to the potential gain of PRC has been fairly small in the Caribbean over the last few decades since China is a new player. However, in the past decade China's investment has ramped up rapidly, which is why we have seen Taiwan's allies start to drop. That means the cumulative cost of sticking to Taiwan is growing each year" (Gibson 2021). This problem is compounded by the potential pressure from a regional economic bloc like CARICOM, which at some point may wish to sign a free trade agreement with China. The ongoing diplomatic recognition of St Kitts-Nevis, St. Lucia, St. Vincent, and the Grenadines, Belize and Haiti could complicate trade talks. While Griffith willingly acknowledged that Taiwan is positively regarded throughout the Caribbean for its generous scholarships, agricultural training programs, and language exchange programs, the economic incentives that drive national interest are a strong pull. As he noted, "Taiwan certainly does much better than any other ally in terms of soft diplomacy. Unfortunately, soft diplomacy will always pale in comparison to hard, cold, economic facts."

While Griffith's view has merit, it may be too bleak. There can be denying that Taiwan's diplomatic are shrinking. At the same time, Taiwan maintains trade with a wide range of countries. Taiwan remains a trade partner for many countries throughout the Caribbean despite the loss of diplomatic recognition. It has free trade agreements with Panama and El Salvador despite the rupture in relations. It also has FTAs with Guatemala, Honduras, and Nicaragua. At the same time, China's more aggressive stance against Taiwan has strengthened its position with the United States, Japan, Australia, and France. The challenge ahead is how to parley Taiwan's economic strengths (including its considerable dominance over the global semiconductor market) into a formula that keeps the idea of its sovereignty alive. The option of trade offices was attempted in Guyana in 2021, where China moved rapidly to shut it down. The other case has been in Lithuania, which allowed Taiwan to open a trade office. Although China indicated its displeasure with Lithuania's action, the Baltic country went ahead with allowing the Taiwanese office to open. The result was that China shut its doors to Lithuanian exports and put pressure on German companies not to conduct business in the Baltic country, a form of hardball economic statecraft similar to prior actions against other countries that have displeased China, like its suspension of rare earth exports to Japan, a curb on Norwegian salmon imports and a ban on Australian wine and barley imports. Some countries have been willing to fight back with China, but smaller countries, like Guyana, are less inclined to do so. For now this means that the best glue to bind the remaining small countries in the Caribbean and Central America to Taiwan is through trade and investment, with a view that as the new Cold War deepens, even these loyal bastions are at risk.

CONCLUSION

Taiwan has played a constructive role in the Caribbean and is likely to do so in the future. However, its struggle with China is one of survival. To maintain its claim to be a "country" and not a breakaway province, Taiwan needs to have diplomatic recognition by at least a handful of countries. If nothing else, having diplomatic allies gives Taiwan someone to represent its interest in international forums and to share information. For China, this is not acceptable if the Communist Party is to achieve its historical mission of righting all of the imperialist era wrongs and bring Taiwan back into the fold. China's economy is far greater in size; its ability to be generous is more significant, a critical factor in its use of economic statecraft to lure away Taiwan's overseas partners. Furthermore this plays into China's preference to make an isolated Taiwan see reason; it cannot survive over the long term. In many respects, Taiwan's trials and tribulations with China place it squarely in the new Cold War between the United States and China, both in Asia and the Caribbean. It also pulls Caribbean countries into the struggle between China and Taiwan. The Caribbean may be thousands of miles away, but foreign policy makers in Beijing and Taipei can find Belize, St. Lucia, and the Dominican Republic on the map.

REFERENCES

BBC. 2021. China-Taiwan Tensions: Xi Jinping Says 'Reunification' Must Be Fulfilled. *BBC News*, October 9. https://www.bbc.com/news/world-asia-china-58854081.

Bernstein, Jake. 2017. *Secrecy World: Inside the Panama Papers Investigation of Illicit Money Networks and the Global Elite.* New York: Henry Holt and Company.

Blanchard, Ben. 2017. After Ditching Taiwan, China Says Panama Will Get the Help It Needs. *Reuters*, November 7. https://www.reuters.com/article/us-china-panama/after-ditching-taiwan-china-says-panama-will-get-the-help-it-needs-idUSKBN1DH1FZ.

Castillo, Valeria. 2019. Dominican Republic Warms to China. *Diálogo Chino*, February 14. https://dialogochino.net/en/trade-investment/22177-domini can-republic-warms-to-china/.

Chansoria, Monika. 2018. Yuan Diplomacy: Panama Cuts Ties with Taiwan in Favor of the Mainland. *Japan Forward*, January 9. https://japan-forward.com/yuan-diplomacy-at-work-panama-cut-ties-with-taiwan-in-favor-of-the-mainland/.

Charles, Jacqueline. 2018. The Dominican Republic Ditched Taiwan for China. Is Haiti Next to Cut Diplomatic Ties? *Miami Herald*, May 17. https://www.miamiherald.com/news/nation-world/world/americas/haiti/article21 0790414.html.

Ching, Nike. 2018. Eyeing China, US Scolds El Salvador, Warns Others on Cutting Taiwan Ties. *Voice of America*, August 24. https://www.voanews.com/usa/eyeing-china-us-scolds-el-salvador-warns-others-cutting-taiwan-ties.

Ding Gong. 2018. China, Caribbean Countries More Closely Connected in New Era of Ties. *Global Times*, October 29. https://www.globaltimes.cn/page/201810/1124988.shtml.

Dou, Eva. 2018. China Woos Another Taiwan Partner, Diluting Island's Support. *The Wall Street Journal*, May 1. https://www.wsj.com/articles/china-woos-another-taiwan-partner-diluting-islands-diplomatic-support-1525158328?mod=searchresults&page=4&pos=1.

Ellis, Evan. 2018. The Evolution of Panama-PRC Relations Since Recognition, and Their Strategic Implications for the U.S. and the Region. *Global Americans*, September 21. https://theglobalamericans.org/2018/09/the-evolution-of-panama-prc-relations-since-recognition-and-their-strategic-implications-for-the-u-s-and-the-region/.

Everington, Keoni. 2021. China Sends 200,000 COVID Vaccines 4 Days After Nicaragua Dumps Taiwan, December 14. https://www.taiwannews.com.tw/en/news/4375334.

Fauriol, Georges. 2021. Adrift: US-Haiti Policy. *Global Americans*, October 22. https://theglobalamericans.org/2021/10/adrift-us-haiti-policy/.

Gibson, Liam. 2021. Taiwan Will Likely Have No Caribbean Allies Within 10 Years. *Taiwan News*, August. https://www.taiwannews.com.tw/en/news/4277904.

Gray, Alexander B., and Peter Navarro. 2016. Donald Trump's Peace Through Strength Vision for the Asia-Pacific. *Foreign Policy*, November 7, 2016. https://foreignpolicy.com/2016/11/07/donald-trumps-peace-through-strengthvision-for-the-asia-pacific/.

Hemmings, John, and Janjan Sun. 2017. Panama Has Ditched Taiwan. Here's Why It Matters for America. *The National Interest*, June 22. https://nationalinterest.org/feature/panama-has-ditched-taiwan-heres-why-it-matters-america-21275.

Herrera, Luis Carlos, Markelda Montenegro, and Virginia Torres-Lista. 2020. The Diplomatic Context Between China and Panama and Their Agreements. Working Paper, London School of Economics. https://www.lse.ac.uk/international-relations/assets/documents/global-south-unit/Working-Paper-No-3-2020.pdf.

Horton, Chris. 2018. El Salvador Recognizes China in Blow to Taiwan. *The New York Times*, August 21. https://www.nytimes.com/2018/08/21/world/asia/taiwan-el-salvador-diplomatic-ties.html.

Hughes, G. Philip. 2019. Is the Dominican Republic's Pivot to China Paying Off? *Latin American Advisor*, May 9. https://www.thedialogue.org/analysis/is-the-dominican-republics-pivot-to-china-paying-off/.

Hunt, Katie, and Kristie Lu Stout. 2016. Taiwan Elects Its First Female President; China Warns of 'Grave Challenges'. *CNN World*, January 17. https://www.cnn.com/2016/01/16/asia/taiwan-election/index.html.

International Trade Centre. 2019. List of Supplying Markets from Latin America and the Caribbean for a Product Imported by China Product. In Petroleum Oils and Oils Obtained Bituminous Minerals, Crude. Geneva, Switzerland: International Trade Centre. https://www.intracen.org/itc/market-info-tools/sta.

Kraska, James. 2001. How the United States Lost the Naval War of 2015. *Orbis* (Foreign Policy Institute, Winter): 35–46. https://papers.ssrn.com/sol3/papers.cfm?abstract_id=1648631.

Lai, Johnson. 2020. Taiwan Says Virus Aid Sent Quietly to Avoid Beijing Protests. *AP*, August 11. https://apnews.com/article/beijing-virus-outbreak-alex-azar-international-news-health-5af2dab4fd701e38918b7ff85889b058.

Mendez, Alvaro, and Chris Alden, 2019. China in Panama: From Peripheral Diplomacy to Grand Strategy, *Geopolitics*. September 6. https://www.tandfonline.com/doi/abs/10.1080/14650045.2019.1657413.

Myers, Margaret, and Ricardo Barrios. 2019. Is the Dominican Republic's Pivot to China Paying Off? *Latin American Advisor*, May 9. https://www.thedialogue.org/analysis/is-the-dominican-republics-pivot-to-china-paying-off/.

Phillips, Tom, Nicola Smith, and Nicky Wolf. 2016. Trump Phone Call with Taiwan President Risks China's Wrath. *The Guardian*, December 3. Quoted from Tom Phillips, Nicola Smith, and Nicky Wolff, Trump Phone Call with Taiwan President Risks China's Wrath. *The Guardian*, December 3, 2016. https://www.theguardian.com/us-news/2016/dec/03/trump-angers-beijing-with-provocative-phone-call-to-taiwan-president.

Republic of China (Taiwan). 2017. President Tsai's Remarks on Termination of Diplomatic Relations with Panama. Office of the President, Republic of China (Taiwan), June 13. https://english.president.gov.tw/News/5161.

Sevastopulo, Demetri, and Kathrin Hille. 2021. Nicaragua Cuts Diplomatic Ties with Taiwan and Recognizes Beijing. *Financial Times*, December 9. https://www.ft.com/content/20be9454-8f04-47d5-a55f-58bbb3b57b0f.

Thorburn, Dana. 2007. Remapping Caribbean Geopolitics. *NACLA*, September 25, 2007. https://nacla.org/article/remapping-caribbean-geopolitics.

Xinhua. 2019. Xi Says 'China Must Be, Will Be Reunited' as Key Anniversary Marked. *Xinhuanet*, January 2. http://www.xinhuanet.com/english/2019-01/02/c_137714898.htm.

Zheng, Sarah. 2019. As Taiwan's Allies Dwindle, St. Lucia Stands Firm Against China Pressure. *South China Morning Post*, October 28. https://www.scmp.com/news/china/diplomacy/article/3035240/taiwans-allies-dwindle-st-lucia-stands-firm-against-china.

CHAPTER 7

Realignments, Tensions, and Asymmetry: Russia and Iran

The more significance presence of Russia and Iran in the Caribbean reflects the broadening nature of the slide into a new Cold War in the Caribbean. Although the combination of China-Russia-Iran is not a monolithic bloc of countries to counter the West, they share commonalities, including a projection of power into the Caribbean. In this Russia and Iran are more limited than China. The first two countries are more selective in how they project power and with whom. In this Venezuela looms large. Beyond that Russia has greater engagement, especially with Cuba. Consequently, Russia's and Iran's Caribbean ventures must be observed as part of a global new Cold War-like geopolitical realignment, which is generating its own set of tensions with the United States. At the same time, Russia's and Iran's activities in the Caribbean have a certain asymmetry in that their power projections are overwhelmingly closer to home (Eastern Europe and Central Asia for Russia and the Middle East for Iran). For Moscow and Tehran, the Caribbean is of lesser consequence, but nonetheless is worth the reach, something that will be discussed in this chapter.

This is a pledge to stand shoulder to shoulder against America and the West, ideologically as well as militarily. This statement might be looked back upon as the beginning of Cold War Two.

Robert Daly, Director of the Kissinger Institute of China and the United States at the Wilson Center following China's and Russia's declaration at the February 2022 Beijing Winter Olympics of a "new era" in which the two Eurasian counties announced that they would challenge

© The Author(s), under exclusive license to Springer Nature Switzerland AG 2022
S. B. MacDonald, *The New Cold War, China, and the Caribbean*, https://doi.org/10.1007/978-3-031-06149-3_7

the United States as a global power and offer a different model from Western liberal democracy (Wright 2022).

It is 2026 and Russia is reopening a naval base in Cuba. The United States is protesting and threatening some type of action, but Washington is distracted by its deeply divided politics, unrest in its major cities and impeachment proceedings against the winner of the 2024 election. Russian security personnel earlier returned to Cuba since the near-toppling of the Cuban Communist Party by nation-wide riots in 2024, but the sending of Russian naval ships has raised tensions, some analysts claim back the same levels of 1962, the Cuban Missile Crisis. To bolster its Cuban ally, President Putin worked with China to cobble together an economic package to tide over the Caribbean regime, including guaranteeing a steady flow of food. Iran, already active in Venezuela, is also doing its part to help keep Cuba out of the clutches of democracy and Western influence. While this scenario sounds like the beginning of a futuristic political thriller, Russia has already returned to Cuba, playing a role in backing the sclerotic Cuban regime, while Iran is active in Venezuela. To be certain, Russia and Iran lack the economic heft of China, but they share a similar incentive to poke at the U.S. geostrategic underbelly in the Caribbean, a trend that is likely to continue through the upcoming decade.

In the first two decades of the twenty-first century Russia, Iran and China have drawn closer together. While there is no formal alliance, the three countries oppose U.S. hegemony, prefer a multipolar world order, have authoritarian governments, are under U.S. economic sanctions, and have traditions of being great powers. Russia is the most hostile to the United States, largely due to the U.S..-led effort to punish it from absorbing Ukraine and arming the government in Kyiv. Equally important, China, Iran and Russia find themselves on the same side in the Caribbean, presenting themselves as alternatives to United States and Western power. As global geopolitics realign into a more competitive environment closer China-Iran-Russian relations are likely to continue. Indeed, Jamsheed K. Choksy and Carol E.B. Choksy observed in *Foreign Affairs* in November 2020: "...the Islamic Republic has joined forces with the People's Republic and the Russian Federation to improve its military position and shore up its economy. China and Russia are now integrally involved in Iran's affairs from its oil and port infrastructure to its defense capabilities" (Choksy and Choksy 2020). In this regard, there is a realignment of power dynamics between Beijing, Tehran, and

Moscow, which can translate into better cooperation in a number of strategic arenas, including the Caribbean. It is also worth noting that Chinese–Russian relations are closer than either those countries is with Iran. The joint announcement by presidents Putin and Xi at the Beijing Olympics stopped just short of a formal alliance, but clearly sent a message that Beijing-Moscow are challenging the United States as a global power, Western alliances (like NATO and Five Eyes), and Western liberal democracy (Wright 2022). This is a major realignment. The war between Russia and Ukraine is one manifestation of the new Cold War-like mindset.

It is important to clarify that the China–Russia–Iran axis is an important development, but it is far from being a monolithic force. There are areas of friction and different national interests at play. China is a world power, with aspirations to be the leading hegemonic state. Russia wants to be acknowledged as a great power and is willing to strategically intervene in an opportunistic fashion and apply pressure on the United States in its "near abroad." Russia's use of a threat to further build up military assets in Cuba and Venezuela in January 2022 certainly has a new Cold War feel to it, especially as it linked tensions in Eastern Europe and the Caribbean. The Russo-Ukraine only adds one more layer of complexity of declining East-West relations. Iran is a struggling regional power, but can project power beyond its region in a very limited, perhaps more symbolic fashion. While the two countries share an interest in eroding U.S. hegemony in the Caribbean and Latin America, they compete in some spheres, such as arms sales and rights to oil fields. China's resources are greater and its interest are broader. Russia has a more narrow focus in terms of countries, but it has deep ties to those states (Gurganus 2018). Despite frictions and tensions, Russia and Iran have surfaced in the Caribbean's geopolitics in the early twenty-first century and it is worthwhile to have at least a basic understanding of their role, especially with a hot war in Eastern Europe.

Russia's Return to the Caribbean

President Putin is a firm believer in geopolitics and is motivated by a sense of history. For a Russia traumatized by its collapse as a world power and worried about the rolling back of its influence from Eastern Europe and elsewhere, his arrival was pivotal. Putin's stamp on contemporary Russian history is substantial. He has been the dominant political figure in Moscow since 2000. Appointed acting president by an ailing President Boris Yeltsin in 1999, Putin won the 2000 elections and served as

Russia's chief executive from that year to 2008; then was prime minister under his colleague Dmitry Medvedev; and re-elected president in 2012. He remains in power. Changes to the Russian constitution allow him to run for office in 2024 and 2030.

What is important about Putin for the Caribbean is that he is the force for re-engagement with the region. Shaping his policy outlook is a sharp sense of grievance over the Soviet Union's end, a view shared by nationalist groups, many of them in the security apparatus and military. In 2005, he stated that the breakdown of the Soviet Union was the "greatest geopolitical catastrophe of the century" (Taylor 2018). Putin saw his nation transit through economic and political collapse and a subsequent need of revival. Part of this revival includes the return of Russia to its former glory as a great power, one that is taken seriously.

During Putin's first term as President, he sought to restore stability at home and work with the West overseas. He overlooked lingering resentment from the 1999 U.S. bombing of Serbia (a Russian ally); cut his country's nuclear arsenal by two-thirds; raised little objection to the stationing of U.S. troops in Central Asia; offered flyover rights and intelligence cooperation to the United States and NATO during the war in Afghanistan; and in 2002 closed down the main Russian listening post in Lourdes, Cuba. Yet from Putin's later perspective, Moscow got little in return from the United States. By 2007, the Russian leader's view about the United States and the West had hardened (Treisman 2011).

The Return of Russia as a Great Power

Beginning in 2008, when the world was watching the Beijing Olympics, Putin began to reclaim what Russia has traditionally called the "near abroad," that is most of Eurasia that was once under the Tsarist and Soviet flags. Georgia, a small former Soviet Republic in the Caucasus, had steered too close to the West and Russia used the cause of South Ossetians (a separatist region) to give the Georgian military a dubbing. The message was simple; Georgia is part of the Russian sphere of influence and closer engagement with the West will have consequences. The Western response was weak and ineffective; Georgia was not worth a major crisis with Russia.

Two more actions followed. The first was Putin's move to become more heavily involved in Ukraine's murky politics. This ultimately resulted in Russian support for two breakaway regions in its neighbor and the annexation of Crimea in 2014. The latter was the first major land grab in Europe since the Second World War and resulted in tough Western economic sanctions against the Russian economy. The significance of Putin's Ukraine actions was caught by Dmitri Trenin, the Director of the Carnegie Moscow Center: "Thus, Russia broke out of the post-Cold War system in Europe and openly and forcefully challenged the U.S.-dominated world order" (Trenin 2019: 164). At the same time, the resurgence of Russian power and its use of Ukraine reinforced a growing perception that the world was increasingly divided between autocratic or authoritarian regimes, like China and Russia, who were willing to support like-minded regimes elsewhere and more liberal Western democracies, favoring open and inclusive societies.

The second action in Putin's tougher foreign policy was a refocus on the Middle East. In 2015 Russian provided military support to an old ally, the al-Assad regime in Syria. Although Bashir al-Assad had the support of Iran and Hezbollah, his military still struggled against the radical Islamic State and other rebel forces. The Russian intervention in Syria was decisive, based on air power and missiles as well as Moscow-backed mercenaries. By 2022 the al-Assad regime remained in power and had recovered considerable parts of the country. The Russian message once again was that Moscow was back and needed to be taken seriously.

Russia's return as a global power was also evident by its seeking to influence elections in Europe and the United States as well as being actively engaged in cyber-hacking the West. With a pool of well-educated and technology-savvy people, Russia found that malign influence activities were another way of leveling the playing field with the West. These activities are defined as covert, coercive, and corrupting and designed with the objective of manipulating public discourse, discrediting the electoral system, biasing policy formulation, and disrupting markets for the purpose of advancing a political or strategic objective (Conley et al. 2020). In essence, Russia used sharp power. The Russian approach was comprehensive and used multiple actors, including Sputnik and RT, state-owned media outlets, augmented by Russian intelligence agencies and trolls, some officially state-sponsored and some operating as independent contractors in the service of the state. Russian malign influence activities have been evident in elections in the UK, Germany, France, and the United States (becoming a controversial issue in the aftermath of the 2016 presidential contest). They have also expanded into Latin America and the Caribbean (Global Americans 2021).

Rounding out Putin's foreign policy overhaul was a reset in relations with China. Russia was Communist China's early backer and up into the mid-1950s relations between the two countries were close. However, following Stalin's death in 1953, friction developed in a number of areas and by the 1960s the lengthy Asian border between the two was a heavily militarized zone, marked by occasional and bloody skirmishes. In the 1970s, China and the United States slowly moved to repair their relationship, which eventually led to President Richard Nixon's trip to Beijing and the normalization of relations. This left the Soviet Union out.

Relations between China and Russia finally thawed by the 1990s, when the two countries shared concerns about what increasingly appeared to be a unilateral world order, headed by the United States. Both countries were also wary about U.S. support for pro-democratic movements and had watched the various "color" revolutions in Central Asia and the Middle East with considerable trepidation. As Russia's relationship deteriorated with the West so did China's. It increasingly made sense for old slights to be forgotten and a new relationship forged on having a common rival, the United States. This was evident in the formation of the Shanghai Cooperation Organization (SCO), increased Sino-Russian trade (which reached a record $146.9 billion in 2021); the construction of natural gas pipelines from Russia to China; and a more coordinated approach on some foreign policy questions, including support for the leftist regimes in Venezuela, Cuba, and Nicaragua.

Vladimir Putin was a well-feted guest at the 2022 Olympics, where the two leaders did the usual big leader photo session and condemned the United States and its allies for stoking the arms race in Asia–Pacific and expressed joint opposition to the expansion of NATO in Eastern Europe. Russia also backed China's claims on Taiwan and the Russian leader walked away with a new oil deal. As part of their "new era" communique China and Russia took their rivalry with the United States and the West up a notch. For anyone that has studied Sino-Russian history, the autocrat photo opt brought back memories of Chinese Communist and Soviet leaders doing the same thing and the communique signaled that the world is heading a little further down the road on a new Cold War.

By the end of the first decade of the twenty-first century Russia found itself in a unique place in the global system. While it had declined in terms of power vis-à-vis China and still lagged behind the United States in terms of economic and military might, Russia still had the tactical savvy to be an opportunistic disruptor. It also remained a nuclear power and upgraded its military, including developing a sophisticated cyber warfare capacity. Russia had already demonstrated an ability to dominate the near abroad, those countries which were once former Soviet republics, it has also regained the capacity and will to project power into the "far abroad," the Middle East, and increasingly in parts of Africa. Moreover, Moscow maintained a significant role in European politics, especially through being a major energy supplier. The Caribbean beckoned.

The Caribbean Beckons

After the Georgian War Russia felt compelled to broaden its range of diplomatic relations, including to the Caribbean and Latin America. This push was renewed with greater vigor in the aftermath of Russia's annexation of Crimea in 2014, when the United States and European Union imposed tough economic sanctions. Considering the changing nature of the geopolitical picture, Russia's foreign policy needed to reach out to non-Western countries, including those in Latin America that did not adhere to the sanctions. Equally important, the gaining of support in the Caribbean provided an avenue by which (even if symbolically) to help construct a new multipolar world order that would challenge the existing United States-led world order. Cuba offered a point of reference as did, in a more limited sense, Grenada, both of which figured prominently in Moscow's Cold War experience (Ashby 1987). At the same time, the Caribbean provided new opportunities for Russian state-owned and privately owned businesses, in particular those sectors where the Russian government believed it had a comparative advantage—that is, energy, mining, and armaments (Rouvinski 2021: 24). The Russian approach also worked better where the governments were more authoritarian and anti-United States This, of course, had a Cold War feel.

The Russians were willing to show the flag by visits of naval and air units and high-ranking officials. In 2008, two Russian nuclear-capable bombers landed in Venezuela and flew training missions for several days before returning to Russia. This was followed by a small Russian naval flotilla, which included the nuclear-powered *Peter the Great*, which conducted joint military exercises with Venezuela and stopped in Cuban and Nicaraguan ports. Russian attention to the region continued with a November 2008 visit by then President Dmitry Medvedev who visited Peru, Brazil, and Venezuela, ending his trip in Cuba, where he met with Raúl Castro. In 2009, Moscow played host to Venezuela's Chávez,

Nicaragua's Daniel Ortega, Bolivia's Evo Morales, and Ecuador's Rafael Correa, none of them friends of the United States. Seeking to touch base with this increasingly more important group of countries, in July 2014 Putin visited Cuba, Argentina, Brazil, and Nicaragua, where he signed security and economic agreements. Significantly, many Caribbean and Latin American countries did not join United States and E.U. sanctions against Russia.

Russia maintained its showing of the flag with the visit of a Russian intelligence ship, the *Viktor Leonov*, docked in Cuba later in 2014, which was followed in 2015 by Russian Defense Minister Sergei Shoigu's visits to Cuba, Nicaragua, and Venezuela. In each case he met with leaders to discuss potential Russian access to airports and ports. Rounding out the picture, in November 2016 Russia's Ministry of Foreign Affairs in its Foreign Policy Concept paper laid out its priorities, noting of the region: "Russia remains committed to the comprehensive strengthening of relations with the Latin American and Caribbean States taking into account the growing role of this region in global affairs" (Russian Federation 2016).

Deteriorating U.S. relations with Cuba, Nicaragua, and Venezuela, which accelerated with the arrival of the Trump administration in 2016, were to be reflected in a more active Russian approach to the same countries. Rekindling the Cuban relationship was an easier process than dealing with Venezuela (which played a significantly larger role in the world economy via energy markets). After all, Russia had largely paid to keep Castro's communist experiment afloat through the 1960s to the early 1990s. Cuba offered a degree of familiarity. Moreover, Cuba's ongoing need to find external support in the face of the Communist Party's flaccid economic reform effort provided Moscow with an opening. As already noted, China had little interest in a large-scale bankrolling of bad economic policies (especially considering its high-risk lending record in Venezuela).

The ongoing shuffle of Russian and Cuban leaders to each other's capitals eventually resulted in a deepening in economic and investment relations. One of the first results was Russia's willingness to forgive $32 billion of Cuba's external debt, left over from the Soviet period. Cuba still had to repay $3.2 billion over ten years. This came in 2014, when Putin visited Havana as part of a regional tour. The debt forgiveness made a 90 percent reduction from what Cuba previously owed. It also removed a sticking point in relations between the two countries.

For Russian companies, Cuba gained greater attention. Although Russia is not in the same league as Spain and China on the trade front, it has steadily increased its involvement with Cuba. Bilateral trade between the Caribbean and Eurasian country was $180 million in 2013; by 2019 it peaked at $450 million, which made Russia Cuba's fifth most significant trade partner. It was to fall to $356 million in 2020, reflecting the depth of Cuba's economic crisis related to the Covid-19 pandemic and the tightened U.S. embargo. The trade balance has been largely in Russia's favor, especially following the restarting of Russian exports to Cuba in 2017. Helped by Russian credit lines, Cuba bought Russian cars, trucks, minivans, aircraft, locomotives, and spare parts.

While Chinese investment in Cuba slowed (before and during the 2020 Covid-19 pandemic), Russian investment increased. The main projects pushed by Moscow are a $2 billion overhaul of the railroads over the next decade and the installation of four 200 megawatt generators by 2024. The first project is being managed by RZD, a fully state-owned company headquartered in Moscow. The second project is managed by electrical power generating company Inter RAO, which is a private sector firm with close ties to the government. For a struggling Cuban economy hit hard by renewed U.S. sanctions and Covid-19, Russian investment is clearly welcomed.

Russian support for Cuba has been visible in other ways. In 2019, Russia sent one of its newest ships, the *Admiral Gorshkov*, and three other ships on a visit. The small flotilla had left its base in the Barents Sea in northern Russia, transited the Suez Canal, made stops in Djibouti, Sri Lanka, China, Ecuador, and entered the Caribbean through the Panama Canal. The ship arrived in Cuba in July 2019 and was greeted by a 21-gun salute. The *Admiral Gorshkov* was an important symbol of support for Cuba, especially considering the close U.S. military attention to the little fleet and the new technology built into the ship.

Russia also remained active in high-level person-on-person relations. Putin has visited Cuba as have a stream of other Russian leaders. These included Moscow's top security official, Nikolai Patrushev and in February 2020 it was the turn of Foreign Minister Sergei Lavrov. Upon his arrival on the island Lavrov gave an interview with the local media, *Prensa Latina*, where he reaffirmed his rejection of U.S. sanctions and highlighted his country's support of Cuba. He also noted that through its economic sanctions the U.S. violated human rights, with people (Cubans) being the most affected (Telesur 2020). Cuba's president, Díaz-Canel, visited Moscow in November 2018 and again in October 2019, indicating the importance of Russia (though did not return with any new breakthroughs in Russian aid).

Russia's commitment to Cuba was tested in July 2021, when the island was hit by widespread protests against the government. The main causes were frustration over gross economic mismanagement (characterized by a severe contraction over the last two years) and a spike in Covid-19 which put the medical system under pressure. While the U.S. economic sanctions hurt the economy as well, the main target of the protests was the Castroite state. Protesters took to the streets in 40 cities, shouting "Freedom," "Down with the dictatorship," and "We're hungry." For the Communist regime this was one of the most significant challenges to its rule, probably in the last 30 years. For Russia, popular protests are not a positive development as any political opening in Cuba probably would not favor Moscow's support for the authoritarian government. In the aftermath of the protests, Russia warned against any "outside interference." While Russia did not rush to Cuba's side with new loans, it did send 88 tons of humanitarian support, including food, personal protective equipment, and more than one million medical masks. Cuba will represent a growing political risk challenge for Russia going forward as the pressures for change on the Caribbean island is only likely to rise, but it will remain important to Moscow from a global geopolitical viewpoint.

Cuba again reappeared in Russian-Western tensions in late 2021 and 2022, with Moscow stressing its "special relationship" with Havana. While the Cuban government and Cuban Communist Party are quite happy to have Russian attention, the announcement came as a surprise to Havana. Putin spent time via phone with Cuba's leader, Diaz-Canel, discussing ways to enhance their special relationship, including greater cooperation in the technical military sphere. In realist politics the message was clear, in balling hardball with the West over Ukraine, Russia is quite willing to stoke up tensions in the U.S. backyard with Cuba and Venezuela. The Russo-Ukraine War brings all of this up to another notch, raising questions as to what can Russia actually do to stir up trouble in the Caribbean (considering its stretched resources in Eastern Europe) and how far down the road to confrontation do Caracas and Havana want to go with the United States?

Russia's Role in Keeping Venezuela Afloat

Russia's relations with Venezuela were much like China's; there was not a warm and friendly relationship during the Cold War era, but with the coming of Hugo Chávez to power in 1999 that changed. From the Venezuelan side, Chávez was quick to recognize the benefits of warming up to Russia. He was willing to offer something Russia wanted—recognition that Moscow was again the capital of a great power.

Russo-Venezuelan relations drew closer in the 2000s and were characterized by high-level visits and the signing of economic deals and arms sales, all of which played to Moscow's strengths. Beginning in 2005, Russia became a major arms seller to Venezuela, with a price tag running into the billions. At the same time, the two countries ran joint military maneuvers in 2008 and Chávez made two visits to Moscow in July and September 2008. A number of agreements were also signed between the two countries, which included plans for the building of an aluminum plant (which never occurred after Russians inspected the facilities), the creation of a bi-national development bank (the Moscow-based Evrofinance Monsnarbank), and possible automobile construction (which never took off). The bank was launched to fund joint Russia-Venezuela oil and infrastructure projects and has offices in Caracas and Beijing. Russian assistance was also sought for the development of gold mines and housing projects. Chávez visited Moscow again in 2010, where he signed an agreement to construct Venezuela's first nuclear plant and buy $1.6 billion worth of oil assets. Furthermore, Venezuela in 2011 borrowed $4 billion from Russia to finance the purchase of Russian weapons.

When Venezuela came under the control of Maduro in 2013, Russian support continued. This became more important as President Maduro reaped the whirlwind of an implosion in global oil prices, a collapsing economy, and growing opposition to his rule. The political crisis that followed his fraudulent re-election in 2018 resulted in closer Russian support. In a show of support for their beleaguered ally, in December 2018, Moscow sent two Tupolev Tu-160 bombers. But Maduro's problems worsened, in the January 2019 with the opposition-held National Assembly declaring that the dictator's re-election was invalid and that its president, Guiadó, was now recognized as head of state. Russia, along with China, Iran, and Cuba, backed Maduro. Indeed, in February 2019, Russia, along with China, vetoed a United Nations Security Council resolution calling for new presidential elections in Venezuela.

By 2019, Russia's role in Venezuela had expanded considerably. Key to that expansion was one of Russia's major energy companies, Rosneft, which had become very active in the local oil industry. Rosneft is one of the world's largest energy companies, with a market capitalization of around $48 billion. Headquartered in Moscow, it operates globally with operations in Brazil, Cuba, Egypt, Venezuela, and a number of other countries. Rosneft (50.1 percent owned by the Kremlin) presides over, along with the other state-controlled energy company Gazprom, the core elements of the Russian economic engine and, as such, who runs the company has considerable influence in Russia. The company's CEO is Igor Sechin, a close ally of President Putin and considered the country's most powerful oligarch. Indeed, the *Financial Times* Henry Foy noted in 2018 that Sechin is "...widely considered second only to Vladimir Putin as the country's most powerful man" (Foy 2018). Foy also noted, "He was described as unafraid of conflict, ruthless and opportunistic, a man whose political apprenticeship under the president's wing has taught him that might is right."

Sechin is an experienced Russian insider, having graduated from Leningrad State University with a PhD in economics and a proficiency in French and Portuguese. His ability in the Portuguese language was to take him as a military translator as to Angola and Mozambique (both former Portuguese colonies with left-leaning governments upon independence in 1980s). Upon returning to Russia, he served in the St. Petersburg mayor's office, where he worked closely with Putin. He followed Putin into the presidency, where he was deputy chief from 1999 to 2008. However his big move came in 2004, when he was made the chairman of Rosneft, functioning as the government's overseer in the energy business. Sechin is regarded as a member of the *silovki*, a group of former and current members of Russia's security services who believe in state control of the economy and authoritarian principles. Considering Sechin's political clout at home and active involvement in international markets, Rosneft often appears to function as an arm of Russian foreign policy.

Sechin and Rosneft's involvement in Cuba and Venezuela certainly gives the appearance of being an extension of Moscow's foreign policy. In 2008 before he became CEO, he was able to convince pro-Russian governments in Latin America to recognize the two breakaway areas of Georgia (long supported by Russia), Abkhazia, and South Ossetia. Nicaragua was the first country to do this; Sechin soon thereafter visited the Central American country and pledged new investments. Venezuela followed in 2009 with recognition; shortly thereafter Caracas received a $2 billion loan to buy Russian weapons. (The only other countries to recognize the two statelets are Nauru and Syria.)

Sechin's key area of focus in the Caribbean has been Cuba and Venezuela. In 2009, he negotiated with Cuba for his company to become involved in deep-water drilling off its coast and in 2017 it was Rosneft that resumed Russian oil exports. This was significant as Venezuela was increasingly struggling to produce oil and ship it to Cuba. No doubt, Rosneft's actions were helped by personal diplomacy, including his December 2017 visit to the Caribbean country and a meeting with Raúl Castro.

Venezuela, however, was much more important to Russian interests. Indeed, Russia remained committed to the idea that Venezuela's problems were not its own making, but caused by U.S. machinations. As the Wilson Center's Vladimir Rouvinski noted in 2021: "A considerable part of the Russian political establishment has shared Caracas' view that Venezuela's domestic problems are the work of outside forces, primarily the United States. In spite of the economic failures, Russian elites still greatly value their relationship with Venezuela because the leaders of the Bolivarian Republic continue to support Russia politically and are ready to cooperate with Moscow in order to stay in power" (Rouvinski 2021: 34).

China's curtailing of new loans to Venezuela gave Russia a chance to save their ally. As China quietly pulled back, seeking to extract some of their money lent to Venezuela, Rosneft moved in. The Russian oil company not only lent money to PDVSA, it also gained control of two offshore gas fields and large stakes in assets of crude oil. Rosneft also created a consortium with other Russian energy companies to help in investing in Venezuela. Some of the other companies were concerned that they did not have the technology needed to process Venezuelan heavy crude (something U.S. refineries have long been able to do), but Sechin, who headed the consortium, pressed ahead.

Although Venezuela increasingly struggled to repay Russian loans, Moscow emerged as the country's lender of last resort. Since 2015, Rosneft made loans to and purchased crude oil futures from PDVSA for a cumulative amount of $6.5 billion and in December 2016 granted a loan of $1.5 billion against the collateral of 49.9 percent of shares of Citgo, the Venezuelan company's U.S. subsidiary (De la Cruz 2019). Sechin also probably had a hand in extracting loans out of Russia for Venezuela as well, probably around $3 billion. Considering Sechin's clout in the Kremlin and his ability to defeat rivals, he managed to sideline critics within the government over Russia's growing involvement in Venezuela. The logic of the situation was straightforward; for Russia and Rosneft to get repaid, Venezuela needed to sell oil. However, U.S. sanctions were making that difficult. Consequently, one option was to have Rosneft sell Venezuelan crude through its subsidiaries. In 2019 Rosneft Trading and TNK Trading handled a "large percentage" of Venezuela's oil exports and in January 2020, TNK purchased about 14 million barrels of crude from PDVSA (Griffin and Dart 2020).

Rosneft was soon exposed to the cross currents of new Cold War geopolitics in the Caribbean. As part of the effort to tighten the economic noose on the Maduro regime in February 2020, the Trump administration imposed sanctions on Rosneft Trading (a Switzerland-based brokerage firm), which supplies crude to German and Indian refineries and controlled the Citgo stake. The United States claimed that despite well-known sanctions, Rosneft Trading continued operations with PDVSA, concealing shipments and handling more than half of Venezuela's oil exports. The sanctions against Rosneft Trading were followed in March by new ones against TNK Trading (also Swiss-based), for trading Venezuelan crude, arguing that crude allocated to Rosneft Trading was transferred to TNK Trading to evade sanctions (which was true). The penalties would freeze assets of Rosneft Trading within the United States and punish Rosneft's global partners. Rosneft now faced a major dilemma: sanctions is that they could hurt Rosneft's many other business dealings in other parts of the world; as it was Sechin was added to the list of those banned from traveling to the United States None of this was palatable—Rosneft was one of the Kremlin's corporate crown jewels.

The solution was that Rosneft entered into an agreement with a newly created company, Roszarubezhneft, which is 100 percent owned by the Russian government on the sale of shares and termination of its participation in all projects in Venezuela, including shares in a number of production projects in oil service enterprises and trading operations. According to Rosneft, "Based on the results of the agreement, all the assets and trading operations of Rosneft in Venezuela and/or related to Venezuela will be sold, closed or liquidated." As part of Russia's gambit as a gatekeeper for Venezuela's oil flow, the fear of major losses in other areas of operation forced Rosneft's backing down. Despite U.S. sanctions, Russian state support remains in the Venezuelan oil industry, though it is obscured by a high degree of opaqueness, seeking to hide the flow of oil and cash. The advent of the Russo-Ukrainian War and economic sanctions against Russia could bring a return of Russian oil experts, dependent on Moscow's ability to get its people to Venezuela. As it is, tourism has resumed between Russia and Venezuela and Venezuela appears set to join the Mir system, a Russian payment system for electronic fund transactions. The Mir system would help develop the tourist trade and provide Venezuela trade around U.S. economic sanctions (at least with those countries that are members).

The military factor also has been evident in Moscow's approach to Venezuela. While exact numbers are difficult to obtain, Venezuela is thought to have purchased Russia's state-of-the-art S-300 anti-aircraft missiles, imported hundreds of thousands of Kalashnikov rifles and ammunition, and acquired 5000 Igla-S MANPADS (man-portable air defense systems). Russia has also (after a long period of setbacks) established a plant in Venezuela to produce Kalashnikov assault rifles, something that neighboring countries' law enforcement are not pleased by, especially in the Caribbean. Russia has also let its military support demonstrate commitment to keeping Maduro in power; in 2019 Moscow flew in over 1,000 military personnel to help maintain earlier sold arms equipment, including anti-aircraft defenses for Caracas. Another element of the deepening of Russian-Venezuelan relationship is the possibility that the long-delayed establishment of a Kalashnikov rifle production plant, intially planned in 2001, but delayed by corruption scandals, could be finally moving forward. It was also claimed that in Russia hundreds of Russian mercenaries were embedded in Venezuela (Sisk 2019).

Considering that the Maduro regime remains in power in Venezuela, despite pressure from the United States, this has been a success for both Moscow and Havana. Indeed, longtime Russian watcher, Dmitri Simes, observed: "Yet the greatest success for the resurrected friendship between the two countries is undoubtedly Venezuela. Together Russia and Cuba have allowed Venezuelan President Nicolas Maduro to withstand mass protests at home and mounting US sanctions by providing the embattled socialist leader with military, economic and diplomatic support" (Simes 2020). Stirring up trouble in the U.S. backyard also suits Moscow when it plays power politics in the region between Moscow and Berlin. Caracas may be thousands of miles away, but it matters in a global game of geopolitics.

An important point to stress is that Russia's relationships with Venezuela and Cuba is that the primary objectives are to stir up trouble in the U.S. underbelly or the near aboard. Russia may or may not send military advisers, troops, and ships to its Caribbean friends, but the real purpose is to harry its rival close to home. As Douglas Farah, president of IBI Consultants, observed in early 2022: "…Russia is willing and eager to disturb U.S. relations in the region as much as possible, given its limited resources overall and logistical difficulties. The optics of flying intercontinental bombers or docking war ships in harbors is less important than the willingness to sustain U.S. adversaries and implement unconventional methods to undermine U.S. influence and policy while seeking permanent military bases in Nicaragua and Venezuela" (Farah 2022).

RUSSIA AND THE REST OF THE CARIBBEAN

Russia's engagement with the rest of the Caribbean has been small, with the exceptions of bauxite operations in Guyana and Jamaica, some offshore oil exploration in Grenada's waters, and an on-and-off again military agreement with Suriname. Russia's trade with Caribbean countries, with the notable exception of Cuba, is minimal. The second largest Caribbean trade partner for Russia in the region is the Dominican Republic, which imported $68.2 million of Russian goods in 2020 and exported $9.27 million to the Eurasian country. Trade between Russia and the Eastern Caribbean, Dutch Islands, and British overseas territories is tiny. Only in Jamaica did Russia break into the top 10 trade partners in terms of the Caribbean country exporting goods. Compared to the United States, China, European countries, and inter-Caribbean trade, Russia has little to trade in goods that the region needs.

Russia's bauxite/alumina business in the Caribbean is dominated by one company, Rusal (also known as United Company Rusal). It was founded in 2007 out of a merger of a number of companies and is the world's second largest aluminum company. In the Caribbean the company's main operations have been in Jamaica and Guyana. In both countries Rusal has not found great success.

Rusal arrived in Jamaica in 2007, having assumed control of the Swiss commodity trading company Glencore's Jamaican operations (as part of the company sale of its aluminum assets). Rusal's intention was to use Jamaica to supplement its already existing operations, sending what it produced there to Ukraine where the company ran a smelter and for a period, it came to control 65 percent of the island's alumina production capacity and prospects were more encouraging. However, Rusal's Jamaican operations ultimately failed to produce the hoped-for-profits and in 2016, it sold 100 percent of one of its operations to the Chinese state-owned Jiuquan Iron & Steel Group (JISCO). The company's remaining facility became a point of dispute with the Jamaican government, which in 2018 revoked the Russian company's license. The company has disputed this and the matter ended up in the courts (Wilson 2019).

Rusal's other operation in the Caribbean, Guyana, has also been plagued with problems. The Russian company arrived in Guyana in 2006, buying 90 percent of the Berbice operations at Aroaima and Kurubuka, in the Kwakwani, Upper Berbice region. Once one of the leaders in world bauxite production, Guyana's bauxite industry since independence has gone through a period of high profits (many of which did not stay in the country), nationalization, a driving out of foreign companies, mismanagement, and an uneven record in restoring it to economic health. The main company is the Bauxite Company of Guyana Incorporated or BGCI.

Rusal's experience in Guyana raises more questions than answers. Has the company made profits? Did it pay any dividends to the Guyanese government? And what about the way it treats its workers? As a letter to the editors piece in the *Stabroek News* asked in June 2021: "While the government's 10% equity in BCGI gets it only a token board seat, how much of the 1.5% royalty on bauxite production has the company paid? …what is the status of the company's compliance with the Guyana Extractive Industries Transparency Initiative (GYETI)?" (Lowe 2021).

There is another interpretation of Rusal's actions, political meddling in Guyana's March 2020 parliamentary elections. Maximilian Hess, then head of Political Risk Analysis at AKE International in London, noted, "Yet, the timing of Rusal's decision to suspend mining – just four weeks before the vote – suggests potential political intent. Rusal has a long history of political meddling from Montenegro to Tajikistan" (Hess 2020). Adding to the murkiness around Rusal and suggestions that it was engaged in malign activities in regard to the election was the report that three persons with Russian background with cyber equipment were seized and deported. Considering Rusal's track record in political meddling elsewhere, it is possible that there was something going on, though strong evidence remained elusive.

RUSSIA AND THE OFFSHORE CARIBBEAN

The Caribbean has one other use for Russia, the utilization of its offshore financial centers. At one point or another, the Bahamas and Bermuda, the Cayman Islands, British Virgin Islands, Curacao, and Panama have played a role in this, offering a safe harbor for Russian money, some of it from criminal organizations and from high-ranking members of the government and business oligarchs. According to the most reliable estimates, Russia has the world's largest amount of dark money hidden abroad at $1 trillion, with an estimated one-third of this controlled by President Putin and his close associates (Asland and Friedlander 2020; Novokmet et al. 2017).

There is a certain irony to Russia's use of offshore finance. According to the late political scientist Karen Dawisha, Putin's regime is a combination of secret police and organized crime, a "kleptocracy" (Dawisha 2015). This political-economic system has three circles, one law enforcement and the courts (which facilitates control over the state and civil society); the second circle is made up of the major state-owned companies and their bosses who make Putin and his associates as well as themselves wealthy; and the third circle that entails Putin's oil friends from the St. Petersburg business world who obtained companies that substantially benefited from public procurement and asset stripping from the large state firms. Anders Aslund, an economist and long-timer Russian economy watcher, adds a fourth circle to this: offshore assets. He notes: "Ironically, the Kremlin's executive control of the courts have deprived Russia of real property rights, and not only ordinary rich Russians but also its rulers transfer their assets abroad to keep them safe. They must have three requirements for their money's destination: the country must have sound rule of law, allow anonymous ownership, and have deep asset markets, because their assets are substantial" (Asland 2018).

Among the largest listed investors in Russia are the Bahamas and Bermuda, alongside of Cyprus, the Netherlands, Luxembourg, Ireland, and the United Kingdom. This is not a case of Bahamians and Bermudians waking up one morning and deciding that they would make large investments in Russia; rather it is that Russian nationals have used Caribbean (and other countries) countries for their offshore financial services, much like they long used Cyprus, which is much closer to home and for a time had relatively loose regulation.

The challenge of accurately tracking foreign direct investment into Russia (and for a number of other countries) is greatly complicated by the use of "conduit countries," broadly defined by the United Nations Conference on Trade and Development (UNCTAD) as "jurisdictions that are not offshore entities (though some of them are included in the Tax Justice Network list) but are jurisdictions through which large volumes of foreign direct investment (FDI) transit because they host special purpose entities or other entities that facilitate transit investment and offer advantages to investors" (UNCTD 2015). According to the UNCTAD, between 30 and 50 percent of FDI transits through conduit countries. Table 7.1 demonstrates the importance of conduit countries to Russia's foreign direct investment. The key point is that part of foreign direct investment going into Russia is Russian money that has been parked offshore in jurisdictions that offer some type of protection for the ultimate beneficiaries of that money.

One of the major users of the Caribbean's offshore financial services was President Putin, his cronies and companies created to serve the movement of hot money. As investigative journalist Jake Bernstein observed in his examination of the Panama Papers:

> Vladimir Putin haunts the Mossack Fonseca files. The Russian leader managed to be both present and invisible at the same time. No documents exist with his signature. No company form carries his name. He is not officially the director or owner of anything. Nevertheless, he is the

Table 7.1 Breakdown of countries and their foreign direct investment in Russia (2017)

Investing country	Percent
Cyprus	36.8
Netherlands	9.2
Bermuda	7.2
Bahamas	5.8
Luxembourg	4.4
U.K	4.2
Germany	4.1
Singapore	3.7
France	3.4
Switzerland	2.9

Source Bank of Russia. https://www.bloomberg.com/opinion/articles/2019-11-06/where-russia-s-foreign-investment-really-comes-from

North Star in a vast constellation of offshore companies. (Bernstein 2017: 95)

One of the key links in Putin's shell game has been Rossiya Bank, headed by Dmitri Lebedev, whose career like so many around the Russian president, emerged from St. Petersburg. Known as "Putin's bank" Rossiya Bank used Panamanian firm Mossack Fonseca to create a shell company, Sandalwood Continental, which was then registered in the British Virgin Islands in 2006. Over the next seven years as much as $2 billion flowed through the shell company. As noted by Bernstein, "Sandalwood sucked money from the Russian Commercial Bank of Cyprus – which was partially owned by Russia state bank VTB – engaged in questionable loan arrangements, and consistently benefited from curiously advantageous share deals. There are approximately a hundred separate transactions involving Sandalwood and four additional companies as part of the Rossiya Bank network" (Bernstein 2017: 95).

Bank Rossiya was also an active backing classical musician and close friend to Putin, Sergei Roldugin, in his business efforts run through another Panamanian-registered company, Sonnette Overseas. The bank further helped the musician create yet another shell company, Roldugin International Media Overseas (IMO). Although the musician had little business experience, he soon showed a deft hand at complex deals and profit-making, conducting business with Rostec, a Russian military company, and Kamaz, the country's leading truck maker. It is believed that the two Roldugin-linked companies received at least $69 million from 2008 through 2010 from a system of at least 75 offshore entities dubbed the Troika Laundromat (Bernstein 2017; Cerniauskas 2019).

While Eastern Europe has loomed large in Russian money laundering, the Caribbean connection remains important, especially in terms of getting dark money into the United States. As the Atlantic Council's Anders Asland and Julia Friedlander observed: "...the money often moves from the Cayman Islands to the United States – mainly through the State of Delaware – and the United Kingdom. There are the two countries that have the deepest financial markets in the world and accept anonymous companies" (Asland and Friedlander 2020). While regulations in the United States have finally tightened on real estate, it has been alleged in The Washington Post and Financial Times that dirty Russian money reached into many Trump businesses.

Another linkage between Russia and the Caribbean has been in the selling of what are called "golden passports," something that countries such as Antigua and Barbuda, Dominica, and St. Kitts-Nevis have done to help supplement revenues for their governments. Caribbean governments are willing to provide citizenship for an investment. This has attracted Russians, some of whom are thought to have criminal connections. The risk to the Caribbean countries is that if the programs are run poorly and opaquely, they could lead to corruption, including inadequate disclosure of the number of passports issued and revenues collected. Concerns have risen due to connections to alleged Russian criminals, such as Alexander Grigoriev (a Moscow banker who sought St. Kitts-Nevis citizenship) and Pavel Melnikov (who bought a passport from St. Kitts-Nevis and is suspected of money laundering in Finland) (Harding and Pegg 2021). Russian efforts to hide money offshore, ranging from golden passports to secret bank accounts and assets, have become more difficult in the face of Western sanctions because of the Russian-Ukrainian War. That said, the world of hot money is very much like a balloon, squeeze at one end and it comes fills out at the other end.

IRAN AND THE CARIBBEAN

There is nothing like high-seas drama. In 2020–2021 Iran held out a lifeline to the Maduro regime in the face of intense U.S. pressure. Responding to Venezuelan requests for help in meeting gasoline needs, Iran sent a number of tankers, bringing badly needed gasoline. U.S.–Iran relations, already tense on a number of fronts, hit another low. Iran's motivation to become involved in Venezuela is similar to Russia's; Tehran is opposed to a U.S.-led world order; has a historical sense of grievance; it has suffered from U.S. economic sanctions; and likes to believe it can play the role of a great power. To the last point, since the founding of the Islamic Republic in 1979, Iran has survived many lean economic years, fought off an invasion attempt from Iraq, and built a Shiite arc of influence that ranges from Iran through parts of Iraq, all of Syria and into Lebanon (the home of Hezbollah). It played a role in keeping al-Assad in power in Syria and intervened in Yemen's brutish civil war. Moreover, it has pushed ahead to develop its own nuclear power industry (which has worried the United States and the West that the real intent is to build nuclear weapons). Although much of the younger generation would prefer change (i.e. better relations with the West and a functioning economy), the older generation of "revolutionary leaders" in the Revolutionary Guard and, its special forces unit Quds as well as in the theocracy, have little interest in loosening the government's hardline approach to foreign policy and control at home. In this light, Iran's reach into the Caribbean, in particular, Venezuela is part of its claims of being a great power and having the ability to cause trouble for the United States.

Relations between Iran and the United States are complicated. Since the Iranian seizure of the U.S. embassy in 1979, the two countries have not had an "official" relationship, but have operated through third countries. The taking of U.S. diplomats as hostages remains a major grievance from the U.S. side as well as Iran's efforts to destabilize pro-U.S. regimes, like Saudi Arabia and the United Arab Emirates, and Tehran's support of terrorist groups hostile to Israel, a key U.S. ally. From the Iranian side, grievances stem from the Central Intelligence Agency's coup in 1953 which knocked out of office the democratically elected Mohammad Moseddegh, who nationalized the Iranian oil industry. For many Iranians, he was an important force of secular democracy and standing up against foreign domination. U.S. support for the Pahlavi regime also placed the United States on the side of what eventually became an out-of-touch autocratic regime. This combination of grievances and Middle Eastern geopolitics has left relations between Washington and Tehran largely frozen. The exception to this came in 2015 when the United States and several world powers were able to secure a deal (Joint Comprehensive Plan of Action or JCPOA) whereas Iran's nuclear program would be placed under significant restrictions in exchange for sanctions relief. In 2018 the Trump administration walked away from the JCPOA in 2018, claiming it failed to curtail Iran's missile program and regional influence.

What advantages did Iran gain from its relationship with Venezuela? Mahmoud Ahmedinejab, Iran's president from 2005 to 2013, was the main force behind Iran's push into the Americas. Along with Africa, he found opening relations with Caribbean and Latin American countries compelling. His worldview was similar to the old Third World liberation struggle and in Venezuela, Nicaragua, Bolivia (under Evo Morales), and Ecuador (under Rafael Correa) he found soulmates. Indeed, one of the Iranian leader's favorite themes was the imbalance of power between the United States and the developing world. In his speeches he often repeated the following: "The days when a handful of nations could sit around a table and dictate to all other nations of the world are coming to an end. The language of force and threats and colonial attitudes will have to be replaced with a respect for logic, fairness and justice (Ghazvinian 2021: 442–443). Ahmadinejab greatly expanded the number of embassies throughout the Caribbean and Latin America. Taking this into consideration, Venezuela offered Ahmandinejab and his successors a beachhead for diplomatic and commercial expansion into the Americas, while taking a poke at the United States. As CSIS's Moises Rendon and Antonio De La Cruz observed: Chávez ushered the Iranians to his regional allies, opening up channels of communication that led to agreements between Ahmadinejab and the governments of Ecuador, Bolivia, and Nicaragua. As Iran faced increasing financial isolation due to U.S. sanctions, Venezuela, through its Bolivarian Alliance for the Americas (ALBA), helped open up vital trade links" (Rendon and De la Cruz 2020).

Chávez and Ahmadinejab changed the Iran–Venezuela relationship. While the Iranian leader was an Islamic hardliner, he shared two things with his Venezuelan counterpart; both men were populists and had a strong dislike for the United States (Johnson 2021). Having a certain personal chemistry, the two men visited each other in their respective capitals several times and met at the sidelines of international meetings. On a state-to-state level, Iran invested in Venezuela's oil industry and the two countries established the Banco Internacional de Desorrollo (International Development Bank). The bank was funded with startup money of $200 million and according to Bosworth functioned as a "slush fund for projects tied to corruption" (Bosworth 2021: 204). The bank was eventually hit by U.S. sanctions due to its being used by the Ahmadinejab government to fund Hezbollah. Other Iranian projects in Venezuela, such as tractor, bicycle, cement, and plastics plants were attempted, but were largely duds (Johnson 2021: 7–8).

Iran and Venezuela also used the nuclear weapons card to poke at the United States. Washington saw Iran as a major supporter of and participate in international terrorism; the idea of Tehran gaining control of weapons of mass destruction was something taken very seriously. Iran and Venezuela's signing of a nuclear cooperation agreement in 2008 was not well-received in Washington. This was followed by reports that Iran was helping Venezuela look for uranium in 2009 (Reuters 2009; Johnson 2021). In 2008 it was reported that Venezuela had given the Iranian firm Impasco rights to a gold mine concession in the Roraima Basin, located along the Brazilian and Guyanese borders. Although nothing appeared to have emerged from this, Chávez was a supporter of Iran's nuclear power program and with Russian aid had started to work on his own country's nuclear power program.

Iran–Venezuelan relations ebbed following Chávez's death in 2013 and Ahmadinejab's presidential term ending. Trade between the two countries remained small, though the two countries remained supportive of each other in international forums. One area that appeared to maintain the link between Iran and Venezuela was Hezbollah, which received some of its weaponry from Iran and used Venezuela as a base as a hub for the convergence of transnational crime and international terrorism (Humire 2020).

Another dimension of Iran's engagement in Venezuela is that it helps facilitate Hezbollah's activities through its Caracas operations and from there, to the rest of the Caribbean and Latin America. Hezbollah is a major Lebanese political party/organization which emerged from dissatisfied Shiite groups during the Middle Eastern country's civil war that broke out in the 1970s. It has strong backing from Iran, including a steady flow of weapons and money. Part of the Hezbollah organization functions as a military force (which has fought against Israel and most recently in Syria) and is part of outreach through terrorist acts, some conducted in Latin America, such as the 1992 attack against the Israeli embassy in Argentina that killed 29 people and the Israeli Mutual Aid Society in 1994 that killed 85 people. The United States and other Western countries have designated Hezbollah as a terrorist organization.

Hezbollah's push into transnational crime was motivated by the need for money: the flow of cash and weapons from Iran could be sporadic. One of the earlier examples of Hezbollah's dipping its toe into the Latin American and Caribbean drug trade came in 2009, when 17 people were arrested in Curacao for alleged involvement in a drug trafficking ring. This criminal enterprise connected Hezbollah, with traffickers using cargo ships and speed boats to import the drugs from Colombia and Venezuela for shipment to Africa and beyond to Europe. Among those arrested were four people from Lebanon and others from Cuba, Venezuela, and Colombia.

Another case linking Hezbollah, Iran, and Venezuela came in 2020 when the U.S. Department of Justice announced multiple narcoterrorism indictments against the Maduro administration, including the president. This was followed by the indictment of Abel El Zebayar, a former member of Venezuela's National Assembly. According to The U.S. State Attorney's Office, Southern District of New York, El Zebayar, a Venezuelan of Syrian descent was a key member of the Cártel de Los Soles (Cartel of the Sun/a mix of the upper part of the Maduro government and the country's armed forces). Accordingly, "El Zabayar, in particular, has, among other things, participated in weapons-for-cocaine negotiations with the FARC, obtained anti-tank rocket launchers from the Middle East for the FARC as partial payment for cocaine, and recruited terrorists from Hezbollah and Hamas for the purpose of helping to plan and organize attacks against United States interests" (U.S. Department of Justice 2020). He was also alleged to be a liaison between the Venezuelan government and the Syrian president Bashir al-Assad.

One of the key players in the development of Venezuela's Middle Eastern connections has been former vice president and former oil minister, Tareck El Aissami. El Aissami is of Syrian descent, has openly pro-Hezbollah sympathies, and as governor of the state of Aragua is said to have allowed Qods Aviation (from Iran) and sanctioned under the 2007 UN Security Resolution (1747) to operate. It was also rumored that he was recruiting Arab Venezuelans to train with Hezbollah. In many regards, El Assami represents the murky underside of Venezuela's criminal enterprises used for keeping the regime afloat. If anyone could help maintain relations with Hezbollah and Iran it was certainly within his ability and positions in the government. He has been sanctioned by the U.S., Canada, the European Union, and Switzerland for a combination of drug trafficking, money laundering, and human rights violations.

While Iran–Venezuelan relations drifted from 2013 to 2019, many of the same reasons that initially brought the two countries together remained in place. This became evident in 2020, when Iran stepped up to help its ally. By 2020 China and Russia had both pulled back (but not abandoned) their operations in Venezuela. The Maduro regime was struggling both in terms of getting food to its population (because of the embargo and bad distribution) as well as not having enough gasoline to keep the country's autos running as the country's refineries were run down from a lack of experienced staff and maintenance.

Iran's response to Venezuela's shaky gasoline situation was to send engineers and other technicians to help repair some of the refineries. While this brought production up, it hardly met the country's needs. Iran next sent five tankers across the Atlantic and into the Caribbean to Venezuela, where they were unloaded. According to one report, the tankers were loaded with 1.53 million liters of gasoline which covered Venezuela's needs for one month (Al-Barrack 2020). Venezuela was said to have paid for the gasoline and food supplies with gold, some of which was smuggled out of the country.

Iran's willingness to send tankers to Venezuela was a major development intended to help a friend and rile the United States. While the United States had seized other tankers carrying Iranian gasoline, they were registered in third countries, like Liberia. Iran used a certain brinksmanship in sending the tankers, which were carefully watched by the U.S. Navy. The Biden administration, wishing to avoid trouble with Iran and Venezuela, was concerned with what a seizure of an Iranian vessel would do to the flow of international shipping in the Persian Gulf. Considering that the Biden administration would like to return to the negotiating table with Iran, caution was exercised.

Upping the ante one more level, Tehran in June 2021 threatened to send two Iranian Naval ships to Venezuela. The Makran, a converted tanker, has considerable capacity to carry weapons, including missiles. The other ship, the Sahand, was designed for long missions in rough seas like the Atlantic. If the Makran was indeed carrying weapons it would have put the ships in violation of the U.S. sanctions. As it was seven camouflaged Zolfaqar speedboats were visible on the Makran's deck. The speedboats are capable of carrying anti-ship missiles and a 12.7 mm machine gun. Although Iran did not proceed with the weapons delivery by ship, it was a reminder of Iran's growing ability to launch ships into Atlantic waters and the Caribbean. As the Washington Institute for Near East Policy's Farzin Nadimi noted: "Although delivery of these boats would not alter Washington's strategic calculus substantially, the prospect of Venezuela engaging in longer-term asymmetric naval cooperation with the Iranian Revolutionary Guards Corp is worrisome" (Nadimi 2021).

Another picture into the Iran–Venezuela relationship emerged with the 2020 arrest in Cape Verde and 2021 extradition to Miami of Alex Saab, a Colombian businessman of Lebanese descent and international financial fixer for Maduro. Saab had also served as Maduro's secret envoy to Iran's Supreme Leader Ayatollah Ali Khamenei. It is speculated that in April 2021 the Colombian helped facilitate a number of cargo flights (possibly between 12 and 17) by Tehran-owned Mahan Air of Iranian missiles, bombs, and other military equipment to Venezuela in 2021 (Semana 2021). It was reported that two Iranian teams arrived in Venezuela to help train local military forces in the new equipment (Humire 2020). To help facilitate some of the deals, Venezuela made the gasoline purchases by paying in gold, which possibly went through Turkey. According to veteran

Miami Herald reporter Andres Oppenheimer, "Iran's main reason for such weapons transfers…would be to threaten the United States with retaliation in its own neighborhood if the U.S. military were to attack Iran or its allies in the Middle East" (Oppenheimer 2021).

THE HIDDEN HAND OF OIL TRADING

The more active involvement of Iran in Venezuela's oil industry has a link to China. The U.S. embargo on Iranian and Venezuelan oil has not sit well with China. Although Chinese companies cannot be prohibited from trading with Venezuela or Iran, the U.S. government can hurt companies by reducing their access to international finance necessary to conduct day-to-day business. Officially China has not bought any oil from Venezuela since September 2019, but evidence shows that a considerable trade goes on (Saul et al. 2021). Venezuela's leading export destination in 2020 was China, at $1.9 billion. Considering that Venezuela and Iran are mainly oil exporters, it appears that China is willing to circumvent international sanctions. What would happen if Iran and Venezuela colluded to sell their oil to China? It appears that this is what occurred in 2020 and 2021, with the help of a Chinese logistics firm, the China Concord Petroleum Co (CCPC).

CCPC's role in facilitating the flow of Iranian and Venezuelan oil was broken by *Reuters* news agency in July 2021, which used as sources one Chinese-based source familiar with CCPC operations, Iranian officials and a source at PDVSA (Saul et al. 2021). According to the report, CCPC got involved in the Venezuelan oil trade in 2021, chartering ships in April and May carrying over 20 percent of Venezuela's total oil exports in that period (worth close to $445 million). CCPC's engagement fit part of the desire of Iran and Venezuela to sell oil through a system of ship-to-ship transfers (many of them offshore of Malaysia), a mixing of crude with chemicals and giving it a different name (and point of origin), shell companies and middlemen who operate outside of the U.S. financial system. China's buying of Iranian and Venezuelan oil rose in the first half of 2021, indicating that the U.S. economic embargo has some holes in it.

While the activities of China and Russia appear much more above the surface, Iran's ties to Venezuela and, for that matters the Caribbean, are more murky, less well-defined, and much more out of public sight. This leaves more questions than answers as to how the relationship functions beyond Iranian food, gasoline, and diplomatic solidarity for the Maduro regime. As Bosworth noted: "Why are there Qads and Iranian Revolutionary Guard Corp personnel in Venezuela? Is Hezbollah still laundering money in Venezuela, and are there active threats from Hezbollah cells. How much gold has been transferred from Venezuela to Iran?" (Bosworth 2021).

Iran has also made some forays into other parts of the Caribbean and Latin America beyond Venezuela. President Ahmadinejab visited the region in 2009 and his 2012 tour touched ground in not only Venezuela, but also Ecuador, Guatemala, Cuba, and Nicaragua. Despite Iranian commentary on promoting greater cooperation with Latin American countries, Iran's ability to deliver infrastructure projects and other programs has not matched the rhetoric. In Nicaragua it promised to build a $230 million hydroelectric plant and a $350 million deep-water port in 2007; neither has seen construction (Maradiaga and Meléndez 2008). For Iran the reach-out to Caribbean and Latin American leftist governments beyond Venezuela and, to a lesser extent Cuba, is more symbolic than anything else, especially when considering what China and, even Russia, has delivered much more over the past decade.

It is worth a few comments on the Cuban–Iranian relationship. When the Islamic Republic came into power in 1979 it found a ready friend in Fidel Castro. Both countries were strongly anti-American and in need of international friends. This allowed a long history of cooperation in the areas of trade, science, security, and diplomatic alignment. While the trade relationship is small, the two countries have made more headway on joint science effort, including the transfer of technology of Cuba's Sobermnoma-2 vaccine to Iran (Giambertoni 2021). On the diplomatic front, the two countries are also supportive of each other. Indeed, Iran made the right diplomatic narrative of support for Díaz-Canel's government during the 2021 riots. Human rights are not a driver in Cuban–Iranian relations; realpolitik is the main force and is linked back to a mutual animosity vis-à-vis the United States.

Iran's role in the Caribbean fits the new Cold War narrative—to a degree. Although the leadership in Tehran has changed a number of times since 1979, it remains conservative, hardline, and anti-American. There have been a few openings, such as the nuclear deal struck during the Obama administration, but the narrative is dominated by mutual distrust and a willingness to use violence on both sides. Hassan Rouhani, president from 2013 to 2021 was considered a moderate and willing to negotiate a nuclear deal with the U.S. and Western countries. The Trump administration walked away from the deal, taking a hardline on Iran, especially for its terrorist activities throughout the Middle East. The assassination of Major General Qassem Soleimani, the head of Quds Force and architect of Tehran's proxy wars in the Middle East in January 2021 was done to preempt his plans to attack U.S. diplomats and service members in Iraq and throughout the region. Although the Biden administration has indicated a willingness to return to the bargaining table with Iran over the nuclear issue, the winner of Iran's 2021 election, Ebrahim Raisi, is a hardliner and not likely to open to go too far down the road of giving away Iran's nuclear program. The U.S. embargo is proving to be leaky and Iran has allies, including China, Russia, and Venezuela. The last gives Iran and, by extension, Hezbollah, a pressure point on the United States.

CONCLUSION

When thinking of Caribbean geopolitics, Iran and Russia do not automatically leap first to the mind. However, in a global system undergoing realignments, the two countries are playing a role, which is not defined so much by the relationship between Caribbean countries and Iran and Russia, but how these external powers relate to the United States. Considering the level of tensions between Washington and Tehran and Moscow, there is an incentive for the latter two to be active within certain parameters in the Caribbean. The asymmetry of the United States and Europe having NATO right up against the Russian border and the conflict between Russia and Ukraine, Moscow has an incentive to use its distant connections in the Caribbean as a means to stir up trouble for the United States, even if its resources are stretched and Ukraine. The same can be said of the United States has spent the last several decades being able to sail in and out of the Persian Gulf; now Iran can put ships in the Atlantic and mobilize a small presence in the Caribbean. It also weakens the impact of U.S. economic sanctions. This is evident in the flow of Venezuelan oil to China, via Malaysia, helped along by a Chinese company that conducts the same trading activities to getting Iranian crude to Chinese refineries. At the same time, Hezbollah's activities in the Caribbean are mainly criminal in nature and erode the rule of law in those countries where it is active. What makes all of this significant is that Iran's and Russia's Caribbean ventures complement China's more active presence in the region, giving it more of Cold War feel. This is likely to be reinforced by ongoing cooperation between the three countries over a number of issues, many of them involving energy. How far that cooperation develops is questionable, but it does give credence to the idea of a loose counter bloc to the United States, something that Caribbean policymakers will increasingly need to consider.

References

Al-Barrack, Jaafar Mohsen. 2020. What Does Iran Do in the Caribbean? Al-Bayan Center for Planning and Studies, Baghdad, Iraq. https://www.bayanc enter.org/en/2020/06/2082/.

Ashby, Timothy. 1987. *The Bear in the Backyard: Moscow's Caribbean Strategy.* Lexington: Lexington Books.

Asland, Anders. 2018. How the United States Can Combat Russia's Kleptocracy. Atlantic Council, July 31. https://www.atlanticcouncil.org/in-depth-res earch-reports/issue-brief/how-the-united-states-can-combat-russia-s-klepto cracy/.

Asland, Anders, and Julia Friedlander. 2020. Defending the United States against Russian Dark Money. Atlantic Council, November 20. https://www.atlanticcouncil.org/wp-content/uploads/2020/11/Russia-Dark-Money-Printable-PDF.pdf.

Bernstein, Jake. 2017. *Secrecy World: Inside the Panama Papers Investigation of Illicit Money Networks and the Global Elite.* New York: Henry Holt and Company.

Bosworth, James. 2021. Venezuela's Relations with Iran: Maduro's Lifesaver in 2020. In *Venezuela's Authoritarian Allies: The Ties that Bind?* ed. Cynthia Anson. Woodrow Wilson Latin American Program. https://www.wilsoncen ter.org/sites/default/files/media/uploads/documents/LAP_210510-Venezu elas%20Authoritarian%20Allies-V5.pdf.

Cerniauskas, Sarunas. 2019. Money for Nothing: Putin Friend Sergei Roldugin Enriched by Troika Laundromat. *OCCRP*, March 7. https://www.occrp.org/en/troikalaundromat/money-for-nothing-putin-friend-sergei-roldugin-enriched-by-troika-laundromat.

Choksy, Jamsheed K., and Carol E.B. Choksy. 2020. China and Russia Have Iran's Back. *Foreign Affairs*, November 17. https://www.foreignaffairs.com/articles/united-states/2020-11-17/china-and-russia-have-irans-back.

Conley, Heather A., Cyrus Newlin, and Tim Kostelancik. 2020. Countering Russian & Chinese Influence Activities. Center for Strategic & International Studies. https://csis-website-prod.s3.amazonaws.com/s3fs-public/pub lication/200714_Newlin_FullReport_v4_WEB%20FINAL.pdf.

Dawisha, Karen. 2015. *Putin's Kleptocracy: Who Owns Russia?* Simon and Schuster.

De La Cruz, Antonio. 2019. Putin Continues to Stick His Neck Out for Maduro. Center for Strategic & International Studies, November 8. https://www.csis.org/analysis/putin-continues-stick-his-neck-out-maduro.

Farah, Douglas. 2022. What Are Russia's Military Intentions in Latin America? Latin American Adviser, February 1. https://www.thedialogue.org/latin-america-advisor/.

Foy, Henry. 2018. We Need to Talk About Igor: The Rise of Russia's Most Powerful Oligarch. *Financial Times*, March 1. https://www.ft.com/content/dc7d48f8-1c13-11e8-aaca-4574d7dabfb6.

Ghazvinian, John. 2021. *America and Iran: A History 1720 to the Present.* New York: Alfred A. Knoff.

Giambertoni, Marzia. 2021. The Enemy of My Enemy: The US and Cuba-Iran Ties. The Middle East Institute, December 17. https://www.mei.edu/publications/enemy-my-enemy-us-and-cuba-iran-ties.

Griffin, Rosemary, and Jonathan Dart. 2020. Rosneft to Cease Venezuela Operations, Sell Assets to Russian Government. *S&P Global*, March 28. https://www.spglobal.com/platts/en/market-insights/latest-news/oil/032820-rosneft-to-cease-venezuela-operations-sell-assets-to-russian-government.

Global Americans. 2021. Measuring the Impact of Misinformation, Disinformation, and Propaganda in Latin America. Global Americans. https://theglobalamericans.org/wp-content/uploads/2021/10/2021.10.28-Global-Americans-Disinformation-Report.pdf.

Gurganus, Julia. 2018. Russia: Playing a Geopolitical Game in Latin America. Carnegie Endowment for International Peace. https://carnegieendowment.org/2018/05/03/russia-playing-geopolitical-game-in-latin-america-pub-76228.

Harding, Luke, and David Pegg. 2021. How 'Golden Passports' Firm Lays on VIP Service to Colorful List of Clients. *The Guardian*, April 22. https://www.theguardian.com/world/2021/apr/22/how-golden-passports-firm-lays-on-vip-service-to-colourful-list-of-clients.

Hess, Maximilian. 2020. Rusal's Bauxite Mine and Potential Russian Meddling in Guyana's Election. Foreign Policy Research Institute, April 8. https://www.fpri.org/article/2020/04/rusals-bauxite-mine-and-potential-russian-meddling-in-guyanas-election/. The author followed up with an interview with Hess on September 29, 2020, where some of the ideas were expanded upon which are in the text.

Humire, Joseph M. 2020. The Maduro-Hezbollah Nexus: How Iran-Backed Networks Prop Up the Venezuelan Regime. Atlantic Council. https://www.atlanticcouncil.org/wp-content/uploads/2020/10/The-Maduro-Hezbollah-Nexus-How-Iran-backed-Networks-Prop-up-the-Venezuelan-Regime.pdf.

Johnson, Stephen. 2021. Iran's Influence in the Americas. Center for Strategic & International Studies, February. https://csis-website-prod.s3.amazonaws. com/s3fs-public/legacy_files/files/publication/120223_Johnson_IranInfluence_ExecSumm_Web.pdf.

Lowe, Sherwood. 2021. Opportune Moment to Resolve RUSAL Issues, Adjust Mining Policy. *Stabroek News* (Guyana), February 16. https://www.stabroeknews.com/2021/06/16/opinion/letters/opportune-moment-to-resolve-rusal-issues-adjust-mining-policy/.

Meléndez, Javier, and Felix Maradiaga. 2008. Iranian-Nicaraguan Relations Under the Sandinista Government: Rhetoric or Anti-Establishment Foreign Policy? In *Iran in Latin America: Threat or "Axis of Annoyance"*, ed. Cynthia Arnson, Haleh Esfandiari and Adam Stubits. Woodrow Wilson Center. https://www.wilsoncenter.org/sites/default/files/media/documents/publication/Iran_in_LA.pdf

Nadimi, Farzin. 2021. Iran's Atlantic Voyage: Implications for Naval Deployments to Venezuela or Syria. The Washington Institute for Near East Policy, June 15. https://www.washingtoninstitute.org/policy-analysis/irans-atlantic-voyage-implications-naval-deployments-venezuela-or-syria.

Novokmet, Filip, Thomas Piketty, and Gabriel Zucman. 2017. From Soviets to Oligarchs: Inequality and Property in Russia, 1905–2016. NBER Working Paper No. 23712. Cambridge, MA: National Bureau of Economic Research, August. https://www.nber.org/system/files/working_papers/w23712/w23712.pdf.

Oppenheimer, Andres. 2021. Colombian Man Extradited to Miami May Know Secrets of Iran Arms Shipments to Venezuela: Opinion. *Miami Herald*, October 20. https://www.miamiherald.com/article255155672.html.

Rendon, Moise, and Antonio De la Cruz. 2020. Understanding the Iran-Venezuela Relationship. Center for Strategic & International Studies. https://www.csis.org/analysis/understanding-iran-venezuela-relationship.

Reuters. 2009. Iran Helping Venezuela Look for Uranium. *Reuters*, September 25. https://www.reuters.com/article/us-nuclear-iran-venezuela-sb/iran-helping-venezuela-look-for-uranium-idUSTRE58P03T20090926.

Roth, Andrew. 2019. Russian Mercenaries Reportedly in Venezuela to Protect Maduro. *The Guardian*, January 25. https://www.theguardian.com/world/2019/jan/25/venezuela-maduro-russia-private-security-contractors.

Rouvinski, Vladimir. 2021. Venezuela: Russia's Gordian Knot in Latin America. In Cynthia Anson's Venezuela's Authoritarian Allies: The Ties That Bind? Wilson Center Latin American Program. https://www.wilsoncenter.org/sites/default/files/media/uploads/documents/LAP_210510-Venezuelas%20Authoritarian%20Allies-V5.pdf.

Russian Federation. 2016. Foreign Policy Concept Paper of the Russian Federation (approved by the President of the Russian Federation Vladimir Putin on November). The Ministry of Foreign Affairs of the Russian Federation. https://www.rusemb.org.uk/rp_insight/.

Saul, Jonathan, Chen Aizhu, and Marianna Parraga. 2021. China's CCPC Takes Centre Stage in Iran, Venezuela Oil Trade—Sources. *Reuters*, July 22. https://www.reuters.com/business/energy/exclusive-chinas-ccpc-takes-centre-stage-iran-venezuela-oil-trade-sources-2021-07-22/.

Semana. 2021. Colombia en peligro: SEMANA Revela las Pruebas de los Misiles, bombas y radars que Maduro le Compró a Irán. *Semana* (Colombia), October 9. https://www.semana.com/nacion/articulo/amenaza-los-misiles-bombas-y-radares-que-maduro-le-compro-a-iran-y-ponen-en-serio-peligro-a-colombia/202146/.

Simes, Dmitri. 2020. Putin Is Resurrecting Russia's Cold War Pact with Cuba. *The Spectator*, February 6. https://www.spectator.co.uk/article/putin-is-resurrecting-russia-s-cold-war-pact-with-cuba.

Sisk, Richard. 2019. Hundreds of Russian Mercenaries Now in Venezuela, US Adminral Says. *Military.com*. October 4. https://www.military.com/daily-news/2019/10/04/hundreds-russian-mercenaries-now-venezuela-us-admiral-says.html.

Taylor, Adam. 2018. Putin Says He Wishes the Soviet Union Has Not Collapsed. Many Russians Agree. *The Washington Post*, March 3. https://www.washingtonpost.com/news/worldviews/wp/2018/03/03/putin-says-he-wishes-he-could-change-the-collapse-of-the-soviet-union-many-russians-agree/.

Telesur. 2020. Russian FM Lavrov Starts Latin America Tour in Cuba. *Telesur*, February 5. https://www.telesurenglish.net/news/Russian-FM-Starts-a-Tour-of-Latin-America-in-Cuba-20200205-0022.html. Accessed 24 Sep 2020.

Trenin, Dimitri. 2019. *Russia*. Cambridge: Polity Press.

Treisman, Daniel. 2011. *The Return: Russia's Journey from Gorbachev to Medvedev*. New York: Free Press.

UNCTD. 2015. *World Investment Report 2015*. https://unctad.org/system/files/official-document/wir2015_en.pdf.

U.S. Department of Justice, The U.S. Attorneys' General Office. Southern District of New York. 2020. Former Member of Venezuelan National Assembly Charged with Narco-Terrorism, Drug Trafficking, and Weapons Offenses, May 27. https://www.justice.gov/usao-sdny/pr/former-member-venezuelan-national-assembly-charged-narco-terrorism-drug-trafficking-and.

Wilson, Nicky. 2019. Bauxite Battle: Russians Take Govt to Court for Revoking License. *The Gleaner* (Jamaica), January 24. https://jamaica-gleaner.com/article/lead-stories/20190124/bauxite-battle-russians-take-govt-court-revoking-licence.

Wright, Robin. 2022. Russia and China Unveil a Pact Against America and the West. *The New Yorker*, February 7. https://www.newyorker.com/news/daily-comment/russia-and-china-unveil-a-pact-against-america-and-the-west.

CHAPTER 8

Europe, Canada, the Caribbean, and the New Cold War

The slide into a new Cold War between China and the United States in the Caribbean is not just an issue for those two countries. As reflected by the earlier chapters on Taiwan and this chapter on European countries and Canada, other actors are affected. France, the Netherlands and the United Kingdom maintain territories in the Caribbean, while Spain maintains close ties with its former colonial possessions, namely Cuba and the Dominican Republic. Canada has thought of itself having a "special relationship" with the English-speaking Caribbean and to some degree with French-speaking Haiti. The entrance of China into the Caribbean as well as its active role in Europe and areas of European national interest (like the Balkans, Middle East, and Africa) has caused a reassessment of Europe's, the UK's and Canada's role in the Caribbean. The European situation is more complicated in that the European Union has 27 member countries, with the largest economy in that Union, Germany, having little direct national interests in the Caribbean. Germany's interest are more weighted to its economic ties to the rest of Europe, the United States, China, and Russia. This chapter argues that it is complicated to have a unified European policy on the Caribbean; that sensitivity to China's larger role in the region is a point of concern for those countries with interest there; and that if the new Cold War deepens, there could be a divergence in European views on the importance of the Caribbean.

On December 4, 2021 Barbados made a change of direction. Its long-standing relationship with the British monarchy ended as the island state became a republic. Instead of having the Queen as the head of state, that role was now assumed by a president. The handover ceremony included a declaration of Barbados' constitutional independence, a speech (described as "contrite") by Prince Charles and the international singer Rihanna was formally declared a national hero (Ivens 2021). Barbados is not the first former British colony in Caribbean to go down this path; Guyana, Trinidad and Tobago, and Dominica have left the royal fold, having created presidential positions to replace the monarch as head of state (though the Queen remains recognized as the head of the Common-wealth). While pro-monarchy Barbadians may be sad over the policy shift, one of the more surprising twists in this story came when Tom Tugendhat, chair of the UK Parliament's Foreign Affairs Committee, earlier suggested that Prime Minister Mott's government in Barbados had been manipulated by China in an effort to undermine London's historical status as a key partner with Caribbean countries. Indeed, he stated, "China has been using infrastructure investment and debt diplomacy as a means of control for a while and it's coming closer to home for us" (Fisher 2020). Other British media fell into line with this sentiment, with *The Times* (London), headlining a story with the following, "Little England? Not Any More – Barbados Becoming Little China" (Ivers 2021; Tylecote 2021; Campbell 2021).

There were two things to take from Mr. Tugendhat's comments. First, China may be guilty of many things, but it is questionable that President Xi has decided to strike at the British by pushing Barbados to become a republic. The second thing is more significant; the UK is more sensitive to China's greater role in the Caribbean. The same can be said of a number of other European countries, especially those with a presence in the region, which include France and the Netherlands as well as Spain which has maintained special interest in its former colonies, Cuba and the Dominican Republic. But the European countries are not alone in watching China's rise and the slide to a new Cold War in the Caribbean; Canada has a longstanding relationship with the region. Faced with its own challenging relationship with China, Canada has gradually become aware of the Asian country's growing role in the Caribbean (as well as Russia's talk of upping its military assets in the region), which raises questions as what Ottawa should be doing to define its interests and how to protect them.

It is the purpose of this chapter to examine how the geopolitical realignment taking place in the Caribbean is playing out with Europe's and Canada's role in the region. There is a growing awareness that China has made inroads into regional trade and investment, some of it at the cost of European and Canadian economic interests. There is also concern that as China seeks to recast the global system more to its vision, the Caribbean is beginning to offer Beijing allies in international forums, which are regarded as important to Europe and Canada in terms of liberal democracy, human rights, good governance practices and anti-money laundering actions. An added layer to the complexity of the drift to a new Cold War in the Caribbean is a growing divergence in what Europe and the United States want in terms of a global system. Simply stated, "the West" is not what it used to be during the old Cold War; in the new Cold War-like situation thus far there appears to be much less cohesiveness as to grand strategic goals. And there are also different views on the role of the Caribbean in European foreign policy. The British, Dutch, French and Spanish assign some strategic importance to the Caribbean for trade, investment and cultural ties. In that sense it is worth playing a role in the region. For Germany, the European Union's economic locomotive, the Caribbean is far away and it is peripheral to its core interest. For Eastern European nations, such as Poland, Estonia and Lithuania, the Caribbean is a distraction for EU policy as the new Cold War is up front and close in the form of Russian troops on their national borders, spying, propaganda and cyberwarfare. Nonetheless, European-Caribbean ties and those with Canada have some significance in the greater scheme of the new Cold War that are worth exploring.

THE EUROPEAN CARIBBEAN

Europe has been in the Caribbean since the late fifteenth century, radically altering the region's demographics, and shaping its modern societies and economies. In the 2020s Europe maintains a number of jurisdiction in the region, most of which are relatively small islands with scant resources, limited populations and dependent on tourism as the economic mainstay. The exception is French Guiana, which is located on the northeast shoulder of South America, between Brazil, Suriname, and the Atlantic Ocean. Its economy is dominated by the Centre Spatial Guyanais in Kourou, which accounts for 25 percent of GDP, fishing, and forestry. Other economic activities in the mix of islands include offshore financial

218 S. B. MACDONALD

services (as in the British Virgin Islands and Cayman Islands), some agricultural production (as in Guadeloupe and Martinique), and oil refining (as in Curacao). Because of this the Dutch and French Caribbean territories have opted to remain closely linked to their metropoles, which makes them part of the EU.[1]

China is present in the European Caribbean, but its trade and investment substantially trails that of the United States and Netherlands in the Dutch islands and behind France in the French departments. In Guadeloupe, Martinique, and French Guiana, for example, the top trade partner is France (with over 60 percent of imports and exports), with the rest of trade left to other European, Caribbean and North American countries. China factors more in Aruba and Curacao, but still lags well behind the United States and the Netherlands. One area where Chinese companies have shown some activity is Curacao with listings on the Dutch Caribbean Securities Exchange (De Feijter 2020).

Relations between China and the EU cooled in the late 2010s and early 2020s. In the Caribbean, this was felt when the Dutch government assumed a tougher stance on Chinese investment in their Caribbean territories. As part of the Kingdom of the Netherlands, any major investment deals being conducted in the Dutch islands are under Dutch jurisdiction. In 2019, the Dutch government announced: "The Caribbean countries of the Kingdom are economically autonomous, while their foreign policy remains a matter for the kingdom. Because China linked economic and foreign policy, effective cooperation within the Kingdom is needed with regard to China. In cases where China is looking to invest in other parts of the Kingdom, the government has therefore agreed to work with the other Kingdom countries from the outset and share expertise" (Government of the Kingdom of the Netherlands 2019).

Europe's relationship with the rest of the Caribbean is largely driven by trade and investment. A quick perusal through ECLAC's *Direct Foreign Investment in Latin America and the Caribbean 2019* gives a broad idea of the scope of Europe's investment in the region: French and Spanish companies are active in investing in hotels throughout the Caribbean,

---

[1] The Dutch Caribbean evolved from being first under the constitutional framework of the Netherlands Antilles, but when this fragmented in 2010, the current arrangement of treating Aruba, Curacao and St. Maarten as countries under the Constitution of the Netherlands (along with Holland) and making Bonaire, Saba and St. Eustatius into special municipalities was put in face.

including in Cuba and the Dominican Republic; an Icelandic company, Reykjavik Geothermal (along with Canada's Emera Inc.), signed an agreement with the St. Vincent Electricity Services Limited for the construction of a geothermal power plant; and a French company, Rubis, purchased Haiti's main fuel distributor, DINASA. Although European investment lags behind U.S. investment in the Caribbean, it remains a more potent force than China, especially in tourism (Chinese investment has usually been linked to infrastructure, mining, and energy).

European trade with the Caribbean is largely focused on the larger countries, the Dominican Republic, Cuba, and Jamaica. One of the largest Caribbean-European trade relationships is between Spain and Cuba, which was worth a little over $1.1 billion in 2019, just ahead of China, making the Iberian nation the Caribbean country's major trade partner. Italy, Germany, and France were also significant Cuban trade partners (mainly with the import of European goods). The Netherlands is the other major European country participating in trade with the Caribbean: according to the IMF Direction of Trade statistics, Dominican-Dutch trade amounted to a little over $700 million in 2019 and 2020. Dutch trade is also significant in Suriname, Jamaica, and Barbados.

One of the instruments for Caribbean-EU trade has been the CARIFORUM-EU Economic Partnership Agreement signed in 2008. On the Caribbean side this covered the English-speaking Caribbean countries, the Dominican Republic and Suriname as well as the British, Dutch, and French territories. The main purpose has been to facilitate trade between the EU and Caribbean countries. Taken as a whole, the EU countries are CARIFORUM's second largest trading partner, after the United States.

Europe's other major economic link to the Caribbean came through what was known as the Africa, Caribbean, and Pacific (ACP) group, which was established in 1975. In 2020, the group was renamed the Organization of African, Caribbean, and Pacific States, with 79 states as members. Initially providing a forum for trade and development assistance for former colonies and overseas territories, its importance faded through the end of the twentieth century and early twenty-first century as the ties built around shared colonial experiences became less relevant. At the same time, Europe's development focus turned closer to home in Eastern Europe and the western Balkans and the demands of free trade (which challenged preferential trade agreements). Along the lines of the last point, the EU had long maintained a preferential trade regime for bananas, which was a major boost for the economies of Dominica, Grenada, St. Lucia, St. Vincent, and the Grenadines and was important to Jamaica (Bernal 2020). This was given up in the early 2000s after the Clinton administration, pushed along by the multinational corporation Chiquita, took the matter to the World Trade Organization. It was also a damaging blow to the Caribbean countries that had depended on banana exports.

Europe, the New Cold War, and the Caribbean

In the 2020s Europe faces multiple challenges which impact its ability to play a larger role in Caribbean affairs or to act as a counterforce to China. After a period of considerable EU membership expansion in the 1990s and the first decade of the twenty-first century, the 2010s proved to be a period of considerable stress. This came in the form of economic imbalances as well as fiscal and debt management problems in the aftermath of Greece's debt default in 2012. In the mid-2010s migration from the Middle East and Africa added to pressures on the EU, as it created a sharp divide between those countries like Germany and Sweden which were initially willing to take in refugees and those that were not, like Hungary and Poland. This mix of developments helped fuel the rise of leftwing and rightwing populism, which, in turn, fueled nationalism, one manifestation being the 2016 United Kingdom vote to leave the EU, known as Brexit.

The international environment also became more challenging. Europe faced a more aggressive Russia. Europe's relations with the other major powers, the United States and China, also became increasingly more complicated. U.S. demands that Europe carry its fair share of the costs of NATO and the Obama administration's "pivot to Asia" reflected a growing divergence between Washington and Brussels, Paris and Berlin. Indeed, U.S. and European thinking about the global system had shifted incrementally from the Bush and Obama administrations, a process which accelerated more sharply under President Trump, who disdained multilateralism, preferred nationalism, and believed that international relations is a zero sum game. The Dutch think tank, The Hague Centre for Strategic Studies, observed how many European countries viewed this shift in relations, "...the global balance of power...is changing rapidly, and the multilateral system is under pressure. Erosion or even collapse of the multilateral system could potentially have disastrous consequences for the Netherlands: it would expose the country to geopolitical forces over which we have no control and relegate it to a toy of the major powers" (de Wijk et al. 2020). This view encompassed the Trump administration's harder stance on China, pushing the "us v. them" argument, leaving Europe increasingly in the crossfire of the two major powers.

The new geopolitical landscape was particularly disappointing for many European countries. The Trump administration's launching of a trade war in 2018 against China and China's retaliatory measures had a major negative effect on Europe, home to some of the world's major exporting giants, such as Germany, the Netherlands, the United Kingdom, France and Italy. Indeed, the EU as a whole constitutes the world's largest exporter. European concerns about the U.S. shift to protectionism were not helped by the Trump administration's imposition of tariffs on steel as well as ongoing threats to start a trade war with the EU. At the same time, relations with China, also a major trade and investment partner, shifted as Chinese investment increasingly came to challenge European dominance in other markets. Furthermore, a number of Balkan countries signed memorandums of understanding with China to be part of the BRI, among them Bulgaria, Croatia, Cyprus, Greece, and Hungary. Even longtime EU members, such as Austria and Italy signed up. China's buying up of ports and actively engaging in road building, selling of telecommunications products (through companies Huawei and ZTE), and extension of cheap loans through its state-owned banks increasingly concerned European policymakers.

China has also emerged as a competitor to many European companies in a wide range of sectors, including automobiles (electronic models and otherwise), alternative energy, and telecommunications equipment and services (including 5G), and precision engineering equipment. This has been a shock to many European companies, in particular those from Germany, which long counted upon China as a secure major market. Chinese high quality goods are now competing with German and other European companies, even within Europe. As one observer noted, "Now, Chinese companies are supplying wind turbines in France, buses in Norway, power grids in Poland and advanced industrial machinery across the world. In Sweden's capital, a Chinese group recently secured a contract to dig three big tunnels for the Stockholm metro" (Fairless 2020).

The Chinese economic juggernaut has increasingly come under European scrutiny, especially with the use of Huawei products and whether to use the Chinese company to build Europe's 5G networks. Initially this did not appear to be a problem, but growing pressure from the United States on the issue as well as increasing concerns over compromising security within Europe led to friction with China. As already outlined in previous chapters, the main concern is that Huawei's equipment could be used for espionage by China. Moreover, China in the late 2010s ramped up disinformation activities to support populists and threats by senior diplomats. Probably the most notable case of this came in 2019 when the Chinese ambassador to Sweden said on Swedish public radio, "we treat our friends with fine wine, but for our enemies we have shotguns." This came in the midst of Swedish criticism of Chinese human rights violations and the detention of a Swedish citizen. China also took tough measures (suspending Lithuanian beef imports) against Lithuania in 2022 over the Baltic country allowing Taiwan to open a trade office.

Other factors soured Europe's once positive view of China, "including the deepening authoritarianism under Xi; the abandonment of hopes for meaningful economic reform in China; a comprehensive reassertion of the role of Chinese Communist Party throughout societal and economic life; the externalization of the Chinese government's most problematic political and economic practices through the Belt and Road Initiative (BRI); and the acceleration of Beijing's techno-nationalist agenda through the Made in China 2025 strategy and China Standards 2035 plans" (Small 2020). The Covid-19 pandemic also played its part. China's claims that the pandemic was actually caused by U.S. spies failed to gain traction in Europe. There was also resentment over the manipulation of Chinese "mask diplomacy." One case in particular caused a degree of irritation: in 2020 days after Beijing had announced it was sending urgent medical supplies to Italy, Chinese state media showed Italians on their balconies and in the streets applauding the Chinese national anthem, which evidence made questionable (Johnson and Yang 2020). However, it fit the narrative that China wanted to show its own citizens of how well-loved they were around the world, despite the pandemic. China's approach at this time—when Europe was struggling to contain the virus—included a propaganda push highlighting the weaknesses of democracy compared to authoritarianism in being able to enact the right policies. This did not endear Beijing to European leadership.

In the 2020s Europe faces a geopolitical chess board in which China is busy reshaping international organizations to its national interests and the United States is reducing its global role but has adopted a more geopolitical approach to its intercourse with the world. This reflects different views of reality. Europe, in particular, Germany, wants to live in the world that emerged in the early post-Cold War period, where "history ended," an expression derived from the U.S. political scientist Francis Fukuyama's book, *The End of History*. As German foreign policy expert Nora Mueller of the Koeber Foundation observed: "While the tectonic plates of geopolitics are shifting, one thing remains constant: Despite the deterioration in Germany's security environment, the want their country to be a kind of great Switzerland – not a creative international actor...only four out of ten German citizens are in favor of a more active German role in the world" (Mueller 2019).

Accordingly, the ideological frictions of the Cold War ended and a new multilateral world has replaced it, one where defense spending can be scaled down and economic well-being was central. Europe is very reluctant to give up this perception of reality. The problem is that the Chinese probably never believed in the end of history and the United States has returned to geopolitics. Much of Europe remains committed to the end of history mindset when it has gone out of fashion with one major power (the United States) and is being manipulated by the other (China). While this has led to friction with the United States, it has also left Europe dealing with China's push for dominating the narratives at such bodies as the WHO, FAO and the UN Human Rights Council.

EUROPE, CHINA, AND THE CARIBBEAN

How have Chinese-European relations influenced Europe's relationship with the Caribbean? The simple answer is that Europe has become more cautious about allowing Chinese investment in its territories and is less welcoming to China's activities in the rest of the region—to a point. One of the key lines in the EU report outlining China as a strategic rival was the issue of what has been called debt diplomacy, mentioned in prior chapters. While the EU recognizes that Chinese financing has helped facilitate economic growth, it has come with strings. As the European Council 2019 report noted: "...these investments frequently neglect socioeconomic and financial sustainability and may result in high-level indebtedness and transfer of control over strategic assets and resources. This compromises efforts to promote good social and economic governance and, most fundamentally, the rule of law and human rights" (European Council 2020). This message was mainly directed to Chinese penetration in the Balkans and Eastern Europe, it was also part of the message for the Caribbean (though hardly with the same drum beat as U.S. policy).

While Europe and the UK have hardened their views, they also have differences with the United States over Caribbean issues. While the broad brushstrokes of U.S. and European policies are supportive of democracy, human rights, and open markets, the Caribbean is a far lower priority to Brussels and Berlin than to Washington. Additionally, the European approach has generally been supportive of multilateral approaches, lengthy negotiations and, when appropriate, economic statecraft, including sanctions. The U.S. approach during the Trump years was more broadly focused on a mixed economic statecraft strategy, occasionally backed by the threat of military force and heightened policing (i.e. using anti-drug trafficking as a means of cutting down on the illicit financing of the Maduro regime in Venezuela). U.S. Caribbean policy under the Trump administration was more hardline, seeking to force countries to pick a side. Although the Biden administration has been less hardline than its forerunner, the new Cold War policy line has remained largely intact. Although Europe is more concerned, it remains less inclined to take a stand on the Caribbean, at least one that has any commitment of resources.

The two major cockpits of the new Cold War, Cuba and Venezuela, are instructive of the complexity of European relations with the Caribbean, the United States, China and Russia. With Cuba, Europe has enjoyed a lengthy relationship, which though it had low points during parts of Fidel Castro's long reign, benefited European business. While the United States has maintained an embargo on Cuba since 1960, most European nations kept trade relations alive. When Cuba was forced to develop its tourist industry during its Special Period (when Soviet aid dried up and before Venezuelan assistance flowed), it was European (and Canadian) companies that moved into the island. European tourists also became one of the largest groups to visit Cuba. The European approach was backed by the idea that engagement between democratic Europe and Cuba on a long transition to social democracy was important. This provided a sharp contrast with the United States, which believed that sanctions and isolation were the best way to achieve regime change. Both Europe and the United States wanted a transition from the Castro authoritarian regime to a more open society, but their strategies differed considerably.

The contrasting strategies between Europe and the United States also differed on the end-game for business. When regime change comes in

Cuba, the new government would be expected to respect European trade and investment. In contrast, the U.S. vision of the next stage would be a government presiding over a market economy that offers compensation for past property expropriations and offers a major role for U.S.-based Cuban exiles (Erikson 2009).

When Spanish, French, and other European companies conducted business in Cuba, they always ran the risk of falling afoul of the 1996 U.S. Helms-Burton Act (Article III) that would allow the original owners of nationalized businesses in Cuba to take new buyers to court in the United States. The U.S. legislation, however, was written in such a fashion to allow the President to suspend that clause every year. Starting with the Clinton administration and stretching through the Bush and Obama administrations the clause was suspended, largely guided by concerns for U.S. relations with its European, Canadian, and Asian allies. This was not an issue for European and other nations conducting business in Cuba until the Trump administration. As the Trump administration increased the level of economic sanctions on Cuba, Europe, in particular, France and Spain, worked to maintain a political dialogue, partially with an eye to protect their investments. This was evident in the 2019 trip to Havana by Secretary-General of the Ministry for Europe and Foreign Affairs of France Maurice Gourdault-Montagne, who met with his local counterpart First Deputy Foreign Minister Marcelino Medina. The result was that France and Cuba confirmed the "good state" of bilateral relations as well as the "positive development of relations between Cuba and the European Union" since the implementation of the Political Dialogue and Cooperation Agreement signed in Brussels in December 2016 (On Cuba News 2019). The agreement came into force in November 2017 and marked the end of the "common position" that made the EU's relations subject to advances in human rights in Cuba and ended the isolation of the Caribbean country as the only one in the region with which the Union did not yet have a bilateral accord. As a policy it was largely ineffectual.

Cuba, therefore, is an unresolved issue between Europe and the United States. It could be said that as Europe generally resisted being deeply involved in the Cuban–U.S. standoff during the old Cold War, it appears to be attempting to do the same in the new Cold War. European policymakers are watching the Biden administration to see if there were any changes in Cuban policy. The widespread protests throughout the island in July 2021 came as a surprise to Europe. The EU responded by stating that it was "very concerned about the repression" and called upon Cuban authorities to respect human rights and "release detained protesters" (Von der Burchard 2021; Le Monde 2021). The Cuban response was to reject EU claims, claiming they were "lies."

Europe has also been relatively quiet about the growing role of China and Russia in Cuba. European concerns over this have remained muted for two reasons. First and foremost, European companies still play a sizable role in the Cuban economy, Spain in particular in trade. Stirring trouble could backfire on Spanish and French investment. The second reason, is that both China and Russia have not pushed as hard to make Cuba a client state as the Soviet Union due to their own concerns over the mismanagement of the economy, including its track record in repaying debt. Although the Trump administration opened the door to allow aggrieved parties to sue European (and Canadian and any other companies that bought or managed nationalized companies in Cuba) under Title III of the Helms-Burton Act, the expectation is that the Biden administration will return to not enforcing the provision as did the Bush and Obama administrations. Consequently, European policies vis-à-vis Cuba are a balancing act of papering over human rights abuses and China's and Russia's increased presence and protecting their corporate investments. In a sense, European investors want to ignore any slide into a new Cold War, despite Cuba's very obvious human rights violations.

Venezuela has been a different experience. During the Chávez years, European companies were on the receiving end of the socialist caudillo's push to drive out foreign business and nationalize the economy. The more the Venezuelan state under first Chávez and then his successor Maduro took over parts of the economy, the more business prospects dimmed. As outlined in earlier chapters, the escalation of events around the 2018 fraudulent election, the emergence of Guaidó as an alternative to Maduro, and U.S. pressure on the regime helped push European policy to back a negotiated outcome, and in doing so, the EU dropped recognition of the Venezuelan dictator.

The EU's original concerns were articulated in 2016, when it urged Venezuela to bring about a political reconciliation. This was followed in 2017 by an embargo on arms and on equipment for internal repression (at which time Russia and China were already selling weapons to the Maduro regime) and began targeting individuals for economic sanctions. Those sanctions were renewed in 2018 and 2019, accompanied by many declarations warning the Maduro government not to misbehave. In June 2020, the Maduro gave the EU ambassador 72 hours to leave the country and in 2022 Maduro still holds sway, backed by China, Russia, Cuba and Iran.

While Venezuela put the EU at odds with China, Russia, Cuba and Iran, relations with the United States over policy also showed divergence. The EU and United States agreed on the legitimacy of the National Assembly and Guaidó's claim to the interim presidency, but there were differences over the new elections for a new National Assembly set by the Maduro regime for December 2020. The U.S. response was to demand Maduro's exit as a pre-condition to a political settlement, releasing a joint declaration with 28 other countries (including a number of Caribbean countries) that called for the establishment of a transitional government. What was evident was that most European countries had not signed the declaration, with the exception of the Baltic states, the United Kingdom, Ukraine, and Hungary. Instead, the EU (led by Germany, France, Italy, and Spain) pushed for a postponement of the elections to help foster a free and fair process, indicating that if Venezuela played along (by allowing international observers) it might recognize the outcome of the elections. The United States, in contrast, preemptively declared the election fraudulent and vowed to ignore any results. The elections were held in December 2020, were boycotted by the opposition and considered fraudulent.

The situation was worsened by the Trump administration's criticism when the EU Foreign Minister Josep Borrell dispatched an envoy to liaise with Maduro about the election. U.S. Special Envoy for Venezuela Elliott Abrams referred to the EU's action as "cowboy diplomacy." The nub of the issue between the United States and EU was caught by the *Washington Post's* Anthony Faiola: "The dispute suggested a growing divide across the Atlantic over how to handle Venezuela's socialist government. The Europeans have tended to see Washington's hardline position as harsh and ineffective. Washington has viewed Brussels as too willing to deal with Maduro" (Faiola 2020).

In the new Cold War context, the EU was clearly opposed to the Maduro dictatorship and its external backers. However, it also believed that the right approach was through negotiations and economic sanctions, but not the threat of force. This approach was taken by Europe during the Bosnia-Herzegovina War (1992–1995), which was only resolved by U.S.-led bombings and diplomacy and in Kosovo in 1998 (which included a U.S.-led NATO bombing of Serbia). The negotiation dialogue approach was also used when Russia invaded Georgia in 2008 and again when

Russia annexed Crimea. One could argue that there is a pattern. The bottom line is that while most Europeans found the idea of a Chinese-Russian-Cuban-backed thuggish regime abhorrent, a tougher line was not justified by European core interests. Venezuela and, for that matter, Cuba do not represent red lines in the new Cold War, certainly not on the same level as Ukraine or the Baltic States. It also leaves China, Russia and, for that matter Iran and Cuba, calculating that Europe's tougher approach in the new Cold War can bring pain in terms of economic sanctions, but there is no threat beyond that—at least until the Russo-Ukraine War and Europe's shift to reassessment its military capabilities.

In looking ahead, European activity in the Caribbean is likely to remain more of a national focus than led by the EU. And the triangular relationship between China, the Caribbean, and European countries will be conditioned by how European countries deal with China. Although Germany has been strongly opposed to the Maduro regime and has raised concerns about the loss of German business at the hands of the Chinese in other parts of Latin America, France, the Netherlands, and Spain have more at stake in the region. This is decidedly the case of the Dutch in regard to their special relationship with their former colony of Suriname. Since the departure of Bouterse from the presidency in 2021, Dutch relations to Suriname have warmed considerably. At the same time, the Dutch, French, and British armed forces participated in a joint military exercise in Guyana in August 2021, which was a statement to Venezuela to back off its territorial claims on the smaller country. The last development was notable in that the Dutch and French, both with forces in the region, were involved. Germany did not.

THE UK AND THE CARIBBEAN

One of Antigua and Barbuda's most articulate statesmen, Sir Ronald Sanders, now ambassador to the United States, outlined in 1991 the UK's relationship with the Caribbean as broken into two periods. The first was 1962–1982 and was defined by "Britain's obvious determination to withdraw from the Caribbean, giving up influence over the area, and responsibility for policing it, to her NATO ally the United States" (Sanders 1991). The second period started with the Falklands/Malvinas War in 1982 and was marked by a "desire by Britain to once again exert some influence in the region." British interests vis-a-vis the Caribbean were articulated by Timothy Eggar, then the Under-Secretary of State in the Foreign and Commonwealth Office, in 1987:

- The Caribbean's influence in the United Nations;
- The importance of the area as a transit point for trade and resupply from the United States to Europe in the event of hostility;
- The Caribbean's value as a market for British exports; and
- The rapid development of the region, including the British dependencies, as a center for drug trafficking and money laundering.

The British withdrawal from the Caribbean in the 1960s and 1970s and the push to reduce the costs of its dependencies to the government's finances that marked the 1962–1982 period set in motion a change in economic orientation. The former British colonies found that independence took them in a different direction, which elevated the importance of the United States and multilateral institutions, such as the Inter-American Development Bank, the World Bank, and the IMF. These trends were reinforced by the Brexit referendum in 2016 and the rise of China in the Caribbean. China's infrastructure program was something with which the United Kingdom could not compete, especially in the aftermath of the 2008–2009 financial crisis. London did pull together £300 million to help in new infrastructure in the Caribbean such as roads, bridges, and ports to help promote economic growth and development across the region. This was announced by Prime Minister David Cameron in an official visit to Jamaica in 2015. Unfortunately that bit of news was lost in the controversy over the demand by CARICOM for reparations for slavery and colonialism.

The distance from the Caribbean for British policymakers became evident in 2017, when extensive hurricane damage hit a number of territories. Compared to the responses of the French and Dutch, the British response was considered slow. Part of London's problem was that it lacked any regular base for its military in the region, which both France and the Netherlands held.

Probably the most significant hurdle to a more active Britain in the Caribbean was Brexit, which led to a political rollercoaster in the UK and considerable uncertainty over trade issues. Considering that the UK is their largest European market, Brexit left a major question market over the conditions trade would continue (Byron 2019). When the UK departed from the EU in 2020 it was assumed that rules and regulations would need to be updated to reflect the change. In a sense, the UK's move out of the European Union opened the door to a reset in Caribbean ties; London could benefit from being seen to publicly embrace every nation in CARIFORUM no matter their stance on Venezuela (Jessop 2020b). This would signal that in the future what the UK offers would be different from the approach taken by the United States, China, and other nations now seeking a greater role in the region. But the UK's role in the Caribbean cannot be entirely dismissed. The UK is still the principal European importer of Caribbean commodities, an important source of visitors, the facilitator of offshore financial services, the home to one million members of the Caribbean Diaspora, and remains supportive of the region, albeit in future less influentially (Jessop 2020a, b).

Large numbers of people from the Caribbean settled in the UK. Some of the earliest arrivals came on the ship, MV Empire Windrush, which delivered Jamaicans, Trinidadians, and other islanders in 1948. Despite many challenges, including racism, the Windrush generation (1948–1971) was successful in becoming part of British society. The problem came in Home Office decided in 2018 that the Windrush generation were illegally in the UK and sought to deport them. This was taken by many as racist and intentional. Considering that when most of the Windrush generation came to the UK they came from British colonies and were considered British citizens at the time, the orders were strongly resisted. The government finally backtracked and offered compensation to the aggrieved. Nonetheless, the Windrush incident left a bad taste in the Caribbean over the racism and the British government.

Brexit, the rise of China, trans-Atlantic tensions, and economic recovery from the Covid-19 pandemic all are pushing the UK to rethink its role in the world. In this, the Caribbean has a place, considering the colonial era ties, and the Caribbean diaspora. Part of London's approach to the Caribbean could include the establishment of a military base in the region, which has been speculated to potentially in Guyana due to that country's problems with Venezuela (Vitor Tossini 2020). For Guyana, it would be beneficial to have an ongoing military presence with a view to Venezuela; for the UK, Guyana's oil bonanza has to be attractive from a business sense (Miller 2019). The other location under discussion by London was Montserrat, a British territory, in the Eastern Caribbean. The problem there could be the live volcano that has damaged much of the island's economy. Looking ahead, the articulation of China's involvement in Barbados and subsequent comments on China's rise in the Caribbean may seem like old news to the United States and the Caribbean, but for a UK slowly emerging from the Brexit experience, this is part of a bigger refocus. The UK, unlike the EU, may have more of an appetite for a new Cold War, which could result in a bigger profile in the region regardless as to whether the Queen remains the head of state in Barbados.

CANADA, CHINA, AND THE CARIBBEAN

Canada's relationship with the Caribbean commenced during the colonial period, with the northern country's ties to the region based on trade and eventually investment. Ships from Nova Scotia, Newfoundland, New Brunswick and Prince Edward Island sailed to the Caribbean islands to supply food, livestock, lumber and other staples, in exchange for molasses, rum, spices and sugar. Later Canadian banks became important financial actors in much of the English-speaking Caribbean. All of this generated a certain romance to the "special" relationship between Canada and the Caribbean islands. Throughout the twentieth century and into the twenty-first that special relationship waxed and waned, doing more of the latter over the past decade. A question that looms in the halls of Ottawa is—will the slide toward a new Cold War and spillover into the Caribbean revive the special relationship? Directly related to this question is what is Canadian national interest in the Caribbean and what is China's impact?

Canada's national interests are straightforward: maintain independence from its far larger and more powerful neighbor to the south, the United States; seek to have a different persona in international relations; and help advance, where possible, Canadian business opportunities. As Andrew Cohen, a former member of the editorial board of the *Globe and Mail*, stated in 1995: "The truth was that the national interest had become bound up in the global interest. For a country living in the shadow of the United States, attuned to the advantages of wielding influence in a fragmented world, multilateralism was an effective way to preserve freedom and independence. At the end of the day the motivation was probably less moral than practical, though Canadians wore the vestments of virtue comfortably" (Cohen 1995).

Canada's role in the world has been seen as projecting its influence by soft diplomacy. This had included its perception of itself as a middle power, able to play the role of an honest broker, peacekeeper, and active member of international organizations. Moreover, Canada played its role as one of the world's most economically developed countries, with membership in the G7 and Organization for Economic Cooperation and Development. Canada is also part of the West, usually allied to the United States and was an early NATO member. These broad national interests guided Canada through the Cold War and into the post-Cold War era. Indeed, the post-Cold War era appeared to be ideal for Canada; gone were the tensions related to the ideological friction from bipolarity; prospects for a new world order appeared promising; and geopolitics faded before globalization.

U.S.–Canadian relations were generally positive during the Bush and Obama administrations, despite occasional differences. That changed when the Trump administration came to office. Trade policy became a major point of friction, with the renegotiation of NAFTA and its replacement with the United States-Mexico-Canada Agreement. The "America First" mantra of the Trump administration grated on Canadian sensitivities, with one former Canadian diplomat noting that inexperienced amateurs were sprinkled across a wide swath of policymaking agencies; U.S. decision-making had become "completely unpredictable"; and the political situation was "frightening." The advent of the Biden administration was a welcome change, seen with the hope that U.S.–Canadian relations would return to a more balanced and predictable role. Indeed, in their first meeting in February 2021 President Biden and Prime Minister Trudeau agreed on a "Roadmap for a Renewed US-Canada Partnership," though there was disappointment in Ottawa over the new U.S. leader's first day in office cancelation of the Keystone XL pipeline which hurt Canadian business.

While U.S.–Canadian relations dominate foreign policy concerns, China is another major consideration. After the United States and the European Union, China is Canada's third largest trade partner, ahead of Mexico. China is also a major investor in Canada. According to the Alberta-based China Institute, China has invested $82 billion into Canada since 2000 to 2019, more than $51 billion of which was funneled into oil and gas (Synder 2020). The relationship is further complicated by the ties between Canada and Hong Kong, where 300,000 Canadian citizens are living.

While the Liberal government of Prime Minister Justin Trudeau has sought to walk a tight rope between the United States and China, he has found the path difficult. The crushing of the pro-democracy movement in Hong Kong and the persecution of the Uyghurs has called into question

Canada's commitment to human rights. Indeed, the Canadian Parliament voted to call Chinese behavior against the Uyghurs "genocide," which did not go over well in Beijing.

Chinese–Canadian relations were also greatly strained by the "two Michaels" being held by the Chinese authorities in a not-so-opaque tit-for-tat arrest in response for the December 2018 arrest of Meng Wanzhou, the CFO of Huawei, in Canada, pending extradition to the United States. The United States had charged her with misleading HSBC about Huawei's business dealings with Iran, potentially causing the bank to violate American economic sanctions. The two Michaels were Michael Kovrig, a former diplomat and Michael Spavor, a businessman. A third Canadian Lloyd Schellenberg, was tried on drug smuggling charges in 2018, but retried in 2021 as the Chinese authorities decided that his 16 year sentence was too lenient. The new sentence was the death penalty. The word hostages were frequently used to describe the situation.

Considering the changing international relations environment Canada increasingly finds itself being pushed to take a side. As Margaret McCuaig, a longtime government expert on technology issues with China and a Senior Fellow at the Institute for Science, Society, and Policy at the University of Ottawa (among many titles), noted of Beijing's message is that "Canada is not a middle power, but a small power and it should stop leaning towards the United States" (McCuaig-Johnson 2021). This has not gone over well in Canada, where China has steadily risen as a major political issue, behind only the pandemic.

In the run-up to the June 2021 G7 meeting, former Canadian diplomat and China scholar Charles Burton outlined his country's options in the new Cold War-like environment, stating: "There's a desire for there to be more concerted action by an alliance of nations which are affected by China's behavior in the absence of any effective UN ability to respond, because China is a permanent member of the Security Council and therefore able to veto anything significant. Is Canada prepared to stand up for the Australians who are subject to hostage diplomacy as we expect the Australians to stand up for our Michael Kovrig and Michael Spavor? Are we prepared to actually engage in programming which will displease the Chinese government in concert with our allies?" (Dyer 2021). The other option is as follows: "Or do we want to leave this to other powers and hope that if Canada stands relatively neutral, that we will be able to protect our market position in China?".

How does all of the above relate to the new Cold War and Canada's foreign policy for the Caribbean? Through the 1960s and into the 1980s Canadian-Caribbean relations were generally positive. Beyond the fact that Canada was not the United States, the common history made Ottawa a relatively comfortably fit for the English-speaking Caribbean. As former Canadian diplomat Paul Durand observed: "Canada was a logical partner for the newly independent Caribbean nations, one with whom they had much in common through membership in the Commonwealth, similar forms of government, a shared history of trade and immigration going back centuries" (Durand 2016).

The Canadian–Caribbean relationship was bound by a number of practices and policies. These included frequent bilateral contacts and regular meetings between heads of government (which developed important personal relations). Canadian banks were also active throughout the English-speaking Caribbean (as well as in Puerto Rico). In advancing its assistance to the region, Canada joined the Caribbean Development Bank in 1970. Trade continued to be important, which was meant to be helped by the 1986 launching of CARIBCAN (Caribbean-Canada Trade Agreement), Canada's equivalent of the U.S. Caribbean Basin Initiative. At the same time, Canadians became one of the major clients of the Caribbean's tourist trade, especially in the cold winter months. Additionally Canada became an immigration destination for many Caribbean people, in particular to the greater Toronto area and Montreal (with a sizable immigration from Haiti where Canadian has been active on the aid front and shares French linguistic ties). These set of factors reinforced Canadian support for good governance, security and rule of law in the Caribbean. One last factor was that Canadian aid went directly to each Caribbean nation, which reinforced the nature of the relationship as opposed to coming from a larger multinational organization. This set of factors played well in international forums as Canadian and Caribbean governments were often able to work together. The Caribbean bloc was key to Canada's bid to gain a UN Security Council seat in 2010.

The special relationship came under stress in the 1990s and faded in the early twenty-first century. As Canada went into NAFTA, the Caribbean was hit by the new North American trade regime; it was tough competing with Mexico's size and scale and cheaper labor. At the same time, Canadian banks in the 2010s underwent the process of de-risking, which meant a retreat from the Caribbean. This was caused by regulator concerns over money laundering for transnational criminal organizations and terrorist organizations. This complicated business operations in much of the Caribbean, especially in the eastern Caribbean. It also gave China an entry point in the Caribbean's financial system. Equally damaging to the economic/financial changes was the decision by the Canadian government to end the regular meetings by the heads of government. One last factor was that Canada's aid program moved away from being a bilateral process to a multilateral one, which put distance between the donor and receiver. As Durand noted: "The assistance provided is still of value, offering technical assistance in areas like disaster management, tax regimes, and justice systems. However, channeling aid through multilateral institutions has broken the direct link between Canadians and Caribbean recipients, and the Canadian identity formerly attached to our assistance has been lost, along with any sense of loyalty" (Durand 2015).

Despite the divergence of Canada and the Caribbean through much of the first two decades of the twenty-first century, in the last couple of years Ottawa appears to be slowly reassessing its role in the region. Part of this comes as Canadians see the international environment darkening. Former Prime Minister Stephen Harper believes that the world order has returned to a kind of Cold War between the United States and China. As he observed in 2021, China has become more blatantly aggressive and "hegemonic" and has a "system of not just authoritarianism, but a desire to spread that kind of system around the world. This is just not something to be taken lightly" (Canadian Press, 2021). He also noted of the United States: "While the U.S. remains the world's pre-eminent power, I think we're past the day where it is the dominant or overwhelming power."

While not all parts of the Canadian policymaking elite concur with their former prime minister, there is growing concern about control over the country's natural resources and its core data and tech services from China. At the same time, the debate over a new Cold War has functioned to nudge Canada to play a more proactive role in the Caribbean, still regarded as an area of interest. Canada played a constructive role (along with other Western democracies) in reaching a peaceful solution to Guyana's 2021 election crisis; the sending of Canadian armed forces to participate in a joint military exercise in Guyana alongside with the United States, a number of European countries and other Caribbean countries; and providing funding for the Pan American Health Organization (PAHO) in 2020 to help respond to Covid-19 in 23 countries in the Americas, including the English-speaking Caribbean, Suriname and Cuba. Canada has also provided support to the energy sector through grants to the Caribbean Development Bank. Equally significant, Canada and CARICOM held their first Foreign Ministers' Group meeting in February 2021. According to the official communiqué, the ministers "discussed coordinated action to manage the impacts of the Covid-19 pandemic, promoting resilient and sustainable growth and finding solutions to the impacts of climate change." (Government of Canada 2021)

The Trudeau government has sought to walk a careful line between China and the United States, though Canada did sign on to the G7-led infrastructure initiative Build Back Better World (B3W) launched in June 2021 by the leaders of the group. This was done to provide an alternative to China's BRI and aimed at "helping narrow the +$40 trillion infrastructure need in the developing world, which has been exacerbated by the COVID-19 pandemic." Will Canada steer some of that program to Caribbean counties? How engaged Canada be with the B3W? Canada has considerable matters to contemplate for its Caribbean policies as U.S.–China tensions are more than likely to worsen and add pressure in the Caribbean, leaving Canada a potential third party. The bottom line, however, is what role does Ottawa want to play in the Caribbean?

CONCLUSION

Europe, the UK, and Canada have slowly and grudgingly come to acknowledge the rise of Chinese influence in the Caribbean. Although the Caribbean is not a major arena for European policymakers who have more pressing matters in their neighborhood, two EU members have territories in the region as does the UK. Moreover, European concerns over human rights clearly put them in the position of opposing the tyranny of the Maduro regime in Venezuela (while largely giving Cuba a pass). That said, Europe has been cautious in casting Caribbean political ructions as part of the new Cold War. There is a risk that dealing with China, both in Eurasia and the Caribbean, may function more to divide Europe and the United States than unite them as the situation teases out their different approaches to the world. Additionally as China has pursued economic statecraft it has demonstrated that its check book is bigger than Europe's in a number of sectors (such as infrastructure) and access to Chinese development loans is a less onerous process than working with Europe. Looking ahead, the issue facing Europe, the UK, and Canada hinges on its commitment to a democratic and rule of law-driven international system or one that increasingly bows to a new world order dominated by

China and Russia, which prefers a more authoritarian approach and has less concerns over governance issues.

References

Bernal, Richard L. 2020. *Corporate Versus National Interest in US Trade Policy: Chiquita and Caribbean Bananas.* Palgrave Macmillan.

Byron, Jessica. 2019. Relations with the European Union and the United Kingdom Post-BREXIT: Perspectives from the Caribbean. *Études caribéennes*, April. https://journals.openedition.org/etudescaribeennes/14705.

Campbell, Matthew. 2021. Little England? Not Anymore – Barbados Is Becoming Little China. *The Times (London)*, November 20, 2021. https://www.thetimes.co.uk/article/little-england-not-any-more-barbados-is-becoming-little-china-kqlqmjp39

Canadian Press. 2021. Former PM Stephen Harper Sees New Cold War, This Time between U.S. and China. *The National Post*, March 12. https://nationalpost.com/pmn/news-pmn/canada-news-pmn/former-pm-stephen-harper-sees-new-cold-war-this-time-between-u-s-and-china. Accessed 21 Aug 2021.

Cohen, Andrew. 1995. Canada in the World: The Return of the National Interest, Canada International Council, Summer. https://thecic.org/canada-in-the-world-the-return-of-the-national-interest/.

de Feijter, Tycho. 2020. De International Expansie van China. *Atlantisch Perspectief*, 2020, Special Edition, Where is China headed?: 37–42. https://www.jstor.org/stable/48600555?seq=1#metadata_info_tab_contents. Accessed 8 Aug 2020. Also see the Dutch Caribbean Securities Exchange website, which has a list of companies. https://www.dcsx.cw/tag/chinese-market/page/2/.

de Wijk, Rob, Jack Thompson, and Esther Chavannes. 2020. *Adjusting the Multilateral System to Safeguard Dutch Interest.* The Hague Centre for Strategic Studies, September. https://hcss.nl/report/adjusting-multilateral-system-safeguard-dutch-interests.

Durand, Paul. 2015, "Why have Canadian-Caribbean Ties Weakened," Just Ottawa, November. http://justottawa.com/articles/international/323-why-have-canadian-caribbean-ties-weakened-by-paul-durand-article.html.

Durand, Paul. 2016. Who Lost the Caribbean? Canadian Global Affairs Institute, November. https://d3n8a8pro7vhmx.cloudfront.net/cdfai/pages/1307/attachments/original/1477852380/Who_Lost_the_Caribbean.pdf?1477852380. Accessed 21 Aug 2021.

Dyer, Evan. 2021. Biden Says He Wants to 'Confront' China. Is Trudeau Willing to Go Along? *CBC News*, June 9. https://www.cbc.ca/news/politics/g7-trudeau-biden-johnson-china-xi-1.6059816.

Erikson, Daniel P. 2009. *Europe's Cuba Problem: The Limits of Constructive Engagement.* International Institute for Democracy and Electoral Assistance

2009. Stockholm, Sweden. https://www.idea.int/sites/default/files/public
ations/chapters/the-role-of-the-european-union-in-democracy-building/eu-
democracy-building-discussion-paper-10.pdf.

European Council. 2020. *Council of the European Union, Venezuela: The Council's Response to the Crisis.* https://www.consilium.europa.eu/en/policies/ven
ezuela/.

Faiola, Anthony. 2020. U.S. Criticism of European Mission to Venezuela Shows
Growing Divide over Maduro. *The Washington Post*, September 27. https://
www.washingtonpost.com/world/the_americas/venezuela-maduro-guaido-
us-eu/2020/09/27/d13be724-00ea-11eb-897d-3a6201d6643f_story.ht.

Fairless, Tom. 2020. China, Germany Shift from Allies to Rivals. *The Wall Street
Journal*, September 18: A9.

Fisher, Lucy. 2020. China Blamed for Barbados Ditching the Queen. *The Times
of London*, September 23. https://www.thetimes.co.uk/article/china-blamed-
for-barbados-ditching-queen-h3nx66k5g.

Government of Canada. 2021. *Launch of Canada-Caribbean Community Foreign
Minsters' Group: Co-chair Summary.* Government of Canada, February
19. https://www.international.gc.ca/news-nouvelles/2021/2021-02-19-car
icom.aspx?lang=eng.

Ivens, Martin. 2021. Barbados Splits from the Queen, Trading One Empire for
Another. *Bloomberg*, December 4. https://www.bloomberg.com/opinion/
articles/2021-12-04/barbados-splits-from-the-queen-trading-one-empire-for-
another-in-china?sref=8VBJk9tz.

Jessop, David. 2020a. *Brexit—The Caribbean Must Seize the Moment.*
The Caribbean Council. https://www.caribbean-council.org/brexit-the-car
ibbean-must-seize-the-moment/.

Jessop, David. 2020b. *Britain, Brexit and an Impending Crisis.* The Caribbean
Council, May 19. https://www.caribbean-council.org/britain-brexit-and-an-
impending-crisis/. Accessed 11 Oct 2020.

Johnson, Miles, and Yuan Yang. 2020. Allegations of Doctored Films Fuel
Concerns about Beijing's Propaganda. *Financial Times*, May 3. https://www.
ft.com/content/ee8ae647-c536-4ec5-bc10-54787b3a265e.

Le Monde. 2021. Le Monde with AFP, "A Cuba, le gouverne-
ment fait un premier geste face aux pénuries". *Le Monde*, July
15. https://www.lemonde.fr/international/article/2021/07/15/a-cuba-le-
gouvernement-fait-un-premier-geste-face-aux-penuries_6088296_3210.html.

McCuaig-Johnson. 2021. Interview with the author on August 13, 2021.
Margaret McCuaig-Johnston's biography is impressive: she is Senior Fellow at
the Institute for Science, Society and Policy, Senior Fellow with the Univer-
sity of Alberta's China Institute and Distinguished Fellow with the Asia-Pacific
Foundation of Canada. Formerly, she was Executive Vice-President at Natural
Sciences and Engineering Council of Canada where she was responsible for

strategic operations, including research policy and international relations. She was also a member for seven years of the Steering Committee for the Canada-China Science and Technology (S&T) Initiative. From 1991 to 2009 she held senior management positions in the federal government, including being the Assistant Deputy Minister of Energy Technology and Programs at Natural Resources Canada and was appointed to the Assistant Deputy Minister level as General Director in the Department of Finance.

Miller, Phil. 2019. Why Does Britain Want to Build a Military Base in the Caribbean? *VICE*, January 14. https://www.vice.com/en/article/xwjnpa/why-does-britain-want-to-build-a-military-base-in-the-caribbean.

Mueller, Nora. 2019. Didn't Hear the Shot. *Zeit Online*, January 2019. https://www.zeit.de/politik/ausland/2019-01/aussenpolitik-deutschland-europa-vereinte-nationen-internationale-verantwortung/komplettansicht.

On Cuba News. 2019. Cuba and France to Strengthen Bilateral Dialogue. *On Cuba News*, June 15. https://oncubanews.com/en/cuba/cuba-and-france-to-strengthen-bilateral-dialogue/.

Sanders, Ron. 1991. Britain and the Caribbean: A Caribbean Perspective. In *Europe and the Caribbean*, ed. Paul Sutton. London: Macmillan Education Ltd.

Small, Andrew. 2020. The Meaning of Systemic Rivalry: Europe and China Beyond the Pandemic. *European Council on Foreign Relations*, May 13. https://www.ecfr.eu/publications/summary/the_meaning_of_systemic_rivalry_europe_and_china_beyond_the_pandemic.

Synder, Jesse. 2020. As Geopolitical Tensions Rise, Chinese Investment into Canada Continues to Fall, Data Show. *National Post*, July 16, 2020. https://nationalpost.com/news/as-geopolitical-tensions-rise-chinese-investment-into-canada-continues-to-fall-data-show

The Netherlands & China: A New Balance, The Netherlands Ministry of Foreign Affairs. *The Hague*, May 2019. https://globalconnectadmin.com/the-newest-china-policy-of-the-netherlands/

Tylecote, Radomir. 2021. China's Growing Influence Over the Commonwealth's Armies. *The Spectotor*, Novmeber 28, 2021. https://www.spectator.co.uk/article/china-s-growing-influence-over-the-armies-of-the-commonwealth.

U.S. Government. 2021. White House Fact Sheet: "President Biden and G7 Leaders Launch Build Back Better World (B3W) Partnership", June 12. https://www.whitehouse.gov/briefing-room/statements-releases/2021/06/12/fact-sheet-president-biden-and-g7-leaders-launch-build-back-better-world-b3w-partnership/.

Vitor Tossini, J. 2020. A Look at the Considered Locations for New British Military Bases Overseas. *ukdj*. https://ukdefencejournal.org.uk/a-look-at-the-considered-locations-for-new-british-military-bases-overseas/.

von der Burchard, Hans. 2021. EU and Cuba Clash Over Condemnation of Protest Crackdown. *Politico*, July 29. https://www.politico.eu/article/eu-cuba-clash-protest-crackdown/.

CHAPTER 9

U.S. Policy in a Choppy Caribbean Sea

U.S. policy toward the Caribbean has generally been more responsive than proactive in the post-Cold War era. It can be argued that without the external threat of the Soviet Union, the Caribbean as a security concern faded only to be briefly interrupted by the "war on terror" in the aftermath 9/11. U.S. policy remained largely focused elsewhere until the Trump administration when greater attention was given to how China was able to carve out a geo-economic role in the region. It is argued that it was during the Trump years that the move toward a new Cold War in the Caribbean was accelerated. The pressures on Caribbean governments grew as Washington sought to determine who were friends and allies or enemies and Chinese friends and partners. Although U.S. Caribbean policy remained heavy with past buzzwords and concepts, the late Trump administration began a process of rethinking economic statecraft vis-aa-vis the region. U.S. policy is still struggling to bring together a more coherent path to balancing the needs of U.S. hegemony and national security (vis-à-vis new Cold War threats from China and Russia) in the region with maintaining a constructive role in dealing with Caribbean development challenges, ranging from climate change to financing of critical infrastructure.

In March 2021, Navy Admiral Craig S. Faller, former Commander, U.S. Southern Command (that encompasses the Caribbean and Latin America) testified before the U.S. Congress: "This Hemisphere in which we live is under assault. The very democratic principles and values that bind us together are being actively undermined by violent transnational

© The Author(s), under exclusive license to Springer Nature Switzerland AG 2022
S. B. MacDonald, *The New Cold War, China, and the Caribbean*,
https://doi.org/10.1007/978-3-031-06149-3_9

criminal organizations (TCOs) and the PRC and Russia. We are losing our positional advantage in this Hemisphere and immediate action is needed to reverse this trend" (Faller 2021). And according to the admiral, the Chinese challenge is comprehensive, seeking to "gain global influence and leverage across all domains" in the area, including cyber, space, extractive and energy industries, transportation hubs, roads, ports, telecommunications, legal and illegal fishing, agriculture, and military training. Although the United States remains the dominant power in the Caribbean, China has developed the basis from which to construct a more muscular presence and, in the case of hostilities, could conduct sabotage. Yet it is too early to proclaim that the United States has "lost" the Caribbean to China. Rather the United States no longer has the Caribbean to itself and needs to create a more coherent and sustainable strategy for the region, one that balances Caribbean needs with U.S. security concerns.

All of the above should be injecting a greater sense of urgency in Washington. But Washington's response to rising Chinese influence in the Caribbean during the first two decades of the twenty-first century was slow. While China was actively creating stronger diplomatic ties and deepening economic relations with Caribbean countries, the United States was preoccupied with foreign policy issues elsewhere and belatedly recognized the rising level of competition. In a very fundamental way, China's expanding economic influence challenged the casual U.S. assumption that Caribbean countries are always aligned with Washington. All countries have their own national interests, even the small ones in the Caribbean. While the usual mantras of support for democracy and better governance, fighting transnational crime, and promoting free markets remained important to Washington, Chinese economic statecraft changed the dynamic, resulting in a quiet realignment of relations. This sense of strategic realignment has only been reinforced by the Biden administration's ignominious departure from Afghanistan in 2021 and the escalation of tensions between the West and Russia over Ukraine that included Moscow's 2022 threat to become more active in Cuba, Nicaragua, and Venezuela. The challenge of another great power disputing U.S. hegemony in a region regarded as core to security is defining Washington's Caribbean policy in the 2020s and will probably do so through the 2030s, be it China or Russia. The asymmetrical nature of the diplomatic game has yet to fully play out, in large part because it has yet to fully play out in other theaters of global diplomacy, a reflection of the new Cold War tone of the times. If there is a further shift into a new Cold War, which seems likely, the Caribbean looms large to Washington, much more so than it has since the last Cold War.

CONTINUITY AND CHANGE—THE
BUSH AND OBAMA YEARS

There has been considerable thematic continuity in the U.S. approach to the Caribbean from the end of the old Cold War to the 2020s, though the level of engagement has varied considerably. One key element of U.S. policy that has been a constant is the Caribbean Basin Initiative (CBI), which was launched in 1983 by the Reagan administration to respond to Cold War concerns. According to the U.S. Government, the CBI "is intended to facilitate the development of stable Caribbean Basin economies by providing beneficiary countries with duty-free access to the U.S. market for most goods." The program was expanded in 2000 by the U.S.–Caribbean Basin Trade Partnership Act (CBTPA) and again by the Trade Act of 2002. Hardly perfect, the CBI did provide a well-structured framework for trade and was generally supportive of economic growth.

During the George W. Bush administration (the 43rd president from 2001 to 2009) the Caribbean was described as the "third border," with Caribbean nations seen as "vital partners on security, trade, health, the environment, education, regional democracy, and other hemispheric issues" (U.S. Department of State 2021). Although Bush never made an official visit to the Caribbean, the attacks by the terrorist group al-Qaeda on September 11, 2001 brought a renewed focus on the region, much of it security-oriented (Chaitram 2020: 86).

During the Barack Obama years (2008–2015), U.S. Caribbean policy was initially dominated by many of the same themes: support for democracy, drug trafficking, immigration, trade and investment concerns, health issues, and emergency relief. Something new added to the list was the promotion of alternative energy with an eye to climate change. There was a greater emphasis on finding multilateral approaches to problems rather than unilateral action. At the same time, China's growing presence in the Caribbean was not perceived as a major threat. Venezuela was regarded more as a risk.

Much was to change during the Obama years in terms of U.S. foreign policy. When President Obama assumed office in 2009, the United States–China relationship was seen as vital to both countries, but undergoing changes. The Obama administration inherited a relationship between the world's two largest economies heavily conditioned by trade and investment, cross-Straits relations (Taiwan), the South China dispute, and a range of broader international matters, such as climate change, denuclearization, cybersecurity, anti-terrorism, and human rights. The relationship was cemented by economic interdependence, with China becoming one of the largest trade partners as well as one of the foremost holders of U.S. sovereign debt. U.S.–Chinese relations, however, suffered from a "trust deficit," which was increasingly colored by rising Chinese nationalism fueled by the belief in Beijing that U.S. policy was geared to contain its rise to becoming the leading superpower.

The trust deficit was given impetus by U.S. policy initiatives, namely the Obama administration's "pivot to Asia" and the creation of the Trans-Pacific Partnership (TPP). The first was broadly defined by then Secretary of State Hillary Clinton as "strengthening bilateral security alliances; deepening our working relationships with emerging powers, including China; engaging with regional multilateral institutions; expanding trade and investment; forging a broad-based military presence; and advancing democracy and human rights" (Clinton 2011). Washington's objective was to rebalance the U.S. strategic focus out of the Middle East to East Asia, to take advantage of a booming economic region, and deal with security threats such as North Korea and other tensions. The role of the Caribbean did not factor large in this geopolitical policy landscape.

From a Chinese perspective, the pivot to Asia and TPP sounded like containment, a policy that the United States had used against the Soviet Union during the Cold War. At the same time, the superiority of the Western model of development, a mix of private sector-led capitalism and liberal democracy, was increasingly viewed as inferior to China's authoritarian, state-dominated development which appeared to ride through the Great Recession crisis better than the United States and Europe. The combination of such developments was compounded by an increasing view in the West that there was a serious miscalculation about China; the development of a more market-oriented economy did not lead to a more democratic and open political system. Indeed, with the advent of President Xi, China's political system became more authoritarian and aggressive in the pursuit of the country's national interests. In turn, U.S. interest groups, including the U.S. Department of Defense, adopted tougher stances on cybersecurity, China's establishment of the East China Air Defense Identification Zone, and its land reclamation efforts in the

South China Sea. The TPP morphed from being a neutral trade agreement into a counterweight to China's expanding regional influence. The TPP was given further impetus by China's creation of the Asian Infrastructure Investment Bank in 2016, which was perceived in Washington as an effort to rewrite the global rules of engagement, especially as it supported the BRI and threatened to erode the role of the Asian Development Bank, where the United States and Japan maintained considerable influence.

To a backdrop of deteriorating United States–China relations, the Obama administration's approach to the Caribbean was more relaxed. At the Fifth Summit of the Americas held in Trinidad and Tobago in 2009, where 30 heads of state were gathered, President Obama outlined his policy framework: "There is no senior partner and junior partner in our relations; there is simply engagement based on mutual respect and common interests and shared values. So I am here to launch a new chapter of engagement that will be sustained throughout my administration" (The White House 2009). This message was reinforced by the official ending of the Monroe Doctrine in 2013 by U.S. Secretary of State John Kerry: "Many years ago the United States dictated a policy that defined the hemisphere for many years after. We've moved past that era, and today must go even further…it will require courage and a willingness to change, but above all, it will require a higher and deeper level of cooperation between us, all of us together as equal partners in this hemisphere" (U.S. Department of State 2013).

Although Obama's trip to Trinidad and Tobago in 2009 was not followed up by other visits to the Caribbean until his swing through Jamaica in 2015, the Caribbean was not forgotten. The U.S. leader's visit to Jamaica was the first by a U.S. president since Ronald Reagan in 1982, while the trip to Cuba the following year was the first since Calvin Coolidge in 1928. The shift in U.S. policy on Cuba was significant. Obama's effort to normalize Cuban–U.S. relations was a roll of the diplomatic dice; if successful it could end one of the last remnants of the old Cold War in the Western Hemisphere, nudge the island along the path toward democracy, and reduce Cuba's dependence on Venezuelan oil. On the policy side the Obama administration removed Cuba from the international terrorist sponsor list in 2015, the President successfully visited the island, reduced a number of U.S. economic restrictions, and opened the door to U.S. tourists, who soon visited the island in large numbers. Although normalization was opposed by factions of the Republican Party and parts of the Cuban-American community, it had wider public support and the backing of U.S. business, long excluded from one of the largest markets in the Caribbean.

Another major change was the push for the development of alternative energy as a means of dealing with climate change. This action would also counter the influence of Venezuela which had used its Petro-Caribe program to make friends in the Caribbean. With this in mind, Vice President Joe Biden hosted the first Caribbean Energy Security Summit in Washington in 2015. All Caribbean countries with the exception of Cuba participated in the summit as did CARICOM, the Caribbean Development Bank, the European Union, the Inter-American Development Bank, the International Renewable Energy Agency, the Organization of American States, and the World Bank. The meeting marked the launch of the Caribbean Energy Security Initiative (CESI), whose mission was "...to boost energy security and sustainable economic growth in the region by attracting investment in a range of energy technologies through a focus on improved governance, increased access to finance, and strengthened coordination among energy donors, governments, and stakeholders" (U.S. Department of State 2015). Once again, the policy drivers had little to do with China, but were more focused on Venezuela.

The new catch-all of U.S. Caribbean policy came with the United States–Caribbean Strategic Engagement Act of 2016 in which many of the earlier themes were reiterated. While remaining true to democratic rights, the rule of law and economic cooperation, the bill, like many other programs focused on the Caribbean in the post-Cold War era, lacked any substantial heft in terms of new money (Congressional Budget Office 2016). Indeed, U.S. foreign assistance for the Caribbean was to generally decline in the 2011–2014 period due to the lingering impact of the 2008–2009 financial crisis (Congressional Research Service 2021: 8). The United States did pledge ongoing support for the Caribbean Basin Security Initiative (CBSI), which is a shared security partnership started in 2010 to support programs to reduce illicit trafficking, increase

citizen security, and promote crime prevention.[1] Significantly, the U.S.–
Caribbean Strategic Engagement Act of 2016 made no mention of
China.

By the end of the Obama years U.S. influence in the Caribbean was
being quietly chipped away by China. This was evident in the spread
of Chinese diplomats through the region, the economic penetration
of Chinese companies and banks, largescale and visible infrastructure
projects, and a rise in cultural ties. For many Caribbean countries China
was a good partner and its involvement offered an opportunity to
diminish a top-heavy dependency on the United States. Additionally,
while China was willing to establish embassies throughout the region,
the United States refused to address this issue in the Eastern Caribbean,
which was and continues to be serviced out of Barbados. This was inter-
preted in the Eastern Caribbean as evidence that they were of only
secondary importance to Washington. As one local observer stated in the
Jamaica Observer in 2015: "Some people may say these countries are too
small to each have an embassy but Cuba, which has staunchly resisted all
efforts to achieve democracy, will soon have one. Their citizens, at great
expense and inconvenience, have to travel to Barbados to do business with
the U.S." (James 2016).

Although U.S. officialdom claimed that budgetary restraints prohibited
building new embassies in the Eastern Caribbean, this has proven to be
an ongoing sore point in relations, especially as China has done exactly
that. This questioning of Eastern Caribbean diplomatic importance was
only compounded by the Obama administration's inability to appoint an
ambassador to the Bahamas from 2011 through the end of his term; U.S.
diplomacy in Nassau has been the responsibility of the Chargé d'Affaires
(and still was as of 2022).

Probably the main reason for U.S. complacency in the face of a
growing Chinese role in the Caribbean was that the United States
remained the region's lead trade partner, chief source of tourists, and a
major player in foreign direct investment. This was the case in the English-
speaking Caribbean as well as the Dominican Republic. Old business
relationships and geographical proximity helped maintain U.S. hegemony

---

[1] The CBSI has a membership that includes Antigua & Barbuda, the Bahamas,
Barbados, Dominica, the Dominican Republic, Grenada, Guyana, Jamaica, St. Kitts and
Nevis, St. Vincent and the Grenadines, Suriname, and Trinidad & Tobago. Observers are
Belize, Haiti, Montserrat, and the Dutch Caribbean.

during the Obama years. The United States was also the country to which many people in the Caribbean migrated. This mentality gave Washington's political class the opportunity to play games in the holding up of diplomatic appointments, which undermines U.S. global influence. All the same, many in the Caribbean perceived the United States as having a more narrow focus on Cuba, a larger and emotionally connected island, and Haiti, which carried the ongoing risks of political implosion and refugees. The rest of the Caribbean was generally treated to benign neglect.

The Trump Years and the New Cold War

U.S. foreign policy made a dramatic change under President Trump. The new president opposed globalization, had little understanding and was suspicious of multilateral organizations, and had a strong belief that many of the deals the United States made with other countries surrendered national sovereignty for little gain. The world was a zero sum arena, with clear winners and losers. Trump was a strong nationalist, which was captured in his catchphrase, "America First." And unlike his predecessors Trump considered himself a much sharper negotiator, not to mention having a far better belief in his vision of what was good for the United States than the so-called experts (Zakaria 2019). At the same time that Trump pushed U.S. foreign policy in new directions, he was regarded as unpredictable, making one political scientist proclaim early in his tenure: "The inconsistent and erratic character of Trump's foreign policy seems poised to endure well into his presidency" (MacDonald 2018).

Trump's unfiltered comments further injected uncertainty as to how to deal with the new administration. For the Caribbean, the U.S leader came off as racist. In particular, in a January 2018 meeting with several U.S. senators in a discussion about protecting immigrants from Haiti, El Salvador, and African countries, Trump allegedly stated: "Why are we having all these people from shithole countries here?" At the same meeting he also asked, "Why do we need more Haitians?" (Kendi 2019). Haiti's ambassador to the United States, Paul Altidor, stated: "We are surprised, disappointed. Also we want to condemn it if those statements were made" (Dwyer 2018).

Trump's America First came as a dash of cold water for many Caribbean leaders as it was an abrupt departure from the foreign policies of previous postwar U.S. presidents. This was even more so in that the U.S. leader was willing to identify the main U.S. rival as China and start a major trade war, which soon rippled through the global economy. The combination of these factors left U.S. Caribbean policy in a state of uncertainty. While the major themes of U.S. policy vis-à-vis the Caribbean—mutual cooperation in healthcare, helping Haiti and providing support for better governance—were consistent with past administrations, there was a hardening of policy, which was increasingly conditioned by a new Cold War mentality. Catalysts for this were the defections of Panama, El Salvador, and the Dominican Republic from their recognition of Taiwan to China. And there were worries over China's inroads into Panama, key to U.S. trade and security considerations (Ellis 2018).

While the United States slowly woke up to the challenge represented by China, Washington had little new to offer Caribbean countries. The Trump administration was willing to pay lip service to the old mantras of U.S. policy, but was unwilling to commit any new major financial resources to the Caribbean even in the face of Chinese largesse. In a sense, the U.S. message was: do not accept Chinese assistance to finance long-desired infrastructure projects, but we are not going to provide any new major financing. While the Inter-American Development Bank actively provided some assistance (both in terms of loans and technical help), it was hard-put to match China's checkbook. Moreover, the IDB wanted a higher degree of disclosure and transparency in its dealings with Caribbean countries; the Chinese did not.

One easy option for the Trump administration was to ramp-up anti-Chinese rhetoric directed to the Caribbean and Latin America (and the rest of the world). An early stab in this direction came from Trump's first Secretary of State, Rex Tillerson, who surprised much of the Caribbean and Latin America in February 2018 when he touted a return to the Monroe Doctrine, calling it a success and warned that the region must guard against faraway powers, i.e. China. He stated: "Today China is getting a foothold in Latin America. It is using economic statecraft to pull the region into its orbit; the question is at what price" (U.S. Mission to the Organization of American States 2018). He further asserted; "Latin America does not need new imperial powers that seek only to benefit their own people. China's state-led model of development is reminiscent of the past. It doesn't have to be this hemisphere's future." In this China was equated to being an external imperialist power with the goal of subverting Caribbean countries to Beijing's sinister interests. The response to the Trump administration's return to the Monroe Doctrine was hardly positive throughout the Caribbean and Latin America, considering that to many people in both regions the policy was associated with military interventions and coups.

Tillerson's tenure as Secretary of State was short-lived, but a key element of U.S. policy was re-established, stressing a new Cold War rhetoric against China and its allies in the Caribbean and Latin America. National Security Advisor John Bolton followed with a speech in November 2018 in which he noted: "The 'troika of tyranny' speech underlined the affiliations between all three authoritarian governments, laying the basis for a more forward-leaning policy" (Bolton 2020: 249). The reference of course was to Cuba, Nicaragua, and Venezuela, all regarded as Chinese allies in the Americas. In this case forward-leaning meant an "ongoing reversal of Obama's Cuba policy, new sanctions against Cuba and executive orders sanctioning oil and gold sectors from Venezuela. Bolton was to further elaborate": "This wasn't a trade dispute but a conflict of systems. The 'structural issues' we raised with China weren't trade tactics but a fundamentally different approach to organizing economic life." Trump also had stated on occasion that a military option was not off the table for Venezuela, though the idea was strongly resisted by both State Department and Pentagon officials.

While the main thrust of the Trump administration was to address a new Cold War with China, including in the Caribbean, the policy line came out more piecemeal than in the form of a coherent strategy. There were a number of elements to this, including a much more active Secretary of State, Mike Pompeo, making a number of trips to the region (including Jamaica, the Dominican Republic, Guyana, and Suriname); a reaching out to those countries perceived as more friendly to U.S. policy lines on China (and Venezuela and Cuba); pressure from outspoken U.S. ambassadors and an eventual recognition that something needed to be done on economic statecraft side.

Pressure Politics

One of the first sorties into Caribbean policy by President Trump came when the U.S. leader met with his counterparts from the Bahamas, Dominican Republic, Jamaica, Haiti, and St. Lucia in March 2019 at his Mar-a-Lago resort, in Florida. The meeting sought to demonstrate renewed U.S. interest in the Caribbean and rally friendly states to its side on the issue of Venezuela at the OAS. In return for Caribbean support for the U.S. position, the possibility of greater U.S. investment was held out. Following the meeting most of the countries that attended broke from other CARICOM members and supported the position of Venezuelan opposition leader Guaidó. CARICOM still officially recognized Maduro as Venezuela's legitimate president. Although the move was considered by those leaders not invited to Mar-a-Lago as a means of dividing up the Caribbean, it underscored that the Trump administration was willing to advance its policy agenda, even if it ruffled the diplomatic feathers of governments not invited.

Trump (who seemed to have delighted in rolling back everything Obama had accomplished) was also willing to stall and then reverse the thaw between Havana and Washington. This came out piecemeal, but was nonetheless damaging to the Castrorite regime and hurt the Cuban economy. Among the different measures undertaken were a limiting of remittances that could be sent from the United States to the island; tighter restrictions on air and sea travel; and prohibitions on conducting business with any of the Cuban military-owned enterprises. While this played to the idea that such actions could coerce Havana to cut its support for Caracas, another motivation was that as Trump looked toward his chances for re-election in 2020, he needed to secure Florida, which is home to a large Cuban and Venezuelan bloc of voters, most of whom were opposed to leftwing regimes.

The imposition of a new Cold War perceptual lens by Washington was to complicate bilateral relations with Caribbean allies. Although Jamaica was considered as pro-U.S., it also enjoyed a positive relationship with China. Indeed, China's help with infrastructure and cheap loans was appreciated in Kingston. This led to a flap in November 2019 when Prime Minister Holness made an official visit to China, where he was well-received. The recently appointed U.S. ambassador, the octogenarian Donald Tapia, a former businessman and Trump supporter, took aim at Jamaica's China connection. Tapia's comments included a warning about China: "When they go into a country, they go after two things – the minerals and ports. I could tell you horror stories of countries where they have taken over ports because those countries could not pay for their investment. China usually has a great propaganda story as to why it has happened." He also warned Jamaica over installing 5G generation mobile technology made by Huawei and ZTE as it would give China an enhanced ability to spy on the Caribbean country.

The U.S. ambassador's comments did not go down well with most Jamaicans. Indeed, *The Gleaner*, one of the oldest and most established newspapers on the island, stated: "Mr Tapia should be given a message about where Jamaica's foreign policy is formulated, which ought not to be Foggy Bottom. Neither is it done, as the former Jamaica Labour Party (JLP) prime minister, Bruce Golding, famously declaimed during the Christopher Cole imbroglio, at Liuanea, where Mr Tapia now has offices."

While Tapia followed the Trump administration's narrative in showing U.S. displeasure over Jamaica's close relationship with China, his approach was overbearing, especially as he came to his new position with little knowledge or expertise in Jamaican affairs, let alone Caribbean international relations. He also underestimated the level of sophistication of Jamaica's foreign policy expertise that had taken the country through the Cold War and its aftermath. Even more irritating, while Tapia was critical of Jamaica's China policy, he came with none of the same infrastructure help offered by Beijing.

Much of the same narrative from the Trump administration came from its ambassadorial appointment to Trinidad and Tobago, another octogenarian, Joseph Mondello. An attorney, university professor, and chairman of the Nassau Republican State Committee in New York since 1983, Mondello followed the Trump administration's line on China and the Caribbean. In his maiden speech in October 2018 given at the Trinidad and Tobago-American Chamber of Commerce he stated: "Firms owned and backed by governments are incompatible with free markets. As we have seen time after time throughout the world, state-owned enterprises invest abroad in ways that are clearly not market-driven and clearly not designed to benefit the people of the countries in which they invest" (Bridglala, 2018; Power and Politics 2020). For anyone reading between the lines, there was a clear reference to Chinese companies which recently announced largescale investments for projects in Trinidad and Tobago, including a dry dock at La Brea and technology park in Point Lisas. Once again, the United States warned about China's creeping influence and to beware its largescale investments, but it offered little in the financing of projects.

Although relations between the United States and Trinidad and Tobago remained generally cordial, Mondello's stances on Venezuela and China often entered into the public realm, with Trinidad's Prime Minister Rowley pushing back. At the end of his term as ambassador in January

2021, Mondello made the point that he believed that relations between the two countries could improve, that the United States had made contributions to Trinidad and Tobago's security apparatus, and had given assistance in the healthcare area, in particular the visit of the U.S. Naval Ship Comfort to treat 7000 patients for free and providing $250,000 in Covid-19 assistance in 2020. At the same time, the former U.S. ambassador took one last swipe at Trinidad and its relationship with China upon returning home to Long Island, noting: "Keith Rowley, although a nice gentleman, made a statement that the United States was their partner of the past and that China was the partner of the future. And that seems to be the thought of the minds of many of the Caribbean island chieftains so to speak." To this he added, "They depended on the United States for many years and the United States has done very well by them. But they are at the point now where they take the United States for very much for granted. There is a real pushing and shoving as to who is going to have the biggest influence in the government...The reason for that is the Chinese coming in and doing a lot of things..." Mondello clearly was not shy in voicing his opinions, with one Trinidadian academic stating, "He did the normal philanthropic things and also got some security items for the government; he is the sort of diehard Republican patrician who has no reluctance to lecture to the natives."

U.S. diplomacy was also active in Guyana and Suriname, both of which were considered more important due to their large offshore oil reserves. In September 2020 the U.S. Secretary of State Mike Pompeo did something no other holder of his office had accomplished; he paid an official visit to Guyana and Suriname. While in the latter country, Pompeo stated, "We've watched the Chinese Communist Party invest in countries, and it all seems great at the front end and then it all comes falling down when the political costs connected to that becomes clear" (Jamaica Observer 2020).

Not to let the slight go, the Chinese embassy in Suriname promptly responded to the U.S. Secretary of State's comments, noting that "any attempt to sow discord between China and Suriname is doomed to fail. We advise Mr. Pompeo to respect facts and truths, abandon arrogance and prejudice, stop smearing and spreading rumors about China." The Chinese embassy in Guyana followed this up by commenting that Beijing "attaches no political strings in bilateral pragmatic cooperation, which brings tangible benefits to countries and peoples in the region." China's

Guyanese embassy also advised Pompeo to "stop spreading rumors and fake news everywhere to confuse people."

In addition to stopping in Suriname and Guyana to meet with top leaders, Pompeo's itinerary also included Panama and Jamaica, showing the U.S. flag and letting all comers know that Washington was still a force in the region. In Jamaica, the U.S. Secretary of State met with Prime Minister Holness and Minister of Foreign Affairs Minister Kamina Johnson Smith. While seeking to shore up the U.S.–Jamaican relationship, Pompeo also led a multilateral round table discussion with other regional leaders under the theme of Expanding America's Commitment to the Caribbean. Those regional leaders included the foreign ministers from the Bahamas, Dominican Republic, Haiti, St. Kitts-Nevis, and St. Lucia. At the larger meeting, Pompeo stuck to the U.S. anti-China narrative: "It's tempting to accept easy money from places like China. But what good is it if it feeds corruption and undermines your rule of law? What good are those investments if in fact they ruin your environment and don't create jobs for your people?" (Pompeo 2020).

While Pompeo's visit was billed as a U.S. diplomatic success, it also generated a certain degree of ill will among a number of CARICOM members. In particular, U.S. policy appeared to be one of dividing CARICOM members into two camps, those supportive of the U.S. policy on Venezuela and those opposed, which included Antigua and Barbuda, Barbados, Dominica, Trinidad and Tobago, Guyana, Suriname, and St. Vincent and the Grenadines. While those in the U.S. "camp" (the Bahamas, Belize, the Dominican Republic, Haiti, St. Kitts-Nevis, and St. Lucia) were invited to attend the Kingston meeting, the other CARICOM members were not. CARICOM's then president, Prime Minister Mia Mottley of Barbados, took exception to the meeting as it was outside of the usual diplomatic conduit of all CARICOM leaders meeting with the United States. Mottley described Pompeo's meeting as "an attempt to divide the region."

Pompeo's Caribbean tour was a warning to the Chinese as well as a heads up call to regional leaders that Washington was closely watching which countries were regarded as kowtowing to China. The deterioration in China–U.S. relations over a wide variety of issues culminated in an out-and-out trade war in 2018 and an increase in sharp rhetoric between the two countries. The discovery of massive oil reserves in the Southern Caribbean only reinforced the view in Washington that if the United States wanted to keep the region secure to its interests, it had to act.

The significance of major oil and gas finds in the Caribbean is important from the perspective that the shift to renewable energy (RE) and
carbon zero economies remains at least three decades off. As Trinidadian
energy expert Anthony Bryan observed: "…it will take decades for the
transition to RE to run its course. It may never phase out fossil fuels
completely. Natural gas and LNG may be important transition fuels even
in the late twenty-first century" (Bryan 2019). U.S. companies are at
the forefront of regional energy development. While Chinese and Russian
companies are involved in oil and gas exploration and production, their
role is much smaller than that of ExxonMobil (which is big in Guyana)
and Apache in Suriname. In Guyana, China's CNOOC is part of the
consortium, along with ExxonMobil and Hess Corporation, producing
crude. Chinese companies, like PetroChina and Sinocham International,
are also active in seeking a role in Guyana.

The Place of Economic Statecraft

The early Trump administration clearly moved to a hardline stance on
China in the Caribbean, but it later embraced the need for economic
statecraft (at least in an optic sense). This was accomplished in two
ways, launching the Growth in the Americas Initiative (*América Crece*)
and taking aim at getting better control of the Inter-American Development Bank. The former was launched in 2018 and expanded and
relaunched in December 2019 to encompass broader energy and infrastructure needs in the Caribbean and Latin America. In particular, "The
initiative fosters jobs and economic growth by catalyzing private sector
investment in energy and other infrastructure across Latin America and
the Caribbean." Beyond public utilities, the expanded version was meant
to encompass all types of infrastructure, including airports, ports, roads,
and telecom networks. Considering the Caribbean's energy picture, the
program generated some interest (Viscidi and Phillips 2020). Under
the auspices of the U.S. International Development Finance Corporation (DFC), the United States signed memorandums of understanding
with a number of Latin American countries (including Argentina, Brazil,
Panama, and El Salvador) as well as Jamaica. One project launched under
the auspices of USAID in 2019 was the Caribbean Energy Initiative
(CEI), with the goal of building resilience in electrical grids in Haiti, the
Dominican Republic, and Jamaica.

Sadly América Crece had a number of problems. First, it was generated out of the Trump White House, generated by the National Security
Council, and as such it was a policy allowed to fade under the Biden
administration. The other aspect that the program raised was the rules
under which such a program launched by the United States plays are
different from those under which Chinese institutions operate. As demonstrated in earlier chapters, Chinese state companies and banks are directed
by their government to work in certain markets and can channel funds
to those projects that will aid their geo-economic policies. The problem
for the U.S. government is that it cannot direct its companies (which
are private sector-owned) to invest in the Caribbean. Nor can the U.S.
government have its banks lend to the Caribbean; indeed U.S. anti-money
laundering rules and regulations have been a turnoff for many banks to
conduct business in the region, not to mention being an ongoing sore
point between the Caribbean and United States. Congress has made some
efforts to address this issue toward the end of the Trump administration
and into the first two years of the Biden administration.

América Crece was followed by the announcement by President Biden
of a Build Back Better World Initiative or B3W Partnership in early
2021, a plan that sounds very similar. Indeed, President Biden's B3W
was announced as "a values-driven, high-standard, and transparent infrastructure partnership led by major democracies to help narrow the $40
trillion+ infrastructure needs in the developing world, which has been
exacerbated by the COVID-19 pandemic" (The White House 2021).
Unlike América Crece, B3W is meant to be global in nature, with a
focus on climate, health and health security, digital technology, and
gender equity and equality. Although the intention of the Trump and
Biden administrations was clearly to address the effectiveness of China's
economic statecraft in the area of infrastructure, the plans lacked significant follow-though. For many U.S. firms conducting business in the
Caribbean, the Biden administration has done little to change the game.

The other major area of economic statecraft involved the Inter-
American Development Bank and can be considered as more effective.
The view within the Trump administration was that China, which joined
the development bank in 2008, had gained too much influence. This
was evident when in 2019 when China canceled the bank's annual
meeting to be held in Chengdu, due to its refusal to allow a representative of Venezuelan opposition leader Guaidó to attend. The meeting
was intended to mark the IDB's 60th anniversary. A spokesperson for

China stated that Beijing "had difficulty allowing" the representative to attend because Guaidó himself lacked legal standing. The United States contended that Guaidó did have legal standing. The Trump administration had earlier recommended that the meeting be scheduled in the Americas, home to the vast majority of the bank's members.

Concern over Chinese influence at the IDB did not diminish. In 2020, when Luis Alberto Moreno stepped down as the bank's president, the Trump administration advanced Mauricio Claver-Carone, a Cuban-American. Described as a political operative in Washington and a hardliner on Cuba (pro-embargo), he served at the U.S. Treasury Department and the International Monetary Fund. He was appointed to the National Security Council in 2018 and soon became one of the most influential voices on the Trump administration's Latin American and Caribbean policy (while serving on the National Security Council). Claver-Carone grasped the need for an economic answer to China's economic statecraft, having a hand in the formulation of América Crece and was an advocate for tougher U.S. sanctions against the Maduro regime. He also emerged as a strong advocate for nearshoring, a response to the push by the Trump and Biden administrations to reduce U.S. supply chain dependence on China to either the United States or closer to home. This gained greater importance during the Covid-19 pandemic and China's trade to the Caribbean and Latin America fell substantially. The IDB president in 2021 made this point at a Wilson Center conference, noting that his push for nearshoring was not an "anti-Chinese thing," but that "the global corporate community realizes that reliance on a single source is not only unwise, but it's dangerous..." (Claver-Carone 2021).

What was significant was that Claver-Carone was the first American to be advanced to assume the multilateral development bank's presidency. Although there were a handful of countries opposed to his candidacy— there was an unwritten agreement that someone from Latin America would head the bank—Claver-Carone easily won with 23 out of the 28 countries in the region supporting him. One of the main items on his agenda is to recapitalize the bank, seeking to expand its lending power beyond $20 billion to help the region recover from the negative downturn induced by the Covid-19 pandemic. Although his appointment was controversial, it represented one of the last efforts by the Trump administration in reformulating the U.S. position on China in the Caribbean and Latin America.

258 S. B. MACDONALD

Vaccine Policy—A Stumble

While efforts were made in the last two years of the Trump administration to address some of the economic statecraft issues, one policy area where the Trump administration stumbled in the Caribbean was the Covid pandemic. For many in the Caribbean, the United States was traditionally the place to turn for help. Consequently, with the outbreak of the pandemic in early 2020 many Caribbean nations turned to the United States for assistance. The Trump administration, through the implementation of the Defense Production Act, blocked the sale of personal protective equipment (PPE) to non-Americans. Ventilators were also on the prohibited list. This was highly problematic for the Bahamas, Cayman Islands, and Barbados which had container loads of PPE they had purchased from U.S. vendors blocked from entering their territories by U.S. Customs and Border Protection. The administration's main concern was to treat the American public first, even if it meant halting shipments to its allies in the Caribbean and Latin America. The ban went into place after 3M Corporation, which produced N95 respiratory face masks, pushed back on the Trump administration's orders to cease exports of the masks to the Caribbean and Latin America. 3M stressed that there were "humanitarian consequences" to such an action. Exports were shut down soon thereafter. This left many Caribbean countries scrambling and turning to diplomatic channels to get PPE.

Compounding bad feelings over the Trump administration's handling of the medical equipment was its approach to international cooperation. As CSIS's Annie Pforzheimer noted in March 2021: "One reason was the very public U.S. withdrawal from the World Health Organization (WHO), its funding dispute with the Pan American Health Organization (PAHO), and its rejection of other forms of international cooperation. That posture gave the strong public impression that the United States was letting the rest of the world go it alone." The U.S. position was also undermined by China's "mask diplomacy," which sought to demonstrate the Asian country's being a good partner despite the unsettling fact that the pandemic started in that country. China got considerable mileage out of Caribbean leaders praising Chinese medical help, though not all of its equipment worked and there was a questioning of motives.

U.S. efforts to provide assistance were to pick up late in the Trump administration. The United States, through USAID, would eventually deliver ventilators to 13 Latin American and Caribbean countries, including the Dominican Republic, Haiti, and St. Kitts and Nevis. The United States also helped UNICEF install more than 3500 handwashing stations throughout Haiti. Vaccines were also eventually made available for Caribbean buyers. Nonetheless, there was an element of catching up to China, Russia, and Cuba (which developed its own vaccine).

By the end of the Trump administration, the key points of the anti-China policy for the Caribbean were formulated. In its 2020 overview of the Western Hemispheric Strategic Framework, the U.S. National Security Council tagged the following points for what it perceived as China's negative influence on Latin America and the Caribbean (U.S. Department of State 2020). The significance of these points should not be underestimated as they continue to shape the U.S. approach in the post-Trump era. The key points are as follows:

- China does not play by the same rules as the United States and other Western economies in how it pursues state-driven trade, investment, diplomatic, technology, media, security, and health outreach.
- China is aggressively pursuing telecommunications control over the Caribbean in spreading 5G infrastructure by Huawei and other state-affiliated technology firms.
- China is pursuing "debt trap" diplomacy by increasing the region's dependence on non-market debt financing. (This is usually a reference to the case of Sri Lanka in South Asia, which became highly indebted to China, among other lenders. China, through China Merchant Port Holdings, obtained control of the Sri Lankan port of Hambantota for 99 years in a debt deal.) (White House 2020)
- The study also noted: "Such activities empower corruption, weaken intellectual property protection, exploit cyber vulnerabilities, unfairly disadvantage United States and host nation businesses, harm the environment, and pressure nations to adopt policies inconsistent with democratic values and the long-term interests of their own people."

Any questions over the United States being in an adversarial relationship with China were clarified. The National Security Council also advanced "priority actions" to deal with the Chinese threat. These encompassed increasing awareness of the downsides of non-market-based financing; continuing to construct close links between the United States and regional private sectors; promoting free, fair, and reciprocal trade; and working with partners to develop frameworks for constructing responsible commercial relationships that do not undermine U.S. jobs and investment opportunities or threaten intellectual property. Other actions were to support development and investment opportunities in the region, including through the U.S. International Development Finance Corporation (DFC). The "action plan" also stressed the importance of promoting citizen-centric governance to ensure that government decision-making is in a country's long term interest.

At the same time the Trump administration pulled together an anti-Chinese game plan for the Caribbean, it cut aid to the region (see Table 9.1). Probably one of the most hardnosed decisions was to suspend aid for the Pan American Health Organization (PAHO), the regional organization that the United States helped found more than a century ago to protect the health of the hemisphere. The Trump administration's action was due to PAHO's allegedly not fully disclosing its role in "Mais Médicos" involving Cuban doctors providing health in remote parts of Brazil. The suspension of aid came when the Covid-19 pandemic was hitting the Caribbean. It also dovetailed with the Trump's negative stance on the WHO as being too pro-Chinese.

Table 9.1   U.S. Foreign Assistance to the Caribbean by Country: FY2016-FY2021 (Thousands of U.S. dollars)

	FY 2016	FY 2017	FY 2018	FY 2019	FY 2020	FY 2021
Bahamas	270	173	138	196	200	200
Belize	1243	1241	1143	235	1250	200
Dominican Republic	21,615	13,736	20,174	36,777	28,661	15,500
Guyana	243	277	239	176	200	200
Haiti	185,076	164,522	181,319	193,752	172,520	121,155
Jamaica	5065	10,587	1335	1598	1600	600
Suriname	215	269	167	195	200	200
Trinidad and Tobago	325	343	341	326	350	300
Barbados and Eastern Caribbean	26,425	26,629	24,027	3456	13,950	3550
USAID Caribbean Development	3000	4000	4000	4000	13,950	0
Total	243,262	221,777	232,542	239,289	232,881	141,905

Source U.S. Foreign Assistance to Latin America and the Caribbean: FY 2021 Appropriations Congressional Research Service, January 7, 2021

One other factor needs to be considered—the impact of U.S. domestic politics on Caribbean perceptions of the United States as well as Chinese messaging about the superiority of its political-economic system over that of the North American country. In 2020, China was handed a public relations coup, as U.S. cities were caught up in a series of riots and demonstrations sparked by longstanding racial issues. Chinese media widely reported on looting and rioting and blasted the U.S. government for failing to address its racial inequality. As Orville Schell, director at the Asia Society's Center on U.S.–China Relations observed: "I think the Chinese Communist propaganda apparatus is very grateful to have some burning cities in the United States right now, having had to suffer and feel deeply humiliated by the specter of Hong Kong being in a state of chaos" (Ruwitch 2020).

The President's refusal to accept his loss in the 2020 election and the storming of the U.S. Capitol on January 6, 2021 further benefited China as they were able to offer up the Chinese model of single party rule and stability and a guided economy in contrast to the upheaval rocking the United States. China was quite happy to state that the United States needed to face up to its own "democracy deficit" instead of trying to promote democracy around the world. Indeed, one of China's top officials, Wang Wenbin, indicated that the attack on the U.S. Capitol "shocked the world and provoked deep thoughts" presumably about the suitability of democracy in general and American democracy in particular (Zhao 2021). To emphasize the superiority of the Chinese model, Beijing published a 50-page white paper in December 2021, with the title, *China: Democracy That Works*, an eerily Orwellian document. As the document stated: "Whole-process people's democracy integrates process-oriented democracy with results-oriented democracy, procedural democracy with substantive democracy, direct democracy with indirect democracy, and people's democracy with the will of the state" (Liu 2021). Instead of changing the way democracy is conducted in China, the Communist Party has found it easier to change the definition of democracy, making a document that has all of the clearness of a Kafka-like world, guided by the hand of the Communist Party and for those doubters of a new Cold War, the Chinese document is noteworthy in that it takes a direct shot against the U.S. vision and practice of democracy, something with a distinct Cold War feel to it.

Game or no game of extracting benefits out of the United States or China, Caribbean countries should have a greater awareness of the contempt the Chinese Communist Party has for their political systems, based on the vote and the people's will. It is obvious that Caribbean countries are not going to construct better democracies and improve governance by turning to China. Indeed, the future of democratic governance is going to be a major theme of U.S.–Chinese competition in the Caribbean in the decades ahead. U.S. support, therefore, needs to be upped in helping Caribbean organizations that promote democracy throughout the region. There have been some notable efforts in this in Guyana and Suriname, but more is required. This may take on greater urgency if there is greater slippage in democratic governance in not only the Caribbean, but also in neighboring Latin America.

U.S. Caribbean Policy—So Much Unfinished Business

Part of the problem for the United States in dealing with the Caribbean and the idea of a new Cold War is a lack of depth in much of the U.S. policy community. There is an ongoing rotation of personnel in officialdom as it is difficult to make careers advance by working on St. Lucia or Dominica compared to Colombia, Russia, or China. At the same time, the Caribbean was very much out of vogue in the think tank world until the issue of China emerged and large quantities of oil were discovered in Guyana and then Suriname. Even then, some of the work produced has been more a rehash of old ideas and platitudes. The result is that Caribbean policy until the late Obama and Trump years was allowed to drift. While the Obama administration brought change in terms of Cuba and alternative energy and climate change, the Trump administration rolled back or stalled these initiatives and refocused on the Caribbean in a more muscular transactional approach, though some thought was eventually given to how to counter China's economic statecraft.

President Biden entered office in January 2021. He inherited a Caribbean struggling to recover from the Covid-19 pandemic, economic dislocation, high debt levels, a near-total breakdown of law and order in Haiti (soon to be followed by the assassination of that country's president), and major riots in Cuba in 2021. On the southern border, the Biden administration soon faced a new migrant crisis. While there was talk of a major $4 billion economic package for Central America and a trip by Vice President Kamala Harris to Guatemala and Mexico in 2021 to deal with the root causes of migration, matters south of the U.S. border did not improve. Instead, much of Central America shifted to more autocratic leadership; Nicaragua held fraudulent elections and dropped its recognition of Taiwan; and Cuba's communist party engaged in a new round of repression following the island-wide 2021 riots and demonstrations. Moreover, the new Cold War competition with China remains very much of the geopolitical landscape, with concerns that Beijing will press hard on Taiwan's last diplomatic outposts in the Caribbean and Central America to shut the upstart island down. Rounding out the picture, Russia, seeking to put pressure on the United States over Ukraine and Eastern Europe, threatened in January 2022 to put more military assets in Cuba and Venezuela. Although the Biden administration promptly responded that it would "deal with it decisively," Moscow's line of reasoning clearly captured the idea of geopolitical asymmetry. As Russian Deputy Foreign Minister Sergei Ryabkov stated in January 2022: "We are constantly facing a provocative military pressure intended to test our strength. How would Americans act if our bombers fly within 15 kilometers off some U.S. bases on the East or the West coast?" (Isachenkov and Lee 2022). All of this poses tough questions for the United States at a time when it faces substantial challenges both in Europe and Asia as well as at home.

Climate Change, Energy Alternatives, and Transitions

In the mix of policy concerns one of the most significant areas of future U.S.–Chinese rivalry is likely to be over energy resources in the Caribbean, which is closely related to climate change. The Biden administration is clearly different from Trump's; out is the denial of climate change and in is a much more aggressive emphasis on green policies. This matches Caribbean concerns about climate change and its effects— drought, rising sea levels, and more powerful hurricanes. Climate change was addressed early by the Biden administration's policy vis-à-vis the Caribbean; two Caribbean leaders were invited to a Virtual Leaders Summit on Climate Change hosted by President Biden. These were prime ministers from Antigua and Barbuda and Jamaica, Gaston Browne and Andrew Holness, respectively. Antigua and Barbuda was a particularly sharp critic of the Trump administration. The invitations went to 38 other world leaders concerned with the risks represented by climate change.

The Biden administration will most likely remain a strong advocate for a green economy, something which should complement Caribbean efforts to more fully develop what is called the blue economy. According to the World Bank, "The blue economy concept seeks to promote economic growth, social inclusion, and the preservation or improvement of livelihoods while at the same time ensuring environmental sustainability of the oceans and coastal areas" (World Bank 2017: vi). It touches on a broad range of economic activities, including aquaculture, marine biotechnology, shipping and maritime transport, and renewable energy. The challenge for any Biden initiative on energy and a green transition is how to balance transition with energy security, something more challenging than initially expected by many.

The path forward on climate change is not simple or straightforward and is complicated by transitional factors. The Biden administration has adopted "climate-friendly infrastructure," which is re-orienting government spending to help promote a sustainable greening of transportation and providing help for the more rapid development of solar and wind power. While all of this is positive for a greener future, there are hurdles. There are a number of factors that are slowing the energy transition in the United States and Europe and, for that matter, in China and India. First and foremost, the global economy is still mainly powered by oil, natural gas, and coal. For economic growth, employment and keeping the lights and heat on for many homes, wind and solar power have not reached the point of being able to replace fossil fuels. Another challenge is that the green transition will cost trillions of dollars. Considering the already high level of debt racked up by most governments during the Covid-19 pandemic, funding is a concern.

Then there is the issue of many developing countries believing that they should not be on the same timeframe as the advanced economies. The reasoning is that advanced economies, like the United States, United Kingdom, and Japan, have already had their industrial revolutions; it is time for China, India, and Turkey to have their own industrial-tech revolutions. Although this view is slowly changing, countries like China, India, and Indonesia are still building coal-fired electricity power plants—while these are being phased out in the United States and Europe.

Oil and natural gas should be phased out, but it will take longer than expected for the green revolution to take off. In his *The New Map: Energy, Climate and the Clash of Nations*, Daniel Yergin asserts that the transition will happen: "But it is based on the reality of all the investment made, lead times for new investment and innovation, supply chains, its central role in transportation, the need for plastics as the building blocks of the modern world to hospital operating rooms, and the way the physical world is organized. As a result, oil – along with natural gas, which now is also a global commodity – will not only continue to play a large role in the world economy, but will also be central in the debates over the environment and climate, …certainly in the strategies of nations and in the contention among them" (Yergin 2020: 428–429).

All the above means ongoing geopolitical competition over oil and gas resources. It pushes the idea of greater competition between the U.S. and China and Russia. Yergin catches the significance of shifting tides in geopolitics and energy by noting: "How and why new cold wars are developing between the United States on one hand, and China and Russia on the other, and energy's role in them. How swiftly – and potentially perilously – the overall relationship between the United States and China is changing from 'engagement' to 'strategic rivalry' and what begins to look like an emerging cold war" (Yergin 2020: XIV). The lasting nature of oil politics was clearly revealed by the Russo-Ukrainian War, which was marked by the West's radical reduction of its use of Russian oil, gas, and coal, which, in turn, caused international fuel prices to skyrocket. In the United States, the Biden administration's strong anti-fossil fuel approach added to the problems as much of the energy industry had either cut spending on future projects, were forced to shut down operations on federal lands, or had reduced capacity. This, of course, was felt in the Caribbean, where the majority of countries are still heavily dependent on oil for electrical power generation.

Considering the size and location of the oil and gas fields offshore Guyana and Suriname, not to mention Trinidad and Tobago, the southern Caribbean will be important for some time to come (Bryan 2021). While these new petro-states look to oil and gas as a path to a better life for their citizens, the need for the fuel they provide puts them in the line of fire for global competition. The Trump administration grasped this reality as did China. So has the Biden administration: in early 2021 his administration responded to Venezuela's aggressive behavior promptly, stating: "The U.S. supports a peaceful resolution of the maritime boundary controversy between Venezuela and Guyana and condemns Maduro's intimidation through the seizure of fishing vessels and detention of crews" (Charles 2021). But the Biden administration is also conflicted over Caribbean policy—while supportive of alternative energy in the Caribbean, it has sought to cut any founding for anything linked to fossil fuels at multilateral development banks. Most notable was the denying of the Guyana Shore Base Incorporated of a $180 million loan (after a two-year process and environmental testing), which would have expanded Guyana's ability to export oil and import other goods, develop a waste management facility, and install solar photo-voltaic (PV) capacity on some of the facilities. While this probably has pushed Guyanese policymakers to consider Chinese loans, it also reflected a certain rigidness to green policy. What really caused irritation within Guyana and other oil/natural gas producers was that the Biden adminis-tration, feeling the pressure of higher oil prices at home, was apparently willing to open talks with Venezuela and Iran about loosening economic sanctions to put more oil on the market. At the same time, the Biden administration turned to Saudi Arabia for more oil, a situation compli-cated by the U.S. president's strong human rights stance. The conflicted nature of U.S. Caribbean policy was seen as Washington being willing to pressure fellow democracies in the region to go green (at the coast of giving up their oil programs), but willing to negotiate with authoritarian oil producers. From a Caribbean perspective, what does the United States stand for; human rights and democracy or a willingness to sit down with dictators and ask for oil?

Where does this leave U.S. Caribbean policy? There are calls to create a new version of the Energy and Climate Partnership of the Americas created during the Obama years; the challenge remains very much one of commitment and money. This was evident at the Ninth Summit of the Americas, where the emphasis was again placed on renewable energy and talk of financing, but little in hard numbers. The idea of a twenty-first century version of the Caribbean Basin Initiative has also been raised, though it has made little headway in Washington (Fauriol 2021: 3). The United States could certainly differentiate itself from China in taking a more aggressive stance on climate change and transitioning of energy sources in the Caribbean. In any consideration of a new Caribbean policy climate change and energy need to be core issues. Among items for consideration in such policy initiatives would be the expansion of clean electricity by deploying new and existing technologies; assistance for the development of technologies for low-cost building retrofits and efficient appliance manufacturing supply chains; and there should be a pooling of U.S., bilateral, regional, and multilateral development banks of resources to provide funding for innovation in clean energy technologies, including electric vehicles and charging stations, battery storage, negative emissions technologies, next generation building materials, and renewable hydrogen

(Cárdenas and Fitzmaurice 2021). Although the list is extensive, some of it is already applied. The question though remains, how committed is the United States to the Caribbean? Enough to help pay the bill for an energy transition, which is taking longer than expected in the United States?

Puerto Rico and the New Cold War

There is another piece of unfinished U.S. business in the Caribbean—Puerto Rico. As part of the United States, Puerto Rico has generally been absent in the discussion of power realignments in the Caribbean. However, Puerto Rico's strategic value could return depending on how far down the road the new Cold War travels. If U.S.–Chinese tensions escalate and the Caribbean observes an uptick in Chinese and, for that matter, Russian, Cuban and Iranian activities, Puerto Rico offers a key location between the Greater and Lesser Antilles. It is also a major transportation hub and has one of the Caribbean's largest populations after Cuba, the Dominican Republic, and Haiti.

Why does Puerto Rico matter in the new Cold War? It matters because it is a regional example of U.S. governance. That has not been a good thing over the past decade. For historical and political reasons, Puerto Rico has an odd relationship with the North American mainland. While Puerto Ricans are citizens of the United States, they cannot vote for the president nor do their representatives in Washington have a vote in Congress. One of the main challenges in the Caribbean for the United States was and continues to be: what does the North American country stand for in terms of political systems? The United States must rely on the strength of democracy as a critical element of its positioning in the new Cold War with China and Russia. The U.S. narrative has been that as a liberal democratic country, it wishes the same for its Caribbean friends.

However, the track record in Puerto Rico has been problematic, especially in the first decades of the twenty-first century. During that period the United States (along with pro-statehood politicians) ended the 936 Program, which had earlier created incentives for pharmaceutical companies to invest in the island. Unable to find other industries to fill the gap from departing pharmaceutical companies (many of which went to other countries like Ireland, China, and India), successive Puerto Rican governments turned to borrowing from the U.S. municipal bond market (Maldonado 2021). U.S. mutual fund companies were happy to purchase high-yielding Puerto Rican bonds, put them in mutual funds, and sell them to investors, including retirees. The upshot of this was that the Puerto Rican government failed to reform the economy, but racked up a debt of $74 billion, which by 2017 it could not repay. Adding to the daunting nature of the crisis was that the Puerto Rican government had $49 billion in unfunded pensions at the time.

Puerto Rico has struggled to find the exit ramp from its debt crisis. An oversight board, PROMESA (Puerto Rico Oversight, Management, and Economic Stability Act), was created by the U.S. Congress in 2016, but has struggled in dealing with what has been the largest municipal government bankruptcy in U.S. history. On top of that the island has an aging population, high costs for its social programs, and was hit with considerable devastation by Hurricane Maria in 2017. The hurricane reinforced the severe problems facing the Puerto Rican Electric Power Authority (PREPA) and its inability to provide adequate electricity for the island, a situation worsened by its inability to meet debt obligations.

Part of the problem facing Puerto Rico has been leadership that has exhibited corruption and a disregard for voters. In 2019 this resulted in an angry population taking to the streets to demand the resignation of then governor Ricardo Rosselló, following the leak of Telegram app messages in which the governor and his inner circle made light of the casualties caused by Hurricane Maria and disparaged political opponents using vulgar, homophobic, and sexist language (Aleem 2019). The leaked texts came days after the FBI arrested two former top officials in Rosselló's government as part of a corruption probe over their handling of $15.5 million in contracts. Rosselló eventually resigned, setting off a political crisis, which saw two more governors enter office in quick succession. The dismal nature of the island's political life was caught by one observer: "There is a sense in Puerto Rico that politics as usual has been permanently broken. The citizenry is dismayed with the political parties and their leaders" (Cabán 2019).

A massive debt problem, high unemployment, austerity, a lengthy period of economic contraction, and poor governance are reflected in Puerto Rico's declining population. According to the U.S. Census Bureau, Puerto Rico's population declined by 14.3 percent between 2010 and 2019. Around 2000, the total population stood at a little over 3.7 million people; it is now estimated to be around 3.2 million (U.S. Census Bureau 2022).

Puerto Rico's demographic profile is one of a population either aging or leaving the island. The island's women are having on average less than one child each, which puts the island among the lowest fertility rates in the world (Ortiz-Blanes 2021). This has raised concerns about a brain drain of the young and better educated. The other island with the same demographic profile is Cuba, where the population is rapidly aging (much like Greece, Italy, and Japan). Indeed, Cuba's population of 11.3 million is expected to shrink to 10.2 million by 2050, a 10.3 percent decline. According to the *World Population Review*: "The young people leaving the country and low birth rates are resulting in an increasingly aging population. Cuba's population is expected to be the ninth-oldest in the world by 2050" (World Population Review 2021). A key inhibitor in population growth is that many of the young believe that their country offers very little in terms of opportunity for self-betterment.

Part of the Cuban malaise is that the Cuban Communist Party does not wish to share power and is exceedingly reluctant to make badly needed economic reforms, leaving Cuban society stifled. This pertains to the entrepreneurial as well as the artistic. Although Puerto Rico does not have an authoritarian political system, it appears to have a similar sense of malaise as that found in Cuba. What makes matters a little better in Puerto Rico is that the public can drive out corrupt officials, including governors. They can also leave for the mainland or other parts of Latin America or Europe far easier than the Cubans.

In returning to a new Cold War in the Caribbean, one of the policy options for the U.S. government is to resolve some of Puerto Rico's issues, such as moving beyond the bankruptcy issue (which appears to be occurring in 2022), injecting greater transparency and disclosure into government finances, and supporting whatever result emerges from a new referendum even if that includes statehood or the status quo. Moreover, the push under the Trump and Biden administrations to return global supply chains either to the United States or close by is something that Puerto Rico should be taking advantage of, especially in the areas of medical equipment and pharmaceuticals. Last, but hardly least, having the lights stay on would be a great start, especially when Washington promotes its democratic-capitalist model elsewhere in the Caribbean.

Where does this leave U.S. Caribbean policy? The United States is on the right track with climate change, support for better governance and better regional healthcare programs. The push for the IDB to be more active in the Caribbean and Latin America is also a positive step in counteracting Chinese economic statecraft and advancing nearshoring which could help create good jobs in region. That said, there are other policy lines for the United States to follow. As mentioned above Puerto Rico remains unfinished business. But there is more that can be done in a more comprehensive fashion under the flag of U.S. Caribbean policy—providing debt relief for the middle income Caribbean countries at the World Bank and other multilateral organizations, establishing a clearer infrastructure-assistance program (figuring out what works from the América Crece and B3W policy initiatives and making the process clearer), deciding what to do about Haiti (perhaps allowing the island-state to sort out its own problems), and clarifying U.S. policy on Cuba. Cuba is heading toward major changes; it would be constructive to have a policy in place.

Equally important, Congress needs to take foreign policy matters more seriously and stop the partisan sniping and delays over diplomatic appointments. When stalling the appointment process, do Senators actually give any thought as to how pathetic it looks when the world's leading economy cannot do the simple thing of sending a diplomat to represent itself, not to mention the disrespectful nature of lacking a representative? It is difficult for President Biden to assert that "America is back," when it lacks ambassadors in 68 out of a total 190 postings as of January 2022 (*The Economist* 2022). As of December 2021, there were no U.S ambassadors in the Bahamas, Belize, Cuba, the Dominican Republic, Haiti, Jamaica, the Organization of American States, Trinidad and Tobago, and Panama. The U.S. diplomatic corps has considerable expertise, but the political house is not in order, rather it is dysfunctional.

CONCLUSION

U.S. policy in the Caribbean is complicated, composed of a mix of strictly Caribbean-U.S. issues, compounded by the sustained penetration of external powers into the region. The latter is forcing U.S. policy-makers to give greater attention to the Caribbean, something that they had not done since the old Cold War. Although the risk factor from the new Cold War is not yet at the same levels as the old Cold War, the ground is set for such a development. The region's political life can become more militarized, democratic government can slip, and countries like Cuba and Venezuela remain potential flashpoints. The lessons of the past two decades are that the United States cannot take Caribbean support for granted and that while the region slipped in importance for Washington, it increased for China and Russia.

Washington's ability to keep the Caribbean secure for U.S. national interests will require more than platitudes and rehashing old formulas. China's role in the region has demonstrated that it can be considered a viable alternative to what the United States offers, though is beginning to show that it has a harsher, more Machiavellian side. The critical factor here is developing policy momentum. Washington's failure to gain momentum and pull together a coherent overarching strategy runs the risk of leaving China's economic statecraft the most attractive game in town. China has its own set of problems, but to be a disrupter in the Caribbean costs little, especially when considering the more substantial sums it has sunk into a number of African and Asian countries. Moreover, it is scalable and could be stretched to have military application. The United States needs to build policy around both greater economic statecraft and the importance of democracy. Climate change also needs to be part of that policy, reflecting increasing regional needs. The rest of the 2020s and 2030s loom and are going to be a test of U.S. resolve around the world, including the Caribbean. Failure to grasp the challenge is a real risk and the consequences could set the stage for new political crises. Considering Russia's declaration in early 2022 of its "strategic relationship" with Cuba, Nicaragua, and Venezuela and China's deepening economic engagement with the region, one is left wondering how far the global system has traveled since the Cuban missile crisis in 1962. The answer sadly could be not as far as we hoped. Washington needs to wake up.

References

Aleem, Zeeshan. 2019. Puerto Rico's Week of Massive Protests, Explained. *Vox*, July 22. https://www.vox.com/2019/7/20/20701898/puerto-rico-protests-ricardo-rossello-resign-ricky-renuncia-text-scandal.

Bolton, John. 2020. *The Room Where It Happened: A White House Memoir*. New York: Simon and Schuster.

Bridglala, Carla. 2018. Mondello's Maiden Speech Slams State Enterprises. *Trinidad and Tobago Newsday*, October 25. https://newsday.co.tt/2018/10/25/mondellos-maiden-speech-slams-state-enterprises/.

Bryan, Anthony. 2019. Geopolitics and Renewable Energy. *Caribbean Intelligence*, February 2019. https://www.caribbeanintelligence.com/content/geo politics-and-renewable-energy.

Bryan, Anthony. 2021. The Southern Caribbean Energy Matrix and the Consequences of the Regional Push for Renewable Energy. Florida International University Caribbean Working Paper Series, March. https://lacc.fiu.edu/res earch/publications/lacc-caribbean-working-paper-series/bryan_southern-car ibbean-energy-matrix_wps2-2021.pdf.

Cabán, Pedro. 2019. The Summer 2019 Uprising: Building a New Puerto Rico. *NACLA*, October 21. https://nacla.org/news/2019/10/11/puerto-rico-political-future-protests.

Cárdenas, Mauricio, and Laurie Fitzmaurice. 2021. Building an Energy and Climate Coalition with Latin America and the Caribbean: An Agenda for the Biden Administration.

Chaitram, Samantha S.S. 2020. *American Foreign Policy in the English-Speaking Caribbean: From the Eighteenth Century to the Twenty-First*. Palgrave Macmillan.

Charles, Jacqueline. 2021. Venezuela's Border Dispute with Guyana Just Got Even Testier. *The Miami Herald*, January 28. https://www.miamiherald.com/news/nation-world/world/americas/article248798040.html.

Claver-Carone, Mauricio. 2021. Selected Quotes from Wilson Center's "Widening the Aperture: Nearshoring in Our 'Near Abroad'" Program. https://www.wilsoncenter.org/event/moving-day-nearshoring-opportuni ties-latin-america.

Clinton, Hillary Rotham. 2011. America's Pacific Century. *U.S. Department of State through Foreign Policy Magazine*, October 11. https://foreignpolicy.com/2011/10/11/americas-pacific-century/.

Columbia/SIPA. June 9. https://www.energypolicy.columbia.edu/research/commentary/building-energy-and-climate-coalition-latin-america-and-caribb ean-agenda-biden-administration.

Congressional Budget Office. 2016. Cost Estimate H.R. 4939. United States-Caribbean Strategic Engagement Act of 2016. May 31. https://www.cbo.gov/sites/default/files/114th-congress-2015-2016/costestimate/4939.pdf.

Congressional Research Service. 2021. U.S. Foreign Assistancve to Latin America and the Caribbean: FY 2021 Appropriations, January 7, 2021. https://sgp.fas.org/crs/row/R46514.pdf.

Dwyer, Colin. 2018. Racist and 'Shameful': How Other Countries Are Responding to Trump's Slur. *NPR*, January 12. https://www.npr.org/sections/thetwo-way/2018/01/12/577599691/racist-and-shameful-how-other-countries-are-responding-to-trumps-slur.

The Economist. 2022. Diplomacy Minus Diplomats. *The Economist*. January 15, 20–21.

Ellis, Evan. 2018. The Evolution of Panama-PRC Relations Since Recognition, and Their Strategic Implications for the U.S. and the Region. *Global Americans*, September 21. https://theglobalamericans.org/2018/09/the-evolution-of-panama-prc-relations-since-recognition-and-their-strategic-implications-for-the-u-s-and-the-region/.

Faller, Craig S. 2021. Statement of Admiral Craig S. Faller, Commander, United States Southern Command, Before the 117th Congress Senate Armed Services Committee, March 16. https://www.southcom.mil/Portals/7/Documents/Posture%20Statements/SOUTHCOM%202021%20Posture%20Statement_FINAL.pdf?ver=qVZdqbYBi_-rPgtL2LzDkg%3D%3D.

Fauriol, Georges. 2021. The Caribbean Potential: Reimagining the Region's Policy Frameworks. FIU Kimberly Green Latin American and Caribbean Center, January. https://lacc.fiu.edu/research/publications/lacc-caribbean-working-paper-series/fauriol_caribbean-potential_wps1-2021.pdf.

Isachenkov, Vladimir, and Matthew Lee. 2022. Russia's Talk of Troops in Latin America Called 'Bluster'. Fox 13. January 13. https://www.fox13memphis.com/news/world/russias-talk-troops/LGVBEN6RZ2KSZPPSMZ4MTN6CYM/.

Jamaica Observer. 2020. Pompeo Pitches US Business Over China in Suriname, Guyana. *Jamaica Observer*, September 17. https://www.jamaicaobserver.com/latestnews/Pompeo_pitches_US_business_over_China_in_Suriname,_Guyana.

James, Ewin. 2016. President Obama and the Caribbean. *Jamaica Observer*, December 18. https://www.jamaicaobserver.com/columns/president-obama-and-the-caribbean_84120.

Kendi, Ibram X. 2019. The Day Shithole Entered the Presidential Lexicon. *The Atlantic*, January 13, 2019. https://www.theatlantic.com/politics/archive/2019/01/shithole-countries/580054/.

Liu, Natalie. 2021. Chinese White Paper Seeks to Redefine Democracy. *Voice of America*, December 24. https://www.voanews.com/a/chinese-white-paper-seeks-to-redefine-democracy-/6369108.html.

MacDonald, Paul K. 2018. America First? Explaining Continuity and Change in Trump's Foreign Policy. *Political Science Quarterly*. Fall, 401–434.

Maldonado, A.W. 2021. *Boom and Bust in Puerto Rico: How Politics Destroyed an Economic Miracle*. University of Notre Dame Press.

Ortiz-Blanes, Syra. 2021. A New Maria: How Puerto Rico's Population Decline Could Be the Island's Next Crisis. *Miami Herald*, May 25. https://www.mia miherald.com/news/nation-world/world/americas/article251583678.html.

Pompeo, Michael R. 2020. Expanding America's Commitment to the Caribbean. U.S. Embassy in Cuba. January 22. U.S. Department of State. https://cu.use mbassy.gov/expanding-americas-commitment-to-the-caribbean/.

Power and Politics: Ambassador Joe Mondello discusses his time spend in Trinidad and Tobago. 2020. https://www.youtube.com/watch?v=Ou0F3J J1SqI. Accessed 25 Apr 2021.

Ruwitch, John. 2020. In George Floyd Protests, China Sees a Powerful Propaganda Opportunity. *NPR*, June 3. https://www.npr.org/2020/06/03/868 566978/in-george-floyd-protests-china-sees-a-powerful-propaganda-opport unity.

The White House. 2009. Remarks by the President at the Summit of the Americas Opening Ceremony, April 17, 2009. https://obamawhitehouse.archives. gov/the-press-office/remarks-president-summit-americas-opening-ceremony.

United States Census Bureau. 2022. Quick Facts, Puerto Rico. https://www. census.gov/quickfacts/PR. Accessed 20 Oct 2021.

U.S. Department of State. 2013. Remarks on U.S. Policy in the Western Hemisphere. Remarks by John Kerry at the Organization of American States. November 18. https://2009-2017.state.gov/secretary/remarks/2013/11/ 217680.htm.

U.S. Department of State. 2015. Caribbean Energy Security Initiative, 2015. https://www.state.gov/caribbean-energy-security-initiative-cesi/

U.S. Department of State. 2020. The Elements of the China Challenge, Policy Planning Staff, Offrice of the Secretary of State, November 2020. https://www.state.gov/wp-content/uploads/2020/11/20-02832-Ele ments-of-China-Challenge-508.pdf

U.S. House of Representatives (H.R. 4939)—United States-Caribbean Strategic Engagement Act of 2016. https://www.congress.gov/bill/114th-congress/ house-bill/4939/text.

U.S. Mission to the Organization of American States. 2018. "Secretary Tillerson Delivers Address on U.S. Engagement in the Western Hemisphere". February 1. https://usoas.usmission.gov/secretary-tillerson-delivers-address-u-s-engagement-western-hemisphere/.

Viscidi, Lisa, and Sarah Phillips, 2020. Countering China through Infrastructure Investments. *Global Americans*, March 31. https://theglobalamericans.org/ 2020/03/countering-china-through-infrastructure-investments/.

White House. 2021. Fact Sheet: President Biden and G7 Leaders Launch Build Back Better World (B3W) Partnership, June 13. https://www.whitehouse. gov/briefing-room/statements-releases/2021/06/12/fact-sheet-president-biden-and-g7-leaders-launch-build-back-better-world-b3w-partnership/.

World Bank. 2017. *The Potential of the Blue Economy: Increasing Long-Term Benefits of the Sustainable Use of Marine Resources for Small-Island Developing States and Coastal Least Developed Countries.* https://openknowledge.worldb ank.org/handle/10986/26843.

World Population Review. 2021. Counties with Declining Population 2021: Cuba. *World Population Review*, October. https://worldpopulationreview. com/country-rankings/countries-with-declining-population.

Yergin, Daniel. 2020. *The New Map: Energy.* Climate and the Clash of Nations: Penguin Press.

Zakaria, Fareed. 2019. The Self-Destruction of American Power. *Foreign Affairs*, July/August 2019. https://www.foreignaffairs.com/articles/2019-06-11/self-destruction-american-power.

Zhao, Jla. 2021. FM Spokeman Denounces US 'Democracy Summit'. *China Daily*, August 12, 2021. https://www.chinadaily.com.cn/a/202112/08/WS61b0bbeaa310cdd39bc7a2c2.html.

CHAPTER 10

Conclusion

The world is shifting into what increasingly appears to be a new Cold War. This chapter addresses alternative scenarios for the future. The first is based on China achieving global hegemony and what that would mean for the Caribbean. The second is based on China being undercutting by its many internal problems while facing a more concerted and united international opposition. For the Caribbean leaves it facing the United States with major questions as to what comes next, a return to benign neglect or taking a partnership role up to a new level with an eye to climate change, transnational crime and infrastructure challenges. The last scenario represents a muddle through in which the Caribbean finds that the new Cold War intensifies, but the tensions generated by Chinese-U.S. friction will be contained. The worst risk in all three scenarios is that the major actors sleepwalk into a new major crisis in the Caribbean reminiscent of the Cuban Missile Crisis or in the worst case, an outright war along the lines of the First World War, which would overlap into the Caribbean due to its strategic location. It is argued that there is plenty to think about in terms of risk when looking to the future for the Caribbean, which should provide an incentive for greater efforts in developing pan-Caribbean forums and mechanisms to carry more weight in a system dominated by larger powers.

If one does not know which port one is sailing to, no wind is favorable.
Seneca

© The Author(s), under exclusive license to Springer Nature
Switzerland AG 2022
S. B. MacDonald, *The New Cold War, China, and the Caribbean*,
https://doi.org/10.1007/978-3-031-06149-3_10

278 S. B. MACDONALD

The above quote is by Seneca the Younger (4 BC–AD 65), who was born in what is today Spain and raised in Rome. Seneca lived in a turbulent time riding the tides of fortune, being exiled, returning as first a tutor to Nero and then an advisor, but ultimately being forced to take his own life for alleged complicity in a conspiracy to assassinate the Emperor. His quote reflects the need to select a direction because without it one goes nowhere. This is sound advice for the Caribbean as it navigates its way through a new Cold War.

This book began with a simple question: is there a new Cold War in the Caribbean? The answer is yes, but as reflected by the chapters in this book the answer is complicated. China and the United States have clearly identified each other as their major rival. Each country has its own narrative about this transmitted by propaganda instruments, while there is a search for allies. Although China may disguise this under the flag of supporting and seeking to lead a multipolar world order, it is quietly busy around the planet corralling friends and allies.

While a cold war between China and the United States is not something either country wants, it is difficult to see how Beijing and Washington are going to take the steps necessary to avert it, especially when taking domestic politics into account (Heer 2021). Indeed, Zhou Bo, of the Center for International Security and Strategy at Tsinghua University, speaking at the annual Valdai Discussion Club meeting in Sochi, Russia in October 2021 was content to say that "the center of gravity is moving irreversibly to the East," but the current situation "is more dangerous than during the Cold War" (Escobar 2021). The new Cold War is not going to skip over the Caribbean.

What does a new Cold War mean for the Caribbean? The introduction of another major power in the Caribbean is both positive and negative. On the positive side of the ledger, Caribbean countries benefit from having another power capable and willing to provide what is to their small countries considerable assistance; competition between China, the United States, and Europe and, to a lesser extent, Russia and Canada, creates a sense of competitive assistance bidding; and it provides Caribbean countries with a role to play well beyond the confines of their waters. Antigua and Barbuda, Cuba, and Jamaica have a more significant voice in global affairs at a time when every vote counts in international forums.

On the negative side, the new Cold War runs the risk of putting Caribbean countries in the middle between two hegemonic powers, which carries downside in the form of possible tough economic measures (cutting off of assistance, sanctions, badmouthing a particular country as a tourist destination or complicating the entry of a country's goods into the Chinese market); opens Caribbean countries to another hegemonic power which may eventually seek to bully them; and potentially leads to unsustainable debt buildups, which have been evident in the cases of Sri Lanka, Laos, Pakistan, and Ecuador.

The new Cold War raises tough questions for the Caribbean. Can Caribbean countries navigate between Chinese largesse, behind which possibly looms debt traps and loss of control over parts of their economies and the power of the United States, which has "re-discovered" the region and is seeking to re-engage? Can that U.S. re-engagement be channeled better to Caribbean national interests? Do Caribbean countries want to be associated with China, an authoritarian power, that has a dismal track record of how it treats its own minority groups (Uighurs and Tibetans)? Will Chinese–Caribbean relations sour if the Asian giant invades Taiwan? Do Caribbean countries want to align themselves to one side or another? What measures can the diverse set of countries take to ensure that they do not get dragged into the new Cold War rivalry on one side or another? There are no easy answers to any of these questions.

The biggest risk for the Caribbean is that it is caught between two larger forces that suffer a trust deficit, have a global reach, and are well-armed. This is not to argue that the Chinese or Americans are spoiling for a fight. The potential black swan disaster is that China and the U.S. sleepwalk into a major conflict, something seemingly minor unexpectedly escalates into a major conflagration. In his *Sleepwalkers: How Europe Went to War in 1914*, historian Christopher Clark makes the case that World War I was not started by a diabolical, plotting James Bond-like villain; rather it was ignited by "a chain of decisions made by political actors with conscious objectives, who were capable of a degree of self-regulation, acknowledged a wide range of options and formed the best judgements they could on the basis of the best information they had to hand" (Clark 2014: iv). He further notes: "Nationalism, armaments, alliance and finance were all part of the story, but they can be made to carry real explanatory weight only if they can be seen to have shaped the decisions – in combination – that made war break out." It is this combination of decisions, made by different actors looking through very different perceptual lenses that risks taking the planet down the road to a new conflict.

In many ways China and the United States find themselves in a situation similar to Clark's European sleepwalkers. As in 1914 it is not inevitable that the two countries are doomed to an economic, political, and ideological struggle that will end in war, but the machinery of intelligence gathering, decision-making, and policy consideration creates some of the same landscape. Most of all there is a trust deficit between Beijing and Washington that has been deepening over the past decade. From a realist perspective, great powers fear each other and, considering the international system is anarchic, they need to defend themselves against any threats. As the University of Chicago's John J. Mearsheimer, a proponent of the realist approach to international relations, noted: "The logic is straightforward: a scared state will look especially hard for ways to enhance its security, and it will be diposed to pursue risky policies to achieve that end" (Mearsheimer 2014: 42–43).

The pursuit of risky policies is what worries Caribbean countries, considering that the fall-out could be catastrophic, touching everything from tourist flows to the potential for actual warfare. It is often forgotten, but the Caribbean was a warzone during the Napoleonic wars, both World Wars, and the Cold War. The Cuban missile crisis remains one of the closest brushes between the United States and the Soviet Union. Indeed, if the new Cold War intensifies the Caribbean could see a ratcheting up of tensions akin to the last Cold War, something that no one wants in the region. And some would argue that the Caribbean is already being used by China to spy on the United States by using unsuspecting Caribbean telecommunications companies (which use Chinese equipment), not an act of a friendly country (Kirchgaessner 2020; Hartnell 2022).

The Caribbean faces what we shall call the Belgium dilemma, which is when a small country in an important geopolitical location is caught between two major powers that are threatening to go to war without consideration of the small country's neutrality. Like the Caribbean, Belgium sits in a geopolitical pivot. Located between Germany and France, whose historical enmity dates back to when Bismarckian Germany defeated France in the Franco-Prussian War in 1870. The Kingdom of Belgium was established in 1839 and its sovereignty and neutrality was guaranteed by the major European powers of the time, including France and Germany. In 1914, the Germans found its expeditious to maneuver past heavily protected French border fortifications. The easiest route to the rear of French lines and victory was through Belgium. Sadly Belgian neutrality meant little in a case of realpolitik. German forces invaded

Belgium, which resisted, eventually losing over 90 percent of its territory to a four-year occupation. Again in 1940, Germany swept through Belgium on its way to invading France.

The purpose of this short story about Belgium and the two world wars is that Caribbean countries like the European country are small, but located in a piece of geography where more powerful and aggressive countries like to transit. If a new Cold War intensifies or turns hot, the risk is high that Caribbean neutrality will be treated in the same fashion as Belgium's—there is a strong possibility it will not be respected.

THREE POSSIBLE SCENARIOS

What kind of future geopolitical scenarios does the Caribbean face? Some of the potential outcomes could be negative, others more positive. While crystal ball gazing is always a challenge, three possible scenarios are presented, which are the most grounded in current trends and developments.

China Uber Alles (China Above All)

This scenario makes the following assumptions: China continues its economic expansion (albeit at a more moderate pace); captures the commanding heights of technology and sophisticated weaponry by 2030; the Communist Party maintains its control over the population; and socioeconomic problems in the United States are not fully addressed, leaving a badly divided society and a declining military establishment. The decline of the United States as the world's leading power is evident. China establishes itself at the apex of the global system and the Caribbean complies.

It is 2040 and China has established naval bases in Cuba, Trinidad, and Panama. The Chinese also have military training teams in Antigua and Barbuda, Dominica, and Barbados. The main weapons merchants throughout the Caribbean and Latin America are China, followed by its ally/sometimes rival, Russia. China also shares military training duties with large Russian missions in Venezuela and Nicaragua. China's military presence is not the only evidence of its hegemonic status in the Caribbean. Indeed, it is only a small part of it.

For several decades, China's leadership grasped that if it was going to overtake U.S. influence in the Caribbean and elsewhere it needed more than military power. While upping their military budgets and building a powerful blue water fleet, especially after their conquest of Taiwan in 2026, China continued to use trade and investment, development assistance, strategic communications (propaganda, disinformation, and misinformation), targeting technological sectors with subsidies, and excluding foreign imports from strategic sectors to build and expand its reach into the rest of the world, once again making it the Middle Kingdom.

In the Caribbean, most electric cars and buses are now made in China as are the photovoltaic panels that help power those cars and other segments of the local economies. Many public utilities companies are owned by Chinese state-owned companies, which provide dependable electricity and phone service. The power generators are made in China as are the portable phones used by local populations. Chinese engineers are actively upgrading everything from roads and bridges to harbors and airports, while Chinese tourists fill the hotels and resorts. At the same time, the ranks of young Antiguan, Dominican, and Belizean students heading off to China to study are large and increasing. Chinese universities now host more Caribbean students than U.S. and Canadian universities. China is also the major buyer of Trinidad's natural gas, Guyana's and Suriname's oil and timber, and Cuba's sugar and rum (which has been revamped by Chinese investment). Although the United States still retains some influence, Washington's clout is diminished, especially since the new renminbi replaced the U.S. dollar, alongside China's cryptocurrency, the Mao.

China's rise has been helped by domestic U.S. conditions. By 2040, the United States is still a country badly divided and its democratic institutions have eroded into an uneasy and volatile mix of multiple political parties and regional interests, barely disguising major national fissures. The Chinese Communist Party leadership has thus far been correct that the American experiment with democracy is slowly terminating, much like the Soviet Union; pressured by external forces, mainly economic and technological, while rotting from within. The same can be said for the neoliberal economic system and the decline of its institutions, such as the World Bank, IMF, and NATO. The Middle Kingdom has returned as the center of the world, this time its influence reaching every continent, with Beijing guiding other nations. Chinese hegemony is much like an iron hand in a velvet glove and for the countries that play ball, there are benefits. This is particularly the case of China's allies, Russia, Iran, and

Venezuela where strongman leaders share similar authoritarian values and corruption still greases the wheels of business.

Under the Pax China the Caribbean is allowed to maintain its domestic political arrangements—as long as they do not impinge on China's national interests. While authoritarian regimes in Cuba, Nicaragua, El Salvador, and Venezuela are favored by Chinese largesse, the southern Caribbean, rich in oil and gas as well as other natural resources, is given particular attention by Beijing. Most of its oil and natural gas flows to China. No one messes with the Middle Kingdom. The Caribbean has become dependent on China and its center-periphery relations are characterized as a "dependency with Chinese characteristics."

The China Fade Scenario

Scenario two differs radically. The key assumptions are that China's problems ultimately undermine its ability to project its power into the Caribbean on a sustained basis. For all of the depictions of China as an economic and political juggernaut, the Asian country has fragilities. In the "China fade" scenario the fragilities erode Beijing's goals and aspirations in the Caribbean. Key to this scenario is the view that China's power has peaked. As historians Hal Brands and Michael Beckley postulate, a country on the upswing of power, with a strong economy and military and growing weight in global affairs has more to lose by starting a war. Rather the risk is that China peaks and opts to take what it wants before it becomes too weak. As they note:

> A dissatisfied state has been building its power and expanding its geopolitical horizons. But then the country peaks, perhaps because its economy slows, perhaps because its own assertiveness provokes a coalition of determined rivals, or perhaps because of both of these happen at once. The future starts to look quite forbidding; a sense of imminent danger starts to replace a feeling of limitless possibility. In these circumstances, a revisionist power may act boldly, even aggressively, to grab what it can before it is too late. The most dangerous trajectory in world politics is a long rise followed by the prospect of a sharp decline. (Brands and Beckley 2021)

It is 2040 and China has been forced to reassess its role as a global power. While it continues to be a major exporter throughout the Caribbean, the sharpness of its economic statecraft has declined. At home, China has severe problems: ongoing energy shortages; a heavy dependence on imported coal, oil, and natural gas; more severe pollution problems; water scarcity; and food insecurity. Although the Chinese Communist Party still holds sway, it is mainly propped up by a police state, backed by AI, and other forms of technology. Innovation has disappeared, stifled by overwhelming regulation that was imposed during the Xi years. The old contract between the population and the Party—citizens stay out of politics and the Party will give you a good economic life—no longer holds sway. The Party is held in contempt by most Chinese and regions of the country are restless, following years of high food and rent costs. Moreover, the aging population is hard-pressed to enjoy retirement, while the less numerous younger generations grapple with stifling controls over daily life, fewer chances at self-enrichment, ideological drudgery, and lessened chances of marriage due to the preference for sons during the one-child policy years. All of this is made all the more frustrating for China's population as many countries have defaulted on the debts they owe China. The close to $400 billion owned by countries to China in 2021 had peaked in 2025 at close to $600 billion before the BRI partially unraveled due to major problems in Pakistan, Southeast Asia and Africa, including massive outright sovereign defaults and a new round of Central Asian Islamic-fueled conflicts (Pei 2021).

China's more aggressive foreign policy also failed to bring the dividends it expected. An effort to take Taiwan failed in 2027, in part due to the support from the Quad+ (which expanded beyond the founding four—U.S., Australia, Japan, and India—to include South Korea, Singapore, Indonesia, and Vietnam). Although the conflict was largely confined to the Taiwan Straits and South China Sea, it did involve Chinese efforts to sabotage the Panama Canal. At the same time, Europe took tougher economic measures on China and pulled Russia from its close embrace of China. This was the work of German diplomacy. Berlin found China's state capitalism, protected markets, and industrial espionage enough of an incentive to induce Russia to leave China's side. Russia was long secretly worried about the risk of China re-activating its claims over its Far East regions, which are sparsely populated and have considerable natural resources. This development was helped by the dissolution of NATO and considerable weakening of the European Union.

China's other "allies" also put space between themselves and Beijing, especially as the lending and assistance flows slowed to a trickle. The BRI helped create a more pan-Asian transportation system, but its utility was compromised by local political problems and changing alliances, most of them against China. Moreover, the combination of wolf warrior diplomacy and the crushing of an ill-fated Uighur rebellion in 2025 (which was abetted by Afghanistan's Taliban regime) hurt China's international image as a highly successful development model.

As for the United States, it managed to recover from a politically traumatic 2020s. Despite deep-set challenges to the political system and a substantial debt build-up, the 2030s witnessed a period marked by economic and social renewal at home, helped by the re-domestication of supply chains, significant upgrades in the national infrastructure, and considerable improvements in military and civilian technology. While NATO broke up due to pressures stemming from Germany's eastern economic interests, the Quad + functioned well in the same capacity in the Asia–Pacific area, especially after the brief war over Taiwan.

For the Caribbean, China's fade reduced the Asian country's role in the region. This was felt by the consolidation of Chinese embassies throughout the region with Antigua and Barbuda being the new diplomatic hub in the Eastern Caribbean, but closed embassies in Grenada and Dominica. It also saw the return of Taiwan to a number of countries. Other examples of the Chinese decline were reflected by a sharp cut in scholarships, the closure of a number of Confucius Institutes, and fewer visits by high-ranking Chinese government officials. Beijing's primary concerns are more an issue of maintaining allies in countries like Cambodia, Laos, and Sri Lanka; rebuilding its navy after the short war over Taiwan, and containing a massive refugee flow out of a North Korea racked by a civil war.

Chinese power, in particular, its economic statecraft, is missed in the Caribbean. Having China as an active partner, despite concerns over debt traps and losing control over telecommunications and public power systems, has been beneficial. If nothing else, it kept the United States engaged, forcing Washington to listen to Caribbean needs as partners. There is little desire to swap U.S. hegemony (in its bad days) with Chinese hegemony. The Chinese interlude brought upgrades to infrastructure and financial aid. The challenge ahead is keeping the United States–Caribbean dialogue alive as well as maintaining momentum with the North American Free Trade Union, which now encompasses most of the English-speaking Caribbean, Suriname, Cuba, and the Dominican Republic and moving ahead with key climate change projects.

The Muddle-Through Scenario

The most likely scenario for the Caribbean is that it will be an arena of competition in a new Cold War between China and the U.S. That does not mean that the Chinese Navy will seek to base warships in the region or that it will send ground troops into Cuba or Venezuela. Any such development would be a line in the sand moment in U.S.–China relations, probably along the lines of the Cuban missile crisis. Rather the trend line is that the two powers are likely to spar for influence and that will be largely by economic statecraft. The intensity of that competition is likely to be determined by the temperature of overall U.S.–Chinese relations, in particular their differences in the Asia–Pacific region. This, however, does not preclude the potential for a crisis in the Caribbean.

The key assumptions of this scenario are that China's ascent will continue through the 2020s, but begin to cool in the 2030s, short of Beijing's goal of overtaking the United States. Nonetheless, China's ongoing push will keep international relations relatively tense and focused on the United States–China new Cold War. That dynamic is likely to change, especially as the Chinese Communist Party applies the brake to what made their country so successful—innovation. As political science professor Minxin Pei, observed: "The party's existential fear of losing control will impel it to maintain a tight grip on the economy, making it less efficient. Giant but ossified state-owned enterprises will continue to waste resources. The CCP's arbitrary exercise of power – as exemplified by its sweeping crackdown on China's most successful tech companies, such as Didi and Alibaba – will stifle the innovation and growth of its tech sector more effectively than America's sanctions" (Pei 2021). All the same, China will remain the United States' most formidable rival and according to Pei the most likely outcome will be a strategic stalemate, which will first pass through a dangerous 2020s before reaching a relationship where "…both countries may be able to agree on a set of rules confining their rivalry to a small number of realms unlikely to trigger a full-fledged conflict."

It is 2040 and the so-called decline of the West has failed to materialize. The liberal democratic-capitalist order has not dissolved into chaos. At the same time, China remains a major power, reflected by its dominance of the Eurasian land mass. Africa, the Middle East, and the Pacific areas are arenas of Chinese and Western power competition, a situation complicated by the engagement of other powers, namely Iran, Russia, Turkey, and India. In the Caribbean, the United States remains the dominant hegemonic power due to its geographical proximity and longstanding cultural and economic linkages. It has revamped its military capacity in the region, including by building up a larger presence in Puerto Rico.

China remains a partner to the Caribbean due to its trade and investment interests, though its heyday as a big spender appears over. At the same time, there is some resentment of Beijing's unwillingness to condemn Venezuela for its abortive attempt to grab Guyanese territory and the fact that many of the weapons used by Caracas in the conflict came from China. The United States and other Western countries and most of the Caribbean backed Guyana. The Asian country also did not make friends over its attempt to disrupt the newly democratic government in Cuba in 2028 through a relentless cyber warfare and misinformation campaign. China also stumbled from a second Covid pandemic, which originated in another one of its inland cities in 2029. This time the pandemic's spread from China was well-documented and the United States and other western countries were much more rapid in helping other countries, including those in the Caribbean.

In the muddle-through scenario it is likely that the United States will grudgingly up its diplomatic game. This comes in the form of top leadership giving the Caribbean attention on a more regular basis (something that the Canadians started to do under the third Trudeau administration). Equally important to maintaining the United States' role in the region are assigning more diplomatic personnel; adding a couple of embassies in the Eastern Caribbean; increasing scholarships to U.S. universities; boosting infrastructure assistance (albeit on a targeted basis), and implementing new economic and political reforms to help improve the standard of living in Puerto Rico and the U.S. Virgin Islands.

Under this scenario, the United States plays an important role in Cuba's shift from Communist Party-authoritarianism into a democratic-work-in-progress. This is being done with technical assistance in a number of areas as well as help from a number of non-profit organizations that work on issues such as governance and transparency. The overall upgrade in U.S. Caribbean policy was assisted greatly by a more uniform approach to foreign aid and an upgrade in Washington's propaganda machine to better counter China's and Russia's misinformation and disinformation campaigns. Better cyber-security measures also helped U.S. effectiveness in fighting the war for hearts and minds.

The new Cold War returned the Caribbean to its traditional role of being a geopolitical pivot. In that, local issues run the risk of becoming magnified into international ones, something that Caribbean leadership handles carefully. Although the muddle-through scenario has a downside in that it includes the existence of a more pronounced realignment of international forces, it also has provided an opportunity for Caribbean countries to cautiously outline and pursue their own policy objectives, the most important of which is to maintain their sovereignty in more rough and tumble world. While each of the three scenarios is hypothetical, they represent the challenging position in which the Caribbean is finding itself in the early twenty-first century.

To be certain there are other potential future scenarios. The United States and China could both have severe enough domestic problems to force them to reduce their global competition. This has left other countries able to pursue more regionally oriented policies, such as Russia's recreation of a large part of its empire, including direct control over the eastern section of Ukraine and a weak government in the western part of the country; an outright takeover of Belarus and Moldova, and indirect control over Georgia, Azerbaijan, and Armenia as well as most of Central Asia. For the Caribbean, this has led to an effort toward greater unity, while fending off an authoritarian reconstructed Venezuelan state, armed with Chinese and Russian weapons and helped by Russian military personnel. It has also meant a greater leaning toward the United States as the only more significant power in the region capable of standing up to Venezuela.

Certainly all of this has a science fiction feel to it. Another scenario is that Chinese has a democratic revolution, the United States assumes a less stringent anti-China stance, and the two powers seek to work together in concert in the Caribbean. Everyone is happy. But that returns the outlook to the world of science fiction. The three scenarios outlined are probably the most realistic, though not necessarily the most desired.

FLASHPOINTS AND OPPORTUNITIES

As exemplified by the three scenarios, there are potential flashpoints, both external and regional in nature. On the external side, the major flashpoints are Taiwan, the South China Sea, and the Sino-Indian border. Another outlier is North Korea. Far from the Caribbean, an outbreak of hostilities from any of these locations will be felt in an asymmetrical fashion. A hardening of U.S. and Chinese stances could easily show up in Panama, a development that would certainly impact Caribbean economies. It would also put all Chinese operations in the Caribbean, official and private sector, under close scrutiny by U.S. intelligence agencies, concerned about possible Chinese sabotage. That could impact Caribbean telecommunications and internet access as well as the Panama Canal.

Within the Caribbean the major potential flashpoints are the potential for the Chinese to establish military bases or the selling of high caliber missiles (capable of reaching the United States) to Cuba or Venezuela. It is one thing for China and, for that matter, Russia and Iran to send their ships to the Caribbean. It is something very different to put offensive weapons with the capacity of causing massive damage in the continental United States into the hands of hostile regimes.

Another potential flashpoint is between Venezuela and Guyana. The Maduro regime has repeatedly brought up the issue that the old claim on two-thirds of Guyana's territory is valid and has used its navy and air force to harass Guyanese fishing vessels. Efforts to scare away international oil companies have left part of the highly strategic southern Caribbean energy matrix exposed to possible conflict. China is very quiet on the issue, while the United States has actively stepped up in supporting Guyana. What happens if Venezuela actually makes a military attempt to occupy part of the disputed area? Would China back Venezuela? It is after all, one of the major international economic props for the Caracas regime. An invasion would be something to wrap the national flag around the Venezuelan dictatorship. The worst case scenario would be if the situation rapidly escalated eventually causing the United States and China and probably Russia to line up against each other. This face-off between China and the United States would probably start in a non-military fashion, mainly coming as an economic tussle. The risk is that it spirals into a bigger crisis and comes at a time when other points of tension are high. A China in decline (as mentioned in scenario 2) might also feel that it may do something more supportive of the regime in Caracas to keep a major oil producer safely exporting its chief product to the Asian country.

Panama looms as a potential flashpoint. As one U.S. government study noted: "The Panama Canal is the Western Hemisphere's most important and logistical hub and serves as a vital sea lane of communication of both the United States and China" (Koleski and Blivas 2018). As already pointed out earlier in this book, the Panama Ports Company is a subsidiary of the Hong Kong-based Hutchinson Whampoa, and operates two ports, Balboa and Cristobal, located on either side of the waterway. While a U.S. shutdown of the Panama Canal would hurt China's flow of soybeans, iron ore, and oil from Latin America and the Caribbean, Chinese sabotage would complicate U.S naval movements in the case of war. China's strategic vulnerability could be partially offset if Beijing was able to advance its plans for a megaport in Chancay, Peru, located north of Lima. Other Chinese plans call for a railway system to transport Brazilian goods through Peru, which would bypass the Panama Canal. China has clearly made an effort to gain greater influence in Panama. However, there has been considerable push-back from the United States, which continues to regard Panama as a critical link in its communications and transportation network. Any efforts for a more overt Chinese presence with military capabilities would be a flashpoint for the United States.

One last potential major flashpoint is Cuba, one of the Caribbean's largest islands and home to 11 million people. With the exit from center stage of the Castro brothers, the nomenklatura (which includes some Castro family members, top military and bureaucratic leaders, and party members) is increasingly at odds with the majority of Cubans, who do not share their privileged lifestyle. The wealth gap between the ruling class and the general population will probably increase through the 2020s and tensions are likely to increase. China and Russia are supportive of the Communist regime, but without substantial economic reforms, Cuba is likely to continue a brutal, downward descent with its younger population leaving in greater numbers. If a rebellion were to break out (which is not currently expected), it would be of keen interest to the United States as well as China and Russia. Would the last two be willing to sit by and watch a friendly regime potentially be turned into a democratic government and friend to the United States? If China and Russia were to become more engaged in seeking to prop up the Communist state, would the United States do nothing or would it respond, possibly calling on the Monroe Doctrine as justification to up its role in Cuba, which could bring it into collision with China and Russia?

CONCLUSION

China and the United States have entered what increasingly resembles a new Cold War. It seems that every day a new point of tension is discovered, with the two sides squaring off against each other. Worryingly the new Cold War narrative has seeped into trade relations, cross-border investment, tourism, and development lending. The emphasis remains more economic than political, but China's role in a new Cold War is increasingly influenced by its closer ties to Russia, which is demonstrating a willingness to use military force or its threat to use military force to gain what it wants—the recreation of Russia as a great power with total dominance in its near abroad and a global reach (as with Cuba, Venezuela, and Nicaragua). As the process of two rival camps slowly forms, the rivalry of gaining friends and allies in distant points on the map is well-advanced. The contours of a new Cold War are materializing. One need only to listen to the rhetoric and posturing in Africa, the Pacific, and Latin America. The Caribbean is not immune to this. It cannot be. Its geostrategic position puts it on the map for Beijing and Moscow. Washington has taken it for granted, with some of its past foreign policymakers content with benign neglect. The problem is that the days of free-wheeling globalization are over; geopolitics have returned and this sucks the Caribbean into a new Cold War vortex. All of this is more compelling as it comes at a time when other major issues are pressing the Caribbean, such as climate change, transnational criminal organizations trafficking everything from drugs to gold and timber, and healthcare.

Where does this leave the Caribbean in the 2020s and 2030s? For the United States the answer is straightforward; if it wants to play a constructive role in the Caribbean it has to put up or shut up. Stated in more political science terms, the United States needs to focus the right resources and personnel on the region if it wants to compete with China and Russia. It has to walk the narrow path between being a caring, yet powerful neighbor as well as a tough geopolitical competitor. Caribbean countries are sensitive to their larger neighbors past heavy handed efforts to control regional events, while China and Russia need far more forceful reminders of great power push back. Achieving such a balance is not easy, but the stakes are rising. As for the Caribbean, the need to play their cards wisely has increased. This means there is a pressing need to band together and make regional organizations like CARICOM, the Caribbean Development Bank, and Caribbean Court of Justice work more effectively.

Although it is difficult to maintain unity, there is an advantage to strength in numbers. Indeed, the words of Haiti's revolutionary hero, Toussaint Louverture are worth noting, "Unite; for combination is stronger than witchcraft." It is good to be stronger than witchcraft, especially in a cold war. And as we look toward the rest of the 2020s and into the 2030s the new Cold War is likely to be less of a debating point and more of a reality.

References

Brands, Hal, and Michael Beckley. 2021. China Is a Declining Power—And That's the Problem. *Foreign Policy*, September 21. https://foreignpolicy.com/2021/09/24/china-great-power-united-states/.

Clark, Christopher. 2014. *The Sleepwalkers: How Europe Went to War in 1914*. Harper Perennial.

Davidson, Helen. 2021. China Owed $385 Billion—Including 'Hidden Debt' from Poorer Nations, Says Report. *The Guardian*, September 30. https://www.theguardian.com/world/2021/sep/30/42-nations-owe-china-hidden-debts-exceeding-10-of-gdp-says-report.

Escobar, Pepe. 2021. Sochi Probes the Utopia of a Multipolar World. *Asia Times*, October 20. https://asiatimes.com/2021/10/sochi-probes-the-utopia-of-a-multipolar-world/.

Hartnell, Neil. 2022. Investigation Demanded Over China's Alleged Btc 'Spying'. *The Tribune (The Bahamas)*, December 16.

Heer, Paul. 2021. There Will Be a U.S.-China Cold War. *The National Interest*, October 3. https://nationalinterest.org/feature/there-will-be-us-china-cold-war-194791.

Kirchgaessner, Stephanie. 2020. Revealed: China Suspected of Spying on Americans Via Caribbean Phone Networks. *The Guardian*, December 15. https://www.theguardian.com/us-news/2020/dec/15/revealed-china-suspected-of-spying-on-americans-via-caribbean-phone-networks.

Koleski, Katherine, and Alec Blivas. 2018. China's Engagement with Latin America and the Caribbean. U.-S.-China Economic and Security Review Commission, Staff Research Report, October. https://www.uscc.gov/sites/default/files/Research/China's%20Engagement%20with%20Latin%20America%20and%20the%20Caribbean_pdf.

Mearsheimer, John. 2014. *The Tragedy of Great Power Politics*. New York City, NY: W. W. Norton & Company.

Pei, Minxin. 2021. Minxin Pei on Why China Will Not Surpass the United States. *The Economist*, August 30. https://www.economist.com/by-invitation/2021/08/30/minxin-pei-on-why-china-will-not-surpass-the-united-states.

INDEX

© The Editor(s) (if applicable) and The Author(s), under exclusive   293
license to Springer Nature Switzerland AG 2022
S. B. MacDonald, *The New Cold War, China, and the Caribbean*,
https://doi.org/10.1007/978-3-031-06149-3